D1546333

THE I TATTI
RENAISSANCE LIBRARY

James Hankins, General Editor

ALBERTI

BIOGRAPHICAL AND AUTOBIOGRAPHICAL WRITINGS

ITRL 96

LEON BATTISTA ALBERTI

✦ ✦ ✦

BIOGRAPHICAL AND AUTOBIOGRAPHICAL WRITINGS

TRANSLATED BY

MARTIN McLAUGHLIN

THE I TATTI RENAISSANCE LIBRARY

HARVARD UNIVERSITY PRESS

CAMBRIDGE, MASSACHUSETTS

LONDON, ENGLAND

2023

Series design by Dean Bornstein

First printing

Library of Congress Cataloging-in-Publication Data

Names: Alberti, Leon Battista, 1404–1472, author. | McLaughlin, M. L.
(Martin L.), translator. | Alberti, Leon Battista, 1404–1472. De commodis
litterarum atque incommodis. | Alberti, Leon Battista, 1404–1472. De
commodis litterarum atque incommodis. English. (McLaughlin) | Alberti, Leon
Battista, 1404–1472. Vita S. Potiti. | Alberti, Leon Battista, 1404–1472. Vita S.
Potiti. English. | Alberti, Leon Battista, 1404–1472. Vita. | Alberti, Leon
Battista, 1404–1472. Vita. English. | Alberti, Leon Battista, 1404–1472. Canis. |
Alberti, Leon Battista, 1404–1472. Canis. English. | Alberti, Leon Battista,
1404–1472. Musca. | Alberti, Leon Battista, 1404–1472. Musca. English.
Title: Biographical and autobiographical writings /
Leon Battista Alberti ; translated by Martin McLaughlin.
Other titles: I Tatti Renaissance library ; 96.
Description: Cambridge, Massachusetts ; London, England : Harvard
University Press, 2023. | Series: The I Tatti Renaissance library; ITRL 96 |
Includes bibliographical references and index. | Texts in Latin with English
translation on facing pages; introduction and notes in English.
Identifiers: LCCN 2022042111 | ISBN 9780674292680 (cloth)
Subjects: LCSH: Alberti, Leon Battista, 1404–1472. |
Italian literature — 15th century — Early works to 1800.
Classification: LCC PQ4562.A6 Z46 2023 |
DDC 878/.0403 [B] — dc23/eng/20230301
LC record available at https://lccn.loc.gov/2022042111

Contents

ॐ𑀰ॐ

Introduction

※❀※

Leon Battista Alberti (1404–72) was one of the most famous figures of the Italian Renaissance. His extraordinary range of abilities as a writer, architect, art theorist, and even athlete earned him the title of the first "Renaissance man," to use Jacob Burckhardt's famous but problematic phrase in his highly influential work, *The Civilization of the Renaissance in Italy* (first published 1860).[1] Alberti was a prolific author, but only a few of his works are well known today: these are his vernacular dialogue on the family (*De familia*, 1433–43); his treatise on painting, which he wrote first in the vernacular and then in Latin (*Della pittura/De pictura*, 1435–36; 1439–41); and his Latin treatise on architecture, *De re aedificatoria* (*On the Art of Building*, 1443–72). Yet these represent only the tip of the huge iceberg of writings that he composed. Consequently, one of the first aims of this volume is to bring to the attention of a wider public five significant Latin compositions that have largely been neglected even though they tell us much about Alberti's literary aims and development and contain a strongly biographical and/or autobiographical dimension.

The pieces that make up this volume are the early treatise/invective *De commodis litterarum atque incommodis* (*On the Advantages and Disadvantages of Literature*, 1428–32; henceforth, *On the Advantages*), which partly reflects his experiences as a student in Bologna in the 1420s; the biography of an obscure Christian martyr, *Vita sancti Potiti* (*The Life of St. Potitus*, 1432–34), which also contains autobiographical projections and was to have been the first in a series of lives of saints, but Alberti completed only this one biography; a mock funeral oration for his dead dog, *Canis* (*My Dog*, ca. 1438), which however also has distinct autobiographical overtones; his own autobiography, entitled *Vita* (*My Life*, 1438–44), one of the first autobiographies of the early modern period, and the main source for Burckhardt's portrait of Alberti; and a comic encomium of the fly, entitled *Musca* (*The Fly*, 1441–43), inspired by one of Lucian's works, but this too contains many elements of his own self-portrait. These works thus revolve around the author's own lived experiences, the ideal biography of an exemplary Christian saint and the portrait of an ideal dog, writer, or fly. Despite the elements they have in common, these five titles and brief descriptions already offer us an idea of Alberti's variety and originality as a writer: they provide us with a cross-section of his development as an author as he moves from conventional invective from a university ambience to a hagiography commissioned by his first patron in the Roman Curia, Biagio Molin, then the brilliant comic portrait of his dog, the unfinished autobiography, and last, the mock encomium of the fly. This is very much an evolution from tradition to originality.

These five Latin works, written over a space of fifteen years, provide an insight into a crucial phase of Alberti's growth as a writer, as he gradually finds his own voice in these biographical and autobiographical writings. In particular, the last three works here—*My Dog, My Life,* and *The Fly*—from the period around 1440, have a more distinctive voice and constitute a kind of autobiographical trilogy, as the humanist finds one of his main themes, the portrait of the ideal life, with a strong emphasis on humor. Even when writing about a dog or a fly, Alberti is always writing about himself. But let us say a word about each of these five pieces in turn.

On the Advantages and Disadvantages of Literature

Alberti began *On the Advantages* in 1428 and finished it in late 1431.[2] This lengthy, disillusioned complaint about society's lack of respect for those who study literature belongs to that tradition of invectives written by early humanists about rival university disciplines, such as law or medicine, that had found recent expression in Petrarch's invectives.[3] It may also be part of a longer medieval practice of complaining about the lack of appreciation of any form of erudition, such as can be found in Pietro Alfonsi's twelfth-century collection of tales, the *Disciplina clericalis*.[4] Before *On the Advantages*, Alberti had written only one work, his youthful Latin comedy *Philodoxeos fabula*, the first redaction of which was composed when he was barely twenty, in 1424.[5] As we shall see, humor and comedy would remain an integral part of Alberti's literary DNA in his more mature works. However, there is little that is comic in the first two works in this volume. Despite the fact that he was only in his mid-twenties when he wrote *On the Advantages*, the work already displays many of the hallmarks of the author's mature style. There is the strong emphasis on his family: the work is dedicated to his brother Carlo, who had also been born illegitimate, like Battista, and it opens with a brief encomium of their father, Lorenzo Alberti, who had died in 1421 (*On the Advantages* 1.1). Another characteristic Albertian note sounded at the outset is the desperate pursuit of originality in a literary world where the ancient authors appeared to have covered every subject, serious or comic (1.7–14). A final typical motif from the early paragraphs is what we could call his work ethic, his dedication to continuous study and the constant practice of writing (1.1–2, 1.15). Even in terms of style, the humanist already aspires in this work to succinctness and brevity (2.24, 4.210), though these terms are rather relative and are simply part of a modesty topos, since the work is really quite long and not without repetitions.

After the two introductory sections, the bulk of the invective shows how the goals that most people pursue in life, such as pleasure, wealth, and honors, are all largely incompatible with the life of literary study. It is notable that at this early stage Alberti includes travel and the observation of beautiful architecture in foreign cities as well as music among the pleasures of life denied to the literary scholar (3.7–11). Yet throughout the rest of his existence he would not see these arts as incompatible with the life of the writer; on the contrary, he would aspire to include both architecture and music among his own accomplishments. Similarly, in this treatise he excludes the scholar from the enjoyment of sports and fine arts (3.51–56), yet he would boast about his own athletic prowess and his interest in the arts in his autobiography.

Having dealt with pleasures in section 3, Alberti then moves on to wealth in the next section. Here he is even more pessimistic, since from his experiences as a student in Bologna he concludes that studying is costly and that it does not lead to riches, unless after graduating one pursues a lucrative profession such as law or medicine. Any literary scholar who is wealthy can be rich only through good fortune, he declares. He calculates that out of a thousand students only three will survive to the age of forty and go on to make money (4.110).

Finally, Alberti deals with honors and recognition and points out how little public esteem is enjoyed by scholars of literature. Again, he draws on his own experience, this time not in Bologna but in Tuscany (he had probably been to Florence after 1428 when the exile of the Alberti family ended). He observes that people in Tuscan cities are highly critical and outspoken about everyone, so literary scholars will also be a target for their criticisms (5.51–53). As for political honors, he advises literature students to avoid politics entirely since time spent in public administration will never bring them civic dignity or honor (5.75–77). In his peroration, the author uses the rhetorical figure of prosopopoeia to allow books themselves to be personified and to speak to the scholar, urging him to ignore everything else and simply pursue virtue (6.21–39). Even at the beginning of this final section, the author had already enunciated his pessimistic conclusion about the literary scholar's relationship with these three topics of pleasure, wealth, and honor: "the study of letters involves much labor, no pleasure, much expense, minimum profit, many difficulties and dangers and very little prestige" (6.2). Despite this, as the first American translator of the work notes, On the Advantages "ends in a statement of quasi-religious devotion to secular learning."[6]

So this early treatise contains many of the themes and attitudes found in our author's later works: his concern for the family, the restless aspiration to hard work and originality in literature and the arts, the pursuit of virtue and condemnation of avarice and other vices, along with his negativity as regards women and politics. What will change is that he later makes travel, architecture, music and sport ideally compatible with the life of scholarship. As Cecil Grayson put it, "no limited definition of the studia humanitatis, of the humanities, as formulated and practised in the fifteenth century, applies to Alberti."[7]

One final striking feature of this early treatise is the already formidable range of classical sources that underpin it. Apart from the many canonical Latin authors cited or alluded to, such as Cicero and Quintilian, Alberti quotes from "new" texts he has read such as Cicero's On the Orator and the Brutus, both discovered in 1421;[8] but he also draws on other newly fashionable authors in humanist circles such as Martial and Plautus, as well as two Greek authors who will remain permanent favorites of his, Lucian and Plutarch.

The Life of St. Potitus

One of Alberti's first patrons at the Papal Curia was Biagio Molin, archbishop of Grado, who commissioned the young Battista to write a series of lives of Christian saints in the early 1430s.[9] Alberti completed the first biography, The Life of St. Potitus, between the end of 1432 and March 1434. The work is preceded by a Prohemium, which is a letter to his patron, and is followed by two other paratexts. One of these is a letter to his friend and fellow human-ist Leonardo Dati, which outlines the historiographical challenges that faced the author when composing the biography, particularly the reliability of sources and the difficulties in meeting the new standards for humanist historiography. The other is a letter to Marino Guadagni. Alberti provided no indication as to where it should be placed in relation to the biography, unlike the *Prohemium*, which he insisted should precede the main text. However, critics have argued that the letter was meant to accompany the biography when he sent it to Guadagni.[10]

The biography of the obscure second-century saint Potitus was significant for Alberti not just as his first attempt to recount the story of someone's existence but also in that to a certain extent he projected his own life onto the biography of the saint. The early description of the young man contains motifs that the humanist would elaborate in his own autobiography, particularly the young saint's almost divine intelligence, the dazzling rays that his face seemed to emanate, and the outstanding position he held in his city because of his modesty (*Life of St. Potitus* 3). Similarly, in *My Life* (1, 29) he describes himself as having a versatile mind (*ingenio versatili*) and being so accomplished in every appropriate art that he was prominent among the outstanding young men (*inter primarios*) of his age and says that he lived amid the envious with great modesty (*tanta modestia*). In some sense the subject of Alberti's autobiography is a secular equivalent of the young martyr. The author even claims in the account of his own life that he possessed in his breast a kind of ray (*habebat pectore radium*) that allowed him to sense in advance the goodwill or hatred of men toward himself (*My Life* 78). There are also links with other Albertian works: the condemnation of earthly riches (*Life of St. Potitus* 37–38) parallels similar statements in *On the Advantages*, while the denunciation of avaricious holders of church benefices (42) is found in other works of his, such as *Pontifex*, a dialogue on the duties of bishops. In terms of sources, in *The Life of St. Potitus* we find evidence of his reading of Christian authors, including Tatian, Eusebius, and Tertullian, but also the Roman *Martyrology*.

One final point to note is that even in this early work we see the emergence of Alberti's ambivalence, or "double focus," a technique that has also been observed in the writings of other humanists, such as Petrarch.[11] Thus the emperor Antoninus' condemnation of Christians as idle people, who shun society, hard work, and the arts turns the pagan emperor into an advocate of classically Albertian values (83–85). Antoninus is then an ambivalent figure who, although an enemy of Christianity, seems to espouse Alberti's own ideals: his commitment to society, his work ethic, and his pursuit of the arts, ideas championed by the author in many other works.

My Dog

The mock funeral oration, *My Dog*, was cited in the autobiography, so it must have preceded *My Life*, though it seems that the composition of the two works was broadly contemporaneous, belonging to the period around 1438 (though Alberti continued to work on the autobiography until about 1443–44). It is thus not surprising that there are overlaps between the two works.[12] Burckhardt mentions *My Dog* as the ultimate example of the humanist's virtuosity as a writer, a eulogy for his dead dog, written in elegant, classical Latin, with a vast range of allusions to both Latin and Greek authors. But on closer analysis it becomes clear that *My Dog* is much more than this. It certainly belongs to the *serio-ludere* tradition associated with the works of the Greek satirist Lucian, which were being translated into Latin in this same period by a number of humanists.[13] It may also have been inspired by Teodoro Gaza's Greek encomium of the dog, though the dating of the Greek scholar's eulogy is problematic and was probably written after

Alberti's work.[14] However, *My Dog* is substantially more serious than any of the Greek satirist's works. When set alongside the autobiography, many similarities emerge between the portrait of the dog and the self-portrait in *My Life*: both works project beings who are highly versatile, possess a strong work ethic, pursue a deep cult of friendship, have a good sense of humor, and so on.[15] In addition, it has been shown that Alberti wrote the speech in order to show a rival orator how a funeral oration should be written, even when the subject is a dog.[16]

My Dog is also characterized by a greater emphasis on humor than is found in Lucian, so it is both more serious and more ludic than anything in the Greek writer's oeuvre. One major comic element in the oration is the deployment of the author's deep erudition to talk of the potentially banal subject of his dead dog. The two main sources for the many legendary dogs mentioned in the speech were Pliny the Elder (*Natural History* 8.61.142–50) and Plutarch (*On the Intelligence of Animals* = *Moralia* 969C–971A), but Alberti adds many more allusions to other ancient texts.[17] In the mosaic of classical quotations in the speech, he still tries to pursue some originality by avoiding the order in which the ancient sources had listed the famous dogs of antiquity, systematically splicing Pliny's long list of thirteen famous dogs with episodes from Plutarch's work. In another bid to innovate, Alberti also expands the content of the classical exempla: an analysis of the details he added shows that they nearly always emphasize the dog's cult of friendship with human beings (the classical ideal of *amicitia* was embraced by Alberti in many works, including the whole of the fourth book of *De familia*).[18]

Another dimension the reader will appreciate is the clear classical structure of the oration, which begins with an account of the dog's ancestors followed by first his warlike qualities (bravery, mercy, and so on), then his peaceful virtues (cult of friendship, impeccable moral character), his philosophical talents, and a final summary of his victories and virtues.[19] A stylistic element that Alberti uses to comic effect here is the rhetorical figure of *praeteritio*, where the speaker says he will not mention a particular ancient example but then proceeds to mention several of them (*My Dog* 23–25).

One final element to note is the mention of the famous deeds and sayings of the dog's ancestors (10), a topic brought up again toward the end of the oration, when he remarks on how his dog would reproach lazy dogs with his sayings (62). One of the reasons for the inclusion of this detail in the speech is that in the 1430s Diogenes Laertius' *Lives of the Eminent Philosophers* had been translated from Greek into Latin by Alberti's fellow humanist, Ambrogio Traversari, and many of these biographies ended with a list of the philosopher's famous sayings.[20] In addition, a good number of Plutarch's *Lives* were translated into Latin by other humanists in the first decades of the Quattrocento, and some of these also contained lists of the subject's famous sayings.[21]

Thus, Alberti turns *My Dog* into a kind of biography of an exemplary philosopher, soldier, or statesman, complete with great deeds and quotable sayings. This dimension is taken to comic extremes when we are told that his dog would attend debates where he would ask other dogs whether they were Stoic, Peripatetic, Epicurean, or a follower of the Academy (61). Not surprisingly this witty speech ends by stressing the dog's sense of fun and festivity (74): in fact it has recently been suggested that *My Dog* is a deliberate parody of the many funeral orations written by humanists (such as Leonardo Bruni) in the early Quattrocento.[22] Although nothing like this mock encomium had been written by Alberti or other humanists by this stage of the Quattrocento, there are several links with *On the Advantages* and *The Life of St. Potitus*, especially in the contempt for wealth and emphasis on bravely tolerating what life throws at the dog, but the new element here is that of humor, a strand that would remain prominent in Alberti's later and more substantial works, most notably the *Intercenales*, or *Dinner Pieces* (ca. 1434–43), and the satirical Latin novel *Momus* (1443–50).[23]

My Life

Alberti's *My Life* is a fascinating document both for what it tells us about the existence and thought of this major Renaissance author and for what it reveals about his own highly individual brand of humanism. The autobiography was Jacob Burckhardt's main source for his influential but extremely idealized verbal portrait of Alberti as the prototypical "Renaissance man." However, the original Latin text of the autobiography sheds crucial light on the darker sides of Burckhardt's "sunny" Renaissance man, aspects that the Swiss historian suppressed. As has been pointed out by Anthony Grafton and others, Burckhardt says nothing about potentially negative aspects of his life, such as his physical weaknesses, his nervous exhaustion, his constant, sometimes violent, quarrels with members of his family, and his many battles against envy, which led him to burn many of his works.[24] Conversely, Burckhardt does not mention two key positive features emphasized in *My Life*, namely Alberti's prodigious work ethic and his sense of humor: words such as *festivus, iocundus*, and *risus* recur throughout this and other autobiographical works.

Apart from these substantial omissions, the Swiss historian also distorted some of Alberti's quotations from the autobiography. This happens in at least two passages that illustrate Alberti's more open attitude to knowledge, but which Burckhardt felt he had to modify in order to make him seem more of a traditional humanist. First, in the famous passage where the author says he would often ask of "artisans, architects, ship-builders, and even from shoemakers and tailors" (*My Life* 29) the secrets of their arts, Burckhardt's list of such encounters begins with two rather more prestigious categories not present in the original, namely "artists and scholars." A second distinctive trait of Alberti's humanism omitted by the historian is his openness to technical writers such as Pliny the Elder and Vitruvius, authors who were dear to him for their content if not for their style. In fact, in *My Life* he even states that any account that helped explain a discipline was of such value that even bad writers were worthy of praise as long as they expounded their subject clearly (88). None of Alberti's fellow humanists would have admitted spending time on *malos scriptores*, so Burckhardt cuts out this detail as well.

Finally, there is another passage toward the end of the autobiography (83) that the Swiss historian distorts by putting it into a more elevated context: where Alberti had said of himself that men can do all things if they will, this was in the potentially trivial context of how he managed to overcome another one of his weaknesses, namely his aversion to garlic and honey. Burckhardt avoids any mention of his subject's fragilities, so instead inserts the quotation immediately after the more impressive passage about his powers of prophecy, saying that an iron will pervaded the author's personality (a sentence not present in the original) and adds that, like all great men of the Renaissance, Alberti said that men could do all things if they will. Burckhardt's Alberti is anachronistic, closer in spirit to Schopenhauer than to the Stoic philosophers that the humanist embraced.

My Life is arranged around ten major topics, most of which are also found in ancient biographies. The work begins not with Alberti's birth, as in classical lives (no doubt because of the fact of being born illegitimate and in exile), but instead with a list of his physical and intellectual achievements. His education in literature and law is then described, followed by a list of his literary works and an outline of his struggles against envious critics. Next, his character, particularly his wide intellectual curiosity, his achievements in painting, and his appreciation of humor are illustrated. This leads to a list of over thirty of his witty sayings, followed by details of his prophetic powers and, then, examples of his Stoicism in overcoming physical weaknesses and pain. Subsequently, the powerful effects that nature had on him, which mostly served to heighten his own already considerable work ethic, are documented. The work finishes off with another, shorter but unfinished, list of witty sayings.

From the episodes recounted in this work, it is clear that Alberti drew on two great classical traditions to compose his autobiography. The first is biographies of poets, epitomized by the late antique life of Virgil by Donatus (fourth century CE), especially the sections on the author's ill-health, his desire to burn some of his works, his battles with envious critics, his witty replies. The second tradition includes the two "new" Greek authors, mentioned before, whose works were being translated into Latin by contemporary humanists: Diogenes Laertius' *Lives of the Eminent Philosophers* and Plutarch's *Lives*. As Diogenes Laertius ended most of his biographies with a list of the philosopher's famous sayings, so in *My Dog* and *My Life* (and later in *The Fly*) there will be a mention of the subject's celebrated aphorisms.

So we should read Alberti's autobiography not just to counteract Burckhardt's distortions, but also to read a remarkably secular life story. The only precedent for a humanist writing an autobiography was Petrarch's *Letter to Posterity* (ca. 1350, revised 1370), but that text is deeply indebted to St. Augustine's *Confessions*, structured around the seven deadly sins, and its overall tone is one of denunciation of the *vanitas vanitatum*. There is none of this Christian framework in *My Life*, no mention of God, sin, religion, or the afterlife.

The Fly

It seems that Alberti continued working on his autobiography until 1444, so in chronological terms it is close also to *The Fly*, which was finished in 1443. As with *My Dog*, so with the mock encomium of the fly there are many overlaps with *My Life*. This too is a substantial, idealized portrait, but this time of an insect! The Lucianic model here is more specifically identifiable in the Greek satirist's own *Encomium of the Fly*, which had been recently translated into Latin by a fellow humanist, Guarino da Verona, and then sent to Alberti by the Veronese scholar.[25] This gift inspired him to compose, not another translation of Lucian's original, but a free rewriting of it. He embroiders Lucian's theme and rewrites his eulogy as a wittier but also more emphatically ethical oration, with a much denser series of allusions to antiquity, though always permeated from beginning to end by a sense of fun and inventiveness.[26]

As with *My Dog*, so here Alberti organizes the oration in a classical structure, celebrating the animal's family, its achievements in warlike and peaceful activities, its moral qualities, and its work ethic. The fly, like Alberti's dog, is noted for its versatility and wide-ranging erudition, and it is particularly praised for its links with Pythagoras and its contribution to mathematics and music.[27] The insect is also celebrated for other Albertian concerns: its work ethic, its cult of friendship, its patience and affability in dealing with critics, its battles against envy, and its sense of fun.

But these heroic qualities are undermined by the tone of mockery and humor in the work. In fact, *The Fly* is by far the wittier of Alberti's two mock-heroic orations on animals. When praising the fly's boundless knowledge, the humanist inserts a series of learned allusions to characters from classical mythology, saying that the fly is so knowledgeable that it even knows which cakes Circe made in order to turn her guests into monsters; it has learned where Osiris lies hidden; it even knows what blemishes Helen of Troy has on her bottom; has fondled all of Ganymede's hidden parts; and knows how bitter is the taste of Andromache's ancient breasts (*The Fly*, 26). The fly's knowledge here is either banal or simply an excuse for the humanist to indulge in comic sexual innuendo, something very rare in his works. Another source of humor resides in the fact that Alberti elevates the ordinary quotidian activities of the fly into heroic achievements: its buzzing around cattle is exaggerated into a valiant pursuit of an enormous bull (14); its love of food is linked not to greed but to its religious sensibilities, since it is always the first to arrive at and last to leave feasts set out for the gods (23); and the copulation of flies in midair is transformed by the orator into a very different vision, since the speaker sees their aerial mating as one fly nobly carrying a tired fellow insect in an act of *pietas* that would outdo that of Aeneas, who carried his ancient father from Troy (19).[28]

Yet, although *The Fly* contains more humor than Lucian's original *Encomium Muscae*, there is also a strong ethical tone to the work, as the orator praises the fly's tireless research and its humane qualities as opposed to the inhumane cruelty of its enemy, the treacherous and envious spider. This serious side to the oration is also in evidence in many allusions to Roman culture, such as the insect's claimed descent from the goddess Bellona, the allusions to the early history of Rome, and its emulation of the tireless research of Pliny the Elder.[29] *The Fly* is a more humorous but also a more serious portrait of the humble insect than the Greek original: Alberti's is a brief oration that epitomizes the author's own values and strives to outdo several Greek, Latin, and even contemporary writers, such as Guarino.

The reader of this volume of five Alberti works will, I hope, get some idea of the quality of writing and the variety of interests in this "chameleon-like" author.[30] The five texts chart his development as a writer from the first two works of the late 1420s and early 1430s (*On the Advantages* and *The Life of St. Potitus*) to the last three pieces from the late 1430s and early 1440s. The budding author begins with a rather conventional invective/treatise, bemoaning the lack of respect and prospects for scholars of literature, followed by a specially commissioned saint's life as he begins his career in the Roman Curia. Alberti's letter to friend and fellow-humanist Leonardo Dati expresses his difficulties in researching and writing this work, so it is not surprising that he did not write any more hagiographical works for this series.[31] Instead he turned to other, distinctly secular subjects. The last three works in this volume, *My Dog*, *My Life*, and *The Fly*, move in much more original directions and together they form a humorous, autobiographical triptych. For the mature Alberti originality, humor, and the recounting of his life and ideals become more urgent and emerge as the hallmarks of his later works.

One of the most striking aspects in all five works is the staggering, perhaps unequaled range of reference to classical texts, both Greek and Latin (as is attested by the many footnotes in this edition, even those accompanying the shorter texts, i.e., *My Dog*, *My Life*, and *The Fly*). Few humanists of the time had read as widely as Alberti (though some had read fewer authors more deeply). But his classical allusions are as remarkable for their quality as for their quantity. He was always a pioneer in terms of sources, often citing "new" works, such as the Cicero texts rediscovered in 1421 in Lodi (he had his own copy of the *Brutus*), or Greek works by authors such as Plutarch, Diogenes Laertius, and Lucian, which were being translated into Latin by contemporary humanists. These last three authors were a favorite section of Alberti's library, quoted by him on many occasions, and it is interesting that when he turns to Greek culture in these works it is not to philosophers, such as Plato and Aristotle (though he does of course quote them occasionally), or to poets, but to biographers and humorous writers.[32] But he turned to the classical past not just because of his antiquarian interests, though he certainly had them, but to see what it could tell him about the problems of the present. His mind was agile, and constantly in movement: as he tells us in the autobiography, when young he turned to embrace also mathematical and "scientific" subjects, and this "turn" was to prove productive, particularly in his treatises on painting and architecture. Similarly, he moved between Latin and Greek and the Italian vernacular, deriving from Cicero's *Brutus* fundamental ideas about how the arts and also a language such as the vernacular might develop. But the humorous element in *My Dog, My Life,* and *The Fly* will remain fundamental to Alberti, and it will permeate his more substantial final compositions: the satirical novel *Momus* and even the treatise on architecture, *On the Art of Building.* I hope the reader of the last three works in this volume will agree with Alberti's recommendation in the final words of *The Fly:* "We wrote the above laughing, and you too should laugh."

For the Latin texts of the last four works translated in this volume, I am extremely grateful to Roberto Cardini for his kind permission to use the editions established by him and his colleagues in Leon Battista Alberti, *Opere latine,* ed. Roberto Cardini (Rome: Istituto Poligrafico e Zecca dello Stato, 2010). This work is cited throughout as "Cardini 2010" with page number. For *On the Advantages* I am very grateful to Mariangela Regoliosi for permission to make use of her recent edition of the work for the Edizione Nazionale delle Opere di Leon Battista Alberti: for full details see the Note on the Texts at the end of the volume.

In preparing this volume, I accumulated many debts of gratitude. I would like to offer special thanks to the Director of Harvard's Villa I Tatti, Alina Payne, for her kind invitation to spend a semester as Visiting Professor at the Villa, January–June 2019, where the bulk of the work was carried out. I am very grateful also to the Fellows at I Tatti that semester for their helpful comments on this research project, both at formal seminars and in convivial conversations, especially Philippe Canguilhem. I would also like to thank a number of colleagues who have helped me with various queries: first and foremost, Stephen Harrison and Elisabetta Tarantino, who offered precious advice in several different areas; but also Peter Hainsworth, Catherine McLaughlin, Christopher Pelling, Richard Rutherford, Oliver Taplin. I am grateful as well to Marta Celati for precious bibliographical information on the historiographical issues that lie behind the *Life of St. Potitus*.

I owe a particular debt of gratitude to James Hankins, who supported this project from the outset and with his vast knowledge of humanist culture followed it through its various stages with meticulous, insightful editing.

NOTES

1. Jacob Burckhardt, *The Civilization of the Renaissance in Italy: An Essay*, translated by Samuel G. C. Middlemore, new introduction by Peter Burke, notes by Peter Murray (Harmondsworth: Penguin, 1990), 102–4 for the passage on Alberti. For a recent monograph in English on Alberti, see Pearson, *Leon Battista Alberti: The Chameleon's Eye*. (Full references for short-title citations in this Introduction and in the Notes to the Translations may be found in the Bibliography).

2. He seems to have composed the treatise in 1428–29 and "published" it (for circulation in manuscript) in late 1431–32: see Alberti, *De commodis litterarum atque incommodis*, ed. Regoliosi, 1:36–38. See also Roberto Cardini, "Quando e dove l'Alberti conobbe il nuovo Plauto (e qual è la cronologia del *De commodis* e dell'*Ecatonfilea*)," in *Itinerari del testo: Per Stefano Pittaluga*, ed. Cristina Cocco et al. (Genoa: Università degli Studî: Da. Fi.St./D.Ar.Fi.Cl.eT., 2018), 141–94, esp. 189–90; and Luca Boschetto,

"Nuovi documenti su Carlo di Lorenzo Alberti e una proposta per la datazione del *De commodis litterarum atque incommodis*," *Albertiana* 1 (1998): 43–60.

3. For the texts of Petrarch's invectives, see Francesco Petrarca, *Invectives*, ed. and trans. David Marsh, I Tatti Renaissance Library 11 (Cambridge, MA: Harvard University Press, 2003).

4. *Die Disciplina Clericalis des Petrus Alfonsi*, ed. Alfons Hilka and Werner Söderhjelm (Heidelberg: C. Winter, 1911). For this reference I am indebted to Elisabetta Tarantino and to her article, "The Dante Anecdote in Gower's *Confessio Amantis*," *The Chaucer Review* 39.4 (2005): 420–35. The English translator—in Alberti, *The Use and Abuse of Books*, trans. Renée Neu Watkins, 54, note 2—notes some similarities between Alberti's text and Nietzsche's *The Use and Abuse of History*. In this volume, Watkins' translation is cited as "Watkins" with page number.

5. Alberti would later write a definitive version of the comedy in 1437, with a lengthy commentary/introduction, dedicating it to Leonello d'Este: for the texts of the two redactions, see the edition of Lucia Cesarini Martinelli, "Leon Battista Alberti, *Philodoxeos Fabula*," *Rinascimento*, ser. 2, 17 (1977): 111–234. An English translation with Cesarini Martinelli's text of the second redaction is available in *Humanist Comedies*, trans. Gary R. Grund, I Tatti Renaissance Library 19 (Cambridge, MA.: Harvard University Press, 2005), 70–169.

6. Watkins, 4.

7. Cecil Grayson, "*De commodis litterarum atque incommodis*," *Modern Language Review* 83 (1988): xxxi–xlii, esp. xxxix.

8. The many echoes of Cicero's *Brutus* in *On the Advantages* (see the footnotes to the translation in this volume, as well as in the editions by Goggi Carotti and Regoliosi) suggest that Alberti had read this work, rediscovered barely ten years previously, with the enthusiasm of a convert to a newly fashionable text: see Mariangela Regoliosi, "Per un catalogo degli *auctores* latini dell'Alberti," in *Leon Battista Alberti: La biblioteca di un umanista*, 105–13 (esp. 107).

9. After his friend Gabriele Condulmer became Pope Eugenius IV in 1431, Molin moved to Rome, where he became head of the Papal Chancery.

10. Guadagni had a career as papal secretary in the Curia and was a canon of several churches in Tuscany, including the cathedral of Santa Maria del Fiore in Florence; he died in 1438. For the views of the editor (Elena Giannarelli) and Donatella Coppini on the three letters, see the Notes to the Texts.

11. For the idea of "double focus" in Renaissance texts, see Giuseppe Mazzotta, *The Worlds of Petrarch* (Durham, NC: Duke University Press, 1993), 1; for its presence in Alberti's *The Fly*, see Arielle Saiber, "Quadrivial comedy in Alberti's *Musca*," in *Alberti Lvdens* 23.2 (2020): 191–205, esp. 194. For the same technique in a historiographical work by Alberti, see Marta Celati, "Irony, Historiography and Political Criticism: The *Porcaria coniuratio*," ibid. 207–24.

12. Maria Letizia Magnini Bracciali, "L. B. Alberti, *Canis* 10–27: Fonti e problemi," in *Nel cantiere degli umanisti: Per Mariangela Regoliosi*, ed. Lucia Bertolini, Donatella Coppini, Clementina Marsico (Florence: Polistampa, 2014), 2:777–826, considers *My Dog* to be a kind of dress rehearsal for the autobiography (p. 782).

13. See Marsh, *Lucian and the Latins*, 148–67.

14. Marsh, *Lucian and the Latins*, 155, 157, argues for Gaza's encomium being a source for Alberti's work, but it may simply be the case that the two writers used the same classical sources; in any case, Alberti deploys many more allusions to classical texts and writes a much longer encomium than Gaza. Gaza's text can be found in *Patrologia Graeca*, ed. J.-P. Migne, vol. 161 (Paris: Migne, 1866), 985–98. Magnini Bracciali, "L. B. Alberti, *Canis* 10–27," 779–81, is skeptical about Gaza's encomium being a direct source, especially as Gaza seems to have composed his encomium around 1440.

15. For these similarities in the depiction of the dog and of Alberti himself, see McLaughlin, "Alberti's *Canis*, 76–83.

16. Mariangela Regoliosi, "Un'orazione funebre umoristica: Il *Canis* dell'Alberti," in *Alberti Lvdens* 23.2 (2020): 161–69. Regoliosi defines the *Canis* as "una nuova autobiografia albertiana" (p. 169).

17. See the notes to the English translation for the other classical sources; and see also Mariangela Regoliosi, "Un'orazione funebre umoristica,"

166n14, for an important allusion to Cicero, *On the Nature of the Gods* 2.63.158.

18. For details see McLaughlin, "Alberti's *Canis*," 74–76; and Magnini Bracciali, "L. B. Alberti, *Canis* 10–27," 810–23.

19. For structural details of both *My Dog* and *The Fly*, see Martin McLaughlin, "Alberti's *Musca*," 9–10.

20. For Diogenes Laertius' translations, see Marcello Gigante, "Ambrogio Traversari interprete di Diogene Laerzio," in *Ambrogio Traversari nel VI centenario della nascita*, ed. Gian Carlo Garfagnini (Florence: Olschki, 1988), 367–459.

21. For versions of Plutarch in Latin, see Marianne Pade, *The Reception of Plutarch's Lives in Fifteenth-Century Italy*, 2 vols. (Copenhagen: Museum Tusculanum Press, 2007).

22. David Marsh made this intriguing point at a seminar given by Michel Paoli on Alberti's *My Dog* and *The Fly* at the Kunsthistorisches Institut in Florence (July 19, 2022).

23. For the dating of the *Intercenales*, see *Leon Battista Alberti: Opere latine*, edited by Roberto Cardini (Rome: Istituto Poligrafico e Zecca dello Stato, 2010), 194–200; and for *Momus*, ibid., 1258. For a Latin text with English translation of the *Momus*, see Alberti, *Momus*, ed. and trans. Virginia Brown and Sarah Knight, I Tatti Renaissance Library 8 (Cambridge, MA: Harvard University Press, 2003). A Latin text by Roberto Cardini with an English translation by David Marsh is forthcoming in this I Tatti Renaissance Library series.

24. See Grafton, *Leon Battista Alberti: Master Builder*, 9–18. For an account of how the Swiss historian distorted other elements of Alberti's autobiography, see McLaughlin, "Alberti and Burckhardt."

25. For a specific comparison of Guarino's and Alberti's rewritings of Lucian's encomium, see McLaughlin, "Humanist Translations and Rewritings."

26. For details, see McLaughlin, "Alberti's *Musca*."

27. For further details on the fly's links with mathematics and related subjects, see Saiber, "Quadrivial comedy in Alberti's *Musca*."

28. For a more detailed account of the anti-Vergilian dimension of *The Fly*, see Hartmut Wulfram, "Alberti's Attack on Virgil in the *Musca*," in *Alberti Lvdens* 23.2 (2020): 171–90.

29. For further details on the Roman dimension, see McLaughlin, "Alberti's *Musca*," 18–20.

30. Cristoforo Landino was the first to use this metaphor of his mentor when he said that Alberti, like a new chameleon, takes on the color of the thing that he is writing about ("come nuovo camaleonta sempre quello colore piglia il quale è nella cosa della quale scrive"): see Cristoforo Landino, *Scritti critici e teorici*, ed. Roberto Cardini, 2 vols. (Rome: Bulzoni, 1974), 1: 120.

31. Donatella Coppini, "Leon Battista Alberti si corregge. Il caso della *Mosca* Riccardiana," in *Leon Battista Alberti. La biblioteca di un umanista*, ed. Roberto Cardini et al., 56.

32. See Lucia Bertolini, "Per la biblioteca greca dell'Alberti," in *Leon Battista Alberti: La biblioteca di un umanista*, 101–3, esp. 102.

BIOGRAPHICAL AND
AUTOBIOGRAPHICAL WRITINGS

DE COMMODIS LITTERARUM ATQUE INCOMMODIS

I

1 Laurentius Albertus parens noster, vir cum multis in rebus, tum in educanda familia temporibus suis facile nostrorum omnium princeps, ut meministi, Carole, solitus erat nos ita instructos velle
2 et domi et foris videri, ut nunquam essemus otiosi. Qua ingenua et preclara patris nostri disciplina instituti atque imbuti, tu semper aut gerendis negotiis aut in litterarum cognitione versaris, ego autem, qui me totum tradidi litteris, ceteris posthabitis rebus, omnia posse libentius debeo quam diem aliquam nihil aut lectitando aut
3 commentando preterire. Qua ex re illud quidem nos assecutos gaudeo, ut adversas quibus diutius premimur erumnas partim ferre moderate, partim vitare prudenter licuerit documentis litterarum.
4 Ac mihi quidem studiis nostris non modo ut nobis tantum prosint, sed magis etiam ut amicorum expectationi satisfaciant
5 enitendum videtur. Namque in dies nostri, quibus et dignitas mea cara est et fama, omnes exposcunt ut fructum aliquem depromam vigiliarum mearum, quo intelligant me meo studiorum labore et
6 assiduitate aliquid profecisse. Itaque et mea et meorum causa sepe ac multum animo et cogitatione plurima ipse mecum versans, meditabar quidnam possem dignum adinvenire in quo vires ingenii mei periclitarer, tum meis iubentibus, si quid in me esset, obtemperarem.

ON THE ADVANTAGES AND
DISADVANTAGES OF LITERATURE

I

Carlo, as you will remember, our father Lorenzo degli Alberti was   1
easily the most outstanding man of his time in many walks of life
but particularly in bringing up a family.[1] He always wanted us to
be educated both within the family circle and outside it in such a
way that we should never be idle. We were brought up imbued   2
with this noble and famous paternal discipline, so that now you
are always busy either conducting business or increasing your
knowledge of literature, while I, having set aside all other pursuits
and given myself over entirely to literary study, would gladly do
anything else rather than let a day go by without reading or writing something.[2] As a result of this, I rejoice that we have achieved   3
this goal of being able partly to tolerate with moderation the ill
fortune which has oppressed us now for too long, and partly to
avoid it altogether through prudence, thanks to the instruction
contained in literature.[3]

   In my view, I feel that we must strive through our studies not   4
only to be of service to ourselves but even more to satisfy our
friends' expectations. For now, day after day, those who are close to   5
us, who care about my dignity and fame, are all demanding that I
deliver some fruits from my education, so that they can see that I
have made progress through hard work and assiduity in my studies. Thus both for my own sake and for that of my friends and   6
family, I often turned these things over in my mind and thoughts,
wondering what I could find as an area appropriate for me to test
the strength of my talent, and how I could obey to the best of my
abilities those who were encouraging me.

7   Nihil mihi unquam pervestiganti in mentem subiit, quod ipsum
a priscis illis divinis scriptoribus non pulchre esset occupatum, ut
neque eam rem viro hac etate doctissimo quam iidem illi melius
dicere neque mihi similia illis apte et condigne agere relictum sit;
ita et seria omnia et iocosa veteres ipsi complexi sunt, nobis tantum legendi atque admirandi sui facultatem et necessitatem dimi-
serunt.

8   Tum hac etate qui maiores adsunt natu nonnulla que fortassis a
superioribus scriptoribus neglecta latitabant laudis et nominis gra-
9   tia deprehenderunt: nam prestantius esse recte opinantur, his qui
laudem cupiant, quippiam, etsi non omni ex parte perfectum atque
absolutum, conari quam in litteris silentio consenescere.

10   Quid igitur nos? Num, parum commode, Isocratem illum rhe-
torem imitabimur qui Busiridem nequissimum tyrannum laudasse
ac Socratem optimum et sanctissimum philosophum conditis ora-
11 tionibus vituperasse fertur? Sane sic censeo: multa ingenium ex-
ercentibus nobis presertim iuvenibus concedi, que alioquin matu-
ris et perfecte eruditis viris denegarentur.

12   Condant illi quidem historiam, tractent mores principum ac
13 gesta rerum publicarum eventusque bellorum; nos vero iuniores,
modo aliquid novi proferamus, non vereamur severissima et, ut ita
loquar, nimium censoria illorum iudicia, qui cum ipsi infantes et
elingues sint, tantum aures ad cognoscendum nimium deliciosas
porrigunt, quasi doctis sat sit non pectus sed aures eruditas gerere.

14 Nobis, magnis vigiliis, non prisce in primis eloquentie et elegantie

However, although I investigated these things thoroughly, I 7
never discovered any subject that had not already been wonderfully written about by those godlike classical writers. In fact even
the most learned man in this age would not be able to write about
the same topic better than those ancient authors, and I myself
could not discuss even subjects similar to them in a fitting and
worthy manner. Those writers of antiquity have written about all
the serious and comic matters in such a way that they have left us
only with the chance or rather the obligation to read them and be
astonished by them.

After them, in our own times, in the pursuit of praise and fame 8
our predecessors took up some subjects which happened to have
been neglected by previous writers and lay untouched. For they 9
rightly think that for those who pursue glory it is better at least to
attempt to write something, even if it is not completely perfect
and rounded off, rather than growing old in literary silence.[4]

So what should we do? Surely it would not be to our advantage 10
to imitate that famous orator Isocrates who is said to have written
polished rhetorical exercises, including both a eulogy of Busiris,
that most evil tyrant, and a condemnation of Socrates, the best
and most devout philosopher?[5] This is what I truly believe: that 11
there are many subjects that are open to us when exercising our
intelligence — especially when we are young — which are not available to mature and thoroughly erudite men.

So let others write histories, deal with the ethics of princes, the 12
history of states and the outcomes of wars;[6] as long as we produce 13
something new, we younger writers will not fear the unduly severe
and, so to speak, overly censorious verdicts of others. In other
words, we will not be afraid of those who, since they are unable to
speak or write, simply listen with overly fastidious ears in order to
learn things, as if it were enough for the erudite only to have
learned ears and not have the courage to write. We should not, 14
through our long periods of study, seek praise primarily for our

expetenda laus est, ad quod etsi viribus totis iam diu contenderimus, nunquam tamen ne mediocriter quidem assequi potuimus;

15 verum exercitationum nostrarum vetus consuetudo nostra tenenda est atque id quidem non quo illis placeamus qui per omnem vitam suam nihil plus quam nihil laudare didicerunt, sed hoc ad scribendum instituto accessimus, ut meis, eorum voluntati obtemperando, simus hoc munere gratiores atque acceptiores; in quo bene nobiscum agi arbitrabimur si id assequemur ut nos eruditi non penitus contemnant.

16 Itaque consuetudini nostre et meorum petitionibus operam impertiens hoc de commodis litterarum atque incommodis edidi opusculum, quod quidem, mi frater, tum quod meis morem gesserim, tum etiam quod fuerim materiam nactus non vulgarem neque satis ante hoc tempus explicitam, gratum tibi futurum arbitrabor.

17 Et novi studia litterarum, quibus ad hunc usque diem superiorem etatem omnem traduxi meam, quam sint commoda atque incom-

18 moda. Tu vero (ut tuo in *Ephebiis* utar dicto), mi frater, relege hunc nostrum libellum, corrige, immuta tuo quidem arbitratu, emendationeque tua inventionem nostram effice gratiorem ac digniorem.

II

1 Sepe audiveram plerosque gravissimos eruditissimosque viros de studiis litterarum ea referentes que non iniuria possent a litteris discendique cupiditate ununquenque avertere. Ceteras enim inter persuasiones, quas quidem multas ac varias adducebant, palam profitebantur se minime illos esse, quanquam litteris profecissent, qui, si tempora restituerentur, non quidvis aliud vite genus subire

2 quam ad litteras redire commodius ducerent. Quam sententiam

6

classical eloquence and elegance, since even if we were to strive with all our strength, we would never be able to approach, never mind achieve such an ideal. Instead we should stick to our old 15 habit of practicing writing, not in order to please those who throughout their whole life have only learned never to praise anything, but rather we should deliberately write in order that by obeying the will of our family we should be more welcomed and appreciated by them; in doing this we shall think we have been treated well if those who are learned do not totally despise us.

So following our own habits, and bearing in mind our family's 16 requests, I have produced this little work on the advantages and disadvantages of literature.[7] I hope you will appreciate this book, my dear brother, both because I have obeyed our family's wishes in writing it, and also because in it I have dealt with a subject that is neither common nor has it been adequately dealt with before this time. And I myself know how advantageous and disadvantageous 17 literary studies are since I have spent all my life in them up until now. But you, my brother, (to borrow a phrase from your *Ephebia*)[8] 18 reread this little work of mine, emend it, change what you think should be altered, and make this new work more appealing and dignified with the help of your emendations.

II

I myself have often heard several very serious and learned men 1 talking about the study of literature and citing those things that understandably could deflect anyone from letters and from the love of learning. Among many different arguments which they adduced, they openly admitted that if they had their time over again, even though they had made some progress in literary studies, they would think it preferable to choose any other kind of life than to return to literary study. The fact that particularly those who had 2

esse in eos, presertim qui nullum tempus vacuum litteris preter-
mitterent, a mea tantum opinione aberat, ut non modo aliter
quam sentirent dicere illos arbitrarer, sed eosdem etiam propemo-
3 dum inculpandos existimarem. Nam preter officium videbatur si
docti deterrerent iuvenes a litteris, vel si prudentes viri ea seque-
rentur que parum conducere intelligerent. Ea re fiebat, diligentius
plurimos litteratos cum percunctarer, tum in omnibus fere hunc
ipsum animum comperirem, alienum videlicet ab studiis litterarum quibus essent maximopere dediti.

4   Mihi vero, quamvis multorum auctoritas rationesque obstarent,
tamen nescio quo pacto de litteris aliter videbatur: erat enim eiusmodi apud me opinio ut, dum illi viri eruditissimi suis rationibus
multa litteris incommoda adiudicarent, ego esse litteras censerem
longe iocundissimas, dumque ceteris omnibus disciplinis illi cultum litterarum postponendum putarent, ego litteras rebus omni-
5 bus preponendas ducerem. Denique ita me cognitioni litterarum
dedicaram omnino, ut nihil in litteris preclarum esse diceretur
quod illud animo et voluntate non appeterem, quod laboribus,
cura atque vigiliis non prosequerer, quodve summa diligentia et
6 observantia quantum possem non excolerem. Que posset enim
apud me esse opinio aut institutum laudabilius non videbam; ex-
celsi quidem animi officium putabam labores, vigilias, omnesque
reliquas studiorum curas et difficultates subire ac perferre vel
sciendi causa, vel honoris et fame adipiscende gratia: quas me res
7 posse litteris assequi existimabam. Ac fui quidem in ea opinione
et instituto sane liberali sed parum necessario, quamdiu quid in
hominum usu oporteret ignoravi.

not spent a second away from literature should feel this way seemed so different from my expectations that not only did I think that they were expressing an opinion that they did not really hold, but actually I thought that they even ought to be totally condemned. For it seemed to be going against their duty for learned people to deter the young from literature, or for the prudent to follow those things which they knew were unsuitable. That was how it came about that when I diligently asked many literature scholars, I found this same attitude, namely of hostility to literary study even though these same people were hugely devoted to it. 3

As for me, although the authority and arguments of many people stood in my way, still — I'm not sure how — I felt differently about literature. My opinion on the matter was such that, while those extremely erudite men judged there to be many disadvantages in books, I myself felt that literary works were far and away the most pleasant thing of all, and while they thought that the devotion to texts should come second to all other disciplines, I thought that literature should be preferred to anything else. Finally I so totally devoted myself to literary study, that there was nothing that was said to be in literature that I did not seek out with enthusiasm and determination, that I did not pursue with labor, scholarship and burning the midnight oil, or that I did not cultivate with supreme diligence and observance. For I did not see what opinion or decision could be more laudable for me; I thought that it was the duty of a lofty mind to undertake and put up with hard work, scholarship, and all the other worries and difficulties brought on by study, either for the sake of knowledge, or in order to gain honor and fame. These were things that I believed I could achieve through literature; and I was convinced of this noble but hardly realistic opinion and determination for all the time I remained ignorant of what was really needed to survive in the world of men. 4 5 6 7

8   Postea vero quam usu et tractando hominum mores apertius cognovi, fatebor quas rationes de litterarum incommodis refellere ac despicere solitus eram, eas contra omnes cepisse me tum animo nonnihil approbare, tum, rebus ipsis, non minima ex parte easdem

9   veras esse intelligere: quod perpendi admodum nullam fore vivendi viam quam laboribus et anxietatibus ista ipsa litterarum institutio non exsuperet, a quave vita studiosorum non longe facilitate fortune superetur.

10   Quo fit ut minime intelligam quid tantis laboribus sibi tantisque vigiliis litterati velint, nisi forte cognitione rerum earum que litteris continentur capti ac detenti minus franguntur laboribus

11   quam ceteri. (Ego tamen ob studia litterarum non minus laboribus fractum ac debilitatum me quam omnibus fortune bonis spoliatum

12   undique esse sentio. Sed de meis incommodis alias.) Nunc sat sit non sine causa eorum omnino sententiam non abhorrere, qui, ut

13   diximus, omnia mallent quam litteris consenuisse. Non tamen ita me ab instituto vetere dimovi ut litteras penitus deserendas arbitrarer, quas non esse, ut opinabar, commodas comperirem; sed nos ita in studiis litterarum esse animatos oportere censui, ut pre rerum nobilissimarum cognitione parvi admodum reliqua omnia fortune bona facienda existimaremus, sola quidem sapientia contenti essemus.

14   Quibus autem rationibus adducar ut ita constituam de litteris erit, ut arbitror, non iniocundum, neque id quidem inutile accepisse. Videbis enim maximo in errore versari eos qui sibi aliud ex

15   litteris quam liberam et expeditam sapientiam pollicentur. Ac poteris quidem stultissimos illos recte arbitrari qui divitiarum, amplitudinis aut ceterarum inanium caducarumque rerum cupiditate

However, after I got to know men's morals through my own   8
experience and dealings with others, I admitted that those arguments about the disadvantages of literature that I had been used
to rejecting and despising were actually accurate. I now began both
to approve them to a certain extent against all others, and to realize that they were largely true in the actual experience of things. I   9
calculated that there was really no other way of living that a dedication to literature did not outdo in terms of labor and anxiety,
and no other way of living that did not easily outstrip the life of
the scholar in terms of easily enjoying good fortune.

As a result, I do not know what literary people want with all   10
their labor and study, unless perhaps by being so enthralled and
caught up in the study of those things that are contained in books,
they are less broken by labor than others. (As for me, though,   11
thanks to literary study I feel I am both broken and weakened by
labor and totally deprived of all the goods of fortune. But there
will be another occasion for dealing with my disadvantages.) For   12
the time being, and not without reason, let us not totally reject the
opinion of those who, as we said, prefer anything rather than to
grow old studying literature. Still, I have not so departed from my   13
old frame of mind that I think I should fully desert literary pursuits because I found it not to be as advantageous as I previously
thought. On the contrary, I thought I should be so active in literary study that I should consider all other earthly goods of little
worth compared to the knowledge of these noblest of subjects, and
that I should be satisfied with wisdom alone.

I think it will not be unpleasant nor pointless to learn why I   14
came to think about literature in this way. For you will see that
those who think they will get anything else from literary study
than free and uncluttered wisdom are deeply mistaken. And you   15
will be right to think that those people are extremely stupid who
think that they can put up with all the labors that literary scholars

tantos labores perferant quantos litterarum studiosos perferre opus est.

16   Oportet enim duram et asperam vitam ducere studiosos: de his volo intelligi qui, ut debent, ceteris omissis rebus omnibus, omni
17 animo atque opere litteris dediti sunt. Nulla est enim ars que, etsi minima sit, non te totum exigat, modo in ea velis excellere. Id quidem cum ceteris omnibus artibus ita convenire videamus, tum maxime hec litterarum disciplina una est in qua nulla etate liceat a curis maximis vacare.

18   Nam ab ipsa quidem pueritia litteris deditos videmus volvendis, ut aiunt, chartis in solitudinem relegatos; ferula, magistris, discendi cura, lectitandi assiduitate et labore attritos ita et confectos eosdem videmus ut plerunque appareant frigidiores quam illa etas
19 postulet. Post hec sequitur iuventa etas, hanc vero quam ducant iocundam et letam tu eorum ex vultibus contemplere. Aspice quo pallore, qua tristitia, qua omni facie corporis remissa et pene abiecta ex diutino illo scolarum et bibliothecarum carcere egre-
20 diantur! Miseri! Quam sunt exhausti, languidi longo lectionum tedio, magnis vigiliis, nimia assiduitate, ac profundis animi curis obruti! ut eos cum viderint qui humanitatem sapiunt soleant aut misereri laborum aut ineptias eorum vehementius inculpare, maxime si ulla fortune bona tantis laboribus concupiscantur. Et merito id quidem: nam preter cognitionem ex litteris commodi-
21 tates (ut sic fortune bona dicantur) nulle inveniuntur. Quam ob rem vehementer illi quidem inculpandi sunt qui tantum in hoc studio opere cureque posuerint, ut non maiore in optimum fortune et dignitatis statum vita humana collocari posse videatur.

have to endure solely because they desire wealth, greatness and the other pointless and perishable things.

The fact is that scholars have to live a hard, demanding life: by 16 scholars I mean those who do as they ought to and, forgetting about everything else, are dedicated to literary study with all their mind and might. For there is no art, however humble, that does 17 not demand our full attention, as long as we want to excel in it. While we see that this is appropriate in all other arts, in the subject of literature it is particularly so: it is the sole discipline where one is not allowed to be without major worries at any time of life.

For from childhood onward we see those who are devoted to 18 literature turning page after page, as they say, and being confined to solitude. We see them so worn down and exhausted by beatings, by their teachers, by worry about learning, and the constant labor and assiduity required for reading, that for the most part they appear more gloomy than is appropriate for that age. After childhood comes youth, but how happy and carefree their 19 youthful age is you can gauge from their faces. Look at the pallor, the depression in their looks, how they come out of that daily prison of the school and library with every aspect of their body expressing surrender and abjection! Poor souls! How exhausted 20 they are, how lifeless and overwhelmed with profound mental anxiety they seem through the long tedium of reading, the many hours of study and their excessive dedication. As a result, those who have some sort of humanity about them feel sorry for the students' labors when they see them, or they strongly condemn their foolishness, especially if they desire any earthly benefits from so much hard work. And rightly so, for apart from the knowledge gained through reading, they find no advantages (if we might call the goods of fortune this). For this reason they are indeed strongly 21 to be condemned, who have invested so much hard work and anxieties in this pursuit, since with the same amount of study any human life could reach an optimal level of wealth and respect.

22 Nam caput rerum caducarum omnium, que maxime apud mortales commode putantur, eiusmodi est ut aliis divitie, aliis honores, aliis voluptates res digne videri possint, pro quibus maximopere contendant. Preter eas quid in primis fortune commodum putandum sit ignorari arbitror, nam extra hec inveniri puto in bonis fortune nihil quod commodum dici aut putari debeat.

23 Ab huiusmodi tamen omnibus studiosi excluduntur: quod ut dilucidius sic esse ostendam, principio dicam quam maximis voluptatibus perfruantur, proxime litteratorum divitias perscrutabimur, reliquum erit ut de honoribus exquiramus.

24 At erit quidem omnis nostra oratio succincta et pro rei magnitudine brevis, veluti que una cum re ipsa prodeat in medium, non ut se ostentet, verum ut commoda que insunt litteris atque incommoda apertissime intuens rectius quid agendum sit consulat;

25 multas preterea dicendi rationes que ad motus animorum valent ac denique plures argumentandi modos abiiciet, ne videatur producere disciplinas ad contemptum et litteras velle despiciendas tra-

26 dere. Proderit autem cognita res et nostra, ut existimo, argumentatio ad illos evocandos ab errore qui aliud ex litteris quam meram ipsam eruditionem et sapientiam exposcunt; neque non proderit ad studiosos frugi et prudentes confirmandos ut in litteris sola doctrina et rerum peritia gaudeant, reliqua minimi pensanda censeant. Itaque ad rem proficiscamur.

For the whole question about all earthly goods, which are thought   22
to be the best thing among mortal men, is this, that some people
think wealth, others honors, others pleasures are things that are
worth striving greatly for. Apart from these I do not think that
anyone knows what else is regarded as a chief good of fortune, for
outside of them I do not think that anything can be found among
fortune's goods that must be thought or said to be a real advantage.

But scholars are excluded from all these things. In order to il-   23
lustrate more clearly that this is the case, I will say first how some
people enjoy the greatest of pleasures, then we shall examine the
wealth of literary scholars, and lastly we will consider what honors
they can achieve.[9]

But our whole discourse will be succinct and brief compared to   24
the magnitude of the topic. Our speech will, as it were, take center
stage accompanied only by the subject itself, not to show off, but
in order that by observing the advantages and disadvantages that
reside in literary study it can provide the correct advice on what to
do. In addition, it will reject many rules of speech that can move   25
minds and also several ways of debating, lest this discourse seem
to be bringing disciplines into disrepute and presenting literature
as something to be despised.[10] Once this matter has been studied   26
and, I believe, my argument has been listened to, it will be useful
in removing the mistaken belief from those people who demand
anything from literary study other than pure erudition itself and
wisdom. It will also be of benefit in confirming the resolve of fru-
gal and prudent scholars to rejoice in the only things they will find
in literature, namely learning and expertise in certain subjects, and
to believe that everything else is worth very little. So now let us
turn to our main question.

III

1 Principio sic existimo: qui pauper sit, quod effectrix aut certe optima voluptatum captatrix pecunia desit, nulla in disciplina posse

2 hunc satis multa cum voluptate versari. Quod si voluptas, ut aiunt, ea est que sensus moveat, animum delectet iocunditate quadam atque amenitate, nempe cum omnium earum quibus moventur sensus, epularum, unguentorum et eiusmodi rerum copia nequeat sine pecuniarum suffragio satis excipi, quonam pacto poterit in sensus voluptate pauper consistere? aut quanam animi iocunditate fruetur is cui pro necessitate ad questum sit mens potius quam ad delectationem propensa?

3 Nimirum sunt ista ipsa divitum et ociosorum: varietatem rerum pulchritudinemque sectari atque complecti. Tum etiam sic censeo: minime multos locupletes inveniri qui ipsas litteras, ne dicam litte-

4 rarum voluptates, multi esse faciendas existiment. Nimis enim plereque alie undique divitibus voluptates suppeditant, ut maior illis cura sit notis voluptatibus inter amicos perfrui quam apud litteras investigare ignotas.

5 Quod quidem etsi fortassis hi quesituri erunt, videamus an ex sententia illis succedat res. Illud iam maxima ex parte conspicientibus ex sese patet quod paulo ante a me commemorabatur: studiosorum vitam multis magnisque difficultatibus esse refertis-

6 simam; ab ipsa quidem pueritia omnem per etatem premi ac perstringi laboribus, tum vigiliis diuturnaque cura et sollicitudine nunquam eosdem esse vacuos litteratos videmus, ut eos nemo facile credat tam laboriosa in vita multa comperire que vel me-

7 diocrem sapiant voluptatem. Etenim voluptatum prestantissima et libero homine digna una illa est, per urbes provinciasque vagari,

III

To begin with, here is one consideration: since money brings   1
about pleasure or at least is certainly a great procurer of it, whoever is poor lacks money and thus cannot tackle any discipline
with a great deal of fun. For if, as they say, pleasure is that which   2
moves the senses and delights the mind with a certain happiness
and feeling of wellbeing, then truly since a good supply of all those
things which move the senses, feasting, unguents and suchlike,
cannot be enjoyed sufficiently without the support of money, how
on earth can someone poor enjoy the delight of the senses? Or
what pleasure of the mind can he enjoy whose brain is more
geared by necessity to surviving than to procuring pleasure?

Without doubt the following advantages belong to those who   3
are rich and leisured, namely the ability to pursue and embrace the
variety and beauty of things. I also believe this: that very few
wealthy people can be found who think that literature itself, never
mind the delights of reading, should be rated highly. For they have   4
too many other pleasures in great supply, so that they are more
concerned with enjoying the pleasures they know about with their
friends than investigating the unknown pleasures of literature.

Even if by chance these people were to seek out such things, let   5
us see whether this enterprise would work for them as they hoped.
For those who now consider this matter, on the whole it is obvious
from the nature of the thing that what I said before is true, namely
that a scholar's life is crammed full of many substantial difficulties.
From childhood onward and at every age we see literary scholars   6
burdened and crushed by hard work: they are never free from
study, daily cares and worries, so much so that nobody should easily believe that in such a laborious life many things can be found
that have even a hint of pleasure. The fact is that there is one   7
outstanding delight worthy of a free man, that of traveling through

multa et templa et theatra, menia atque omnium generum edificia spectare, locaque ambire que tum natura amenissima, grata, munitissima, tum manu et ingenio hominum fuerint ad conspectum pulchra adque impetum hostium continendum reddita tutiora.

8 Qua insigni voluptate utrum illi omnino non privantur qui sese litteris dedicarunt? Non quidem proficiscentes per itinera trahere libros, neque novis regionibus contemplandis occupati multa possunt lectitare—quod si parum multa parumve sepius lectitantem fieri te litteratum putabis, nihil erit quod ab hac discurrendi per provincias voluptate retraham.

9 Cave tamen ne omnes profectiones non solum incommode studiis, sed etiam studiosis longe vituperande sint; id quidem, cum ceteras ob res, tum vel maxime quod in ipsa patria litterati paulum

10 proclivius amena prosequentes vituperantur. Namque, ut cetera omittam, celebritates quidem nuptiarum, choreas, cantus, iuventutis ludos, amena hec quis ignoret quam litteratorum presentiam

11 dedignentur atque oderint? Relique omni iuventuti fidium, musice, saltandi eiusmodique dulcissime artes non minimum laudi

12 conceduntur, liberale in illis officium putatur. Qui in his ipsis artibus vel mediocriter periti sunt, hi grati sunt omnibus atque iocundi; itaque invitantur, rogantur omnes qui in eiusmodi artibus aliquid valere existimantur; litterati vero tantum refelluntur, exclu-

13 duntur. Nam si ad hec accesserint pallenti, ut solent, vultu, aut ridiculi sane sint omnibus aut graves, sive se immiscuerint, quan-

14 tos ciebunt risus! quantas continuo audient obtrectationes! Quis non succenseat canenti aut saltanti litterato? Mimos, histriones

cities and regions, gazing on many temples, theaters, walls and all sorts of buildings, walking round places some of which are naturally beautiful, pleasing and very safe, and others which, thanks to the hand and genius of man, are attractive to look at, and made safer for repelling the attacks of enemies.[11] Surely those who have   8
dedicated themselves to books will be deprived of this outstanding source of pleasure? Those who set off on long journeys are not able to drag books with them, nor when they are busy contemplating new places can they read much; but if you think that you can become a scholar of literature without reading much or often, then I have no reason to stop you from enjoying this pleasure of traveling.

However, be aware that all journeys are not only harmful for   9
study, but in fact are highly criticized by scholars; and this is so, apart from anything else, particularly because literary scholars are reviled in their home land if they are even a little inclined to indulge in pleasant activities. For, leaving aside all the other delights,   10
who does not know how much wedding celebrations, dancing, music, youthful games and other such delights shun and even hate the presence of literary scholars? All other young people are highly   11
praised for playing stringed instruments and indulging in the enjoyable arts of dancing and similar activities, and this is seen as a worthy duty in them. Those who are even tolerably skilled in these   12
same arts are welcome and attractive to everyone. All those who are thought to be worth something in such skills are invited everywhere and are in great demand; but literary scholars are only spurned and excluded from such activities. For if they approach   13
such gatherings with their usual pallid face, either they are seen as ridiculous by everyone or as a burden, and if they join in, how much laughter will they arouse, how many insults will they be forced to hear! Who would not get angry with a literature scholar   14
who sings or dances? They will see themselves regarded actually as

levissimosque se haberi prorsus conspicient: penitebit, dolebit, si sapiant.

15 Itaque quod aliis alacritatem affert, id ipsum istis litteratis tristitiam refert; quod aliis datur honori, his ad vituperationem im-

16 pingitur; quo alii invitantur, isti expelluntur; ut non stulte deditis litteris adolescentibus, meo iudicio, precipiatur ne per alienas provincias solatii causa discursitent, cum ne propria quidem in patria rebus amenis et iocundis sine ignominia inservire liceat.

17 Quare si quid fame et laudi consulendum putabunt, pulchre domo sese occlusos detinebunt, resque omnes foris elegantes, amenas admirationeque dignas abdicabunt a se atque proscribent, quo maiori, ut opus est, assiduitate ad litterarum cognitionem sese of-

18 firment; ac denique nullam patientur apud se visendi voluptatem tantum valere ut animo alias ad res distracti non queant multam litteris atque necessariam, quam debent, operam contribuere.

19 Proxime his amatorie sunt voluptates, a quibus litteratos admodum cupio esse omnino alienos; nam cum illas quidem omni hominum generi maxime nocuas esse sapientes omnes persuaserint, multo tamen magis studiosis admodum pestifere ac pernitiosis-

20 sime sunt. Quis enim amore occupatus poterit circa litteras mente integra et firma inherere? quis animo ad disciplinam incenso, ad preceptiones intento, ad communiendam memoriam solerti, quis, inquam, furoribus amoris captus, aut voluntate aut ingenio aut

21 opera satis constanti et firma esse ad bonas ullas artes valebit? An ignoramus quid soleat amor? Vires labefactare, mores depravare, ingenia hominum pervertere, animum curis conficere, mentem erroribus obruere, ad insaniam redigere: hec quidem amoris munera et dotes sunt.

mime artists, actors, people not to be taken seriously, and they will regret it and be pained by this, if they are wise.

Thus what gives happiness to others, only brings grief to those 15 dedicated to literature; what is an honor for other people, brings insults to literati; where others are invited, they are shunned. It is 16 not foolish to instruct young men who are dedicated to books not to travel around other regions for the sake of enjoyment, since they are not even allowed in their home country to indulge in pleasant and enjoyable activities without ignominy.

So if they think they must attend to their own fame and praise, 17 they will consider it best to keep themselves shut up at home. They will cut themselves off from and veto all the elegant, pleasant, and praiseworthy activities outside, in order that they can devote themselves with greater assiduity to the study of literature, as they feel they must. In the end they will allow no pleasure in 18 seeing things to be so important that their mind can be distracted by anything else which would make them unable to devote the necessary large amounts of time to books.

Next to these satisfactions are the delights of love, from which 19 I would want literary scholars to be totally removed; for while all wise men have convinced us that love is harmful to everyone, it is much more damaging and indeed highly pernicious to scholars. For who is able to be embroiled in love and still study literature 20 with a clear and constant mind? Or who can be in love and still have their mind focused on this discipline, on instruction, on fortifying the memory? I mean, what person caught up in the frenzy of love will be able to have the will, the intellect, the constant, unwavering dedication for any of the noble arts? Are we not aware 21 what love usually does? It whittles away our strength, depraves our morals, perverts our intellects, destroys our minds with cares, oppresses our brains with errors, and drives us to insanity: these are the gifts and rewards of love.

22   Sed de istiusmodi voluptatibus omnibus (eas ut omnes amplec-
tar), non insisto illis quam difficilius litterati quam ceteri potian-
tur, non quid inter venustatem competitorum et litteratorum tristitiam intersit; non vestium splendorem, non licentiam sectandi,
23   non hec omnia prosequor. Eadem missa omnia faciamus, in quibus certe, omnium iudicio, longe sunt inferiores litterati.

24   Sed sic haberi hoc loco velim: voluptates omnes neque non vi-
25   tuperandas esse in litteratis neque non maxime nocuas. Conviviorum et Veneris consuetudines animum in primis in desidiam et
negligentiam (quod nemo ignorat) evocant atque a perseverantia
lectitandi avertunt, sine qua perseverantia, et ea quidem ingenti,
26   fallitur qui se fortassis putat egregie litteratum fore. Habent enim
studia litterarum in se nescio quam vim ut, cum plura didiceris,
tum semper multo plura ignorare te multoque tibi ardentiore stu-
27   dio esse opus dignoscas. Tum etiam fit epularum et vini exhalatio-
nibus atque Venere ut mens evacuetur sensu, oppleatur tenebris,
crassetur ingenium, perspicuitas obtundatur, tum memorie sedes
multarum suspicionum recordatione ac variis amatoriis imaginibus
28   occupate assiduo perturbetur. Denique etiam fit ut voluptatibus
implicitus et amatoriis facibus incensus animus infinitis levibus
ac instabilibus voluntatum et expectationum motibus et fluctibus
29   sempiterne exagitatus vehementer estuet. Quo homine ob amorem
sic animo et mente affecto quis poterit ad concipiendas amplissimas disciplinas et artes esse inutilior atque ineptior?

30   Sit idcirco studiosis ex cibo et Venere nulla aut perexigua voluptas, sit somni et quietis brevissima copia, sitque iocorum et
31   festivitatum rarissima modicaque licentia. Denique ita se in omnibus gerant ac si laboribus ea lege astricti sint ut a longa rerum

But as regards all those other kinds of delights (with no excep- 22
tions), I am not going to repeat how much harder it is for scholars
to possess them compared to the rest of men, nor do I stress the
difference between the attractiveness of courting and the gloomi-
ness of literary scholars; I am not going to deal with the splendor
of clothes, the fun of pursuing someone — none of all this. Let us 23
dismiss all those things in which, in everyone's view, scholars' lives
are certainly inferior.

Instead now I want to make this point that all pleasures must 24
be vituperated by scholars: they are highly damaging. The habits 25
of feasting and lovemaking lure the mind initially into laziness and
negligence (as everyone knows) and distract it from persevering in
reading: he who thinks he will be an outstanding literary scholar
without huge dedication to study is greatly mistaken. Literary re- 26
search has a certain kind of power such that, once you have
learned many things, you understand that there are many more
things you do not know, and you realize that you need a much
greater appetite for study. In addition, the fumes of wine and 27
feasting and love rid the mind of sense, fill it with darkness, the
intellect becomes dulled, your clear-sightedness becomes opaque,
and the seat of your memory is constantly upset by the memory of
many suspicions and various erotic images. In the end your mind 28
is caught up in delights and fired up by the flames of love, it is
constantly agitated with endless fickle and unstable movements
and fluctuations of your will and expectations, and it is caught in
a ferocious storm. Who can be more useless and unfit for embrac- 29
ing the greatest disciplines than the man who is thus affected by
love in his mind and brain?

So for these reasons let scholars not take any or very little plea- 30
sure in food or sex, let them have very small doses of sleep and
rest, and let them be allowed only very rare and moderate amounts
of games and festivities. Finally, they should behave in all things as 31
though they were bound to their labors by this rule, namely that

meditatione, a sempiternis lucubrationibus, a perpetua studiorum cura non sine ignominia discedere posse opinentur, intelligantque, nisi assiduus fuerit, etiam acerrimum et vehementissimum labo-

32 rem in litteris periturum. Nam habet quidem plus dispendii vel modica interlaxatio studiorum quam habeat compendii multa et bene longa evigilatio, citiusque e memoria elabuntur ea que tene-

33 bantur quam aut ediscantur postea aut recuperentur. Omnes igitur huiusmodi sensuum voluptates si minime litteris conceduntur, minime etiam petende sunt, si plurimum nocent, plurimum etiam fugiende sunt.

34 Ac ne illud quidem vere dici poterit: in voluptatibus animi litteratos habere quippiam, quamobrem possint cum laude non sine

35 multa iactura studiorum commorari. Utrum multa animi voluptate perfruetur is qui eam de se expectationem haberi non ignoret quam si modice adimpleverit nihil se abiectius futurum sciat? Utrum is liberum a curis gravissimis et vacuum animum geret, qui affines, amicos, et notos conspiciat omnes desiderare atque expec-

36 tare ut quam egregie proficiat? Tum idem etiam non sit nescius diversa ex parte emulos, invidos, obtrectatores (quod genus hominum non rarissimum est) omnes esse paratissimos ad derogandum et diffamandum si quid per negligentiam, per luxum, per volupta-

37 tem admiserit, quominus in summam eruditionem devenerit? Ne vero animus huic erit iacens in voluptatibus, qui tanto ac tam laborioso periculosoque negotio fuerit destinatus? An potius sollicitudine, cura et metu quodam vituperationis vehementer perturbato

38 animo vivet? Illum ego, qui has partes suas esse cognoscat per studiorum labores, per summam vigilantiam amicorum expectationibus satisfacere, invidorum obtrectationem effugere, infamiam

they should believe that they cannot depart without ignominy from their long meditations on things, their eternal studies, their perpetual pursuit of scholarship. They should understand that unless their labor is constant, even their most dedicated and intense studies will be wasted. For even a moderate relaxation from study 32 constitutes more of a loss than can be compensated for by many long hours of scholarship, and those things we held in our memory go more quickly from it than the time it takes for them to be relearned or recovered later. Thus all sensory satisfactions of this 33 kind should be allowed only minimally during the study of literature, and so should only be rarely sought after, since the more harmful they are the more they should be avoided.

Nor can this even be said to be true: that in the pleasures of the 34 mind literary scholars have something which they can indulge in with praise and without serious damage to their studies. Can a 35 scholar enjoy great delights of the mind if he is aware that there is that expectation of him which, if he only fulfills it to a moderate extent, he knows there will be nobody more abject than him? Will this man have a mind free from and empty of the weightiest of cares if he sees all his relations, friends and acquaintances wanting and expecting him to make the greatest possible progress? In addi- 36 tion he should be aware that, on the other hand, all his rivals, those who envy him and malign him (the kind of people who are anything but rare) are more than ready to denigrate and defame him if out of negligence or through luxury or pleasure he does something which prevents him from reaching the summit of scholarship? In truth, will this man's mind be able to find any delight in 37 pleasures when he was destined for such a great, laborious and even dangerous role? Or will he rather prefer to live with his mind deeply disturbed by the anxiety, worry and fear of being vituperated? I believe that the person who knows that his role is to satisfy 38 the expectation of his friends through hard work, study and the utmost vigilance, and to avoid the criticisms of the envious, escape

evitare, laudem attingere oportere, eundem hunc ipsum ita esse animatum arbitror, ut plerunque gravissimum durissimumque onus studiorum non subisse malit quam susceptum iam deponere.

39 Quo illud etiam molestissimum inest: quod nisi cum dedecore queas arduam, asperam difficilemque initam litterarum provinciam deserere, quam eandem non sine maximo labore et erumna susti-

40 neas. Accedit quoque quod pertimescis dari ad levitatem si studia iam suscepta sine ingenti causa deseras; adde his etiam quod honestius putas quidvis gravissimum perferre quam aut ingenio te esse inepto ad litteras profiteri aut animo pro virtute ad labores

41 pusillo. Illud preterea odiosum est, quod litterati, aliarum artium insueti et ignari, nullam rem circumspiciunt preter litteras, ad quam, si quid consiliorum mutent, possint cum laude sese conferre.

42 Quid ergo? num erit studiosi animi grandis voluptas, quandoquidem omnino constet se abiectissimum ac pene infamem futurum nisi sempiternis, acerrimis extremisque laboribus insuderit summam in cognitionem discipline cui se dederit evadere?

43 Quid enim erit apud tuos abiectius quam eum non esse te quem per omnem etatem futurum elaborasti? quam non ea in re te prebere doctissimum cui semper fueris deditus? quam non esse in ea disciplina clarissimum in qua diutius commorans potuisti

44 excellere? Num vero is erit modice sollicitus qui, si aliquando se a continuis studiorum laboribus subripuerit, confestim comperiat suum ad consequendam laudem cursum retardari atque rumpi? Miser qui, voluptatibus serviens, vituperantium et obtrectatorum

45 acies offenderit! Preterea non minime in voluptatibus dolendum erit iis qui omni vel etiam modica studiorum intermissione

infamy and obtain praise, that same person I believe will prefer
never to have undertaken this heaviest and hardest of burdens
rather than now to put down what he has taken up. In such a   39
context there is another, very disagreeable risk: that you cannot
abandon without disgrace the arduous, laborious and very difficult
area of literature, even though you cannot sustain it without maximum toil and labor. In addition, you will be afraid that you will be   40
seen to be rather fickle if you abandon without a serious reason
the studies you have undertaken. Add to this also the fact that you
will think it more honest to put up with the heaviest of burdens
than to be thought of as not having an intellect suited to profess-
ing literature or as having a mind that is weak in facing labor for
the sake of virtue. Besides, there is another unpleasant fact: that   41
literary scholars are ignorant of and inexperienced in other arts,
and so they do not look beyond literature to see to what praiseworthy discipline they can turn if they change their plans.

Well then? Surely there is no great pleasure in the scholarly   42
mind since all agree that such a person will be most abject and almost infamous unless he sweats over his eternal, arduous and extreme labors in order to achieve maximum knowledge of the discipline he has devoted himself to? What could be more abject in the   43
eyes of your family than you not turning out to be the person that
you have worked all your life to be? Than not showing yourself to
be most learned in that area to which you were always devoted?
Than not being outstanding in that discipline in which you would
have excelled had you stayed longer in it? Will a man not be more   44
than a little worried if he eventually removes himself from his
continual scholarly labors and immediately finds his race toward
earning praise slowed down and indeed cut off? Wretched is the
person who by becoming the slave of pleasure will have to face the
onslaughts of his critics and attackers! Besides even in the middle   45
of delights there will be great grief for those who will clearly dis-

multarum lucubrationum suarum perditionem fieri manifeste comperiant.

46   Quas quidem res omnes qui ita futuras non dubitet, ut future quidem sunt, quam iocunditatem poterit degustare? Ne vero in illum poterit cadere amenitas aut suavitas ulla, aut dulcedo voluptatum, quem capessendi honoris acris sollicitudo exanimet ac evi-
47 tande infamie metus vehementer perterreat? Non sane integrum gaudium, non festivitatem aut letitiam aliquam senties, mi studiose, qui in litteris occupatus, inter libros involutus atque inter
48 chartulas sempiterne sepultus fueris. Tibi quidem nullam egregiam voluptatem aut alacritatem amplecti licebit, ubi vastissimum
49 studiorum onus partim cupias, partim metuas deponere. Neque hoc loco memoro quanta sit sollicitudo laudis cupidorum emulos pro viribus superare aut a nullo superari contendentium.

50   Ex quo etiam huius istius vita studiosi, ni fallor, est longe acerbissima, eoque magis si quid inciderit cupiditatis ad eas res ad quas, ipsa duce natura, omnis generosa iuventus admodum prona
51 est. Nam si ad equos, ad canes alendos, si ad palestras exercendas, si ad reliquas res libero homine dignas animo aut opere amplectendas fuerit proclivis, quis tum erit huic animus molestie plenissimus, ubi omnia que iuventuti decus et ornamentum comparant deserere et sese apud bibliothecas obdere verecundia illaudationis cogatur, nullam rem aliam quamvis optimam et nobilissimam pre-
52 ter lucernam et libros tractare permittatur? Non sine ingenti, mihi crede, dolore eadem illa ceteris laudatissima eo a nobis deserentur, quod et studiis adversentur et omnium ora ad obloquendum concitent.

53   Stat tanquam censor ac iudex morum multitudo, in litteratos gravius animadvertit quam aut debeat aut in ceteros consuescat:

cover that even a moderate interruption of their studies will destroy many hours of scholarship.

As for those who do not doubt that all these things will happen, as indeed they surely will, what happiness can they enjoy? In fact, can any pleasure or gratification, or any sweetness of joy seize hold of someone who is exhausted by the profound worry of obtaining honor and terrified by the fear of avoiding infamy? My dear scholar, you will not enjoy unalloyed delight or any happiness since you will be busy with literature, submerged in books and always buried in papers. You will not be allowed to embrace any great pleasure or joy when one part of you wants to lay down this enormous burden of studying, and the other part is afraid of doing so. Nor need I remind you how keen is the aspiration to acquire praise in the ambitious and in those who strive to overtake their rivals to the best of their ability or at least not to be outdone by anyone.

As a result, the life of just this kind of scholar, unless I am mistaken, is far and away of the most bitter kind, and will be all the more so if he experiences any desire for those kinds of things to which all wellborn youths, following their natural instincts, are really quite inclined. For if he has a penchant for horsemanship, rearing dogs or going to gymnasia, or pursuing the other activities that are worthy of a freeborn man, how full of misery will his mind be when he is forced to abandon all the things that bring honor and ornament to the young and has to hide away in libraries for fear of not being praised, and he will end up being allowed to handle nothing except the oil lamp and books? Believe me, if we have to abandon those very activities that are praised in all others simply because they obstruct our studies and arouse all others to criticize us, this will cause great grief.

The multitude acts as a censor and judge of our morals, and it is more heavily critical of literary scholars than it either ought to be or than it usually is of others: "That behavior is not decent at

46

47

48

49

50

51

52

53

'non decere istac hora, preter mores istis vestibus, hanc nolim so-
cietatem, ab honestate is locus, preter officium id factum, preter
54 decus id dictum.' Denique omnes infinitis odiis ad studiosorum
famam dilacerandam pervigilant, ut nisi te velis scurram aliquem
levissimum ac nebulonem haberi, plane non tuo arbitrio et libertate, sed arctissima censura plebis tibi sit vivendum.

55   Quod si dixeris plebis iudicium esse aspernandum, quid illud?
Nonne, si vestes cupiveris, inquiet bibliotheca: 'Has mihi pecunias
debes, veto!'?; si venationem, si musicam, dimicandive artem, aut
palestram prosequare, nonne inquient littere: 'Tu nobis has operas
56 surripis, tibi nos famam et nomen non referemus'?; si ingenia,
picturam, formas exquiras, inquient discipline: 'Hac tu nos occu-
patione defraudas, te nos maximarum rerum cognitione privabi-
mus'?

57   Denique si animi causa rus petere (non dico extremas provincias discursitare) volueris, illico te inde incepta professio detorquet
ad libros et litteras apud quas, nisi sese multo opere et vigilia ex-
cultissimas reddideris, multam infamiam non defuturam littere
58 ipse minitantur. Adde his quod grata atque dulcissima suorum
civium familiaritate privari, solitudine gaudere, sermones fugere
omnes, preter eos qui disciplinam ac senilem tristitiam quandam
59 sapiant, litteratis necesse est. Prescriptum tempus litteratis ad amicos consalutandos, prescripta inambulandi loca, prescripte amicorum copie sunt; alias lectitandi, alias audiendi horas, paucissimas
dispatiandi ⟨habent⟩, ut ferme nulle ad plenas voluptates oppeten-
60 das relinquantur. En igitur maximas voluptates! in quibus palam
est non licere litteratis ullos quibus astricti sint labores dimittere

this hour, those clothes are not moral, I don't want you to keep this kind of company, that place is corrupt, this action goes against your duties, what you said is not suitable." In short everyone has 54 endless hatred and is very vigilant in destroying the reputation of scholars, so much so that unless you want to be taken for some kind of jester or a rascal, you will clearly have to live, not by your own free judgment, but under the strictest censure of the mob.

And if you say that the judgment of the people is to be rejected, 55 what then? Surely, if you want to buy clothes, your library will say, "You owe that money to me, I forbid you." If you want to indulge in hunting, music, fencing, or the gymnasium, the letters on the page will object, "You are stealing this effort from us, we will not spread your reputation and name." If you seek out works of ge- 56 nius, paintings and sculptures, the humanities will reply, "You are defrauding us by these activities, we will deprive you of the knowledge of the most important subjects."

Finally, if for the sake of relaxation you want to retreat just to 57 the countryside (I do not mean traveling round the most distant regions), the profession you have embarked on will deflect you back to your books and literature: unless you cultivate them to perfection with constant work and study, the letters themselves will threaten you that you will incur terrible infamy. In addition to 58 this, literary scholars are forced to be deprived of the pleasant company of their own citizens, to enjoy only solitude, to avoid all conversations, except those that deal with the discipline and bring on a certain senile sadness. Strict time limits are imposed on liter- 59 ary scholars for seeing their friends, the places they can walk in are severely limited, as is the actual number of friends they are allowed to have. They have some time for reading, some for listening, very little for taking a walk, so much so that almost no time is left to fully enjoy anything. So these are their greatest pleasures! It 60 is thus clear that scholars are not allowed to give up or even take a break from any of the labors to which they are bound. They have

aut interlaxare, quibusve obnoxii aliorum arbitrio vivere, iuventutis munera, etatis dulcedinem, vite florem omneque evum inter chartas et mortuas pecudes (ut sic libros noncupem) habere sepultum oporteat, ac veluti perpetuo carcere illic contineri ipsique nature nunquam non adversari necessitas cogat.

61   Itaque si amena omnia valent animum studiosorum distrahere ab studiis, sive infinita (ut videre licet) amenissima studiis litterarum nocent, sive ab illis omnibus litterati se abstineant oportet, que idcirco hominum vita quam istorum litteratorum asperior
62 poterit comperiri? Si studii temporibus nunquam debet studiosus a rerum investigatione ac perceptione neque voluptatibus avocari, neque somno et otio retardari, neque commodis aliquibus distrahi,
63 si rursus modica et rarissima sunt tempora non debita studiis, quis igitur erit qui se voluptatis causa litteris operam dare audeat dicere?
64   Non tamen in eum locum detrudo ac compingo litteratos ut eos dicam omni vacuos voluptate litteris operam dare; tantos enim nequirent labores perferre nisi aliqua voluptatum opinione relevarentur.
65 rentur. Sunt qui non inviti lugeant, quoniam ad voluptatem ducant eo pacto se piissimos et amicitiarum nimium memores haberi. Tum etiam plerisque in rebus, dum institutis et opinioni satisfaciamus, multa nobis videntur aspera minus quam re ipsa
66 sint. Sed eiusmodi litteratorum voluptas est ut eam rectius possis dolorem dicere quam voluptatem: sedere enim sempiterne, continuo lectitare, assidue meditari, perpetuo esse in solitudine, eternum privari festivitate et ioco, hanc ipsam vitam degere, non sum ita agrestis aut durus homo id ut ausim dicere voluptuosum esse.
67 Est quoque in vindicandis iniuriis, in simultatibus inimicitiisque contentione et viribus superandis voluptas quedam insita; concertationes tamen et odia sustinere plenissimum est doloribus.

to live obeying the whim of others; they have to forego the joys of youth, the fun of that age, the very flower of their life, and spend all their time buried amid papers and dead sheepskin (if I might call parchment manuscripts that), while necessity forces them to be kept as if in a perpetual prison and sometimes to oppose the instincts of nature herself.

Thus if all pleasant things can distract scholars' minds from their studies, and if infinite delights (as can be seen) damage the study of literature, and if literary students have to abstain from all these pleasures, then what human life could one find that is harsher than that of these literature students? If during study time the scholar must never be called away from the investigation and discovery of things not even by pleasure, nor delayed in his work by sleep or leisure, nor distracted by any comforts, or if the time not devoted to study is limited and very rare, who is there who would dare to say that they are devoting themselves to literature for the sake of pleasure?

Yet I would not say that literary scholars belong to a category of people devoid of all enjoyment as they work on their books; they could not put up with so much work if they were not relieved by some hint of pleasure. There are those who willingly go into mourning because they consider it an advantage to be thought of as very pious and very mindful of their friendships. Then there is also the fact that in most things, as long as we respect our customs and public opinion, many aspects will seem less harsh to us than they are in reality. But the satisfaction of literary students is such that you could more correctly call it pain rather than delight; for I am not such a rustic or harsh man that I would call it pleasant to lead this kind of life, sitting eternally, constantly reading, permanently excluded from festivity and fun. There is also a certain kind of pleasure in taking revenge for injuries, in quarrels, enmities, struggling and overcoming the strength of others; but having just to put up with rivalries and hatred is something that is full of suf-

61

62

63

64

65

66

67

68 Quod ipsum in litteris persimile evenit: nam satisfacere libidini ediscendi prebet illud quidem voluptatem, sed hic studiorum labos acerbissimus animique hec gravissima sollicitudo semper plus affert quod angatur quam quod gaudeat, vel saltem si quam discendo sumunt voluptatem, eam curis et laboribus maximis obru-

69 unt. Verum iidem in hoc maxime differunt, quod concertationum et inimicitiarum pondus brevius, studiorum vero anxietas diu-

70 turna, infinita immensaque est. Habentur enim in litteris innumerabilia cognitu dignissima, neque facile dici potest quam earum

71 studiosum ingenium ediscendi cupiditas premat. Incidit in difficilem doctissimorum disceptationem, aut rem comperit elegantem, dignam, plenam eruditionum: studiosus non dormit, non comedit, non quiescit, nullam penitus voluptatem sentit; stat mordax cura

72 rem totam recognoscere atque tenere. Ea quidem magno labore apprehenditur, multa solertia detinetur, grandi sollicitudine serva-

73 tur. Post hanc sequitur etiam alia atque alia inaudita, incognita, versuta, subtilis et callida ratio, aut singulare quoddam exemplum,

74 aut ornatissima persuadendi vis. His omnibus in rebus studiosus homo discendi cupiditate nec modum ullum, nec finem invenisse potest; neque enim sedato esse animo licet, nisi omnium rerum

75 occultarum ignoratione sublata. Itaque nimis, ut vides, pertricosa res est studiosus homo; ex quo fit ut nunquam sibi vel minima quidem aut corporis aut animi vacatio adsit.

76 Tristis solitudo, acerbus labor, extrema vigilantia, difficilis sollicitudo, summa occupatio, flagrans cura, ut cum in hoc studioso voluptas nulla reperiatur, tum in omni eius vita nulla penitus sit

77 intercapedo laborum et molestiarum. Que cum ita sint, in litteris constare hoc arbitror: prudentem neminem voluptatis causa ad litterarum labores compulsum iri; honoris et dignitatis gratia

fering. This is very similar to what happens in literature: for satis- 68
fying the desire to learn brings delight, but this extremely hard
work of studying and this very burdensome anxiety of the mind
produce more elements to torment than to please us. Or if scholars take at least some pleasure from learning, that enjoyment is
outweighed by enormous cares and labor. But there is this crucial 69
difference, namely that the weight of rivalry and enmities lasts
only a brief time, while the anxiety brought on by study is long-
lasting, infinite and immense. There are countless details in litera- 70
ture that are very worthy of learning, but one cannot easily say
how much the desire to learn such things weighs on the mind of
the literary scholar. He comes across a complex debate among very 71
learned men, or he finds something elegant, worthy, full of erudition: at that point the scholar does not sleep, eat, take rest or feel
any depth of pleasure; he is hounded by a biting urge to learn
about this whole question and remember it. This subject is learned 72
with great effort, has to be held in the mind with a considerable
amount of care, and is only retained with enormous attentiveness.
After this, he comes across other unheard of, unknown, ingenious, 73
subtle and clever reasonings, or there is some illustrious example,
or highly ornate power of persuasion. In all these things the 74
scholar in his desire for learning cannot find any moderation or
end; nor is he allowed to rest with a calm mind until his ignorance
of all difficult subjects has been removed. So the person of learn- 75
ing, as you see, is a very complex thing,[12] hence he never enjoys
even the slightest rest in his body or his mind.

Sad solitude, bitter labor, studying to extremes, difficult wor- 76
ries, total absorption in work, burning anxieties: these are his lot,
so much so that in this scholar there is no delight to be found, and
in the whole of his life there is absolutely no let up in his labors
and troubles. That being so, I think this is what is true about lit- 77
erature: no prudent person will be driven to study letters for the
sake of enjoyment, but maybe you will think that they have gone

fortassis aut divitiarum aut amplitudinis spe credideris eos ad litteras accessisse.

IV

1 Videamus idcirco quemadmodum littere ad divitias iuvent, qui locus divitiarum post voluptates erat edisserendus. Nego studiis litterarum maximas divitias comparari, qua quidem in re non illud disputo possitne quispiam circa questum versari, qui, ut debet, 2 omnem litteris operam impertiatur; sed hoc haberi volo: ex litteris magnam divitiarum vim etiam ab industriis et cupidissimis minime congregari. Quod si ostendero, constabit sane minime prudentem esse illum qui spe divitiarum se laboribus studiorum dedicarit.

3 Quid hoc rei est quod ex tanta multitudine quantam per omnes provincias intuemur studiosorum, tam paucissimos tamen vide- 4 mus prodire litteratos quorum divitias admiremur? Forte potui nonnullos ipse in litteratorum numero non egenos vidisse, quos non iniuria dixerim aut non egregie divites putandos aut non ⟨ex⟩ 5 litteris, verum aliunde esse factos locupletes. Quod si litterarum adiumentis opes comparantur, cur non eque litterati omnes bene fortunati omnes reperiuntur? Cur tam multos litteris prestantes 6 viros in humili fortuna constitutos videmus? Unde ista disparitas, ut ceteri litteratissimi egestate summa laborent, hic autem unicus haud mediocriter doctus inter divitias gaudeat? An idcirco negabi- 7 mus litteras parum admodum iuvare ad questum? An potius eam ob rem esse litteratos omnes egenos fatebimur, quia, litteris occupati, cetera admodum omnia negligendo, cum valetudinis, tum

to literature for the sake of honor and reputation, or in the hope
of wealth and advancement.

IV

Now let us see how literature can help one achieve wealth, a topic   1
that was to be discussed after the question of pleasures. I say that
a huge amount of money cannot be acquired through literary studies, though on this topic I do not dispute the fact that someone
who, as he should, devotes all his time to literature, can end up
accumulating some profit. Still, I want to persuade you of this: 2
that out of literature a huge amount of wealth cannot be accumulated, not even by the most industrious and willing scholar. If I
prove this, it will be established that whoever dedicates themselves
to the labors of scholarship, hoping to become rich, is clearly not
very prudent.

What is the reason why, out of the great multitude of scholars   3
that we observe in every region, so very few literati are found
whose wealth surprises us? By chance I have been able to see amid   4
the crowds of literary scholars a few who are not impoverished,
but I would be right to say that either they are not regarded as
enormously wealthy, or they have become rich, not from literature
but from some other source. And if wealth is acquired through the   5
help of literature, why are not all literati equally fortunate in
riches? Why do we see many people who are outstanding scholars
confined to a humble condition of life? Whence comes the dispar-   6
ity that means that all the other literary scholars work in extreme
poverty, while this one person who is not even half learned enjoys
a rich life? Is it for this reason that we deny that literature really
can help one become wealthy? Or rather is it that we admit that   7
all literature students are poor because, occupied as they are with
their studies, they totally neglect all other things and are unused

multo magis rei familiaris et pecuniarum curam aut solere aut
8 posse habere non maximam? Mihi sane utraque causa videntur
litterati discludi a copia opum: nam altera cupiditas, altera facultas
9 ditandi tollitur. Que enim bonis litteris comparatur, modestia,
magnanimitas, virtus ac sapientia, ea ingenuum spe studioque rebus magnis deditum prohibet animum questibus infimisque rebus
implicari, rectamque mentem inter caducas res prosterni eadem
10 sapientia et virtus non sinit. Quo circa laudantur qui, abiecta cupiditate, non divitias que studiosis denegantur, sed mirificarum
rerum cognitionem sectari didicerint.

11   Etenim que sit ditandi facultas ac modus queritur. Quod si quis
ad divitias accumulandas dixerit duas patere mortalibus vias, alteram quam fortuna nobis aperuisset, alteram quam ars et industria
12 comperisse soleat, recte is quidem meo iudicio dixerit. Fortuna
enim ditamur veluti hereditatibus, legatis, donationibus et huiusmodi largitionibus que fortune beneficio dedita, non virtute nostra
parta deveniunt; industria vero, sicut mercatura, salariis et huius-
13 modi questibus. Quare in his rebus quantum littere commodis-
sime inveniantur pervestigandum est.

14   Quoniam igitur instituimus de commodis litterarum atque incommodis disceptare, fortassis de litterarum fortuna dicere non
convenit, que quidem omnium litteratorum sententia potius, ut-
15 cunque illa fuerit, ferenda est quam existimatione pensanda. Eam
ob rem de questibus primum disseramus, reliqua, ut in rem inci-
dent, non negligemus, sed ea omnia ita brevissime ut plura possint

or unable to devote the greatest care to either their health or, even more importantly, to their family's wealth and income? Two rea- 8
sons seem to me to exclude literature scholars from amassing wealth, namely the desire and the ability to become rich. For those 9
things that are acquired by the study of good literature, such as modesty, magnanimity, virtue and wisdom, prevent the noble mind that is totally devoted to studying great subjects from becoming involved in the pursuit of material wealth and of the lowest things, and these same qualities, wisdom and virtue, do not allow the right minded person to be crushed amid ephemeral matters. In this context we praise those who, dismissing cupidity, have 10
learned to follow not wealth, which is denied to the scholar, but the knowledge of wonderful things.

Now one may ask what is the way to become rich? If someone 11
says that there are two ways that are open to mortals to accumulate wealth, one opened up for us by fortune, the other discovered by art and industriousness, that person is correct in my opinion. For we are enriched by fortune, for example, through inheritances, 12
legacies, donations and other such presents, which come about through the benefit of good fortune, not through our own virtue. And we are enriched by industriousness: for instance, through being a merchant, through stipends and that kind of income. So we 13
must investigate to what extent literature can be found to be advantageous in these areas.

Since, then, we have decided to discuss the advantages and dis- 14
advantages of literature, perhaps it is not right to discuss the fortune of literary scholars, which in the opinion of all such students has to be borne, whatever it is, rather than weighed and evaluated. For this reason let us first examine wealth, after which we will not 15
neglect other topics as they occur. In any case we will debate all these things so briefly that I might seem to have deliberately left out more things than I have gathered together here through my

a me videri consulto pretermissa quam ingenio et arte collecta; malo enim non censeri obtrectator quam videri curiosus.

16   Iam vero divitias tum grandes fieri et subitas dicunt cum questus magni ac frequentes, tum impense modice atque rare sunt:

17 pulchre dictum hoc quidem. Namque crescit domi cumulus cui addideris plura in dies quam detraxeris; quod quidem apud litteratos cum omnino sit contra, cum minima lucra excipiant, maximas per omnem etatem pecunias dissipent, nimirum idcirco eosdem

18 pauperes esse oportet. Sed si est fortassis quispiam qui dubitet in studiis litterarum maximas pecunias disperdi, habeo sane argumentum ad rem accomodatissimum quo non modo patebit ingentes opes in studiis exarescere, sed omnem penitus familiam multis atque ultimis incommodis affici.

19   Venit in mentem quod apud Bononiam, dum in studiis litterarum illic versarer, de quodam honestissimo cive cui erat filius iurisconsultus plane litteratissimus persepius intellexi: nullius eque rei peniteret ac faceret quod operam litteris filium dare permisisset.

20 Ob id enim multis incommodis affectum se asserebat, primum quod in rebus agendis nunquam utilem esse operam filii senserit, quem voluit nunquam a studiis litterarum agende rei familiaris

21 gratia distrahi. Quamobrem sibi fuisse filium inter domesticos superfluum admodum asserebat. Quod ni illum maluisset occupari litteris, multa per eum quidem esset assecutus que per conductos magnis salariis procuratores efficere sibi necesse fuerit, ex quo lucra plena impensarum atque idcirco perexigua reddita sunt. Nam secus accidisset ubi fuisset in negotiis non extranei, sed filii opera

22 usus. Minime enim forent redditus diminuti salariis, neque in

intellect and knowledge; for I would prefer not to be considered as a negative critic rather than seeming excessively meticulous in listing such arguments.

Now then, they say that wealth is truly great and sudden when 16 profit is high and regular, and expenses are moderate or rare: this is well put. For the wealth you have at home will grow if you add 17 more to it than you spend day by day; and since this situation is the opposite of what happens to literature students, who receive very small amounts of money and have to spend large amounts of it throughout their life, it is no wonder that they are condemned to being poor. And if there is anyone who perhaps doubts that a 18 large amount of money has to be spent in the study of literature, I have an argument that is highly appropriate at this point, one that will show that not only do huge amounts of capital dwindle away in their studies but that the scholar's whole family is affected by many, extreme disadvantages.

I remember that when I was in Bologna,[13] studying literature, I 19 often heard about one very honest citizen whose son was a lawyer, totally devoted to letters: there was nothing the father regretted so much as having given his son permission to spend time on literature. For he said that it was for this reason he was affected by 20 many disadvantages, first of all because he had never felt his son's work useful for carrying out any business, and then because he had never wanted him to be distracted from literary studies in order to attend to family affairs. For these reasons, he stated that 21 among all the people in the household his son was totally superfluous. If he had not preferred his son to study literature, he would have carried out a lot of business through him, things which he had been forced to hire middlemen on large salaries to carry out, as a result of which any profits he made were accompanied by high expenses and thus became very small. For it would have been different if he had been able to use the work of his son in business and not that of others. His income would have only been slightly 22

familia fuissent habende tam inutiles impense, que certe non modo
23 inutiles, sed etiam admodum gravissime exstiterunt. Solutum
magistris, datum grammaticis, contributum dialecticis, adhibitos
ceteros pedagogos, emptos libros, et item alios atque item alios libros comparatos, ut nunquam denique librarii, nunquam expostu-
24 latores defuerint. Preterea super accessisse temerarias illas pompas
quas doctoratum nominant: illic donata et dissipata esse quam
multa, erogatas ingentes pecunias, factas vestes et togas, structum
25 epulum; tum domus refulcita et ornata, ac postremo multis modis
26 insanitum, ut pene fortunas omnes familiares exhauserit. Atque
utinam eo pacto rebus esset impositus modus, ne in dies impense
et domi et foris excrescerent! Suorum enim se maiorum more solitum antea private parce atque honeste vivere, nunc autem, as-
sumpta toga doctoratus familiaque facta celebriori, omnia lautiora
27 et affluentiora requiri. Quo fit ut nunquam sibi tanta rependi pre-
28 mia expectet, quanta pro acceptis incommodis deberentur. Addebat huic aliam multorum iudicio bonam, sed omnino apud me
incognitam, huiusmodi rationem. Sic enim aiebat: 'Si pecunie que
inter libros et vestes filii dormiunt, ipse ille, ut potuissent, pecunie
29 negotiate fuissent, habe hoc, maximam gazam accumulassent, et
quas exposui pecunias in filium tenerem, atque simul, quantum
annuis lucris deberetur excepissem.'

30   Itaque his rebus diligens pater quantum damni et detrimenti
accepisset non raro disputabat. Verum cum hec ita essent, non se
tamen eo vehementius affici enarrabat quod immoderatas et ni-
31 mium dissolutas impensas filius attulerit, sed eo magis dolere
profitebatur quo sibi videbat de filio non optime sperare licere,

diminished by salaries, and he would not have had to have such pointless expenses in the family, expenses which were not just unnecessary but also very high. The father had paid teachers, given money to Latin tutors, contributed to the costs of logic lessons, employed other teachers, bought books and then more and more books, so much so that in the end he was never free of the demands of booksellers and creditors. In addition, there were also those foolhardy ceremonies they call doctorates: for these he had given and dissipated an awful lot of funds, handed out huge sums, had clothes and gowns made, organized a banquet. Then the house had to be refurbished and decorated, and in the end he had to pay up for all sorts of insanity, so that he had exhausted nearly all the family's fortune. If only a limit had been set on such things so that the expenses inside and outside the home did not grow day by day! Before all this he had been able to live like his ancestors had, privately, moderately and honestly, but now once his son had donned the doctoral gown and the family had become famous, they needed everything to be more lavish and expensive. As a result, he never expected to recoup as much money as he had had to lay out for all these inconveniences. To all this he added another reason which seemed sound in the minds of many people, but one that I had never heard before, for he said: "If the money which is now lying idle in my son's books and clothes had been invested in business, you can be sure it would have accumulated a huge treasure of wealth, and I would still possess the money I spent on my son and would have received what was due from my annual interest."

So that diligent father often discoursed on how much loss and damage his wealth had suffered through these things. Yet in these circumstances he claimed he was not so much distressed because his son had brought him excessive and unaffordable expenses, but rather he was even more aggrieved by the fact that he saw that he could not entertain any great hopes for his boy. He saw the young quem intueretur ob litterarum curas esse valetudinarium effectum ac intelligeret imbecilli filio quietem futuram nunquam.

32 Idcirco merore affectus ob pietatem, multis modis filium tentasse a libris in iocum aliquem distrahere sepeque iussisse ne vigiliis et ieiunio sese usque adeo affligeret. At filium instanti sibi sic
33 respondere solitum: 'Desine, mi pater, nos ab hoc instituto deterrere. Te enim scire oportet me hanc pro officio litteris assiduitatem debere; atque si sapis, si nostra tibi dignitas cara est, hoc ages ut vehementius prosequar atque hortabere ut nunquam e bibliotheca
34 progrediar. Cave ne quam nostra cura et diligentia adepti sumus famam velis his monitionibus tuis deficere. Te quidem ego libentius audiam, mi pater, si iusseris ut prestitam clientibus fidem
35 susceptasque amicorum causas omni studio et viribus tuear, siquidem hoc intelligere perfacile potes, quam pro expectatione amicorum ne mediocrem quidem, omnibus meis vigiliis, me patronum exhibeam. Ergo, mi pater, sine me nostrum negotium prosequi.'
36 Itaque homo prudens, pater familias, cum ceteris ex causis, tum quod hoc pacto de vita valetudinarii filii maiorem in modum pertimesceret, omni arte illum ab studiis abducere frustra conabatur.
37 Quamobrem piissimus pater, quod robustum, letum, incolumemque habere filium tametsi imperitum, quam enervatum, tristem, exanguem ac valetudinarium prestare arbitraretur, idcirco indoctum sibi sepius quam hunc quem haberet litteratissimum filium optasse adiurabat.
38 Satis enim commodum esse filium aiebat eum qui nullas patri et familie erumnas afferret; hunc vero sibi esse incommodissimum,
39 quem sustinere in vita sumptibus maximis oporteret. Hec igitur vir ille modestissimus non opinione aliqua motus, sed re ipsa, ut

man had become unwell over his anxieties caused by the study of literature and he realized that his sick son would never have a tranquil future.

For these reasons the father was saddened and carrying out his 32 paternal duties he tried in all sorts of ways to distract his son from his books in order to play, and he often ordered him not to afflict himself so much with study and fasting. But the boy would immediately reply along these lines: "Father, stop trying to deflect me 33 from this path. You must realize that I owe this assiduity as my duty to literature; and if you are wise, if my standing is dear to you, you will behave in a way that lets me study even more, and encourage me never to leave the library. Be careful that with these 34 warnings you do not end up damaging the reputation I have built up through my care and diligence. I would rather hear you, father, ordering me to fulfill the promises you have made to your clients and look after the cases I have taken up on behalf of your friends; for you will very easily understand that in order to live up to the 35 expectations of our friends I will always show myself through all my studying to be no mean defender of that reputation. So, father, please let me continue the career that I have taken up."

So this prudent father, both for the other reasons and because 36 in these conditions he feared even more for the life of his unwell son, tried in vain to lead him away from his studies by any means possible. Now since this loving father thought it was better to have 37 a son who was strong, happy, and safe, even though somewhat ignorant, rather than one who was exhausted, sad, pallid and unwell, he often swore that he would have preferred his boy not to be learned than to have reared this highly literate son.

He said that it was enough of an advantage to have a son who 38 brought no troubles to his father and family; but this boy was a source of great disadvantages since he had to keep him alive at huge expense. This very modest father said all this, not swayed by 39 the opinion of others, but influenced by the reality of what was

videre licet, doctus edisserebat. Quare, si probatissimis viris credendum est, dum hic civis sua in urbe primarius multo cum
audientium consensu hec que rettuli attestabatur, nonne satis
40 edocebat litteras minime ad questum valere? Nonne persuasum
relinquebat non sequenda inde lucra, sed tristem et enervatam vitam prebentes litteras penitus esse graves et laboriosas et fugiendas?

41   Etenim cum ille, filium apud se educando, ita senserit, quid illi
facient patres qui filios longinquas apud civitates habuerunt, quo
loci ex patriis agris nihil deportari, nihil, quanquam minimum,
sine nummo comparari queat, contra quicquid ad victum cultumque corporis attinet id omne ex fortunis parentum emungitur?
42 Si vestis deest, si libros cupiunt, si egrotant (que res persepius ac-
cidunt), quante sunt continuo pecunie illuc profundende? Neque
item facile dici potest maiorum metu atque presentia soluti adoles-
43 centes quantum apud socios sint prodigi. Que tum omnia si ad
calculum referas, comperies procul dubio studiosos litterarum
dum litteris operam dedant, longe plures exposuisse pecunias
44 quam ex ullis litteris recuperaturi unquam sint. Quid igitur?
Questusne tam certi tamque maximi expectantur, ut omnes tibi
domestice fortune primum exponende sint? Optima erit quidem
institutio hec que patria et avita bona primo absorbeat, nihil vero
aliud postea rependat nisi tantum spem ipsam meram!

45   Quod an ita litteris eveniat videamus, ut apertius intelligamus
quam sint ignavi qui in litteris nummum exculpere conantur.
46 Constat quidem ex artibus acquiri divitias, cum premia frequentia
deferuntur, aut cum non frequentia sed amplissima; simul enim
permagna et non rarissima lucra, ni fallor, ars nulla conferret.
47 Grandia namque premia extremis atque ultimis laboribus et artibus pretiosissimis singularibusque rebus debentur, in quorum

happening. So, if we are to believe the most reliable people, this most important citizen in his town swore the truth of what I have just recounted with the broad approval of all who heard him, and surely he taught us convincingly that literary studies do not lead to wealth? Surely he convinced us that large amounts of money were   40
not to be sought from that source, but that, since these studies brought about a miserable, exhausted life, they were definitely burdensome, full of labor and to be avoided?

And if he felt like this about a son whom he was bringing up at   41
home, what will those fathers do whose sons study in distant cities, where nothing can be sent from the family fields; nothing, not even the slightest thing, can be bought without spending money; and conversely, whatever he needs in terms of food and of looking after his body has to all be drained from his parents' fortunes? If   42
he needs clothes, or wants books, or is unwell (which very often happens), how much money will his father have to provide continually for these eventualities? Nor can it easily be calculated how much money adolescents spend with their friends once they are free from the fear and presence of their elders. If you count all this   43
up, you will find without a doubt that literature students, while they are studying their texts, will cost much more money than they will ever recoup from any books. What then? Are the prospects of certain and maximum gain so sure that all your private   44
fortune must first be put at risk? If not, then this is really an excellent setup, which first drains the father's and ancestors' wealth, and then offers nothing in return except idle hopes!

Let us see if that happens with literature, so we can understand   45
more clearly how unwise are those who try to gain money from literary studies. It is agreed that wealth can be acquired from arts   46
when regular rewards are offered, or if they are not regular, they are substantial, for no art would bring at the same time both extensive and frequent profit. Large rewards go to extreme, exhaust-   47
ing labors, to very precious works of art and very rare things, but

48 altero artifex, in altero solet emptor deficere. Velim igitur hoc loco
fieri certior, studiose, speres ne minutissimis illis questibus, veluti
cum puerum instruxeris, cum libellus editus sit, cum causam ora-
ris, febrem curaris, aut cum de lege plurimum declamitaveris, aut
49 istiusmodi rebus ditari. Minime quidem, nam adeo modice sunt ut
ee vix quotidianis necessitatibus satisfaciant; tum adeo rare sunt ut
sero magnum divitiarum cumulum conducere possint.

50 At sunt litterati nonnunquam divites. Nolo hic esse pertinax.
Eos enim esse interdum non egenos fateamur, tamen pecuniosos
51 factos unde vis aliunde quam ex litteris putemus; nisi forte avaritia, scelere ac fraude rem quesitam ostentent, quos quidem questus
turpissimos splendore litterarum honestare cupientes mea sententia bis redarguendi sunt: primum quod ipsos se cumularint vitio,
proxime quod decus litterarum et dignitatem sua obscenitate con-
taminent.

52 Ne ergo honestissimi litterati erunt prorsus egeni? Erunt quidem, si litteris abundare quam nummis, si virtute quam ere, si
animi quam domus suppellectile ornati esse volent. Quid si litteras
una et divitias consectentur? In utroque parum egregie proficient.
53 Quid id? Namque diversa et omnino pugnantia esse studia oportet litteris deditorum et cupidorum hominum; nam illi fenori,
furtis, rapinis et flagitiis advigilent, quo quid potest esse turpius?
isti decori, laudi posteritatique servient, quo quid potest esse pre-
54 clarius? Rursus illi auro quam gloria, argento quam fama, caducis
rebus quam gratia et benevolentia civium abundare malunt; isti res
omnes preter solidam integramque virtutem minime expetendas
55 ducunt. Itaque quod cupidi maximopere sequuntur, litterati et

at times there is no artist, at times there is no buyer. At this point   48
I would like to ask the scholar: do you hope to become rich with
these small amounts of profit you make when you teach a child,
publish a book, plead a case, cure a fever, or when you make long
declamations about the law, or other such things? Of course not,   49
for the returns are so modest that they barely suffice for your daily
necessities; and they are so rare that they will only lead to a substantial amount of riches at a very late stage.

But literary scholars are sometimes rich. I do not want to be   50
obstinate here; let us admit that they are sometimes not destitute,
but we believe that for them to become wealthy would require any
other source than literature; unless perhaps they boast wealth that   51
comes through avarice, crime and fraud. But those who desire to
dignify these kinds of evil gains with the splendor of literature are
in my view doubly to be condemned: first because they have become rich through vice, and secondly because they have contami-
nated the dignity and beauty of literature with their own immo-
rality.

So literary scholars who are very honest will be very poor?   52
They will be, if they want to have more culture than money, more
virtue than cash; if they want to be adorned in their mind rather
than in their homes. What if they pursue both literature *and*
riches? They will not do very well in either field. Why so? Because   53
the pursuits of those devoted to literature and those who are desir-
ous of wealth are different and actually opposed to each other; for
the latter attend only to usury, theft, robbery and crime, and what
could be more immoral than that? The former will pursue praise
and their reputation for posterity, and what can be more noble
than that? Again the latter prefer to abound in gold rather than   54
glory, silver more than fame, ephemeral goods rather than enjoying
the favor and benevolence of their fellow citizens. And the former
believe that nothing is worth seeking out except for solid, impeccable virtue. Thus what the avaricious mostly look for will be   55

bonarum artium studiosi aspernabuntur; quod studiosi expetent, cupidi negligent. Denique in augenda re preda et avaritia cupidi utuntur, cum litterati in amplificanda fama liberalitate et iustitia

56 delectantur. Sed ut negotium hoc statuam, sic ipse censeo: non fieri divites litteratos, aut si ex litteris ditantur, turpiter eosdem

57 ditari. Nemo enim animo ingenuo preditus (ut reliquas cupidorum turpitudines omittam), nemo non turpe ducet elegantiam doctrine suppeditare questibus, nemo non flagitiosum putabit doctrinam facere sibi nundinariam.

58 Quod si tandem, preter mores, preter veterem bonorum consuetudinem, quispiam iuste opulentus erit futurus ex doctrina, is plane sit cui fortuna facilior, scientia profundior, auctoritas prestantior, amicorum observantia cultior longe quam ceteris atque

59 amplior fuerit, cuius item facundia, facilitas, ingenium, versutia, calliditas acceptior atque ad hominum aures et opinionem acco-

60 modatior. Talem enim hunc esse litteratum oportet ut dum ei non dubitet civitas universas fortunas commendare suas, tum frequentissimos questus et premia porrigere assuescat. At vero in eo qui-

61 dem gradu claritatis perpaucissimi reperiuntur; addo quod qui multorum gratiam concupiverit, non parsimonia, non his artibus quibus res et divitie comparantur, sed beneficio, liberalitate prodigalitateque contendat oportebit, rebus, ut vides, ad cogendas divi-

62 tias minime accomodatis. Vel esto sane: sint multi quorum se fidei omnis civitas commendare audeat, preterea fieri possit ut omnes questus qui ex litigiis, qui ex sententiis, qui ex morbis iuste capiuntur, omnes, inquam, hi questus in unum congerantur et uni

63 tantum conferantur litterato, non illi quidem omnes (ita me superi

despised by literature students and those who study the nobler arts; what scholars seek out, the greedy will ignore. Finally, in enlarging their fortune, mercenary people will use robbery and avarice, whereas literary scholars in enlarging their reputation will take delight in their generosity and justice. But to draw this part 56 to an end, here is what I believe: either literary scholars do not become rich, or if they do become wealthy through literature they will have done so in an immoral way. For nobody with a noble 57 mind (leaving aside all the other evils of those who are greedy) will think it anything other than unethical if the elegance of learning is enslaved to profit; nobody will regard it as anything other than scandalous if erudition becomes mercenary.

If in the end there is someone who becomes justly rich from 58 learning, without damaging his morals and good habits, this person should clearly be someone on whom fortune has smiled more, whose knowledge is more profound and whose authority is higher than those of others, and who enjoys greater and more justified respect from his friends. He is someone whose eloquence, fluency, 59 intelligence, cleverness and talent is more acceptable and more suited to the ears and opinions of other men. The literary man 60 must be such that his city will not fear to entrust its entire fortune to him, and it should become accustomed to handing him frequent rewards and benefits. Yet only very few are found to have achieved that level of fame. In addition, he who wants to court 61 the good favor of the many, will not do so with parsimony, nor by those arts that are used to acquire property and wealth, but through competing in generosity, munificence and even prodigality, all things, as you see, which are highly unsuitable for accumulating wealth. Let us suppose that there are many to whose good 62 keeping every city commends itself, and moreover that all gains that come honestly from lawsuits, legal verdicts, or curing the sick, are gathered together and handed over to one man of letters: not 63 all of that wealth (may the gods help me) in my opinion will be

adiuvent) meo iudicio questus aut tanti aut tam frequentes erunt
64 ut divitias existimem deditas esse amplissimas. Et quantos morbos, vel potius pestes, quam multas in civitate discordias agi et
quam solertes questuum aucupatores, superi boni, nos esse oportet, antequam iustis salariis litterarum locupletemur, antequam
non aliorum mercedibus, sed nostris opibus vitam degere honeste
65 liceat! Quorsum hec? Plane ut intelligatur sua rata questuum
parte studiosos nequicquam posse ditari, quandoquidem ex tanta
multitudine vix unum posse fieri divitem persuasimus.

66   Neque hoc loco eos audiendos puto vulgatum illud afferentes
quo aiunt: 'Qui in fide non deficit, opes non facit, qui non decipit,
lucra non capit.' Esset enim ea lucri faciendi ratio ab institutis et
67 laude litteratorum longe alienissima. Ac sunt preterea non pauce
ad certissimas divitias comparandas honeste ac civiles artes, quas
longum quidem esset enumerare. Sed illud non pretermittatur:
nullas fore artes aut disciplinas quibus non multo facilius ditemur
quam ex litteris.

68   Si enim ad rem militarem accesseris, persepius dabitur ut illic
amplissimas quam hic in litteris mediocres divitias assequaris; ar-
matis enim militibus mediis in campis patent complures vie vel ad
ingentes divitias coacervandas, vel ad supremam amplitudinem
69 consequendam. Litteras vero qui esse voluerit questuosas, humi-
70 lem se ac mercenarium prebeat opus est. Quid si te mercatura
exercueris? Nonne tandiu lucraberis quamdiu voles? Nonne undique astant portus provincie ac gentes innnumere que te aliquid
71 conducentem expectent? Quid preterea si te ad agriculturam
conferas? Quenam vita beatior erit? Que uberior, questuosior aut

sufficient or so regular that I would think that the money given will be a huge amount. And how many diseases, or rather plagues, 64 how many quarrels in the city will there have to be and how canny will we have to become in hunting down profits before we will become rich through the just stipends that come from literature, and before we may be allowed to live an honorable life from our own resources, and not from fees paid by others? Where is all this 65 leading? It is to make it clearly understood that scholars can never become rich by their share of the profits when we have shown that scarcely one person can become rich out of such a multitude.

Nor at this point do I think we should listen to those people 66 who come forward with that old idea which makes them say: "He who does not go back on his word, will not make money, and he who does not deceive will not make any profit." That method of making money would be a long way away from the procedures and reputation of literary scholars, and there are in any case many 67 honest and civil arts that guarantee the acquisition of certain wealth which it would be too long to enumerate here. But this we should not omit to say: that there are plenty of arts or disciplines by which it is much easier for us to become rich than from literature.

For if you go into the military, it very often happens that there 68 you can get hold of enormous quantities of wealth compared to the mediocre amounts available from literary study; for there are many ways open to armed soldiers in the middle of battlefields either to amass huge amounts of riches, or even to reach the pinnacle of wealth. He who wants literature to be a source of prosper-69 ity needs to abase himself so that he becomes humble and mercenary. What if you are a merchant? Will you not make enough 70 money and for as long as you want? Surely there are harbors all around as well as provinces and countless peoples who are waiting to do business with you? What happens if you turn to agriculture? 71 What life can be better than that? What richer, wealthier or more

sanctior merces poterit inveniri? Sola enim agricultura pacata et libera indoctis quietem, doctis felicitatem poterit contribuere.

72 Nam cum nulla quidem expectatio certior ex re aliqua est quam que ex agro bene culto suscipitur, tum ager quidem ad bene beate- que vivendum otii plurimum atque ab omni strepitu et molestia

73 vacationem mirificam exhibet. Adde his quod nulla grandior atque perennior utilitas est quam que ex rustico penu trahitur. Sed de laudibus agriculture deque artibus questuosis alias.

74 Sit vero in illis ipsis atque in istiusmodi artibus et rebus omni- bus locupletandi quedam ratio posita: in litteris vero doctrine ele- gantia et laus florescet, qua ducti prudentes solent putare omnes questus esse eiusmodi ut sit pulchrius sapientie gratia ferre pau-

75 pertatem fortiter quam ditari sine laude. Quod si qui ita impu- dentes erunt, ut, spreta religione ac decore litterarum, tantum cu- piditate ducantur ac sibi persuasum habeant fieri posse ut, fraude perfidiaque adhibita, litterarum suffragiis locupletentur, velim se

76 sciant vehementer errare. Nam sunt quidem infiniti casus in vita hominum quibus acti mortales paucissimi istuc perveniunt ubi ip-

77 sas primas litterarum mercedes sint suscepturi. Et omittamus qui- dem illud: patrias prius fortunas esse exhaustas in studiis quam ille tantum litteris profecerit ut auctione litterarum sese sustentet.

78 Exploratissimum est eum qui questum facturus sit ex litteris non prius ad eas venditandas accessurum quam se in eisdem bene egre-

79 gieque eruditum exhibuerit. Nempe videmus ut publicis declama- tionibus disputationibusque ac reliquis scolarum et gymnasiorum causis et certaminibus magnopere quid valeant ingenio et litteris

80 ostentent. Neque vero transire ad questum fas est, nisi prius eam

respectable goods could be found? For only agriculture is peaceful and free, and will be able to bring rest to the unlearned and happiness to the erudite. And since no expectation is more certain from any other thing than what is reaped from a well cultivated field, then the countryside offers both the maximum amount of leisure to enjoy the good life as well as a wonderful respite from all kinds of noise and annoyance. Add to this the fact that there is no greater or more lasting source of utility than that which is drawn from country produce. But we can talk another time about the praise of agriculture and about the arts which make money.

Let us admit there is some sort of possibility of wealth in these and similar arts, and indeed in everything; but in literature only the elegance and praise of learning flourish, which leads the prudent to think that all profit is of such a nature that it is better to tolerate poverty bravely for the sake of wisdom than to become rich without any praise. If there are people who are so impudent that, ignoring religion and the wonders of literature, they are led by so much greed to be convinced that by practicing fraud and treachery one can become rich through literature, I would like them to know that they are very much mistaken. For there are an endless number of mischances in the life of men, and this means that very few reach the point where they are about to receive the first rewards of literature. Not to mention this fact: that the family's fortunes will sooner be exhausted in supporting his studies before the young man will progress so far in literature that he will be able to support himself from literary income. It is a very well-known fact that he who would make a living from literature will not be able to sell his wares until he shows that he is wonderfully erudite in the subject. We ourselves see how in public declamations and debates and in the rest of the cases and contests discussed in schools and academies, the young show off how brilliant they are in genius and literature. Nor are they permitted to move into money earning, unless first they have created the opinion in

de se populo iniecerint opinionem ut docti vulgo existimentur, cum qua se posse ad lucrum magis quam cum virtute existimant.

81 Proxime dici se doctores fibulamque auream demirari volunt, que talia tanti faciunt ut cum his plurimum sapere, sine his nihil didicisse videantur.

82 Verum hoc loco querendum videtur utrumne antequam cum auro et auctoritate ab studiis domum redierint annum vel plus trigesimum insudarint, patrias fortunas labefactarint, se ipsos

83 confecerint. Quid etiam, quod accedunt ad hos anni admodum decem quibus nondum fama et rebus gestis ita claruisse potuere ut

84 quas teneant litteras easdem bene fecerint venales? Anni ergo non pauciores quadraginta prius perditi sunt quam ii cupidissimi lucrum occeperint: hominum pene ultima etas, quam ad etatem

85 quot mihi dabis attigisse? Quot, ex mille viris, quanquam nulla anxietate studiorum, nullis angoribus animi oppressis, vitam omnino alacrem et iocundam ducentibus, putas annum quadra-

86 gesimum excessisse? Profecto cum ⟨e⟩ ceteris bellissimam vitam agentibus paucos, tum longe paucissimos mihi litteratos dabis

87 quadragenarios. Valetudo enim imbecilla, vita fragilis etasque admodum brevis est studiosorum hominum, quorum nemo fuit nature usque adeo robuste quin laboribus, vigiliis ac reliquis studiorum nocumentis non penitus conficiatur.

88 Iuvat hanc rem redigere ad numerum, quo argumentatio nostra

89 clarior sit. Consuevere prudentissimi viri, cum interdum a me rogantur quot ex mille hominum numero censeant ad annum quadragesimum etatis sue pervenire, communi, atque, ut opinor, vera sententia, statuere vix CCC ex mille hominum numero nedum ad quadragesimum, sed ne ad trigesimum annum vitam perducere.

people that they are to be considered learned, and armed with this opinion they think they enjoy a higher standing through lucre than through virtue. Next they want to have a doctorate and be 81 admired for their gold brooch, and they think so highly of such things that they believe that with these trappings they can appear to know very many things, but without them they seem to have learned nothing.

But here we should remind ourselves that before they reach the 82 stage of returning from university with their gold and their new-found authority, they will have sweated over their studies for over thirty years, dismantled their fathers' fortunes, and exhausted themselves. What about the fact that another ten years has to be 83 added to this, during which time they will not yet be able to achieve so much fame and success that they can turn the command of literature they may have into something that can support them? Thus they will have wasted no fewer than forty years before 84 these highly ambitious people begin to earn any money, in other words, almost the last age of their life: how many do you think will reach that age? Out of a thousand men who, without any 85 anxiety about studies, their minds not oppressed by any worries, lead a totally joyful and pleasant existence, how many do you think live beyond the age of forty? Now since only a few of the 86 rest who lead a wonderful life reach forty, you must grant that few, very few literature scholars will reach that age. For scholars enjoy 87 poor health, a fragile life, and quite a brief existence: none of them have a strong enough constitution not to be totally ground down by work, late night studying and the other harmful effects of scholarship.

It would be helpful to reduce this question to precise statistics 88 so that our argument becomes clearer. When I sometimes ask very 89 clever men how many people they think out of a thousand reach the age of forty in their life, they give the common and truthful opinion that scarcely three hundred men would reach, not even

90 Illud etiam iidem peritissimi viri statuunt: eum rarissimum esse
qui ante illam quadragenariam etatem possit familiam suam satis
91 opulentam reddere. Ita quidem illi prudentes viri asserunt dum
rogantur.

92   Nos vero, ne hunc locum pro nostro instituto minime negligendum orationis cursu pretervolemus, repetamus hunc vite compu-
tum, ut litteratos qui per etatem ditari queant selectos habeamus,
atque, si quando in divitiarum cupiditatem inciderimus, sciamus
in quem annorum et litteratorum numerum atque gradum nos
fore asciscendos prius optandum sit. Quare ad rem proficiscamur.

93   Quero abs te, litterate, ex istis ipsis CCC prolixam vitam
ducentibus quot sint per omnem vitam omnibus fortune iniuriis
liberi, quotve sint, qui quotidianis malis atque erumnis ita vacuam,
expeditam et liberam vitam duxerint, ut suis studiis freti, nulla
calamitate interpellante, summam doctrine prestantiam attigerint.

94 An ignoramus quam sint artium rationes prolixe atque amplissime
quamque ad tantam disciplinarum amplitudinem colendam sit
95 ingenium hominum debile? Accedit quod fallax et imbecillis adversus impetum fortune atque adversus reliquas fraudes hominum
est nostra et ratio et facultas mortalium, quo fit ut cum difficile sit
ceteras quasvis artes egregie tenere, tum longe omnium difficilli-
mum mihi videatur totam rem litterariam (ut sic loquar) amplecti.

96 Statuamus idcirco inter nos quot ex CCC in eam longam etatem
viventibus non cogantur variis fortune casibus in medio proficiendi
97 cursu studia litterarum deserere aut interrumpere. Hoc ut rectius
statuamus, considerandum fortassis est quanta dentur discidia ab
studiis maxima et pene innumerabilia; proxime meminisse oportet
omnem pertinaciam studiorum facilius casu abrumpi quam inter-
ruptam postea consilio retexi.

forty, but only thirty. These same experts also agree on this: that it 90
is a very rare person who can make his family wealthy enough before he reaches forty. That is what such prudent men answer when 91
they are asked.

So that we do not pass over this point in the course of my 92
speech, let us, as is our wont, emphasize these statistics again, also so that we can be aware of how few are the literary people who become rich in their lifetime. Thus, if we want to become rich, we will know how many years we have to spend, how much literature we will have to have read, and how few literary scholars succeed in becoming wealthy. So now let us turn to our main topic.

I want to ask you, man of letters, out of these three hundred 93
leading a long life, how many of them are there who throughout their lives are free from the injuries of fortune, or how many are there who lead an existence so free, unhindered and untouched by woes and toils that, devoted only to their studies, and with no calamity intervening, they reach the peak of literary excellence? Or 94
do we not know how long and arduous the study of arts is and how unfit the mind of man is to cultivate this breadth of scholarship? In addition, mortal man's reason and capabilities are unreli- 95
able and weak against the slings of fortune and against the fraudulent actions of other men, so that it is both difficult to master the other arts well, and by far the most difficult thing of all is to master the whole business of literature, so to speak. Let us there- 96
fore decide among ourselves how many of those three hundred men living that long life are not forced by various turns of fortune to abandon or interrupt their literary researches in the middle of their course of study. In order to establish this more precisely, 97
perhaps we must consider how many, indeed how innumerable are the instances of people abandoning literature; then we must remember that any dedication to study is more likely to be broken off completely by an accident than to be duly resurrected after an interruption.

59

98 Tu vero si dixeris litterarum studia nunquam quicquam recipere
ut tibi ab opere intersedendum sit, profecto aut nimium felix es
99 aut minime studiosus; nam id quidem in omni cursu vite in dies
experimur: studia, operas atque instituta nostra omnia variis et
fortune et rerum casibus perturbari, partim vi bellorum, partim
locorum infectione et peste, partim fortune volubilitate, partim
animi aut corporis morbis, partim rebus extrinsecis urgentibus,
veluti paupertate, iniuriis, inimicitiis, reliquisque calamitatibus in-
terpellantibus, infinitisque (ut est hominum vita refertissima) de-
100 trimentis, incommodis et difficultatibus compellentibus. Has ob
res prudentes aliqui familiares, cum de his rebus a me rogantur,
statuisse soliti sunt circiter centum ex CCC esse quorum cepta
101 studia, his malis intacta, possent evadere. Non recusemus hunc a
prudentibus viris constitutum numerum, tametsi pauciores esse
perplures existimassem; nos tamen in hac summa liberales sumus.
102 Centum ergo ex mille studiosis viris fortuna et vita ad lucra ex
litteris excipienda perveniant; iam ad decimam totius summe par-
103 tem devenimus: M posueram, centum delegimus. Rursus quero
quot ex istis centum putes esse memoria validos, mente potentes,
ingenio aptos ad doctrinas. Non enim qui volent omnes, sed quibus fata singulare id munus ita concessere, ad capessendam doctri-
104 narum magnitudinem accomodati sunt; memoria enim atque ingenium pene divinum quo studiosos maximarum artium prestare
oportet, fato quodam, hominibus perpaucissimis ab ipsa natura
105 concessum est. Nam si Hortensio memoriam, Ciceroni ingenium
fata elargita sunt, aliis quidem ex tanto rhetorum numero in his
rebus singularem laudem vix ullam concessere.
106 Sed preter quod polliciti sumus egredimur. Nudam orationem
nostram futuram prediximus, sola veritate contentam et honestam;

But if you say that literary studies never receive any setback 98
which forces you to give them up, then either you are very lucky or
not very studious. For this is something that we experience daily 99
in all walks of life: all our studies, works and education are dis-
rupted by the various turns of fortunes and events, sometimes
through the violence of war, sometimes through infection and
plague in places, at others through the volatility of fortune, or
diseases of the mind or body, or the force of external factors such
as poverty, injuries, enmities, and the other calamities that befall
us, as well as infinite kinds of damage (with which human life is
riddled), disadvantages and difficulties which force us to give up
study. For these reasons, when I have asked some wise family 100
members about this, they have usually answered that there were
about one hundred out of these three hundred people whose studies managed to escape these evils. We will not reject this statistic 101
established by my relatives, even though I would have put the
number at several fewer than that; but let us be liberal about that
figure. Let us say that one hundred manage to make money out of 102
literature in their life and fortune, so we have now reached a tenth
of our original number: I had suggested a figure of one thousand,
we have ended up with a figure of one hundred. Again, I ask how 103
many out of those hundred do you think have a strong memory, a
powerful mind, a genius for learning? For it is not everyone who
wants to, but those to whom fate has given this rare gift who are
suited to mastering the whole breadth of learning in the disciplines; for nature herself allows very few to receive by some fate 104
the memory and divine genius that students of these greatest of
arts have to possess. For if the fates gave Hortensius memory and 105
Cicero genius,[14] they allowed hardly any praise in these subjects to
be obtained by the huge number of other orators.

But we have gone beyond the bounds we set ourselves, when we 106
promised that our discourse would be unadorned, just an honest
account, content only with the truth; so let us avoid all these

idcirco hos omnes amplificationum locos fugiamus, ad rem rede-
107 amus. Hos quidem ingenio et memoria ad doctrinas non ineptos,
aliqui plures, multi vero pauciores comperiri attestantur; nos au-
108 tem quod utranque opinionem sapiat teneamus. Esto, ex centum
ingenio, facultatibus et vita integris decem sint ad perficiendam in
studiis laudem compotes, ex quibus quidem omnibus nescio an ad
summum tres ita litteris affecti, ita disciplinarum amatores et cupidi, ita studiis dedicati sint, ut totas quas recitavi studiosorum
erumnas et anxietates per omnem etatem vel audeant, vel valeant
109 perferre. Nam si ad humanos casus incertosque motus fortune ac
nature imbecillitatem extremi quoque labores accesserint, qui sane,
ut docui, in litterarum studiis et permaximi sunt et interlaxari
minime possunt, quos putas tanti divitias facturos, ut non plus
110 vite sue consultum iri velint? Hac ergo enumeratione compertum
fecimus ex mille studiosis viris tres ad summum in eam etatem
annorum quadraginta cum ea facultate, animo, ingenio, viribus
atque instituto perdurasse quo satis apti ad questum suis litteris
111 esse possint. Et neque latet, tametsi litteris claruerint, tamen eosdem ante futuros senes quam questibus litterarum possint orna-
tam et locupletem familiam reddere. De iis fortassis illud Catonis
persimile dicetur: studuisse istos ut apud inferos divitias pararent.
112 Quod si quis erit litteratus in vita sua ditior, habeat is quidem
gratias fortune, non virtuti, et sciat non meritorum laborum id
premium esse, sed largitatem, vel potius stultitiam fortune; que
cum in ceteris rebus omnes odisse bonos consueverit, hunc tamen
litteratum delegerit cui preter consuetudinem suam donare colli-
buerit.

topics that lend themselves to amplification, and return to our
subject. Some claim that there are several people who have a suit- 107
able mind and memory for this kind of erudition, but many say
that there are rather few to be found; we shall hold to a view that
reflects both opinions. So let us say there are ten out of a hundred 108
who have the right kind of genius, capacities and life to achieve
fame in these studies, and out of all of these I think that at most
three are so competent in literature, so much in love with and eager for the discipline, so dedicated to study, that they dare or are
strong enough to tolerate throughout their lives all the trials and
anxieties I mentioned. For in addition to the accidents that affect 109
man, the uncertain movements of fortune, and the weakness of
our nature, if you then include the extreme labors that, as I have
shown, are everywhere in literary study and which cannot be reduced even minimally, how many people do you think will care so
little about money and will not think it more important than their
own existence? By this calculation we have discovered that out of 110
a thousand scholars only three in the end will reach the age of
forty with the right ability, mind, genius, strength and way of life
to be able to make money from literature. Nor does it escape me 111
that even although some men have become famous through literary scholarship, those same people will be old before they can
make their families adorned and rich through the gains made from
literature. Maybe something very similar to Cato's famous saying
will be said about these people, namely that they have studied so
long in order to accumulate wealth in the underworld. And if 112
some literature scholar does become a little rich in his lifetime, he
should thank his good fortune, not his virtue, and know that this
is not a reward for his well-deserving labors, but the generosity or
rather the foolishness of fortune. Although fortune is accustomed
to hating good people in other things, she will have singled out
this literary person as someone to whom she has decided to be
generous against her usual practice.

113   Ceterum et hoc apud litteratos detrimentum quanti existimabi-
mus, quod nunquam queritur quisnam constantior inter litteratos
aut modestior aut integrior sit, sed illud in primis sciscitantur
quisnam ad forensem strepitum, quis ad insidias et fraudes litigio-
114 rum exercitatior, callidior, audentior atque procacior sit? Non secus atque omnes boni sint cum ab extorquenda pecunia rudes,
115 tum ad causas defendendas inepti. Quod si de litteratorum peritia
recte iudicaretur, fortassis assentationes, dicacitatem ac versutiam
improborum non plus quam modestissimorum simplicissimoru-
116 mque scientiam facerent; sed nunc plus malitia quam virtus, de-
ceptio, levitas, petulantia quam humanitas et modestia valet apud
vulgus: quorum iudicio litterati nisi probentur nunquam erunt
117 non egeni. Iam vero vulgus, cum ea decipiendi et predandi mente
qua ad litigium accessit, patronos nequeat fraudare, cumve fraudem contraria fraude collidi sentit, illico hunc magnificat a quo
118 perfidia superetur. Quod si causam iniustissimam audacissimus
litteratus susceperit, illico hunc summum patronum, optimum
119 virum preclarumque amicitiarum cultorem esse predicant. Ex quo
fit ut fraudem virtutem putent, simulandi ac dissimulandi artem
tanquam doctrine quandam eximiam vim admirentur, malitiamque
ac nequitiam et fallacias ex litterarum cognitione deductas existi-
120 ment; bonum vero, rectum sanctumque virum, ipsa iustitia et
equitate merita causarum metientem, non calliditate et perfidia
disceptantem, iuri ac scientie non tergiversationibus fidendum sta-
tuentem, non decipiendo lucra, sed vincendo laudem exposcentem,
hunc quidem ipsum inutilem, indoctum causarumque naufragium
121 noncupant. Denique odisse simplicitatem ac detrahere virtuti non

And how should we rate this negative fact concerning literary 113
people, namely that nobody ever asks who is the most constant,
modest or blameless among literati. Instead they want to know
this above all: who is more experienced, cleverer, more daring and
impudent when it comes to the noise of the law courts and the
tricks and fraud of lawsuits? As if they thought that those who are 114
honest were incapable of extorting money and hopeless at defending their clients. If people judged correctly about the capabilities of 115
literary scholars, perhaps they would not rate flattery, sarcasm and
trickery higher than the knowledge of these very modest and
straightforward men. But nowadays, in the eyes of the populace 116
wickedness is more highly prized than virtue. Deception, levity
and petulance are rated higher than humaneness and modesty: unless literary people are approved of by the populace's judgment,
they will never be anything other than poor. But now, since the 117
people, using the same mentality of deception and robbery with
which they approached their lawsuit, are unable to defraud their
lawyer, and since they feel that each case is just one kind of fraud
coming up against another, they immediately rate someone great if
he can outdo them in perfidy. But if a very unscrupulous literary 118
man takes on a very unjust case, they immediately proclaim him to
be the top barrister, the best person and outstanding cultivator of
friendships. That is why they think that fraud is virtue, why they 119
admire the art of simulating and dissimulating as if it were the
most outstanding strength in learning, and why they believe that
malice, wickedness and deception have all been derived from literature. And the man who is good, upright and pious, who weighs 120
up the merits of a case with justice itself and equity, not discours-
ing with trickery and perfidy, who believes that one must rely on
the law and its knowledge, not on evasion or deception in order to
make money but rather to pursue praise through winning cases—
well this kind of man is deemed useless, unlearned, someone who
will sink their case. In the end they never stop hating integrity and 121

desinunt, quam ob rem non modo cupidi, sed etiam illi qui quotidianum victum sibi ex litteris suppeditari volent profecto his que
122 dixi perfidiis animum imbuere coguntur. Itaque avaritia et scelere
divitias cupidi litterati adipiscuntur, quandoquidem (ut ipsis oculis
intuemur) versuti et fallaces petuntur, boni et simplices deseruntur.

123   O duram igitur studiosorum sortem! Quid hoc primum mali
est? Mille hominum labores, innumerabiles anxietates, pregrandes
vigilie, iterum maior in dies atque longe incredibilis assiduitas
124 apud studiosos non plus quam tribus fructuosa futura; atque iis
fructuosa futura est, qui perfidia prestent, quibus fortuna ad gratiam comparandam, ingenium ad calliditatem, mens ad mendacium, vita ad turpitudinem fuerit prona et assuefacta, quos indocti
doctissimos attestentur, de quibus temerarium vulgi iudicium vigeat!

125   Itaque unicus bonis litteris adversator, bonorum morum hostis,
iustissimarum causarum inimicus ac ad omne scelus et flagitium
paratissimus universorum litteratorum emolumenta sua petulantia
et protervitate preripiet, laudem aliorum sua temeritate offuscabit,
126 nomen et famam ambitione restinguet. O rem duram, ex mille
studiosis vix unum atque eum quidem nequissimum divitem fieri!
Reliqui omnes mendicabitis, litterati, si probi eritis, si improbi non
tamen omnes eritis locupletes: fortuna enim non semper omnibus,
ex instituto, eadem facilis est.

127   Quas ob res stultissimum esse illum arbitrari oportet qui spe
128 divitiarum se dedicarit litteris. Sunt enim vel non honesta vel non

decrying virtue, and as a result not only the greedy but also those who want just to have their daily subsistence from literature are forced to imbue their minds with the kinds of perfidy I have mentioned. Thus literary scholars who are greedy get hold of wealth 122 through avarice and crime, since (as we see with our own eyes) people look for other crafty and deceptive people, while the good and straightforward are abandoned.

What a hard lot scholars have! What is its main disadvantage? 123 Every day they have to face labors worthy of a thousand men, countless anxieties, enormous hours of study, ever greater and prolonged assiduity. All this bears fruit for no more than three men; and even then it will be fruitful only to those who are out- 124 standing for their perfidy, and who have been given the good fortune to be able to acquire favor, the brains to become clever, the mind to become a liar, and a life that is abjectly enslaved to evil; these are the people whom the unlearned swear are extremely erudite, and about whom only the rash judgment of the multitude counts!

Thus just one opponent of good literature, the enemy of good 125 morals, the enemy of the most just cases, and the person most ready to embrace every crime and disgrace will steal the rewards of all literary men through his insolence and impudence, will darken the praise of others through his own rash behavior, and extinguish the good name and fame of others through his own ambition. What a harsh thing this is to tolerate: out of a thousand scholars 126 scarcely one becomes rich, and that one is the most wicked! The rest of you literary people will have to become beggars, if you are honest; and if you are not honest, not even all of you will become rich: for fortune, deliberately, is not always accommodating to everyone.

For all these reasons we must consider very foolish the man 127 who dedicates himself to literature in the hope of wealth. For the 128 profits to be gained from it are not honest or worthy of a free man,

liberalia lucra litterarum, tum ut vidisti, perexigua atque, postremo, quecunque illa sint, paucissimis et minime bonis concessa

129 sunt, que quidem, etsi magna honestaque exciperentur, non tamen eiusmodi ut superioribus impensis satisfaciant.

130 Iam vero quid hoc loco dicent arguti viri? An vera que a me
131 dicta sunt esse negabunt? Non erunt, ut opinor, ita impudentes ut verissimas notissimasque a me deductas rationes inficientur, sed fortassis illic insistent, ac divitem aliquem litteris tinctum in medium afferent ac rogabunt quidni et ceteros quoque litteratos di-
132 vites posse fieri existimem. Quibus ego si forte dixero quem producant litteratum malis artibus pecunias acquisivisse, plane sim dignus odio quod de meis litteratis invide iudicem; si autem dixero
133 eiusmodi perpaucissimos esse, illi quidem inquient: 'In hoc eruditorum minimo quem videmus numero vel unus admodum sat est,' tum omnes qui sese questus gratia litteris applicarint contra me testes et dictorum meorum reprehensores adducentur.

134 Has igitur ob res liceat nobis causam hanc brevissima quadam excursione membratim resumere copiasque nostras iterum collus-
135 trare. Nam proderit id quidem, ni fallor, ad tollendam cupidorum studentium imprudentiam, quos precor ut, posita (si quam fortassis habent) cupiditate lucri, rationes parumper nostras perlegant;
136 nam hoc si fecerint, posthac nunquam ad libros ac scientias nisi spreta cupiditate accedent. Itaque ad rem procedamus.

137 Ex omni quidem litteratorum multitudine, que infinitas pene in disciplinas distincta est, solas admodum tres esse questuosas professiones constat: unam eorum qui causas et contractus notant, aliam illorum qui iuridicundo presunt; tertia est eorum qui

and then, as you have seen, they are very small and in the end, no matter their amount, they are given to very few and to people who are far from being good. And if these profits were great and honest, they are not on a scale to compensate for the previous expenses. 129

Now then, what do clever men say at this point? Will they deny that what I have said is true? They will not, I think, be so rash as to deny the very truthful and well-known arguments I have set out, but perhaps they will go so far as to bring forward some rich man who has a smattering of knowledge about literature and will ask him why it is I think that everyone else who studies literature cannot become rich like him. And if I say to them that the man they have brought forward gained his money through evil practices, I would deserve their hatred because I would be judging my fellow literature scholars with envy. And if I say that there are really very few like him, they will reply: "Out of this very small number of learned men that we have seen, one rich man is enough"; and then all those who have dedicated themselves to literature in order to make money will be witnesses against me and will be brought forward as critics of my words. 130 131 132 133

This being so, let me be allowed to resume this argument point by point, with a very brief digression, and review once more the strength of our reasoning. For I believe that this will be helpful in eliminating the foolishness of those who study for greed, whom I would beg to set aside their desire for profit (if they have any), and briefly read my arguments; for if they do so, afterward they will never return to their books and knowledge unless they have set aside all greed for money. So now let us proceed with our subject. 134 135 136

Out of the total number of literature scholars, who are spread across an almost infinite number of disciplines, it is agreed that only three professions offer financial gain: one group are those who are notaries and deal with lawsuits and contracts; a second group are the lawyers who administer justice; the third are the doctors 137

138 valetudines curant. Reliquas omnes intueor non magis erudimentis claras esse quam paupertate. Neque id quidem iniuria, nam que solum corporis ac fortune bonis deserviunt, eedem ad questum artes nate et accomodate sunt; que vero artes animum et ingenium

139 alunt, aliquid maius incorruptibile ac sempiternum exposcunt. Tu vero si hec negabis, rogabo utrumne grammatici, rhetores philosophique parum tibi dare litteris operam videantur, proxime rogabo ex illis ipsis quot comperias esse divites. Nonne tu ferme omnes eiusmodi litteras per civium domos pedagogas mendicare animad-

140 vertis? Doceo quid pulchre respondeas: dicito philosophos tanquam ultimum malum sprevisse pecunias, itaque merito iacent

141 inopes, egeni. Denique usque adeo adducta sit res ut scriba, medicus ac iurisperitus, tres hi tantum, prestantes atque utiles didicisse litteras putentur, quoniam easdem bene fecerint nundinarias;

142 relique autem doctrine de ingenio, de natura rerum, de moribus deque ceteris maximis prestantissimis atque elegantissimis rebus inculte et sordide a civibus contemnantur atque reiiciantur, soleque venales littere in pretio sint.

143 Ego tamen minime unquam tanti faciam illorum trium generum opulentiam, ut non sit apud me pulchrius hic sapientie

144 gratia ferre fortiter paupertatem quam illic ditari sine laude; nam honestissimos quidem scribas plures egenos quam quadruplatores aut rabulas divites vidi, ut in toto scribarum ordine dubitem an

145 ulli ferme questus fraude ac perfidia careant. Certe hoc pace bonorum dicere audeam, nam qui succenseat improbis bonis favere

146 existimandus est. Ego de tabellionibus improbis sic censeo: putari posse illud plerunque in eis esse verum quod aiunt vulgo, in tabellionibus signum maxime nequitie tum apparere cum sine calamo

who look after those in ill health. All the other people who study 138
literature are as famous for their poverty as for their erudition.
And that is only right, for those arts that only serve the goods of
the body and of fortune are those that were discovered and made
suitable for profit. The arts that nurture the mind and the intellect
demand something greater, incorruptible and eternal. If you deny 139
this, I will ask you whether grammarians, rhetoricians and philosophers seem to you not to spend much time on literature, and
then ask you how many of those people have you found to be
wealthy? Do you not notice that nearly all literature teachers go
round the houses of our citizens begging? I will teach you what 140
your clever reply will be: you will say that philosophers have
spurned money as though it were the ultimate evil, so it is right
that they are now poor and without resources. Finally, things have 141
reached the stage where only these three, the notary, lawyer and
doctor, are considered prestigious and useful students of letters
since they have made literature marketable. All the other subjects 142
dealing with the intellect, nature and morals, and all the other
eminent and choice disciplines are despised and rejected by our
citizens as uncouth and squalid while only literature that makes a
profit is appreciated.

However, for my part, I would never rate the wealth of these 143
three professions so highly that I would change my view that it is
better to put up with poverty bravely for the sake of wisdom than
to make money from it without praise. For I have seen many more 144
honest notaries who are poor than wealthy snitchers and pettifog-
gers, so much so that in all the ranks of notaries I would doubt
whether any gain is without fraud and perfidy. Of course, I dare to 145
say this out of respect for all good people, namely that those who
get angry with the wicked are regarded as favoring the good. I have 146
the following idea about corrupt notaries: that it could be thought
that what people say is true, namely that the sign of their utmost

147 ad aurem assito deambulent. Non enim licet scribam una et divitias et mores velle ostendere: nam nemo ignorat quam tenue aurum calamus notariorum expuat; ergo qui scriba nolet furtum

148 profiteri, paupertatem pre se ferat oportet. Sed hoc loco de bonis atque improbis notariis credant alii quid velint, mihi certe non fit verisimile notarium quempiam obsignatarum tabellarum mercedulis ditari.

149 Tum de medicis prolixius dicerem, ubi non viderem multos et eos quidem viros et medicos bonos cum egestate luctari semper

150 duros, acres, semper ad convitiandum accinctos; de quibus quidem omnium in ore omnium illud est quod fertur: quas res mortales ducunt tristes et abhorrendas, vulnera, morbos, pestes, mortem, has omnes maiorem in modum cupidi medici hominum generi

151 oppetant et sequantur necesse est. Tum preterea in his ipsis horrendis rebus paulo maiores divitias affectantes, utrum avare, crudeliter desperateque versentur aliorum sit iudicii. Iuvat hunc locum cum brevitatis causa preterire, tum ne quid videar nimis accurate

152 colligere si quid possit ad vituperium litterarum adduci. Taceatur idcirco fraus, perfidia, falsa attestatio, corrupte contractus atque hereditatis formule, taceantur subacta venena, nutrite febres, productus morbus potionibus et pharmacis, multa denique alia scelestissima et nefaria cupidorum tabellionum atque medicorum cri-

153 mina sileantur. Neque insuper enumerentur morbosi aeris atque inimicitiarum pericula que notarios omnes atque medicos cupidiores subire opus est. De opere autem prestatione servili, obscena

154 et omnium sordidissima dicere fedum esset. Verum apud ingenuum presertim atque nobilitatum litteris animum sit par non

155 posse ditari et nolle divitias cum turpitudine. Malint quidem preclara ingenia mores assequi quam divitias, oderint docti scelus et

wickedness is apparent when they walk without any pen over their
ear. For a notary is not allowed to make a show of both his wealth   147
and his morals: for everybody knows how little gold the pen of a
notary can spit out: thus the notary who does not want the cry of
"Thief!" to go up, must bear poverty. But at this point those who   148
want to can believe what they want about good and bad notaries,
but as far as I am concerned, it is not likely that any notary will
become rich with the small rewards he makes out of signing and
sealing letters.

I would say more about doctors if I did not see many of them   149
grown men, and good doctors at that, always having to fight
fiercely against poverty. They always have to fight hard and are
constantly ready to trade insults; people always say that all the   150
things that men consider grim and abhorrent—wounds, diseases,
plagues, death—are those that greedy doctors have to prefer for
mortal men and have to deal with. Then whether doctors, in the   151
pursuit of slightly greater wealth, particularly in these horrific
matters, live a greedy, cruel, desperate life, that is for others to
judge. It is appropriate to leave this question both for reasons of
brevity and lest I seem to be collecting too eagerly anything that
could add to the vituperation of literature. So let us say nothing   152
about fraud, perfidy, false witness, corrupt documents relating to
contracts and inheritance, and say nothing about poison being
administered, fevers being nourished, diseases procured with potions and poisons, and many other outrageous and abominable
crimes committed by grasping notaries and doctors. And let us   153
not list here the dangers of infected air and of enmities which all
greedy doctors and notaries have to face.[15] For it would be foul to
speak of the reality of their servile, obscene and filthy work. But it   154
is right that the person with a particularly free mind, ennobled by
literature, cannot become rich and that he does not prefer wealth
acquired by evil means. Fine intellects should prefer to amass good   155
morals rather than wealth: let the learned hate crime and disgrace

dedecus magis quam paupertatem; nemo sit usque adeo stultus
qui tam turpem ac nefariam cupidorum scribarum et medicorum
156 servitutem non penitus abhorreat. Ceteri enim quos servos nostros
dicimus, aut bello superati aut predonibus capti, servitutem inviti
157 subiere, medici vero atque scribe sponte servitia prebent. Servi, ut
apud dominos gratiam atque perinde libertatem consequantur,
summa et fide et diligentia operas prestant quantum licet honestis-
simas; tabelliones vero et medici, ut pecuniam excerpant, nullas
158 tametsi vilissimas operas respuunt. Servi pro domini salute, in
quem, vel ob expectationem libertatis vel ob facilitatem in se,
summa observantia et amore affecti sunt, pericula atque, si opus
159 fuerit, mortem adire non recusant; medici vero atque scribe vo-
lentes et cupidi ad omnes inimicitias, ad pestes, ad contagiosos
morbos, ad ultima mortis pericula sese pro quovis ignoto, sola
paucorum nummorum mercede adducti offerunt.

160   Ceterum de nostris iurisconsultis quidnam preclarum referam?
Quid de pontificio iure deque civium legibus? Nam ex his grana,
ex ceteris bonis disciplinis atque artibus omnibus colligi paleas di-
161 cunt. Superi boni, grandes littere, amplissimi codices, sarcine, proh
superi, immanes, quas qui ordine similique apparatu in tabernam
apud forum exposuerit quo iurisconsulti domi pompam apertam
atque dispositam ostentant, certe illic plures, procul dubio longe
plures ille pecunias, si pretio ad rem visendam intromittat, accipiet
quam iurisperiti, cum suis omnibus impedimentis librorum ma-
162 chinisque atque architecturis bibliothecarum, sint soliti capere. At
queso, adhibe huc animum: putasne ullius esse vim tantam pecuniarum que in hac tanta tamque amplissima librorum congerie
comparanda non exarescat ac penitus deficiat, ut summe quidem
163 inscitie sit divitias tantis impensis consectari? Quod si quis tam
multis libris, tam grandi impensa divitias concupiverit, nonne is

more than poverty; let nobody be so stupid as not profoundly to hate the corrupt, nefarious servitude of greedy notaries and doctors. The rest of those we call slaves have been either overcome in war or captured in a raid, and undergo service unwillingly, whereas doctors and notaries provide their service voluntarily. Slaves perform very honest services in order to acquire their master's favor and thence their freedom; but doctors and notaries do not reject even the most degrading work in order to get hold of money. For the sake of their master, slaves display the utmost obedience and love toward him, either because they expect to be freed or because of their master's kindness to them, and they do not refuse to face dangers, and if necessary, death itself. By contrast, notaries and doctors willingly and greedily offer themselves up for all kinds of legal conflicts, plagues, contagious diseases, even the ultimate danger of death, all for someone unknown and only led on by the reward of a few coins.

But what uplifting thing shall I say about our legal experts? What about canon law and civil law? For they say that from these things comes grain, whereas from all the other good disciplines and all the arts comes only chaff. Heavens above, look at the huge works, enormous manuscripts, colossal amounts of baggage they carry around. If anyone were to display these in a tavern near the marketplace, in the correct order and with a similar display to that used by lawyers when laying out their open files and books at home, he would definitely make much more profit by charging money just to see these things than lawyers usually take with all their weight of books, reading devices and the whole architecture of their libraries. But, I beseech you, pay attention: do you think that anyone has such a supply of money that it will not dry up and totally disappear in acquiring this huge pile of books, so much so that it is the height of ignorance to pursue wealth with such an outlay? If someone wanted wealth through so many books and such enormous expenditure, surely he will be similar to those who

156

157

158

159

160

161

162

163

164 persimilis erit illis quos Cesar solitus erat dicere hamo aureo piscari? Adde his quod summe stultitie est tantis non modo impensis, verum etiam laboribus atque vigiliis questum exposcere. 'Cras,' inquit, 'causam te orare oportebit,' modica tum porrigit cliens,

165 plura in crastinum pollicetur. Tu quicquid porrigitur accipis, totam deinde noctem inter libros ad nidorem lucerne, pedibus atque manibus algentibus, somnescis, queritans, pervolvens machinas et libros omnes atque te ipsum cura, somno, inedia frigoreque confi-

166 ciens. Ergo prodis ad causam rauca voce, obtorto collo, rubentibus atque gementibus ocellis, astas animo non minus avido et sollicito

167 ad lucrum quam ad ledendum parato atque incenso. Denique ipsis illis vastissimis evigilatissimisque recitationibus legum, paraphorum et glosarum multa voce conclamitas, omnes precordiorum ramices misero tibi erumpuntur, neque vereris contra primarios et prepotentes cives, conductus premio, disceptare atque cavillari.

168 Minitantur, convitiantur, mordent, inculpant: tu infelix ad hec

169 omnia famam ac dorsum tuum venale expositum habes. Siccine idcirco? Qui ita faciunt, qui petita pecunia evigilent, proclament, crepent, qui invidiam pretio subeant, aliorum vices exorent, in rixa

170 aliorum minitentur, ac reliqua omnia in hoc ordine litteratorum quos legistas dicunt desiderata qui faciunt (ut pro viribus iurisperiti omnes lucris impliciti faciunt), an non hi vident sese quam sint

171 publica et deterrima in servitute constituti? O preclare lucri faciendi rationes, que non modo questum non faciunt, sed maximam rei familiaris iacturam patribus tametsi locupletibus afferunt, inimicitias afferunt, nullas nisi serviles cum maximis laboribus mercedes afferunt!

Caesar used to say went fishing with a golden hook?[16] Add to this 164
the fact that it is the height of stupidity to seek out wealth with
such expenditure but also after so much labor and study. "Tomor-
row," someone will say, "you have to plead a case," then your client
will hand over a modest sum, promising more the next day. What- 165
ever he offers, you accept, then you will spend the whole of the
following night sleepless amid your books and the fumes of your
lamp, with your hands and feet aching, searching for an answer,
going through all possible machinations, all your books and wearing yourself out with worry, lack of sleep, hunger and cold. So you 166
end up appearing in court with your voice hoarse, your neck
strained, your tiny eyes red and tearful, and you stand there with
your mind as greedy and anxious for money as it is angry and
ready to injure others. In the end you shout at the top of your 167
voice in those long and exhaustingly prepared recitations of laws,
commentaries and glosses, with all the blood vessels of your lungs
strained to breaking point, and you are not afraid to debate and
cavil with the foremost and most powerful citizens, since you have
been hired for a fee. They threaten you, insult you, attack and 168
blame you: you are miserable and in the face of all this you have
your reputation and your back now up for sale. Is this not so? 169
Those who do this have to seek out money and study all night,
then declaim and roar, undergo envy for the sake of a fee, plead for
the sake of others, issue threats in other people's quarrels, and do 170
all the other things that this order of literati whom they call lawyers are asked to do, as though they were all top lawyers pursuing
wealth to the best of their abilities. But do these people not see
how they have been thrust into public and humiliating servitude?
Oh, what glorious ways of making money, which not only do not 171
make a profit, but bring the maximum loss to the family patri-
mony even when the fathers are rich; they bring about enmities
and they deliver only servile rewards for the maximum amount of
labor!

172   At dixerit fortasse quispiam: 'Quid ni, cum a studiis domum se litterati receperint, parta illis auctoritas cum ad gratiam proderit, tum etiam iuvabit ut ditissimas uxores comperiant? Nemo enim tam insipiens est qui eruditi et famosi viri affinitatem recuset.'

173   Huic pulchre posset in hunc modum responderi: 'Immo quis litteratus non dementissimus divitiarum gratia cuiquam hominum

174   subservire cupiat?' Libertatem in primis vir doctus cupiet in primisque fugiet cum ceteris, tum omnium maxime servire mulieri.

175   Sit enim ab his qui litteras sectantur omne servitutis genus procul: non quidem eam decet auctoritatem studiis litterarum induere cum qua nos in servitio honeste versari putemus; potius omnem auctoritatem et fastum litterarum exuamus quam id velimus ut

176   nos pecunie gratia servitutem iniisse videamur. Nam qui eiusmodi mente ac cogitatione consistunt, ut malint cum servitute divitias quam cum libertate laudem assequi, sunt illi quidem omni auctoritate indignissimi. Etenim quis ignorat magnam servitutis partem esse aliorum causam procurare atque aliorum ad se litigia advo-

177   care? Tum plane ab iis, qui opulentas dotes sectantur, eadem hec semper exposci, quis dubitat? Nonne videmus ut causas sempiternas, que nunquam sopiri, nunquam confici queant, ab affinibus, ab affinium affine atque ab illorum amicis congerantur, litteratique opem atque auxilium gratis petant?

178   Tum preterea quis negabit genus esse turpissimum servitutis eorum qui garrientem suorumque semper divitias et amplitudinem

179   referentem uxorem sibi in animum induxerit perferre? Quibus quidem rebus opulente dotes sunt nunquam non refertissime: homi-

180   num infortunium! Nam est genus mulierum stultum, arrogans, contentiosum, audax, insolens atque temerarium suapte natura.

181   Hanc vero tu qualem futuram uxorem putas, cui maiorem fortuna licentiam dederit quam vel tu vel potius ipsa possit sustinere queve

But perhaps someone will say: "What, when these literary peo- 172
ple go home, will the authority they have acquired not become
useful for gaining favor, and also help them to find the richest
wives? For nobody is so foolish as to reject affinity with an erudite
and famous man." To this man one could offer a fine reply along 173
these lines: "But which literature scholar not completely mad
would want to serve any human being for the sake of riches?" The 174
learned man will above all want his liberty, and so like everyone
else he will especially flee from serving a woman. For all kinds of 175
servitude should be kept far away from literary scholars: it is not
suitable for those who have studied literature to take on that kind
of authority which we think can make our servitude seem more
honorable. We would sooner reject all authority and pomp of literature rather than wanting it to seem like we have entered into
slavery for the sake of money. Those who have this mindset and 176
way of thinking, who prefer to achieve wealth with enslavement
rather than praise with freedom, such people are most unworthy
of any authority. For who does not know that a large amount of
slavery is involved in taking on other people's law cases, being ad-
vocates in other people's quarrels? Then clearly who can doubt 177
that such things are always requested by these same people who
pursue opulent dowries? Do we not see that these eternal lawsuits,
which can never be settled or finished, will be piled up by the relatives and the relatives of relatives and by their friends, who seek
the literary scholar's help and influence for free?

Besides, who will deny that it is a very base form of servitude 178
wherein those who persuaded themselves to put up with a chatter-
ing wife have to listen to her always talking about her family's
wealth and riches? Large dowries are always full of such problems: 179
they are a disaster for men! For women are by nature stupid, ar- 180
rogant, contentious, bold, insolent and rash.[17] What kind of wife 181
do you think she will be to whom Fortune has given greater li-
cense than either you or rather she can manage, and who being

inter delitias educata propter divitiarum affluentiam insaniat? Quot leges imponet et quotiens nullum esse te, o noster litterate, sine suis opibus uxor exprobrabit?

182   Sed de mulierum natura et ineptiis satius est nihil referre quam infinitam rem atque notissimam libare, ut ita dixerim. Illud tamen persuasum esse cupio: femina divite, ut aiunt, esse nihil intolerabi-

183 lius. Que cum ita sint, ne erimus ipsi nos litterati qui tantopere ex dotibus divitias affectemus, ut non servitutem magis quam pauper-tatem oderimus?

184   Verum esto, sane cupiant, deceat uxoribus litteratos ditari. Quis tam erit improbus atque audax qui apud matrem fortunatam et locupletem inopi litterato virginem cum dote opulenta dandam

185 persuadeat? Nonne acclamabit mater: 'Veto, prohibeo illi semivivo, illi incompto ac tristi litterato dari filiam nostram'; nonne rursus

186 reclamabit: 'Filie mee virum dari quero, non magistrum'; ac virgo ipsa nonne sue rei sollicita eadem apud matrem instabit, animo in suum aliquem amatorem pendens atque cupiens aliunde sibi quam ex dictis philosophorum satisfieri? tum fratres nonne preferent

187 urbani ac lepidi alicuius affinitatem? Excludetur igitur malam in rem noster litteratus matris, fratrum ipsiusque puelle iudicio atque sententia. Verum ego quid in his commoror ac si tantum egeni

188 litterati opulentas dotes affectent? Quero, poterintne quoque com-periri divites qui divitem virginem non recusent? Poterunt sane. Iuro idcirco, si aderunt, mi litterate, excludere, abiicere, cum tua

189 omni Minerva et Pallade despicere. Ne certa inops cum locuplete, ne te pallentem ac tristem cum ceteris adolescentibus compara, ne

brought up amid riches goes mad because of them? How many laws will she impose on you and how many times, my literary friend, will your wife upbraid you, saying that you are nothing without her riches?

But it would be better not to say anything about the nature and 182 foolishness of women rather than just grazing the surface, as it were, of an infinite and well-known topic. However, I do want this to be understood: there is nothing more intolerable, as they say, than a rich woman. This being the case, will we literary men be 183 the sort of people to desire rich dowries to the point where we hate servitude less than poverty?

Be that as it may, let them desire this and suppose that it is fit- 184 ting for literary men to be made rich by their wives. Who will be so immoral and rash as to persuade a fortunate, rich mother to give her virgin daughter with a substantial dowry to a penniless literature student? Will the mother not retort: "I veto this, I forbid 185 our daughter to be given over to that literary man who is only half-alive, unkempt and depressed"; will she not also complain: "I am looking for a husband for my daughter, not a teacher." And 186 surely the girl herself will give priority to her own affairs and will insist with her mother that her mind is inclining toward some lover of hers, and she wants to be satisfied with something other than the sayings of the philosophers; and then surely her brothers will prefer to be connected to someone who is urbane and clever? Our literary friend will be rudely excluded on the basis of her 187 mother's and brothers' judgments, not to mention that of the girl herself. But why am I spending time on this topic, as if only needy literature scholars pursued wealthy dowries? I ask you, can we not 188 also find wealthy men who would not refuse a rich virgin? Of course we could. So I swear, my literary friend, that if there are such people, you will be excluded, rejected and despised, despite all your classical wisdom. Certainly a poor person cannot compete 189 with someone rich, so do not compare your miserable, pale self

auctoritatem apud puellas pulchritudini preposueris! Abi, potius,
190 fuge, obde te tuam in bibliothecam! Nam agilis, festivus, venustus
comptusque adolescens suam sibi amatam ne preripias omni arte
et ingenio curat; irrideberis, impexe mi litterate et squallens, si de
191 re uxoria cum nitido et polito amatore contenderis; quod si te fu-
catum exhibueris omnem et auctoritatem et dignitatem litterariam
amiseris.

192   Durum dixeris me, qui uxores nolim dari litteratis: quin volo
esse in litteratos non solum nihil durus, sed etiam non usquequaque mitis, ut velim cupidos litteratos fastidio uxorum carere.
193 Quam ergo dandam iudicabimus? Primo consulo pauperem tanquam ultimum malum fugiant, proxime moneo ne cupiant iuve-
nem: ea est enim etas infensa et parum tuta studiosis; novi quid
194 dicam, verum exempla cessent. Capiat igitur litteratus viduam aliquam vetulam, a qua minus quam a ceteris mulieribus aspernabi-
tur: nam istiusmodi vetule cum filiorum contumacia, tum iniuriis
affinium coacte nimirum se exhibent ut spe divitiarum aliquem il-
195 liciant, cum quo vel apud iudices, ad quos in dies trahuntur ab
infestissimis affinibus, sint tutiores, vel domi sine sollicitudine et
196 solitudine requiescant. Ac recte circa divitias litterati secum agi
existiment ubi istiusmodi dotibus tametsi litigiosis atque refertissi-
mis inimicitiarum ditentur.

197   Quod si fortassis videor in hac uxoria disceptatione iocari,
repete animo coniugia litteratorum, non dico ut de pudicitia

with all the other young men, nor consider your authority over girls as more useful than good looks. Instead, just go away, flee, hide yourself in your library! For the agile, cheerful, charming, 190 well-groomed young man will make sure with all his skills and intelligence that you do not steal his beloved from him; you will be mocked, my squalid, unkempt literary student, if you contend with a sleek, polished lover for the courtship of the girl, because if 191 you show yourself all tricked out, you will lose all your literary authority and dignity.

You will claim that I am harsh in saying I do not want wives to 192 be given to scholars: on the contrary, I do not want to be harsh, but nor do I wish to be so easygoing that I would like covetous literary scholars to be without the annoyance of a wife. So then, 193 what kind of woman should he marry? Firstly, I would advise him to flee someone who is poor as though it were the ultimate evil; next I would warn him not to desire a young woman: for that age is hostile to and not safe for scholars. I know what I am talking about, we do not need any more examples. So let the literature 194 student acquire some elderly widow by whom he will be less despised than by other wives, for such elderly widows are forced by both the arrogance of their sons and the insults of her relatives to put themselves on display, not surprisingly, so that they can entice someone with the hope of riches. With that kind of husband they 195 will be safer either in front of the judges, before whom they are dragged by their fiercely hostile relations, or they can rest at home without anxiety or loneliness. Literature students think they are 196 treated correctly as regards wealth when they are enriched through marriage, even though such dowries can prove litigious and full of enmities.

And if I seem to be joking in this discussion of marriage, con- 197 sider in your mind the marriages of literary students: you should

uxorum, sed de etatibus ac dotibus perscrutere. Facile quidem cerno quid sentias, sed missa hec ridicula faciamus.

198 Meminisse autem oportet quam sint lucra litteratorum minuta, tarda, turpia ac paucis concessa, atque illud superius memoria tenendum est quod docui: quam graves impense, quam multe ac

199 diuturne quamve rebus familiaribus pernitiose sint. Quibus ex rebus constare arbitror litteras non modo ad questum minime valere, verum etiam detrimenti plenas esse ac penitus incommodas.

200 Ex quo duabus primis partibus nostre institute disceptationis

201 plene a me satisfactum esse existimo: quod si dubitarem non satis rei factum videri, alio verterem orationem, ostenderem quidem quam pusilli servilisque animi sit is qui labores litterarum spe divitiarum ductus subierit, neque tacerem quam preclaros eruditosque animos honoris atque animi prestantia et claritas plus quam cupi-

202 ditas et avaritia debeat movere. In qua quidem re possem diutius commorari si placeret ingenii mei vires ostentare aut si ad laudem ducerem hoc loco nostre facundie, que plane minima est, aut copie

203 longius periculum facere. Nam est ea quidem materia patens, ampla, spatiosa, ut quivis laxatis habenis facile possit multa cum oratione per omnes exornationis locos bellissime discursitare; sed frustra atque ab instituto esset in eiusmodi notissimis atque ap-

204 probatissimis sententiis expoliendis vagari. Nam quis est tam imprudens qui hoc dixerit esse non turpissimum: que artes animi morbos, avaritiam, cupiditatem atque libidinem sedare, tollere ex-

205 terminareque debuerant, queve animum illis imbutum flagitiis in libertatem, decus, laudem inque caducarum rerum despicientiam erigere ac stabilire sint solite, easdem ipsas artes et disciplinas avaritie et cupiditatibus subditas et morigeras velle reddere,

84

reflect not on the woman's fidelity but on her age and dowry. I easily see how you feel about this, but let us dismiss these comic matters.

We must remember how minimal, late in the day, shameful and 198 restricted to very few are the rewards of literature students, and we should remember what I taught you earlier: how great are the expenses, how many and long-lasting are the damages they do to a family. From this I think we have to agree that not only is litera- 199 ture of very little use when it comes to wealth, but also that it is actually full of harm and thoroughly disadvantageous.

From the foregoing I think I can say that I have fully satisfied 200 myself as far as the first two parts of the discussion we initiated are concerned. If I still doubted that this has clearly satisfied these 201 demands, I would turn my oration elsewhere and show how pusillanimous and servile is the mind of the person who wants to undergo literary labors led by the hope of riches, nor would I remain silent about how the excellence and fame of honor and of the mind ought to inspire prestigious and erudite intellects more than greed and avarice. I could dwell longer on this topic if I wanted to 202 show off my intellectual skill or if I thought that it would be praiseworthy to try out our eloquence at this point or our rhetorical abundance, even though these are minimal. For this subject is 203 so open, large and spacious that anyone can easily let the reins go and with a copious oration roam wonderfully through all the topics that lend themselves to rhetorical embellishment; but it would be pointless and irrelevant to go around polishing up such very well-known and uncontroversial arguments. For who is so impu- 204 dent as to say that this is not the most shameful situation? Previously, the arts used to sedate, remove and exterminate diseases of the mind, such as avarice, greed and lust, or they usually made 205 upright and stabilized the mind that was imbued with such disgraceful things and led it to liberty, honor, praise and to contempt

206 tum ipsum animum disciplinarum elegantia imbutum sinere
207 turpitudinum mole pressum atque obrutum esse? Est plane ab officio alienum ac turpe cum omni generi hominum, tum litteratis
non extollere animum quantum licet ad laudem et virtutem, turpius tamen pessundari avaritia atque ignominia, turpissimum
208 rerum caducarum illecebris duci sapientem; turpius divitias disciplinis et sapientie titulis aucupari, turpissimum decus et libertatem pro viribus parum tueri; turpius mercedibus illiberalissimis
209 servire. Sed ista omnia omittamus, siquidem mihi ipse imperavi et
nihil non valde necessarium prosequi in hac re et esse omnino
quam possem brevissimus, quod plane quantum in me est hacte-
210 nus effeci. Nam succincta et levis, ut vidisti, nostra fuit oratio
eritque, quoad pro rei qua de agimus magnitudine permittatur,
facillima et brevissima.

V

1 Dixi ex studiis litterarum neque voluptates captari neque accumu-
lari divitias; proximum est ut de litteratorum auctoritate et hono-
2 ribus a me dicendum esse videatur. Honores etenim non negan-
dum est deberi litteratis admodum maximos; nam si bene meritis
honos quasi premium refertur, in exhibendo certe honore quem
preponemus litteratis?

for ephemeral things. Now is this not most shameful that people 206
want to make these very arts and disciplines subordinate and obedient to avarice and cupidity, and to allow the mind that is imbued
with the elegance of these disciplines to become burdened and
overwhelmed by the weight of moral turpitude? It is clearly not 207
part of our duty, indeed it would be shameful to discourage all
types of men and in particular literature scholars as much as possible from pursuing praise and virtue; but it is even more shameful
to be defeated by avarice and ignominy and, most disgraceful of
all, to have the wise man ensnared by the attractions of ephemeral
things. It is more disgraceful to go chasing riches with disciplines 208
and titles of wisdom, and most disgraceful of all not to protect
honor and freedom to the best of our ability; and it really is quite
wrong to become enslaved to highly dishonest rewards. But let us 209
forget all about those subjects, since I have made it a rule for myself both not to pursue any subject not strictly necessary in this
context, and to be absolutely as brief as possible, which is what I
have done to the best of my ability. For our speech has been suc- 210
cinct and light,[18] as you have seen, and it will be very fluent and
very brief as far as the magnitude of the subject we are dealing
with allows.

V

I have said that one cannot seek pleasure nor accumulate wealth 1
from the study of literature. The next thing I should say, it seems
to me, is something about the authority and honors awarded to
literary people. For one cannot deny that really the highest honors 2
are owed to scholars of letters; for if honor is a kind of reward for
those who are meritorious, whom should we put above students of
literature?

3   Si quis bonas inter artes fortiter ac diu labores ferendo, si quis
pro adipiscenda virtute ac sapientia etatem in studiis conterendo,
si quis omnes voluptates aspernando, omnes cupiditates eiciendo
meretur, si quis industrie sudoribus, sumptu, tempore, fortunis
atque vita pro amplissimis et necessariis hominum generi atque
omnium gratia dignissimis rebus comparatis meretur (ut sunt
bone artes, bona instituta, prestantissimi mores atque sapientia),
4   quas in litteris adipiscimur, quis erit tam improbus qui esse litteratos omnibus omnium generum hominibus anteponendos infici-
etur? Sunt ergo litterati omnium iudicio non postponendi.
5   Ceterum cum reliquis animantibus omnibus homo in multis rebus
excellat, tum vel maxime longe superior est quod cognitionis et
rationis vi quadam fruitur, qua facile persuaderi potest hominum
6   mentes esse natura ab celestium genere non alienas: nam constat
quidem et mari et terra queque moveantur omnia ingeniis homi-
7   num subigi et suppeditari. Idcirco hominem in natura rerum esse
animantium honoratissimum atque principem omnes fatentur.
8   Que cum ita sint, homo qui eandem ipsam rationem vel mentem,
qua a natura iam est rerum dominus constitutus, habuerit absolutam perfectamque artibus, cultam et expolitam studio atque solertia, quive eadem ipsa ratione et intelligentia inter homines maxime
9   superior fuerit, nonne idem hic, inter mortales precellens, maximis
10   honoribus atque reverentia ab hominibus erit prosequendus? Denique deus ipse cum ceteris infinitis in rebus prestet, tum non in
postremis ad divinitatem est quod verum a falso secernere, quid sit
optimum eligere, ac rebus ratione et providentia moderari perfecte
11   noverit; homo autem qui in huiusmodi divinis rebus doctum et

Anyone who carries the burden of studying the humanities 3
bravely and over a long period of time, who spends a lifetime in
study in order to obtain virtue and wisdom, who despises all delights and rejects all desires, surely that person deserves a reward.
Similarly meritorious is anyone who uses the sweat of his industry,
his expense, his time, his fortunes and his life in order to acquire
those subjects most rewarding and necessary to human kind and
those that are worthy of men's gratitude (such as knowledge of the
humanities, good customs and wisdom), all of which we acquire
from reading. That being so, who will be so impudent as to deny 4
that when it comes to merit, literary scholars should be placed
above all other kinds of men? Thus literati are in everyone's judgment second to none. But just as man outdoes all other living 5
creatures in many things, in particular he is far superior to them
because he enjoys a strength of knowledge and reasoning whereby
one can easily be convinced that by nature human minds are not
unlike celestial ones; for it is agreed that whatever creatures move 6
upon land or sea are subject and subordinate to man's genius.
Thus everyone admits that man is the most honored and indeed 7
the prince of living creatures in nature. Since this is so, the man 8
who possesses that very reason and mind with which by nature he
is now constituted as the lord of all things, the man who has a
mind complete and perfected by the arts, cultivated and polished
by study and wisdom, or who is by a long way superior to other
men in those same qualities of reason and intelligence — surely this 9
man is preeminent among mortals and should be celebrated with
the greatest honors and reverence? Lastly, God himself is both 10
preeminent in countless other things, and it is not the least of his
divine powers that he knows how to discern truth from falsehood,
what is the best choice to make, and how to control things perfectly with reason and providence; but the man who shows himself 11

eruditum se prebeat, nonne inter homines prope divinis honoribus erit concelebrandus, nonne omnibus hominibus preferendus?

12 Qua igitur ratione compertum est ut equester ordo in publicis cetibus litteratos antecedat, aut quivis ex ordine equestri litterato

13 comparetur? Qua impudentia rudem, inexpertum rerum atque plerunque temerarium militem litteratis omnibus anteponamus?

14 Hec ego non institutis maiorum, sed insolentia et temeritate quadam militum id sibi arrogantium in usum accessisse arbitror.

15 Nisi forte maiores nostri iudicarint litteris quam auro minus ha-

16 bendum esse honoris. Alioquin perversa ratio, turpis mos, iniusta licentia est hunc militem preponere, in quo nullus virtutis, morum aut sapientie splendor inest, quive tantum gemma et auro se velit

17 admodum conspicuum videri; hunc vero litteratum postponere, qui moribus, virtute, ingenio, litterarum ac rerum optimarum cognitione ac ratione sit probatissimus atque clarissimus.

18 Sed missam faciamus hanc disceptationem recte ne miles pre-ponatur, quanquam quidem ea ipsa disputatio esset hoc quoque

19 loco non negligenda. At dicamus militiam esse aliquod publicum munus militisque ipsius munus et officium esse non mediocris

20 negotii: virgines, viduas destitutas atque indefensas atque pupillos atque pauperes omnes eiusmodique afflictos omnes una et rem publicam omnem sua ope, opera, rebus et armis tueri, tegere atque

21 defendere. Eiusmodi esse militis officium arbitror. Quam vero probe pro officio sese gerant milites, quamve idcirco sint honore

22 dignissimi censeant ceteri; nobis tamen cum nemo negaverit lit-teratos suis studiis plurimum et rei publice et miseris omnibus et fortunatissimis etiam civibus conferre utilitatis, quis tum ulla ratione defendet stultos prudentibus, indoctos peritis, inutiles

to be learned and erudite in these kinds of divine matters — surely he should be celebrated with almost divine honors, surely he should be preferred above all other men?

Why then has it become established that the order of knights 12 should precede literary scholars in public ceremonies? What im- 13 pudence makes us place an ignorant and often rash soldier above all literature scholars? I believe that this did not stem from the 14 traditions of our ancestors, but came into usage through some insolence and boldness on the part of knights who arrogate this right to themselves. Unless perhaps it was our ancestors who 15 judged that less honor should be awarded to literature than to gold.[19] Otherwise it is some kind of perverse reasoning, some base 16 custom and unjust lawlessness to award preference to this soldier, who has no splendor of virtue, morals or wisdom in him, and who wants to seem illustrious just because of his jewels and gold; and 17 to downgrade the literary man, who with his morals, virtue, genius, knowledge and understanding of literature and the finest arts has been proven to be utterly outstanding and famous.

But let us set aside this debate on whether it is right that 18 knights take precedence, even though that argument is relevant also at this point. We say instead that knighthood is a public duty 19 and the knight's duty and commitment is of no small import: he is 20 duty bound to use all his strength, deeds, property and arms in order to protect, shield and defend maidens, destitute and defenseless widows and wards as well as all the poor and other similarly afflicted persons.[20] That is the kind of duty a knight has. Let 21 others decide how valiantly knights conduct themselves with regard to this duty, or how worthy of honor they are. But, in my 22 view, since nobody will deny that literary scholars confer maximum utility on their area of study and also on the state and its citizens, both the poorest and the richest, who then with any reason will defend in any sphere the placing of the stupid over the wise, the unlearned over the experienced, the useless over those

commodis, desidiosos agentibus et bene in dies merentibus litteratis ulla in re debere anteponi?

23   Neque solum apud hunc militarem ordinem meritis honoribus
24 defraudantur litterati, sed etiam apud quosvis despiciuntur. Quem
enim in civitate divitiis et amplitudine paulum egregium civem
dederis, qui non se in omni re supremum velit fore, quive non illico paupertatem floccipendat ac studia penitus, artes et ingenia
25 pauperum non oderit? Quis enim ita moratus dives aderit qui non
26 plus deberi fortunis suis iudicet quam aliorum virtuti? 'Enimvero
qua de causa illum mihi litteratum preferes? — inquiunt divites —
Nonne una eademque nobis omnibus patria est? An mihi fortassis
humiliores affines et parentes, an stirps nostra quam istius degene-
27 rosior est? An vero in senatu, quia grammaticen nesciam, sententia
28 et vota minus nostra quam litterati valebunt? Libera nobis est civitas, liber animus, liceat sane nostra materna inter nos lingua loqui,
atque ea quidem sic loquamur libere, ut inviti tacuisse nihil vi-
29 deamur. Gaudeat iste sane litteratus, inter libros, suis exquisitis
vocabulis, nos autem divites curemus ut apud senatum nostra in
primis sententia vigeat, quod, scio, pulchrius nos quam quivis litteratissimus suis preponderatis exercitationibus nostra divitiarum
30 auctoritate assequemur. Nos enim deauratas, illi laureatas senten-
tias proferunt, et cedat auro laurus.'

31   Tu vero si litteratorum causam susceperis, 'Enim desine hunc
tandem litteratum magnificare! — inquient — Quid illi assurgam?
Quid cedam e via aut discoperiam? Quid mihi cum illo est nego-
32 tii? Novit litteras, quid ad me? Regat ille quidem ludum ac ins-
33 truat pueros. Meminit leges, quid ad me? Garriat ille quidem,

who bring advantage, the lazy over literary scholars who day after day are busy and well-deserving?

Nor is it only by knights that literati are deprived of the honor   23
that is their due: they are also despised in everyone's eyes. What   24
citizen in the town can be found who is moderately outstanding
through wealth and fortune, who does not want to be supreme in
everything, or who does not for that reason regard poverty as of
no worth, and does not thoroughly hate the scholarship, arts and
genius of poor scholars? What rich man will be so modest that he   25
believes that he owes more to the virtue of others than to his own
money? "But why do you prefer that literature scholar over me?"   26
the rich man will say. "Surely we all have one and the same fatherland? Or do I have humbler relatives and family, or is my family
more degenerate than his? Or in the senate will the literary man's   27
opinions and votes count more than mine just because I do not
know Latin? We have a free city and a free mind, so allow us to   28
speak among ourselves in our own mother tongue, and let us
speak it freely, so that we will not appear to have kept silent about
anything against our will. Let this literary man enjoy himself to   29
the full with his books and their exquisite words, but we wealthy
citizens will ensure that in the senate our opinion will be supreme.
I know that we will obtain this outcome thanks to the authority
that comes from our wealth, a more elegant thing than the plod-
ding rhetorical exercises of any literary person. For we pronounce   30
golden sentences, based on good earning, while they utter olden
ones, based on university learning: but learning should give way to
earning."[21]

But if you take up the cause of literati, the wealthy will reply,   31
"Stop exaggerating the worth of this man of letters! Why should I
stand up for him? Why get out of his way and take my hat off to
him? What business have I with him? He knows literature: what   32
is that to me? Let him run his school and teach boys. He has
memorized the laws: what is that to me? Let him chatter, make   33

proclamet, inscribat dicas, expilet viduas, predetur litigantes, prodat clientulos ut lubet, patronum se ac consultorem civibus futu-

34 rum prestet, quid ad me? Bene erit orba civitas illa que tales tu-
35 tores complectatur! Medicinam profitetur, quid ad me? Curet ille quidem ebrios, edaces, helluones, venditet pharmaca et venena, pertractet omnia feda spurcissimaque, ut volet, quid ad me?
36 Divina sectatur, quid ad me? Compleat ille quidem vetulas clamo-
37 ribus, deliret in pulpitis, ut volet, quid ad me? Quod quidem male illi succedat litterato! Omnia norit, cuncta didicerit, universa te-
38 neat, quid, inquam, ad me? Istorum ego, si quando mihi aliquis fuerit necessarius, faciam uno nummo omnes horas noctium trium
39 dierumque trium vigilans connumeret. Iam quidem sint illi litterati suis demum nugis et disputatiunculis contenti, non prodeant in publicum suis cum venalibus cavillatiunculis, potius ad quam
40 olent lucernam redeant. Aut denique, superi optimi, abiicite hanc pestem hominum e conspectu, qui, nisi essent, nullus litigiorum strepitus, nulla in litigiis calumnia adesset, iurgia rixeque tollerentur, summa concordia in urbibus vigeret, pax inter cives constituta servaretur, non litigiorum eternitas, non causarum immortalitas perseveraret, sub equo et bono, natura duce, simplici quadam equitate cause discernerentur.'

41 Hec verba (ita me superi ament) ut a multis, neque infimis ne-
42 que vulgaribus, nostris civibus, quam sepissime audivi! Pro rei tamen molestia dignum responsum aliud nullum dedi, nisi putare me eos agere non modeste, qui de re sibi incognita non sensu,

proclamations, declare the day for a trial, strip widows of their money, prey on his litigants, betray his little clients as he wishes, let him say he will be an advocate and consultant for his citizens, what is that to me? A city that has such defenders in it will be   34
truly defenseless. This man professes medicine: what has that got   35
to do with me? Let him cure the drunkards, gluttons and madmen, sell potions and poisons, treat all those disgusting, filthy conditions as he wishes: what is that to me? Another has studied   36
divinity: what is that to me? Let him deafen old ladies with his clamor, let him rave in the pulpit, as he wants, what is that to me? Let that literary man not have any success in any of that. Suppose   37
he knows everything, learns everything, memorizes the whole universe, but what, I say, has that got to do with me? If one day I   38
should need any of these people, I will make the same amount with one coin as he would in all the hours contained in three days and three nights of wakeful study. Now let these literati finally be   39
content with their trifles and petty disputations; do not let them come out into the public with their venal debates; rather they should go back to the study lamp of which they stink. Either that   40
or, gods above, throw this plague away from the sight of men: if they did not exist, there would be no noise of litigation, no calumny in their cases. Instead quarrels and fights would disappear, supreme harmony would flourish in the cities, peace between citizens would be established and maintained, there would not be this eternal squabbling, this everlasting series of lawsuits, and cases would be decided under the fair and good leadership of nature with a simple form of equity."

These words (heaven help me) — how often have I heard them   41
from many of our citizens and not just the lowest and most vulgar of them! But despite the annoyance caused by this I gave no other   42
dignified response except to say that I thought that those people are not acting modestly if they judge a thing they know nothing

43 natura et equitate, sed odio, invidia iudicent; illis tamen aliqua ex parte indulgendum esse qui negligant quod ignorent et vituperent quod negligant, sed ab his optare me ut parcius et modestius de
44 bonis obloquantur. At illi inceptam cantilenam resumunt. O civitatem modestam! Sed quis non eadem ipsa persepius in triviis audiat? Quis non omnino abiecti agrestisque animi parum egre
45 huiusmodi homines ferat audiens? Quis vel minime cupidus honoris non prestare arbitrabitur se divitem putari quam doctum, pre-
46 sertim cum viderit se ad honores inter divites esse nullum? Quid, cum audiet litteratum hunc aut vocari lixam aut coquum, si forte, ut fit, veste non ita lautissima de libris ad civium coronam progrediatur, aut marmoreum bovem aut phreneticum, siquid vehementius suis litterarum meditationibus inheserit, aut ambitiosum latratorem, si quid eloquentia et erudita lingua publice delectetur?
47 Ut profecto non sine auctoritatis et dignitatis iactura sit litteratum inter cives publicos petere honores atque auctoritatem.
48 Tum etiam ad gratiam prestat nos studiosos haberi stolidos quam prudentes. Nam ita consuevere nostri cives, stultos tantum
49 irridere ac ludos facere; gnavos autem et agentes malignos esse et rapaces dicunt, hominum genus fugiendum, quod et naturali astutia et litterarum fraudibus ad omnem iniuriam et perniciem aptis-
50 simi sint. Tu, idcirco, litterate, qualem te illic prestabis? Si simplicitatem ostentabis, bonum te sed rudem atque inutilem dicent, si prudentia callere, malignum te esse interpretabuntur.

about not by common sense, nature and fairness but on the basis of hatred and envy. I thought that we should forgive to a certain 43 extent those who slight the things they do not know about, and vituperate what they disrespect; but from them I would ask that they criticize good people more sparingly and modestly. But they 44 take up the same old song they started with. What a modest city! But who does not often hear these same things at every cross-roads? Is there anyone not entirely of an abject and rustic disposi- 45 tion who would not have great difficulty in listening to such men? Is there anyone in the slightest bit ambitious for honor who does not think it better to be considered rich rather than learned, espe-cially when he sees that among the rich he is not considered to have any honors? If by chance, as sometimes happens, the litera- 46 ture scholar leaves his books in order to go out, without respect-able clothes, among a crowd of citizens, will you not hear him being called either a baker or a cook? Or a marble ox or a mad-man, if he dwells on his literary meditations a bit more vehe-mently, or an ambitious barking dog, if he delights in eloquence and learned language in public? So the man of letters who seeks 47 after public honors and authority amid his fellow citizens cannot do so without serious loss of his authority and dignity.

Furthermore, in order to gain favor it is better for us to be con- 48 sidered dullards rather than wise scholars. For these are the habits of our citizens: to mock and make fun of the stupid, whereas the 49 literati who are diligent and active are said to be wicked and rapa-cious, the kind of people one should flee from, since they are very fitted by both natural astuteness and the deceptions of literature to commit every kind of injury and perniciousness. So you, man of 50 letters, what kind of face are you going to show them? If you pa-rade your candor, they will say you are good but uncouth and useless; and if you exhibit cleverness, they will consider you to be evil.

51   Proxime, de reliqua plebe erga studiosos quid est quod referam? Nam est ea quidem sors hominum cum ceteris in civitatibus loquax et maledica, tum maxime in nostris Hetrurie urbibus multo insolens ac maledicentissima, omnes irridere, nemini deferre, te-

52 mere proloqui, ac multa per insolentiam agere assueta—quod tamen nostris hominibus et nomini Hetruscorum laudi dandum puto: Hetruscis enim civibus ob antiquissimam libertatem multa cum dicere, tum etiam facere licent, que apud tyrannos educatis

53 nimium solute fortassis et intemperanter facta viderentur; laus tamen libertatis et fructus est, quo legibus parueris eo reliquas omnes voluptates et instituta ita gerere tua ut velis.

54   Sed ad plebem redeamus nostram, apud quam semper prime honoris partes fuere auro ac divitiis dedite; neque obscurum quidem est qua mente vulgus non virtutum, sed pompe admiratione

55 moveatur. Movetur enim imperita multitudo rebus his quas oculis intuetur, illis autem quibus mente reddi perspicacior et possit et

56 debeat non commovetur. Itaque cupiunt imperiti quas intuentur divitias, negligunt quam ignorant sapientiam, fortunas consectan-

57 tur, virtutem spernunt. Progreditur dives longo cum amicorum et servorum comitatu, sese multo supercilio et gestibus efferens, non secus atque multa per divitias et amplitudinem polliceatur aut

58 comminitetur. Huic, cuius divitias cupiditate amplectitur, plebs vultu fronteque applaudit, ergo advenienti confestim assurgit;

59 hunc quanti fortuna prestet, tanti esse faciendum et censet et pre-

60 dicat; hunc ergo a quo iuvari favoribus et pecunia queritant cives,

61 non stulte omnibus litteratis anteponunt. Ita demum his omnibus rebus increbruit, presertim in nostre urbis hominibus, opinio, flagranti cupiditate incensa, ut solis divitibus, solis fortunatis in

Next, what can I say about the rest of the common people's at-   51
titude to scholars? For that kind of person is both loquacious and
critical in other cities, and especially in our Tuscan cities they are
very insolent and very prone to speak ill of others.[22] They laugh at
everyone else, defer to nobody, are rash and outspoken, and accustomed to doing many things out of insolence—and yet I think   52
these attitudes bring praise to our citizens and credit to the Tuscan name. For Tuscan citizens, because of their very ancient tradition of liberty, can both say and also do many things which to
those brought up under tyrants would seem perhaps to be too
loose and intemperate.[23] Yet the praise and fruit of freedom is this,   53
that as long as you obey the laws, you can enjoy all other pleasures
and your own ways of doing things.

But let us return to the common people for whom the first ap-   54
portionment of honor was always given to gold and wealth; nor is
it a secret what mentality moves the vulgar crowd to admire pomp,
not virtues. The inexperienced mob is swayed by the things it sees   55
with its own eyes, but is not moved by those which could and
should make their minds more perceptive. Thus the inexperienced   56
desire the riches they see, and neglect things they are ignorant of
such as wisdom; they follow goods of fortune and neglect virtue.
The rich man sets out with a long retinue of friends and servants,   57
strutting along with a haughty brow and gestures, with the look of
someone promising or threatening many things he can do through
his wealth and status. With their looks and their hands the popu-   58
lace applauds this man, whose wealth they covet in their greed,
and immediately rise up to greet him as he arrives; they think and   59
proclaim that as much as his fortune outstrips that of others, just
by so much more should he be valued. So the citizens approve this   60
man by whom they want to be helped with his favors and riches,
and are not foolish in placing him above all literary scholars. Thus   61
in the end, with all these things happening, an opinion, inflamed
by flagrant greed, spreads abroad, especially among the men of our

primis honores deberi existiment, de litteratis vero non amplius
62 cogitent quam de rebus his que usui future minime sint; quin
immo multis modis despectos habent litteratos. Missa facio reli-
63 qua obscena litteratis a plebe imposita ignominia. Illud non preter-
mittamus quod aiunt: nescire se qua re nostros litteratos debeant
magnificare, quos plane videant circa vite usum ea negligere que ad
bene beateque vivendum admodum necessaria sunt.

64   'Tum preterea sit sane illud, inquiunt, ut predicatis: este litteris
docti rerum omnium; hoc si vestris litteris tam amplissimum atque
divinum munus inest, ut nihil rerum omnium sit quod ignoretis,
65 quid est vobis litteratis in hominum genere stultius? Quanta vestra
insania est, dum non in primis discitis esse non egeni, dumque vos
66 paupertatis et miserie vestre non peniteat? Utrum igitur tanti fa-
ciemus istuc ipsum didicisse litteras, ubi pluries detur sitire et
67 exurire, quam sapientiam ostentare? Discite, discite, litterati (si
aliquid sapere videri cupitis) primo sine inopia vivere, postremo
68 optabitis cum laude vivere!' Sunt ergo magna ex parte, ut vides,
litterati apud omnes ordines et apud plebem usque adeo ridiculi,
ab omnibus irrisi, a multis despecti, atque id quidem potissimum
ubi non fuerint valde locupletes.

69   Tum qui (quod rarissime evenit) fortassis fuerint fortunati,
sciant illi quidem non litteris sed divitiis, non virtuti eorum sed
70 fortune honores tribui. Etenim animadvertant quot assurgant, cedant, aut dignentur, nisi eorum oculos toge aurique splendor prius
71 perculserit; desit aurum, deponatur toga, ignorabere. Equidem ita
se res habet: qui veste sunt ornatissimi, iidem sunt honoratissimi

city, that honors should be conferred only on the rich, only on the most fortunate, while people no more think about literati than about those things which will be of minimum use in the future; in 62 fact they look down on literary people in many ways. I leave aside the many obscene ignominies inflicted on literati by ordinary people. But this one thing we should not overlook, namely the well- 63 known view that people do not know why they should extol our literary men when they plainly see them neglecting the very things that are really quite necessary for leading the good, happy life.

They say, "Then again, let us say things are as you say they are: 64 you claim to be learned in everything through literature. If there is such a rich and almost divine gift in literature, namely that there is nothing that you do not know about, who could be more foolish than you literati? What madness of yours is this, that you do not 65 learn first and foremost not to be poor, and you are not ashamed of your poverty and misery? Do we really rate the feat of learning 66 letters so highly when more often literary scholars end up starving and dying of thirst rather than displaying their wisdom? Learn, do 67 learn this, you men of letters (if you want to seem knowledgeable about something): learn first to live without poverty, then once you have done this, you can choose to live with praise!" Thus, as 68 you can observe, most literary scholars are seen in the eyes of all classes, and especially the common people to be ridiculous, mocked by everyone, and despised by many, and this is particularly the case when they are not very wealthy.

Then, as for those scholars who (though this very rarely hap- 69 pens) perhaps are well-off, they should know that any honors are attributed not to their literary knowledge but to their riches, not to their virtues but to their fortune. They should notice how many 70 would rise up, make way or honor them if the splendor of their clothes and gold had not first dazzled their eyes; if there is no gold, if you are not wearing a gown, you will be ignored. In fact 71 this is how things are: those who have very ornate clothes are

apud vulgus, qui ditissimi, iidem honoribus et observantia dignis-
72   simi putantur, ut nemo tametsi prudens, peritus atque rerum pre-
clarissimarum scientia et sapientia excultissimus, nisi auri atque
divitiarum suffragio, quicquam ex se possit in vulgus proferre quod
laude aut admiratione dignum putetur.

73   Sed nos forte maiores circa res, veluti publicis in muneribus,
legationibus, aut magistratibus honorem esse constitutum putare
magis oportet quam circa istas assessionum, locive atque vie prero-
gativas, quibus quidem in rebus aurum, ut plane videmus, partes
74   iam pridem primas sibi vendicavit. Quamobrem fortassis rem publicam gerentes poterunt videri integro atque perfecto in honore
constituti: nam mores et virtus eorum probata esse videtur, quorum fidei et diligentie res publica sese maximum pondus commen-
75   darit. Mihi tamen non persuadeo rem publicam in magistratibus
exposcere copiam litterarum magis quam rerum experientiam
longo usu et tractatione perfectam. Verum brevissime hunc locum
76   transeundum censeo. Nam constare arbitror ut raro de celo aut
planetis atque nunquam de deorum natura, de animorum procrea-
tione et vi apud rem publicam consulatur: de bello sane et pace,
vectigalibus et impensis, deque omni re civili moderanda atque
tuenda, non litteris apud senatum, sed usu ipso atque experientia
77   disseritur. Tum in contionibus quid de septem orbibus aut vagis
planetis, quid de sole aut luna disserendum sit non video, ut profecto omnes litteras ab hoc forensi usu et publico seclusas esse
oporteat.

78   Proxime qui litteras profitentur commodius fecerint si, suis litteris contenti, ea loca effugient quibus nulla cum publica dignitate

highly honored among the people; those who are very rich are thought to be most worthy of honors and consideration, so much   72
so that nobody, however wise, experienced and exquisitely adorned with the science and knowledge of the most famous subjects, will be able to produce anything in public that will be thought of as worthy of praise or admiration unless he is bolstered by gold and riches.

But reflecting on these more serious matters, we should perhaps   73
think it more appropriate if honor resides more in public duties, embassies or magistracies than in those privileges about giving up your seat or giving way in the street, in which things gold certainly, as we have clearly seen, has long ago claimed the first place for itself. Perhaps it is for this reason that those who run the state will   74
seem placed in total and perfect honor, since those to whose faith and diligence the state has entrusted itself and its greatest burden, are thus seen to have their morals and virtue approved. But I am   75
not convinced that the state demands from its magistrates copious amounts of literature more than experience of public affairs, tested over a long period of practice. However, I believe we should pass over this topic very briefly, for I think it is agreed that rarely do we   76
have to consult in the state about the heavens or the planets, and never about the nature of the gods, and the generation and strength of souls. Rather what is debated in the senate is war and peace, taxes and expenditure, and the governance and protection of everything to do with the state, and this is done, not through literature, but with practice and experience. Furthermore, in po-   77
litical speeches I cannot see when they will need to debate about the seven planets or wandering stars, or about the sun and the moon; as a result all literature should be removed from this public and political sphere.[24]

Next, those who profess literature would do better to stay   78
content with their books and avoid those places where they can

versentur, vel, si quid publicorum negotiorum tractasse concupiverint, in eo se tantum exerceant quo non advocantur, non tamen
79 excluduntur. Solas enim pacis et coniunctionum formulas conscribendas et consignandas suscipiant, reliquam vero rem publicam omnem suo pro iure sibi sumant expertissimi ac probatissimi cives,
80 ac volente iubenteque populo capessant. Litterati vero qui non se in usu negotiorum vel magis quam in litteris doctos et peritos videri elaborarint, officio suo tum functi erunt, cum in publicis monumentis redegerint ea que sint coram se, veluti apud testes bene intelligentes gesta.

81 Ergo qui recte sibi consultum volet, publicas istas omnes administrationes effugiat: non enim facile dici potest quanta publica hec omnia munera cum ceteris expeditis et ab omni reliquo negotio solutis civibus, tum maxime artibus et disciplinarum cognitione occupatis animis detrimenta afferant. In publicis enim mu-
82 neribus hec sunt incommoda: quod animum ab studiis privatis distrahunt, trahunt in sollicitudinem et invidiam, opponunt inimicitiis ac periculis, referunt curas, labores atque difficultates acerbissimas, que res omnes quam sint cum ceteris, tum litteratis moleste atque idcirco pacatis ingeniis vetite nemo non discernit.

83 Quod tametsi litteratos in honoris, gratie admirationisque loco esse olim constitutos audierim, nova tamen hec tempora alios mores ideo attulere, quod nimis multos et eos quidem insolentes,
84 vilissimos abiectissimosque homines bone littere suscepere. Ex quo effectum est ut, cum sanctissime pene omnes discipline isthac eadem hominum fece replete dehonestateque sint, tum idcirco nobilissimi et prestantissimi qui litteris affici olim consueverant, admodum dedignentur, tum etiam his artibus inherere negligant in quibus neque honorem neque amplitudinem nanciscantur.

enjoy no civic dignity; or if they do want to deal with some public business, they should train themselves in those subjects to which they have not been called nor yet excluded. They should only un- 79 dertake the writing and sealing of treaties dealing with peace and alliances, whereas all the other political dealings should rightly be taken on by those citizens who have the utmost expertise and approval in this area, and who take charge of these things at the wish or command of the people. But literary scholars who do not strive 80 to be seen as learned and expert in the practice of business or in anything other than literature, will have performed their duty when in public documents they have recorded those things which have been performed in their presence, as though in front of intelligent witnesses.

So whoever wants to do right by himself should flee all those 81 jobs in public administration; for it is not easy to say how much damage such civic duties bring both to all the other citizens who have been freed from any public service, and in particular to those people whose minds are busy with the arts and the study of other disciplines. The fact is that in civic duties there are the following 82 disadvantages: they distract your mind from private study, expose you to worry and envy, lay you open to enmities and dangers, bring you anxieties, labors and extreme difficulties, all things that everyone sees are detrimental both to others and also to literati and for that reason they are prohibited to studious minds.

Even though I have heard that literary men were once placed in 83 a position of honor, favor and admiration, these current times have brought new customs, because the study of good literature has been taken up by too many people, some of them insolent, vile and totally abject. As a result, nearly all these most sacred disci- 84 plines have been overtaken and dishonored by the dregs of society, and in addition, the very noble and outstanding men who once used to have literary ambitions now quite look down on them, and neglect those arts from which they cannot obtain either honor or

85 Atque eo devenimus ut non modo nobilitate et auctoritate prestantes litterarum studia negligant, verum etiam nulli nisi abiectis-
86 simi atque ignavissimi se ad litteras conferant. Nam aut claudi, aut
strume, aut distorti et comminuti, stolidi, hebetes, inertes atque
rebus aliis obeundis invalidi et incompotes, omnes ad litteras de-
portantur: quos autem civilia negotia respuunt, eos putant esse ad
87 otium litterarum accomodatos; quos muliercule maritos reiiciunt,
hos litterarum cognitioni iniungunt, ut aperte sentire istud videantur: prestantissima ingenia pulchrius commodiusque quovis in alio
88 negotio versari quam inter litteras. Eam ob rem quis non perspi-
ciet quam nullo in pretio sint apud cives littere? Quis causam non
discernit quamobrem decus et honos litterarum apud cives interi-
erit? Quis non ante oculos veluti pictam rem prospicit casum
89 atque perniciem disciplinarum et artium? Quis non condoluerit
tantam iacturam tantumque naufragium in litteris factum esse intuens, posteaquam in has ipsas morum tempestates et procellas
incidimus, ut nemo pene animi causa, paucissimi honoris gratia,
infiniti cupiditate et spe questus moti disciplinas sectentur?

90 Iam vero liberales omnes scientie et artes sanctissimaque animi
instituta serviles effecte iacent, iurisperitia, sacrorum disciplina,
cognitioque nature ac forma morum, reliqueve egregie et solis libe-
ris hominibus decrete littere (execrandum facinus!) quasi hasta
91 posita, publico veneunt. Infiniti venalitii licitatores bonarum artium circumvolant, ex agro, silvis, ex ipsaque gleba et ceno emer-
gunt innumerabiles non homines, sed bestie potius ad serviles
operas nate, qui spreto rure ad disciplinas venditandas et profa-
92 nandas irruunt. O pestem litterarum! Itane qui rastra et bidentem
exercere debuerant libros et litteras impudentissimi tractant?

wealth. We have now reached the stage where not only do those   85
who are outstanding in nobility and authority ignore the study of
literature, but also nobody except the most abject and lazy turns to
literary studies.[25] For it is the lame, or the scrofulous, or the dis-   86
torted and diminished, the stupid, dense, inert people who are
unable or incompetent to do any other work who all end up studying literature. The people rejected by public life are thought to be
suited for literary study; the husbands that even uneducated   87
women reject are told to embrace literature, so one should clearly
understand that it would be better and more suitable if the most
outstanding geniuses turn to any other pursuit than literature. So   88
who does not see how letters are of absolutely no value in the eyes
of citizens? Who does not perceive the reason why the glory and
honor of literature has perished in their view? Who does not have
before their eyes like a painting the decline and disaster that has
overtaken the disciplines and arts? Who does not grieve seeing   89
such a loss, such a shipwreck that literature has encountered,
when we have fallen into the current storms and tempests in
which almost nobody for the sake of their mind, very few for the
sake of honor, and an infinite number moved only by greed and
the hope of gain pursue these disciplines?[26]

Now all the liberal arts and sciences and the most sacred pre-   90
cepts of the mind have become servile and lie prostrate: jurispru-
dence, theology, natural philosophy and the whole body of ethics,
and the rest of the outstanding literature which had been only the
preserve of free men, are now up for sale as though an auction had
been declared (what an outrageous state of affairs)! Countless ve-   91
nal sellers of the nobler arts swarm around, and from the fields,
woods, soil and mud emerge an endless number of I won't say
men but beasts, born to do servile work, who reject the countryside and rush off to sell and profane the higher disciplines.
Oh what a plague has befallen literature! Those who formerly had   92
to wield the rake and the pitchfork now most impudently handle

93 Quorum officia erant pecus observare, stabulis insistere, ii de for-
94 tunis hominum diffiniunt atque disceptant; qui bacillo cogere pe-
cora debuere, ii iam sceptra gerunt, ii iam inter magistratus
95 consident; qui denique ab ipsis pecudibus non moribus, sed effigie
et loco segregati atque alienati sunt, tandem nonnihil tincti litteris,
temerarii et, ut ait poeta, hiulca gens, progrediuntur, nullo infamie, dedecoris, aut turpitudinis metu repressi, ad omnem immani-
96 tatem prompti, omni scelere et flagitio coinquinati, nihil pudori,
probitati, rectis studiis aut bonis artibus concedens, non a virtute
et sapientia, sed a cupiditate et avaritia bene et male vivendi rationem ducens, solam paupertatem miseriam, solas divitias summum
97 bonum statuens, ut de fortunis, fama et capite insontis pacisci,
questusque gratia pestem ac perniciem in quemvis machinari
98 minime abhorrescant. Nihil temerarii atque audacis flagranti
pecuniarum cupiditate affecti verentur.

99 Bone idcirco littere, honestissime artes sanctissimeque disci-
100 pline prostant et questum faciunt. Tune igitur divinarum humana-
rumque rerum cognitio, que bonorum morum et glorie tutrix,
optimarum rerum inventrix et parens exstitisti, que animos ornare,
ingenia excolere, laudem, gratiam et dignitatem conferre, rem publicam moderari, ipsumque terrarum orbem summa lege et ordine
101 agere consuevisti, tune, inquam, alumna litterarum, philosophia,
turpissimorum abiectissimorumque hominum cupiditatibus sup-
peditas et deservis?

books and literature! Those whose job it had been to mind herds 93
and deal with stables, these people now define and debate on the
fortunes of men. Those who ought to have driven sheep with their 94
crook, now wield scepters, now sit alongside the magistrates. Fi- 95
nally, those who are different from and segregated from animals,
not in their morals but just because of their appearance and the
place they now occupy, these bold and "greedy people," as the poet
says,[27] with just a smattering of literature, now advance, not held
back by any fear of infamy, shame or turpitude. They are ready for
any kind of base behavior, polluted by all kinds of crime and scan-
dal, give no thought to restraint, probity, upright studies, or the 96
nobler arts. They do not derive their understanding of the right
and wrong way of living from virtue and wisdom, but from greed
and avarice. They decide that only poverty is misery and only
wealth is the utmost good, so much so that they are happy to
bargain in the courts for the fortunes, reputation and life of an innocent man. For the sake of gain they are not in the least deterred 97
from plotting evil and destruction against anyone; driven by their 98
burning lust for money they are not afraid of doing anything rash
or outrageous.

Thus, literature and the most noble arts and most sacred disci- 99
plines are prostituted and sold for money. And you, philosophy, 100
who represent the knowledge of human and divine matters, who
protect good morals and glory, and have been both the inventor
and parent of the best things, you used to adorn the minds of
men, cultivate their genius, confer praise, favor and dignity on
people, rule the state, and run the world itself with supreme law
and order. But you, philosophy, the nurturer of literature, are you 101
now reduced to satisfying the greed of the most corrupt and abject
of men in this servile fashion?

VI

1 Sed iam desinamus casum et interitum litterarum deplorare, tum
etiam finem faciamus pervestigandi quidnam cause sit quamobrem
littere usque adeo abiecte et viles iaceant: nam id quidem cum
2 prolixum, tum ab re et instituto nostro esset alienum. Sit igitur
quantum ad rem nos parce, sed tamen vere, demonstravimus: multos labores, nullas voluptates, multas impensas, minima lucra,
multas difficultates, multa discrimina, perexiguam auctoritatem in
3 litteris comparari. Quibus ego quidem in rebus exponendis ita
studui esse brevis ut multos locos desertos commorationibus, multas argumentationes nudas exemplorum, multas persuasiones va-
cuas amplificationum consulto reliquerim, id quidem ne eius rei
accuratus vituperator viderer cui non mediocriter fui semper dedi-
4 tus. Tum etiam minime sum veritus ne oratio nostra que virtute
ipsa comite proficisceretur, tametsi ieiuna, exilis, atque humilis
5 esset, possit tamen ad iudicia litteratorum tuto pervenire. Satis
enim cultam et comptam orationem existimo eam que nulla in
parte mendacii aut falsitatis queat redargui, satis honesta est que
nullas turpitudines admiserit. Quare nemo reprehendat si malui
parum eloquens quam nimium mordax videri.

6 Nam tantum quidem a me abest ut litteras non maximi faciam,
ut pro litterarum cultu prosequendo multas anxietates, multos labores, multa incommoda, damna, detrimenta, multas erumnas
atque calamitates in vita pertulerim, dum omnino me litteris deditum atque (admodum invitis plerisque quorum ope et suffragio
7 vitam ducebam) dedicatum habui. Etenim paupertatem, inimicitias iniuriasque non modicas neque, ut multi norunt, leves, in ipso
etiam fere proficiendi flore forti integroque animo atque erecto hac
8 una litterarum gratia et amore, sustinui. Atque hoc quidem effeci
non ut voluptatem caperem, non ut questum facerem, ut profecto

VI

But now let us stop deploring the collapse and disintegration of 1
literature, and also let us end this investigation into why it now
lies so abject and lowly: that would be a prolix topic and alien to
our purpose. Let it be agreed that we have set out the case spar- 2
ingly but truthfully: the study of letters involves much labor, no
pleasure, much expense, minimum profit, many difficulties and
dangers and very little prestige. For my part I have tried to be so 3
brief in expounding these things that I deliberately left many topics devoid of development, many arguments without examples,
and many proofs empty of amplification, and I did this lest I
seemed a meticulous attacker of something to which I have always
been much devoted. In addition, I was not at all afraid that our 4
discourse — which proceeded accompanied only by virtue itself —
although it was spare, thin, and humble, would not safely reach
the judgment of men of letters. For I believe that an oration is 5
polished and cultured enough if it is not able to be accused of
falsehood or lying, that it is honest enough if it does not admit of
any baseness; so nobody should rebuke me if I have preferred to
seem not very eloquent rather than too caustic.

For I am so far from thinking literature the least important 6
subject that, in order to pursue literary studies, I have borne
throughout my life many anxieties, much labor, many disadvantages, losses, damages, much toil and many calamities, while keeping myself totally dedicated and devoted to literature (and this
quite against the wishes of most people whose help and support I
needed to live my life). For even in the very flower of my youth I 7
put up with poverty, enmities and serious injuries, ones that were,
as many know, not light: I bore this all with a strong, unshaken,
upright mind, and all for the sake and love of letters. And I carried 8
this out, not in order to pursue enjoyment, nor to make a profit,

9 fecissem si me a litteris ad negotia transtulissem: nam qui aliorum
ductu vixi, non modicas aliorum res meo arbitratu duxissem, qui
10 ab aliis impetravi, potuissem multis rogantibus esse liberalior. Sed
rerum cognitio, bone discipline, occultissime artes plus semper
11 apud me quam omnes fortune commoditates valuerunt; quare
nemo sibi persuadeat velim que a me hactenus dicta sunt ea esse
12 contra litteras odio aut fastidio aliquo exquisita. Nam sunt illa
quidem ita ex sese posita in conspectum clara atque notissima, ut
nostro ad persuadendum ingenio minime aut ullius eloquentia in-
13 diguerint. Velim tamen in eam partem nostra dicta prodesse studiosis, ut cum sua prudentia et ratione cuncta que a me explicita
sunt tenuerint, tum, me adiutore, si quid valeo, excitati diligentius
perspiciant litteras non ad lasciviam, non ad inanium caducarumque rerum expectationem conferre.

14   Nullum enim aut perexiguum fructum bone artes turpissimis
institutis conferunt; idcirco arbitremur stultissimos eos non esse
qui aliquid preter rerum optimarum notitiam in litteris affectant.
15 Decet enim prudentes eos qui probe litterati esse ac videri volunt
sic ad studia incendi, sic inter libros versari, ut suum primum officium putent sese non magis doctrina quam virtutibus ornatissimos
16 reddere. Sit animus studiosorum flagrans cupiditate quadam non
auri et opum, sed morum et sapientie, discantque in litteris non
tantum vim et causas rerum, sed formam etiam cultumque virtutis
17 et glorie; discant preterea fugere voluptates, contemnere divitias,
aspernari pompas, fortunam non metuere, solamque animi quietem moresque, virtutem, sapientiamque apprehendere, siquidem
18 bone huc ferme artes contendunt. Nam quicquid a maioribus

as I would have done if I had changed from literary studies to business: for I, who have lived under the guidance of others, 9 would have looked after substantial amounts of others' goods under my care; I who have successfully asked others, could have been more generous to the many people who asked me. But the knowl- 10 edge of things, good disciplines and uncommon arts has always been worth so much more to me than all the advantages of fortune; hence nobody should believe that what I have said so far has 11 been dug up to attack literature out of hatred or disgust. For these 12 things are so clear to everyone's sight and so very well known that they do not need our genius or anyone else's eloquence in order to persuade people. But I would like what we have said to help schol- 13 ars in this sense, that when they have digested with their own wisdom and reason what I have explained, they will be aroused through my help, if that is worth anything, to see clearly that literary studies do not lead to licentious behavior nor to the expectation of empty and ephemeral things.

For the humanities confer none or very little material reward on 14 those with the lowest of instincts; for that reason we think those people are not completely stupid who aim at something beyond just the mere knowledge of the noblest things in literature. For it 15 is right that those wise people who want to be and to seem to be upright literary scholars[28] should be so fired up to study, so to immerse themselves in books, that they should think that their first duty is to make themselves most adorned with equal amounts of learning and virtue. Let the minds of scholars burn with a desire, 16 not for gold or wealth, but for morals and wisdom, and let them learn from literature, not power and the causes of things, but the form and cult of virtue and glory, and let them learn also to avoid 17 pleasures, condemn riches, despise pomp, not fear fortune, and to acquire only peace of mind, morals, virtue and wisdom, since the humanities on the whole strive to take us in this direction. For 18 everything that is found to have been written by the ancients

conscriptum esse reperitur, id omne eo tendere videtur, ut errori-
19 bus levemur, veritatem simplicitatemque teneamus, que due res ad
bene beateque vivendum fundamenta atque robur sunt, quibus
iactis et constitutis virtutem animis magnificentius instruimus, ratio ipsa virtutis comes florescit, animus intelligentie et sapientie
munere fruitur, mens omni perturbatione vacua contra omnem
20 fortunam victrix persistit. Ergo in litteris sapientie laudem ex-
posces, litterate, tum virtutem totis viribus tuebere atque servabis,
quod ipsum libri ipsi (si loqui per se possent) ut faceres admone-
rent.

21   Nam his verbis uterentur: 'Tantis vigiliis, adolescens, te quo is
perditum? Tanti labores quid iuvabunt? Quid apud nos hac tua
solertia et assiduitate queritas? Quonam tendunt he vigilationes,
cure, et cogitationes tue? Cupis oblectari dum te ipsum excrucias
22 curis? An tibi unquam aliquod indixeris otium? Sperasne tu divitias, idem qui paupertatem apud nos non metuere didicisti? An
te preterit nostrum nihil esse venale? Non te lateat, adolescens,
commodius ducere nos amatores nostros pauperes habere quam
23 divites. Nam experti sumus: nemo est unquam factus ditior studiosus qui non illico delitiis et luxu rerum imbutus ceperit nos-
24 tram consuetudinem nostrumque complexum fastidire. Quid?
Tune potentiam exquiris, gaudes honoribus, affectas dignitates,
25 desideras amplitudinem? Falleris adolescens, falleris, si vulgi assentationes, si plebis plausus preponis virtuti, si fortune ludum, forensem tumultum, popularem auram non longe postponis doctrine et
26 sapientie! Caduca illa, instabilia, fragilia, plena inanium laborum,
plena timorum, plena suspicionum, plena casibus et labe, quis
animi quieti, stabilitati virtutis disciplinarumque pulchritudini

seems to lead us along a path where we can rid ourselves of errors and hold on to truth and simplicity, which two things are the 19 foundations and support for living the good life. And once we have laid and solidified such foundations, we can instill virtue more magnificently in our mind; reason itself, the companion of virtue, will flourish; the mind will enjoy the gift of intelligence and wisdom; and the mind will be empty of all perturbations and will stand victorious against any form of fortune. So you, scholar of 20 literature, must demand the praise of wisdom from the books you read, and then you must protect and keep virtue: this is exactly what books themselves (if they could speak on their own) warned that you should do.

For they would use these words: "Young man, where are you 21 rushing wildly off to with all these studies? How does all this work help you? What do you seek from us with all your cleverness and assiduity? Where are your studies, anxieties, and thoughts leading you? Are you seeking pleasure while you torture yourself with cares? Will you ever give yourself some leisure? Do you want 22 riches even though you have learned from us not to fear poverty? Or did you neglect the fact that nothing about us is for sale? Never forget, young man, that we think it is better for us to have those who are in love with us poor rather than rich. For we have 23 realized this: no scholar has ever become richer who did not immediately steep himself in pleasure and luxury and begin to dislike our habits and what we stand for. What? Do you seek out power, 24 do you delight in honors, pursue awards, want enrichment? You 25 are mistaken, young man, mistaken, if you put the flattery of the mob, the applause of the people before virtue, and if you do not place the games of fortune, the noise of the forum, the popularity of the people a long way behind erudition and wisdom! Who has 26 ever compared those ephemeral, unstable, fragile things, full of pointless labor, fears, suspicions, full of pitfalls and death, who has ever compared these to peace of mind, the stability of virtue and

27 compararit? An fugit, adolescens, te virtutem apud nos undique
circumstare, nullam cupiditatem, nullum fastum, nullam tumidita-
tem, nullam in animis levitatem amare, omni caligine, omni umbra
28 turpitudinum mentem expurgatissimam fieri velle? Tum, adolescens, nonne perspicis quam lumine ac splendore suo hec, cuius
verbis loquimur, sapientia nobis deditos illustres ac clarissimos
29 elaboret reddere? Memento rerum preteritarum vetustissimam
apud nos memoriam integramque prudentiam considere, que te
res omni fortune impetu et casu possit sublevare ac sustinere.
30 Sepone igitur mentem istam cupidam, exue animum istum spe
amplitudinis tumidum, fuge istas divitiarum et futilis fame cor-
31 rupteque laudis famulas, quas litteris adhibes, operas. Stultum est
prosequi voluntate quod opera nequeas assequi, stultissimumque
id adniti opera quod si perficere nequeas peniteat laborum, si as-
32 sequeris turpitudinis doleat. Utere apud nos laboribus parcius,
virtute acrius; neque tantum peritiam doctrinarum, que quidem
merito virtutis comes putatur, apud nos consectaberis, quin te ad
integram potius virtutem spe, ratione et cogitatione in dies reddas
33 aptiorem. Nam ex doctrina et artibus illud preclarum dabitur, ut
ad sapientiam liceat aspirare; ex virtute divinum illud consequeris,
ut quietem animi, laudem, dignitatem et felicitatem adipiscaris.
34 'Quod si, ut debes, ad virtutem, ceteris posthabitis rebus,
contenderis, maxima omnium vitiorum levatio fiet, tum maxima
35 laus et gloria succedet. Prestat enim et excellit virtus, nam ei coniuncta et complexa est divina quedam vis qua levamur a vitiis
atque erroribus omnibus, qua laus, honos, integraque et perma-
36 nens animi voluptas et quies subsequitur et persistit. Quam quidem virtutem qui animo, voluntate et usu comprehenderit, qui

the beauty of the arts? Has it escaped you, young man, that virtue   27
is to be found all around us, that we do not love any desires, any
pomp, any pride, any levity of mind, that with us your mind wants
to become totally cleansed of every darkness, every shadow of
baseness? And then, young man, do you not see how this wisdom,   28
with whose words we speak, endowed with its own light and
splendor, tries to make its devotees very illustrious and famous?
Remember that we possess a very ancient memory of things past   29
as well as pure prudence, and this can lift you above any blast of
fortune or chance and sustain you. So set aside that greedy men-   30
tality, strip off that mind, swollen with the hope of enrichment,
flee those slaves of wealth—futile fame and corrupt praise—which
you are trying to associate with literature. It is foolish to pursue   31
with your will what you cannot attain with your actions, and extremely foolish to struggle to achieve with your efforts something
that, if you cannot achieve it, will make you regret your labors,
and if you do achieve it, will make you ashamed of your wickedness. Use less labor and more virtue when dealing with us; and by   32
reading us you will not just gain knowledge of doctrines, which is
rightly thought to be the companion of virtue, but you also make
yourself fitter day by day for complete virtue through your hope,
reasoning and thought. For out of erudition and the arts comes   33
this wonderful thing, namely that you are allowed to aspire to
wisdom; through virtue you will obtain this divine gift of obtaining peace of mind, praise, dignity and happiness.

"And if, as you must do, you aspire to virtue and leave aside all   34
other things, you will experience the greatest ever elimination of
vices, followed by the fullest praise and glory. Virtue stands above   35
and excels everything else, for allied to it and embracing it is a
certain divine strength by which we are raised above all vices and
errors, and through which we achieve permanent praise, honor,
and complete and lasting pleasure and peace of mind. The person   36
who attains this virtue in his intellect, his will and in daily use,

solidam et expressam virtutem non in plebis iudicio esse, sed in
animi elegantia et splendore sitam meminerit, is nullum sibi cum
fortuna commercium esse volet, is omnia sua in se bona esse posita
putabit; ex quo profecto ornatissimam et beatissimam atque deo-
37   rum persimilem vitam ducet. Que cum ita sint, adolescens, in-
cumbe ad virtutem, ac de his fortune commodis sic iudicato: nihil
eorum esse vehementius cupiendum, nihil animi bonis preferen-
dum, nihil admodum probatissimis viris, preter sapientiam et virtutem persequendum, nihil preter insipientiam et vitium perti-
38   mescendum atque refugiendum. Etenim qui volet suum facere
animum ornatissimum, is quidem sordes istas quas voluptates
nuncupant atque illas virtutum inimicas quas opulentiam et divitias nominant atque alias istas omnes morum animorumque
pestes, quas honores, dignitates et amplitudinem appellant, despi-
39   ciat, oderit et abhorreat necesse est. Quibus omnibus rebus si dili-
gentissimam adhibueris operam, adolescens, comperies litteras
esse voluptuosissimas, utillimas ad laudem, ad gloriam atque ad
fructum posteritatis et immortalitatis accomodatissimas.'

40   Nos idcirco tum nostra superiori, tum hac librorum hortatione
et commonefactione excitati atque erecti sic prosequamur in litteris, Carole, ut nostra apud omnes virtus, mi frater, comprobetur,
et dubitet nemo vel solam a nobis esse quesitam sapientiam.

who remembers that solid and perfectly visible virtue lies not in the judgment of the people, but is situated in the elegance and splendor of the mind, such a man will not want any commerce with fortune; he will believe that all his goods are placed within himself. As a result, he will indeed lead that most decorous, blessed existence, very similar to that of the gods. This being so, 37 young man, pursue virtue relentlessly, and as for these goods of fortune, think of them like this: none of them is to be desired vehemently, none of them is to be preferred to the goods of the mind, nothing should be pursued by the most upright men except wisdom and virtue, nothing is to be feared and fled from except foolishness and vice. Whoever wants to enrich his mind to the full 38 will have to despise, hate and abhor those things that are called pleasures, those enemies of the virtues that are called wealth and riches, and all those other plagues of your minds and morals, which they call honors, dignities and prestige. If, young man, you 39 apply yourself most diligently to all these things, you will find that literature is most pleasant, most useful for praise and glory, and very suitable for achieving the goal of future fame and immortality."

So Carlo, we will be roused and raised up by the encouragement 40 we set out earlier and by this exhortation and warning, issued by our books themselves, to proceed in our pursuit of literature, so that all our virtue, my brother, will be approved by everyone else, and no one will doubt that we have only sought after one thing: wisdom.

VITA SANCTI POTITI

PROHEMIUM

1 Blasi, pater et domine mi, reverendissime patriarcha Gradensis, pax tibi, gratia et gloria a deo patre et Christo Jhesu domino nostro. Martirum sanctorum vitam tuo iussu descripturus, libenter ista salutatione usus sum, qua Galliarum religiosi ad Frygias et 2 Asiaticas ecclesias de suis martiribus scribentes utebantur. Quod vero ad rem attinet, gaudeo abs te viro disertissimo tanti Baptistam fieri, ut que sanctorum martirum vita tuo integerrimo iudicio parum accurate scripta videtur, eam studio meo digniorem reddi 3 posse non dubites. Tamen videto nequid nimis tua in me benivolentia de nobis tibi persuaseris. Nosti enim admodum eruditi et maturissimi ingenii officium esse vitam sanctorum pro dignitate 4 recensere. Et nosti preterea quod multi fortasse recusarent hoc scribendi munus, quo agenda cum maioribus esset ingenii et eloquentie comparatio. Non quidem quo se ita rudes illi diiudicarent ut sua scripta repudianda penitus ducerent, sed quia inprimis fugerent inepti aut arrogantes videri, veluti qui maiorum scripta suis novis ostentationibus oblitterari studuissent.

5 Que res quamquam ita sint, nihil tamen tibi ut me omnino exerceam iubenti denegandum existimo. Nam qui meam eloquentiam in hoc scribendi genere parum dignam iudicabunt, iidem ipsi ut opinor meam in te observantiam non reprehendent.

THE LIFE OF ST. POTITUS

PROHEMIUM

Father Biagio, most reverend Lord Patriarch of Grado, peace be 1
with you, and the grace and glory that comes from God the Father
and Jesus Christ our Lord be with you also.[1] Since at your behest
I am setting out to describe the lives of the holy martyrs, I have
willingly used that form of greeting that the religious fathers of
Gaul employed when they were writing about their own martyrs
to the Phrygian and Asiatic churches.[2] As for the substance of this 2
letter, I rejoice that you, a most eloquent man, hold Battista so
highly in regard that you have no doubt that any lives of the holy
martyrs that seem to your impeccable judgment to have been written less carefully could be made more dignified by my scholarship.
However, please ensure that your benevolence toward me does not 3
make you overestimate my capacities. For you know that it re-
quires the work of a really erudite and mature intellect to recount
the life of martyrs with appropriate dignity. You are also aware 4
that many people might perhaps refuse this writing task, since it
would invite comparison with those who have greater eloquence
and genius. It is not because they would judge themselves to be so
uncultured as to think that their own writings are to be thoroughly rejected, but because primarily they would want to avoid
seeming inept and arrogant, as though they aimed at obliterat-
ing the writings of our predecessors with their own showy new
works.

Yet despite these dangers, I do not feel I can deny you anything 5
you ask, especially when you command me to exercise my intellect
in some way. For even those who judge that my eloquence in this
genre is not adequate will not, I believe, criticize my obedience to

6 Itaque, posteaquam tuis preceptis obsequendum est, iube cuius vitam primam esse velis. Ego pro virili enitar expectationi tue satisfacere. Tu meorum studiorum primicias (ut aiunt) cum primum aliquid scripsero, videbis et emendabis; deinceps vero quid agendum censeas imperabis.

VITA SANCTI POTITI

1 Potiti adolescentis vitam non iniuria primam esse voluisti, qua meas vires periclitarer. Est ea quidem adolescentis constantia et miraculorum multitudine singularis, in qua colenda qui se exerceat multam dicendi materiam inveniat multamque sibi attentionem

2 comparet. Quis enim non libenter legat adolescentis vitam, qui intra quartum et decimum annum queque nos appellamus mala perpessus constanti firmissimoque animo sit — paupertatem, exilium, cruciatus atque extrema omnia non modo dura ferentibus, sed pene incredibilia legentibus? Tantus quidem religionis deique amor adolescentis animo flagrabat, ut immemor domus, patris, patrie omnisque fortune sese totum pro vera Christi religione de-

3 dicaret. Erat enim admodum puer ingenio et forma pene divina preditus, — nam eius faciem non secus atque solem fulgores radiasse referunt quasi presagium futurum illum inter martires splendidissimum, — reliquis vero in rebus ac precipue singulari modestia in urbe Serdica primarius.

4 Hunc eius pater, cui nomen Ylas, vel has ob res vel quod unicus esset filius, omni caritate prosequebatur dabatque operam quoad posset filium reddere non modo bonis fortune verum etiam doctrina et moribus ditiorem. Denique suas supremas delicias in

your wishes. So, since I must obey your precepts, tell me which 6
life you would like me to write first. I will do my best to satisfy
your expectations of me. As soon as I write something, you will
see the first fruits, as they say, of my studies and will let me have
any emendations; after that you may order me to do whatever else
you consider is necessary.

THE LIFE OF ST. POTITUS

You rightly wanted the life of the young saint Potitus to be the 1
first biography in which I should test my abilities. For the youth is
outstanding for his constancy and the large number of his miracles, so much so that whoever wants to exercise his skills in paying
homage to him will find an enormous amount of material and will
attract considerable attention. For who would not gladly read the 2
life of a young man who, before he was fourteen, suffered every
kind of what we call evil with a constant and totally unyielding
mind: poverty, exile, physical torture and all sorts of extreme torments which were not only harsh to bear in reality but almost incredible to read about. Such a love of God burned in this young
man's mind that, forgetting about his home, his father, his country
and all aspects of his fortune, he dedicated himself totally to the
true religion of Christ. While still a boy, he was endowed with an 3
almost divine genius and good looks—for they say that his face
radiated dazzling rays just like the sun, as if this was a presage of
his future splendor among the martyrs—and he was outstanding
in the city of Sofia in all matters, but especially in his extraordinary modesty.[3]

Either because of these qualities or because he was his only son, 4
Potitus' father, who was called Hylas, cherished him with all his
love and made every effort to make his son richer not only in the
goods of fortune but also in erudition and morals.[4] In short, he

5 Potito filio constituerat. Idcirco, quod fore optimum existimabat, prisca illa gentilium superstitione filium imbuebat, nam id vel ad mores vel ad filii salutem arbitrabatur; siquidem per ea tempora Christi religione compleri plurimum orbis ceperat, quam rem principes cum reliquarum urbium tum maxime Senatus regesque Romani gravissime ferebant. Videbant enim ob id fieri plurimos in populo motus neque facile patiebantur suam veterem deorum ob-

6 servantiam antiquari. Eam ob rem, edictis, penis atque omni seve-ritate cavebant ne latius Christi disciplina in plebis animos effun-deretur. Ea res cum ita esset, Ylas, Potiti pater, omni studio et vigilantia puerum observabat et ne patrie ac maiorum suorum reli-

7 gionis inscius ad alios ritus sese verteret ⟨e⟩laborabat. Multa ideo de diis disserens ad aras puerum adducebat, sacrificiis adesse com-pellebat, nihil quod ad instruendum puerum attineret pretermit-tebat.

8 Frustra tamen omnia, nam Potiti animum incesserat dei Jhesus spiritus, forte quidem per Christianos qui non pauci Serdica urbe aderant. Iam deum Christum norat, amabat, tacitusque secum

9 colebat. Cuius rei factus certior, Ylas pater iterum atque iterum ad aras deorum invitum puerum trahere, periculum quo per Antonini imperatoris edictum subiceretur ac mortes eorum qui Antonini

10 voluntatem parvifecissent enumerare. At Potitus sancto dei spiritu plenissimus:

Quam, inquit, erras pater, si de deo te recte sentire existi-mas, aut si minis posse me compelli ut tecum errem tibi

11 persuades. Saxa fictaque simulacra ut adorem, imagines

took supreme delight in his son Potitus. As a result, feeling that 5
this would be the best thing for him, he imbued his child with the
ancient religion of the gentiles: he thought that it would be benefi-
cial to his morals and to his safety, since at that time the Christian
religion had begun to fill the world, a phenomenon that rulers of
other cities, and especially the senate and emperors of Rome,
strongly resented. For they saw that, because of this new religion,
there were many disturbances among the people, and they did not
easily accept that their old worship of the pagan gods was being
put aside. Because of this they used edicts, punishments and all 6
kinds of severity to discourage Christian worship from spreading
further in the minds of the people. In this situation, Hylas, Potitus' father, watched his son with the utmost care and attention and
tried to ensure that he did not forget the religion of his fatherland
and his elders by turning to other sacred rites. So, talking a lot 7
about the gods, he would take his son to the altars and make him
attend sacrifices, not omitting anything that pertained to his son's
education.

But all this was in vain, for the spirit of Jesus had entered Poti- 8
tus' mind, perhaps through contact with the many Christians who
were in the city of Sofia. By this stage he knew that Christ was
God and loved Him and secretly worshipped Him. When his fa- 9
ther Hylas got to know about this, he would drag his unwilling
son more and more to the altars of the pagan gods and would spell
out the danger to which he might be subject because of Emperor
Antoninus' edict and would list the deaths of those who had
flouted the emperor's will. But Potitus, who was full of the holy 10
spirit of God, said,

How wrong you are, Father, if you think your views about
God are correct, or if you are convinced that by your threats
you can compel me to sin with you. Who will force me to 11
adore stones and false images and offer prayers and sacrifices

hominum manu erectas, illis vota sacrificia ut faciam, quis
me compellet? Non tu, Ylas, si sapis, si tibi me carum habes.

12 Nam te errare qui es etate grandior, turpe quidem est, sed
turpius nolle ab errore desistere, siquidem, ut meministi,
Petrus, Paulus, reliquive Christi discipuli et usque in nostra
tempora Christi imitatores, multis miraculis, multis rationibus comprobent solum unicum esse deum, eundemque esse
Christum, eius precepta veram esse religionem, nostros deos
esse demonum illusiones, fraudes.

13 Cum igitur multa per etatem de his verissimis rebus au-
dieris atque videris, an non reprehendendus eris, pater, si

14 nolueris salvam filii animam fore? Tune tanti feceris Antonini edicta, ut ea preferenda summi dei preceptis censeas?
Cruciatus et mortes enumeras eorum qui secus egerint; id

15 timendum asseris, commonefacis. Vide quam sim alienus a
tua ista sententia, — ego is sum qui non genus aliquod tor-
mentorum recuso, non mortem ipsam, qua vitam gloriosam
apud deum adipiscar, — et quam cupio hac eadem in senten-

16 tia te esse. Da, queso, operam ut salvus sis. Sit procul a te
ista vulgi opinio; Martem, Minervam, Jovem ipsum inania
commenta poetarum existima, ut quidem sunt. Desine falsa
deorum opinione te ac me ipsum solicitare. Mihi est animus:
nihil vereri, nihil timere, omnia perpeti pro vero deo Jhesu,
cuius ego quanta sint premia non ignoro. Quod si ulla apud
te veritatis cognitio esset, me scio laudares ac tue saluti esses
minus infensus.

to statues erected by human hands? Not you, Hylas, if you are wise, and if you care for me. For you, who are older than me, to err is a base thing, but it is even more base not to want to desist from this error; for, as you remember, Peter, Paul and the rest of Christ's disciples, as well as those who imitated Christ down to our own times, have proven through many miracles and many rational arguments that there is only one God, and He is Christ. His precepts are the true religion, while our pagan gods are the illusions and deceptions of devils.

Therefore, when you have heard and seen many proofs of these true facts in the course of your lifetime, will you not be to blame if you do not want your son's soul to be saved? Do you really give so much weight to Antoninus' edicts that you think they count more than the precepts of God on high? You list the torments and deaths of those who have acted against the edict: you assert, you warn that we should be afraid. Look how far I am from this idea of yours: I am someone who will not refuse any kind of torture, not even death itself, since that will allow me to gain a glorious life with God. And see how much I want you also to share this view. I beseech you to make all efforts to save yourself; keep the opinion of the vulgar crowd far from you; you must regard Mars, Minerva, Jupiter himself as the empty lies of the poets, as indeed they are. Stop tormenting yourself and myself with this false belief in the gods. My mind is made up: I will fear nothing, I will not be afraid of anything, I will suffer anything for the true God Jesus, as I well know how great his rewards are. If you had any knowledge of the truth, I know you would praise me and you would be less hostile to your own salvation.

17 His Potiti verbis plurimum commotus, Ylas non magis admirari grandia pueri verba cepit quam secum ipse pervestigare quibus preceptoribus novam puer institutionem accepisset, simulque maiorem in modum dedignari novo cum dei cultu eam contumaciam
18 in filium accessisse, ut nihil valeret monitu aut minis flecti. Ob id non nihil subirritatus domi puerum inclusit ac vetuit alimenta, vetuit ipsam aquam dari istic inquiens: 'Tuo cum deo salvum te
19 esse querito.' Sperabat Ylas puerum, qua etate ceteri gule et lasciviis consuescant quave plurimum nutrimenta exposcant, ea ipsa pressum fame puerum sibi obsequentiorem fieri.

20 At vero, posteaquam sitim famemque, non modo forti animo sed etiam libenti, perferre Potitum vidit, motus partim pietate, partim penitentia, denuo filii animum temptare instituit. Igitur apud filium simili persuasione institit, dicens Potitum sibi semper omni re fuisse cariorem, multam in unico filio spem locasse, nunquam illum non ingenuum iudicasse, dolere quod nova insania captus patris monitus tam minimi faciat. Esse hoc contra ipsa illa precepta que Potitus se imitari assereret; plus patris pietati ac pru-
21 dentie credendum esse quam subornatoribus; fruendum preterea bonis paternis, quibus facile abundaret; olim recoligendam esse mentem; dementis esse manifestis periculis se obiectare, desipere quidem qui non prudentia patrem multo prestare quam puerum arbitretur. Se enim previdisse ac pertimescere que ad filii dignitatem et vitam pertineant, delirare profecto qui ita obstinatus sit, ut mortem vite, patris inimicitiam anteponat amicitie. Quod si sui

Hylas was very moved by this speech of Potitus, and began   17
both to be amazed at the boy's powerful words and wondered
within himself what teachers had given him this new education.
At the same time he became more and more indignant that, along
with this new religious cult, his son had been filled with such ob-
stinacy that he was unable to be moved by either warnings or
threats. He was considerably irritated by this, kept the boy at   18
home, forbade him food and even water, saying to him: "Now try
to save yourself with your god." Hylas hoped that his son, who   19
was now at the age when young people become accustomed to the
pleasures of food and sex, or when they demand a lot of food,
would be reduced by hunger at this particular age to become more
obedient to him.

But after he saw that Potitus bore his hunger and thirst not   20
only with a strong mind but seemed actually to be glad of this
trial, his father was moved, partly by pity and partly by regret, and
once more decided to test his child's resolve. So he returned to
him with the same idea as previously, saying Potitus had always
been dearer to him than anything else; he had placed a lot of hope
in his only child; he had never considered him to be anything but
high-minded;[5] and he grieved that his son had been seized by this
new insanity and paid so little attention to his father's warnings.[6]
He said that this was against the very precepts that Potitus claimed
he followed and that his son should give more weight to his father's concern for his son than to the advice of wicked men.[7]
Moreover, he should enjoy his father's wealth which was very   21
abundant; he should finally recover his senses, for it was only a
madman who would expose himself to obvious dangers; and anyone who did not think that a father's prudence was far superior to
that of a child was insane. Hylas had foreseen and was very afraid
of the dangers that threatened his son's standing and indeed his
life, and thought that anyone who was so obstinate as to prefer
death to life and a father's enmity instead of his friendship was

oblitus aliqua tandem in patrem pietas relicta est, orare ne se ita gerat ut patrem quoque vita periclitari oporteat; magistratibus enim iratis facile persuaderi posse puerum, quem Ylas unicum habeat, quem etiam unicum observet, hunc paternis monitis no-

22 vam religionem atque invisam sapere. Adolescenti quidem fortassis mutande opinionis rationem ex tempore futuram vel etatis veniam facile impetrari, sibi vero patri, ni se filius corrigat, presens infortunium paratum esse.

23   At Potitus plenus deo eas omnes patris rationes refellebat tanta eloquentia tantaque scripturarum memoria, ut omnium disertissimus videretur, multa de filiorum officio in parentes, de patris pietate in filios, multa insuper de Christi religione disserens.

24 Postremo ne patri ullum ex se periculum immineret, instituisse aiebat longius proficisci; quam tamen rem magis libenter faceret, si patrem id ipsum institutum sequi intelligeret, aut si ita domi remaneret ut olim sui erroris peniteret. Itaque cum multa de his rebus Potitus disseruisset, ferunt patrem obstipuisse, procidisse, ac non obscure perpendisse puerum non suo ingenio sed dei spiritu eloqui.

25   Puer vero quam potuit repente sese apud Epirum in silvestrem locum proripuit. Dicunt aliqui nebula Potitum septum atque absportatum. In Epiro igitur fere omnem primum adolescentie florem intra silvas atque feras egit sola Christi dei gratia contentus. Carere enim peccatis, Christo gratior reddi, has ille divitias po-

26 tiores ducebat quam omnes patris fortunas. Etenim pulchrius intra feras belluas versari arbitrabatur quam intra crudeles, nefarios

clearly deranged. Lastly, if Potitus, forgetting about himself, still retained any filial piety toward his father, he begged his son not to behave in such a way that his father's life also would be in danger: for the magistrates could get angry and easily be convinced that the boy, who was Hylas' only son, and whom Hylas cherished and also treated as an only son, had come to know about this new and hated religion thanks to his father's instruction. The youth might   22 eventually be pardoned because of his age or because in the course of time he might find reason to change his mind, but unless his son changed his ways, his father would be facing imminent punishment.

But Potitus, inspired by God, rejected all his father's arguments   23 with such eloquence and such a memory for the words of Scripture that he seemed the most eloquent person of all, saying much about the duties of a son toward his parents, about a father's piety toward his children, and many things about the religion of Christ. Finally, he said that, in order that his father should not have any   24 danger hanging over him because of his son, he had decided to go far away, but he would do this much more willingly if he understood that his father would follow him, or if Hylas, while remaining at home, would eventually repent of his error. Thus, after Potitus had made a long speech about these things, it is said that the father was astounded, fell prostrate and clearly thought that his son was speaking not from his own intellect but through the spirit of God.

The young man rushed off as soon as he could to a wild,   25 wooded place in Epirus.[8] Some say that Potitus was wrapped in a cloud that bore him away. So he spent nearly all the first flower of his youth in Epirus among the woods and wild beasts, content only with the grace of Christ the Lord. For he believed that to live without sin and become more pleasing to Christ constituted greater wealth than all his father's fortunes. He felt it was better to   26 live among wild animals than amid cruel, wicked and inhuman immanesque homines, quorum nulla pene urbs non refertissima est; immo nullum cum hominibus commercium non pestiferum ducebat, nisi quo homines instructiores sancte religionis efficerentur.

27 Quam rem cum egregie posse cuperet, desiderio adolescentis favit deus. Nam forte Agathonis uxor, per id temporis principis Senatus, cui nomen Cyriace, lepra incurabili morbo premebatur. In ea igitur primum voluit deus ostendere quantum Potitus fide ac meritis posset.

28 Sed prius quam ad rem accederet eum per angelum cautiorem fecit multas esse diaboli insidias adversus hominum genus, qui corpore infirmo agitationibus vero animi prompti sumus et facile in vitia deducimur. Idcirco cavendum esse ne demonis ostentatio-

29 nibus et persuasionibus a vera Christi via seducamur. Tale dehinc fantasma ferunt Potito per demonem ante oculos advolasse: formosum quendam hominem, multa auctoritate gravem, disserentem quantum civilis vita a solitaria differat, quantum quidem antiquius sit dignitatibus imperiisque versari quam intra ignavam

30 solitudinem algescere. Illic posse multis prodesse, hic nemini; homines hominum causa natos esse; opinione prorsus inani duci homines qui sibi animum inducant omnibus rebus egere ne sua opera et opibus amicis notisque benefaciant; presenti felicitate fruendum esse, non oportere duci stulta illorum opinione qui tantopere paupertatem laudent. Non enim fecisse deum opes, non reliqua bona,

31 ut nulli essent possessores. Vel quidni? deum esse quicquid prosit, divina profecto omnia in illo esse qui possit omnia tibi conferre necessaria, deo etiam simillimum esse qui dare bona quam multis possit; non denique dedignandam plebis gratiam, optimatum

people, since hardly any city was not crammed full of such men. Indeed, he believed that there was no commerce with other men that was not dangerous, unless that whereby men became more knowledgeable about holy religion.

Since he strongly desired that this should come about, God fa- 27 vored the young man's wishes. For it happened that at that time Cyriace, the wife of Agathon, leader of the senate, was suffering from an incurable form of leprosy. It was through her that God first wanted to show how much Potitus' faith and merits could do.

But before the young man embarked on this enterprise, God 28 informed him through an angel that the devil's snares against mankind are manifold, since through the weakness of the flesh and the perturbations of the mind we are all too ready to be drawn into vice. For that reason we must beware lest we are seduced from the true way of Christ by the pageants and persuasions of Satan. Subsequently, it is said that the following phantom flew before 29 Potitus' eyes through the powers of the devil: a handsome man, with the serious look of someone of considerable authority, talked about how much civic life differed from the solitary existence, how much better it was to be involved in the offices and governance of the state than to grow cold in lazy solitude.[9] In the former exis- 30 tence one could benefit many, in the latter nobody; men were born for the sake of their fellow men.[10] It was a completely fatuous idea that led some of them to decide to do without everything in order not to benefit their friends and acquaintances with their deeds and wealth; the happiness of the present has to be enjoyed, and one must not be led by the foolish opinion of those who praise poverty so much. God did not create wealth and all the other goods so that nobody should possess them. So then, God is whatever ben- 31 efits us, indeed all things divine are in that person who can confer on you all the things you need, and the person who can give goods to the largest number of people is very similar to God; finally one should not disdain the people's favor, the approval of the best

consensum, principum amicitias, famam quidem gloriamque esse capessendam.

32 His igitur rationibus Potiti mentem fantasma expugnare plurimum nitebatur. Cui peroranti Potitus cum fortiter obstitisset, non hominis speciem sed monstri hanc esse animadvertit; nam illi calcaneus informis nullo loco recte vestigia imprimens aderat. Quo quidem fantasmate pulchre persuaderi potest simillima esse fortune et presentis vite bona, nullo enim se loco firmare, nihil vestigii, nihil felicis memorie, ex illis caducis et monstruosis fortune
33 bonis relinqui. Et sunt ea quidem monstruosa maxime in quibus omnia vitia versentur. Quid enim monstrum est perdito flagitio-
34 soque homine maius? Certe nullum. Reliqua omnia monstra ex natura produci, nature opus esse nemo negabit; at quis fatebitur malam, libidinosam, invidam, avaram crudelemque mentem, quis ex natura id monstrum profectum dixerit? Etenim quem mihi dabis, bonis fortune prepotentem vel mediocriter quidem abun-
35 dantem, ullas sibi fortunas absque vitio patrasse? Repete istos, quos felices diceres, quorum imperio et ductu urbes gentesque aguntur; illis ego quid detestabilius dici possit nescio. Nam eos
36 pene omnes omni miseria perditos video. Tales igitur fortune fastus monstra esse ac demonem per fantasma perspexit Potitus adolescens. Que quidem mala ut perpetuo liceret effugere multis deum precibus oravit.

37 Orante Potito, ferunt id ipsum fantasma cubitos XV excrevisse. O pulchram rerum caducarum picturam! Nam cum optes fortune bona, quantum illa sint perniciosa haud facile sentis; ubi vero dei beneficio illa potes effugere ac despicere, sane apertius intelligis nihil esse ea peste grandius, hominum vires multo excedere.

people in society, and making friends with princes: fame and glory are to be seized.[11]

With these arguments the phantom strove to capture Potitus' mind. As he finished his speech Potitus stood firm, and noticed that this was a kind of monster, not a man, for he had a deformed heel which left no proper footprint anywhere. This image could be a fine way of persuading us that the goods of fortune and of our present life are very similar to it, for they are not firm anywhere, and from those ephemeral and monstrous goods of fortune, no trace remains, and no happy memory. And such goods are most monstrous of all in those who are involved in every kind of vice. For what greater monster is there than a wicked and scandalous man? Surely none. All other monsters are produced by nature, nobody will deny they are the work of nature, but who will say that an evil, libidinous, envious, greedy and cruel mind is a monster that proceeds from nature? What man can you show me who is powerful through his goods of fortune or even just moderately wealthy who has gained any fortune without vice? Recollect those whom you would call happy, under whose guidance and leadership cities and states are ruled: I do not know anything that could be called more detestable than them. For I see almost all of them damned in all sorts of misery. So through the appearance of this vision the young Potitus saw that such displays of fortune were monstrous and through the phantom he saw the devil. And he said many prayers to God, asking that he be allowed to escape such evils in perpetuity.

As Potitus prayed, it is said that the phantom itself grew to fifteen cubits. What a wonderful image of things ephemeral![12] For when you desire the goods of fortune, it is not easy to perceive how pernicious they are; but when through God's gift you can escape and despise such things, then you understand more clearly that there is nothing greater than that disease and that it far outdoes human strength.

38   At vero cum tantam immanitatem monstri vidisset adolescens, aiunt sufflasse ac monstrum evanuisse, que res etiam ad nostram picturam pulcherrime accedit. Nam vel uno flatu bona per omnem etatem parta morientes perdimus, vel nobis viventibus uno flatu

39 estuque fortune quam repentinum naufragium patiuntur. Non ideo reprehendo qui mundi caducas res demones nuncupant, modo verum demonum genus non substulerint. Tantum enim apud me valet in his fortune rebus tamquam in aliquo corpore versari malum demonem, malas cupiditates, quantum illis esse

40 quod aiunt aereum corpus. Siquidem utrinque est ingenium nocens mensque pessima, denique quod ad salutem noceat, an aliter quam cachodemon dici poterit? Abiicienda igitur est omnis mens rebus caducis affecta, omni opera et industria ab animi actione segreganda et eadem longius fugienda quidem, non secus atque malus teter obscenusque demon, deo ac nature hominum inimicissimus.

41   Etenim demonem aiunt in multas et varias rerum species verti, nempe id ut imbecilles mortales aut in facinus trahat aut ab optimo instituto perterrefaciat, quam ipsam rem apud Potitum fecisse re-

42 ferunt. Nam ex illa immani hominis specie in bovis colorem versum esse demonem multoque mugitu adolescentem concussisse. Porro quid bovis colorem aut bovem ipsum in bonis fortune dici credimus, nisi auri agrorumque divitias vel maxime has nostras beneficiorum possessiones, quibus intemperati ad lasciviam et libidines, paulo modestiores ad pompam et amplitudinem utuntur?

43 At cornu eius hoc pacto exaltari aiunt vel nominis immortalitatem et gloriam comparari. Hec est porro illa tumultuaria bovis vox,

However, when the young man saw the huge dimensions of the   38
monster, it is said that he blew hard and the monster disappeared,
which also fits our image well. For either when we die we lose with
one breath all the goods that we have acquired throughout our life,
or while we are still alive with one breath and surge of fortune
these goods suffer the most sudden shipwreck. So I do not criti-   39
cize those who say that ephemeral things of the world are devils as
long as they do not deny the existence of real devils. For it is as
real for me that in these goods of fortune a wicked devil and evil
desires live just like in someone's body, as the fact that they are
said to possess what is called an aery body.[13] The fact is that in   40
both cases there is an intelligence that wants to do harm and a
very wicked mind; and finally, since it damages our salvation, can
it be said to be anything other than a *kakodaimon* (evil spirit)? So
one must reject any mind that seeks after ephemeral things; it
should be segregated from any action of the intelligence with all
effort and striving; and such a mind ought to be fled from, exactly
like the evil, disgusting, obscene devil, who is full of enmity toward God and the nature of man.

For they say that Satan can metamorphose into many and vari-   41
ous species of things, and of course he does that so that he can
either drag weak mortals into doing evil or frighten them away
from their best resolutions: they say that he did this very thing to
Potitus. For the devil changed from that inhuman image of a man   42
into the color and shape of an ox; and that with a great mooing
sound he struck the young man down. Now what do we believe
the yellowish color of an ox or the ox itself signifies amid the
goods of fortune except gold and the wealth of the fields, especially the income that comes from church benefices which intemperate individuals use for lasciviousness and pleasure, and more
modest people use for ceremony and display? They say that for   43
this reason the bull's horn is exalted so as to mean the acquisition
of the immortality and glory of one's name. Moreover, this is also

que Potiti ac nostram omnium mentem plurimum incutit. Nam
terrene glorie cupiditate corrupta quadam natura ducimur, quam
adipisci dulce arbitramur, fugere vero arduum.

44   Quo fit ut vulgi censura pene omnes pendeant. Non enim vestitus, non incessus, non ulla vivendi libertas est quam ipsi non
subiectam habeamus plebis iudicio. A plebe laudari magnum et
45 honorificum, non approbari ignominiosum. O stultam hominum
opinionem! Gloriam aiunt approbantium, laudem bene de te iudi-
cantium. Ego secus gloriam dixero non dignosci, non approbari a
stulta multitudine: deo notissimum acceptissimum reddi et glorio-
sum adolescentem Potitum dixero, quamquam scio perpaucos huic
46 sententie assensuros. Quem enim mihi dabis qui se ita comparet,
ut Potitum imitandum ducat, ut ea solitudine, eo a patre exilio,
gloriosior apud deum esse quam apud homines malit? Alii enim
questibus inserviunt, alii militie insudant, alii litteris et vigiliis
marcescunt, omnes ut fama clariores in hominum ora quam glo-
riosi in dei conspectum veniant.

47 Sed forte nimis ab instituto digressi sumus. Verum hoc quoque ne
tacerem, commonuit adolescentis Potiti vita, qui quantum interes-
set et hodiernam inter et priscam Christi disciplinam per id fan-
48 tasma quasi per picturam intellexit. Demonis namque illusiones,
hoc est rerum caducarum possessiones, primo hominis effigiem
habuisse quasi non esset alienum ab humanitate bonis terrenis
perfrui; deinde supra hominem crevisse hoc est fastu et superbia

the meaning of the ox's noisy voice, which struck the mind of Potitus and the minds of all the rest of us.[14] For we are led on by our corrupt nature and by our desire for earthly glory, which we think is sweet to pursue and hard to renounce.

This means that nearly all of us are swayed by the view of the   44 crowd. For there is no freedom in our clothes, in our way of walking, no freedom in the way we live that we do not subject to the judgment of the common people. To be lauded by the common people is great and honorable; not to be approved by them is ignominious. Oh, the stupid opinions of men! They say that glory is   45 when people approve of you, and praise is when they judge well of you. I think differently and say that glory is neither recognized nor valued by the foolish multitude; I say that the young man Potitus was made very well known, glorious and most welcome to God, even though I know that very few will agree with this verdict. In   46 fact, can you tell me anyone who thinks Potitus is to be imitated? Would anyone prefer to live in that solitude, in that exile from his father, in order to be more glorious to God than to live among men? For some are in thrall to the pursuit of gain, some sweat over a military career, others waste away studying literature and burning the midnight oil, all of them do so in order to be more famous in the mouths of men than glorious in the sight of God.

Perhaps we have strayed too far from our subject. But the life of   47 the young Potitus has warned me that I should not omit this point either, that through this phantom, as though it were a picture,[15] he understood what a difference there was between the Christian discipline of his own times and that of the old days. For   48 he first had the image of the man as representing the illusions of the devil, in other words the possession of ephemeral things, as if to say that it was not alien from humanity to enjoy earthly goods; then the fact that he grew above the dimensions of man, in other words man swells up through pride and pomp; and finally Potitus

intumuisse, postremo divitiis et opum copia in belluas nostros supremos clericos verti vidit.

49   Id itaque fantasma, facto sibi crucis signo, profugavit Potitus; dehinc e silva ipsa Epiri in propinquam urbem descendit, qua Agathonis senatoris uxor, ut supra diximus, lepra laborabat. Ad huius senatoris edes cum accessisset, Potitus elemosinam dari petiit.

50 Aderat illic eunuchus, cui nomen Jacinto. Is Potiti ingenuam indolem diu conspicatus:

Hen adolescens, inquit, ni fallor, haud humili loco te genitum esse declaras: queso isthac cum indole et etate quid vivendi turpitudo hec commune habet, vel quid eo dici pot-

51 est turpius qui sibi instituerit omnino alieno vivere? Tibi vires, tibi industriam esse existimo; an desunt artes, an desunt apud quos honestius divertas? Videsne me abiectis ex parentibus ruri natum, tam honeste cum his maioribus vi-

52 tam ducere? Vestitus, victus non deficit. Unum cognosco patronum, non ut errones universam urbem. Cum desit aliquid, uni supplico, et ei quidem qui virtute, nobilitate omnique in re sit mihi anteponendus. Tu a quoquo etsi infimo

53 exoras; nullus te quidem, dum id sequaris, miserior est. Indoleo tibi, adolescens. Te indignam rem facis ni ab hac te miseria eripis, quam rem ut facias te et hortor et moneo. Facile invenies qui te suscipiat, quin immo, si velis, dabo ipse operam ut pari fortuna fruaris qua ipsi fruimur: dominum conveniam; est enim ille humanissimus, scio, non recusabit tibi aliquod in domo servitium impartiri.

saw our best clerics being turned into wild beasts through wealth
and the abundance of riches.

Thus Potitus, after making the sign of the cross, put this phan-   49
tom to flight; afterward he descended from the woods of Epirus to
the nearby city where the wife of Agathon the senator, as was said
above, was suffering from leprosy. Once he got to the senator's
house, Potitus asked to be given alms. There was at the door a   50
eunuch whose name was Jacintus. This man, after contemplating
Potitus' unblemished character for a long time, said:

Young man, listen, unless I am mistaken, your looks proclaim that you were born not of humble stock: pray, tell me
what has this disgraceful way of life got in common with
your character and age, or what could be more demeaning
than a man who has decided to live completely dependent on
someone else? I think you possess both strength and dili-   51
gence; do you lack any artistic skills or do you not have any
people with whom you could stay in a more honest fashion?
Do you see that I, born in the countryside from lowly
parents, am living so honestly with these wealthy people?
Clothes and food are in good supply. I recognize just one   52
lord, not like beggars who beg from the whole city. When I
lack something, I beg from one man, and he is someone who
is above me in virtue, nobility and all other things. You plead
for things from anyone no matter how low; while you follow
this way of life, there is nobody who is more miserable than
you. I feel sorry for you, young man. You will be doing some-   53
thing unworthy unless you escape this poverty, and I warn
you and indeed encourage you to do so. You will easily find
someone who will take you in; why I myself, if you want,
will see to it that you enjoy the same fortune as we do: I will
go to my lord, for he is very humane, I know, and he will
certainly let you play some role of service in the house.

54 Jacinto surridens Potitus inquit:

O quam honestius servires tu homo, si tibi hunc velles esse dominum cui ego servio, cui quidem qui servit imperat. Ipse enim est unicus Regum Rex vel potius deorum deus, eius regnum minime caducum, minime fragile, ut nostra hec mundi regna, non est limitibus ullis aut temporibus prefini-
55 tum. Queso, amice, qualem existimas, cui qui serviunt, ea possunt, que nulla hominum manus, ars aut ingenium potest? Fuere eius servi qui incurabiles valetudines, lepram, cecos, mancos sanarint atque restaurarint, quin etiam mortuos in lucem excitarint.

56 Denique his ac plerisque aliis verbis docuit Jacintum se Christi servum esse. Jacintus vero, quoniam tale genus hominum proxima superiori etate per universum orbem non obscurum fuisse audierat, non ideo destitit Potitum adolescentem ad leprosam dominam conducere, multa de prudentia adolescentis, que in superiori ser-
57 mone audisset referens. Leprosa autem, ut est valetudinarium animus credulus, omnia experiri, conducere arbitrabatur. Eam ob rem rogat sibi ad sanitatem queque possit ut conferat. Tum ille:

58 Scito, inquit, mulier, te sanari posse modo in deum Jhesum credere eiusque nomine baptizari velis. Potest enim baptisma non solum corporis, verum etiam animi morbos abstergere. Audisti Silvestrum episcopum Christi servum qua ex infirmitate solo baptismate Constantinum sanarit. Id ipsum in te

Smiling at Jacintus, Potitus replied: 54

Oh, how much more honest would your service be if you
wanted to have as your lord the master whom I serve, for the
person who serves Him actually rules. For He is the only
king of kings or rather the god of gods; his kingdom will
never fall, never be fragile, like the kingdoms of our world,
nor is it bound by either geographical or temporal limits. I   55
beg you, my friend, how great do you think He is whose
servants can do things which no hand or art or genius of
man can do?[16] There have been servants of his who have
healed and restored to health the incurably ill, lepers, the
blind, the lame, and have even brought the dead back to the
light of the world.

Finally, with these and many other words Potitus taught Jacin-   56
tus that he was the servant of Christ. Since Jacintus had heard
that men of this kind had become well known in the world some
time before, he did not fail to lead the young Potitus to his mis-
tress who was suffering from leprosy, telling her much about the
youth's wisdom which he had witnessed in the previous conversation. Since the minds of the sick are credulous, the woman suffer-   57
ing from leprosy was willing to try anything if she thought it
would do her good. For that reason, she asked him to do whatever
he could to restore her to health. Then Potitus said:

Woman, you must know that you can be healed only if you   58
believe in our Lord Jesus Christ and if you are willing to be
baptized in his name. For baptism can cleanse not only the
sickness of the body but also diseases of the mind. You heard
of what illness Pope Sylvester, the bishop of Christ, healed
the emperor Constantine simply by baptizing him.[17] You
must believe that the same sacrament of God can have the

dei sacramentum posse existima. Crede mulier; si credideris, salva eris.

59 His addidit non modicas alias ad persuadendum rationes atque exempla. Quo factum est ut credens mulier multa cum fide et veneratione baptismatis sacramento lavari pateretur, pristine incolumitati restitueretur.

60 Eius facti fama iam per universam urbem vulgata erat. Agathonis domus et fere dimidia urbs Christi religione imbuti Potiti sanctitatem summis laudibus extollebant. Erat adolescens in ore, in oculis omni populo. At vero ille nihil minus facere quam inani

61 glorie aurem prebere. Igitur, plebis mugitum, gloriam, monstrum scilicet illud a se fugare instituit. Ergo in nemus inque solitudinem refugit, quo ex loco cum omne tempus ieiuniis et orationibus conterens ita demonis illusiones, mundi gloriam sperneret, ut in eum cuncte demonis vires essent vacue, rursus novam diabolus

62 rationem invenit seducendi puberis. Nam in Antonini imperatoris filiam ingressus miserandum in modum illam vexabat. Cum vero a magicis ex omni provincia accitis rogaretur quam ingrediendi causam habuisset cur nollet cedere, nihil ille plus responsi dabat quam

63 se id Potiti adolescentis iussu facturum. Ego demonem cupivisse arbitror certiorem facere Antoninum imperatorem esse Potitum christianum, quos ille homines capitali odio prosequebatur, cupivisse etiam eo pacto plebi persuaderi, quod per religionem Christi

64 servi facerent, id malis artibus fieri. Adde his existimasse fortassis demonem nequire Potitum per teneros etatis annos cruciatus et mortis metum ferre, quamquam strenuo animo reliqua omnia perpessus fuisset.

same power in you. Woman, believe; if you believe, you will be saved.

To these he added many other arguments and examples to persuade her. That was how this woman came to believe and with great faith and veneration allowed herself to be cleansed by the sacrament of baptism and restored to her former health.

The fame of this event had now spread throughout the whole city. Agathon's household and almost half of the city had become imbued with the Christian religion, extolling Potitus' sanctity with the utmost praise. The young man was on everyone's tongue and in the eyes of the whole populace. But he would do anything rather than lend his ear to the sound of vainglory. So he decided to cut himself off from the roar of the people, the noise of fame— in other words that monster. He fled from the town to a lonely grove, where he spent all his time in fasting and prayer, and since he spurned the illusion of the devil that was worldly fame, all Satan's strength was powerless against him, but the devil found a new way to try to seduce the youth. For he had entered into Emperor Antoninus' daughter and was tormenting her horribly. But when the devil was asked by the magicians, who had been summoned from the whole province, why he had entered this girl and would not give up, the only answer he gave was that he would do so only on the orders of young Potitus. I believe that Satan wanted to let Antoninus know that Potitus was one of the Christians, whom the emperor pursued with deadly hatred, and I think that the devil also wanted to persuade the populace in this way that what the Christians did as servants of Christ was actually being done by evil arts. In addition to this, the devil perhaps believed that because of his tender years Potitus would be unable to bear torture and the fear of death, even though he had suffered all the other torments with a constant mind.

65   Itaque iussu Antonini Gelasius preses cum L commilitonibus
ad Potitum accessit quo loci per demones commorari adolescentem
intellexerat. Iam enim propius accedenti Gelasio obviam fiunt ferarum caterve in aciem disposite non secus ac pro adolescentis salute
66   dimicature, cum quo quidem plurimum consueverant. Hoc spectaculo primum timuere milites; dehinc magorum ostentationes pu-
tarunt; postremo cum venientem Potitum ac pacem feris impe-
rantem viderunt nullo vestium ornamento, sola paupertate, sola
verecundia atque mansuetudine ornatissimum, subito sunt in ve-
67   nerationem versi eorum animi. Dehinc exponunt veniendi causas,
referunt Antonini precepta. Que Potitus cum diaboli ductus esse
atque fraudem presentiret, non nihil recusavit, narrans gentiles per
Christi servos multa vidisse miracula, duri cordis homines tardos
ad credendum obstinatos in erroribus, frustra idcirco se accessu-
68   rum edicebat. Hec Potiti verba Gelasius, natura superbus, ingenio
militari insolens, impatiens, graviter ferre, precipere audentius reli-
gare adolescentem atque ad Antoninum adducere.
69   Cum igitur ad Antoninum pervenisset, bonis verbis acceptus
est. Multa quidem de Potiti fama que audisset rettulit; cupere
enim se adolescenti meliorem esse fortunam ac libenter illum in
amicitiam accepturum; sic autem solere quos diligat ornare divitiis
et dignitate ut nulli equalium invideant; paratam adolescenti fortunam non minimam, ut eam capescat precari; unum esse in
70   quo Potiti officium requirat: ut filia libera sit demone. Potitus id
sua in potestate haud fore respondit; dei Jhesu arbitrio et nomine

So on Antoninus' orders the military commander Gelasius, 65
along with fifty fellow soldiers, went to Potitus in the place where,
thanks to demons, he had found out the young man was dwelling.
And now as Gelasius was approaching, packs of wild beasts,
ranged in battle order, advanced to meet him as though they were
going to fight for the safety of the young man with whom these
animals had become very friendly. At this sight the soldiers were 66
initially very afraid; then they decided this was an illusion created
by magicians; and finally, when they saw Potitus with no orna-
mental garments, adorned only with his poverty, modesty and
gentleness, approaching and ordering the animals to be peaceful,
their minds were suddenly filled with veneration. After this, they 67
explained why they had come and told him about Antoninus' orders. Potitus felt that these were the maneuvers and deceptions of
the devil, and he initially resisted, saying that pagans had seen
many miracles performed by Christ's servants, but that they were
hard-hearted men who were slow to believe and obstinate in their
errors. As a result, he said it would be pointless for him to go with
them. When he heard Potitus' words, Gelasius, who was arrogant 68
by nature, and through his military training was also insolent and
impatient, took it badly and boldly ordered his men to tie up the
young man and take him to Antoninus.

When he came in front of Antoninus, Potitus was greeted with 69
kind words. The emperor told him many of the things he had
heard about Potitus' fame; he wanted the young man to enjoy better fortune and would willingly accept him into his friendship; this
was what he usually did with those he loved, showering them with
wealth and honors so that they did not envy any of their rivals;
he had prepared for the young man a considerable fortune and
begged him to accept it; there was just one thing where he required Potitus' help, namely that his daughter be freed from the
devil.[18] Potitus replied that this was not within his powers; that 70
through the will and name of Christ the devil would give up,

71 cessurum demonem, modo apud Antoninum Christi nomen plus quam hactenus valeat; sese libenter apud deum fore interpetrem; cuncta ex dei pietate speranda; in eo fidendum neque expectanda pro beneficiis ulla rerum caducarum premia; unum esse quod egregie cuperet, Antoninum et filiam in Christum deum credere, quandoquidem videre liceat Christi nomen esse supra omne nomen Christique servum posse quod omnes Antonini dii nequiverint.

72 His quamquam verbis subirritaretur Antoninus odioque in adolescentem afficeretur, nam Christi nomine nihil erat Antonino molestius, tamen quo magis cupiebat filiam liberari eo iracundiam altius animo comprimebat. Adductam deinde puellam Christi auxilio inpetrato eam alapa Potitus percussit, ex qua demon e vestigio in draconis formam evolavit. Hoc manifestissimum dei ministerium videntes qui non pauci aderant palam Christi religionem

73 admirabantur. Erat vero id imperatori perspicienti gravissimum. Idcirco ne facile crederent, multa se talia vidisse enumerabat per magos pulchrius facta, esse id quidem artis, non religionis; commentum enim hoc religionis ab scurris vilissimisque Christianis inventum quo malas artes obtegant ac plus admirationis in populo assequantur.

74 Proxime convitiis in adolescentem invehebatur: perditum genus vite, siqui⟨dem⟩ furtis et nefariis rebus illam Potiti artem esse accommodatam; solere has magorum artes inter virum et uxorem, inter fratres interque amicissimos inimicitiam gignere, inter alienissimos vincula amoris turpissima iacere; et his similia referebat,

provided only that Christ's name was more highly considered by
Antoninus than hitherto. Potitus said he would gladly intercede   71
with God, since everything could be hoped for from God's mercy;
he had to trust in Him, and not hope for any ephemeral rewards
for good deeds done; there was one thing that he dearly desired,
namely that Antoninus and his daughter should believe in Christ
as God, since it was clear that Christ's name was above all other
names, and Christ's servant could do what all Antoninus' gods
could not achieve.

The emperor was somewhat irritated by these words, and was   72
overcome by hatred for the young man, for nothing was more
hateful to him than the name of Christ; nevertheless the more he
wanted his daughter to be free of the devil, the more he suppressed his anger deeper in his heart. Then the girl was brought
before them and, having obtained the aid of Christ, Potitus
slapped her with his hand, at which the devil immediately flew out
of her, taking the shape of a dragon. There were quite a lot of by-
standers and when they saw the evident ministry of God at work,
they openly expressed their admiration for the Christian religion.
But this was something the emperor took very badly as he looked   73
on. So in order that they should not easily believe what they saw,
he listed many such displays performed even more convincingly by
magi, saying it was something that belonged to an art, not religion,
that this religious trickery had been invented by those scoundrels
and vile people, the Christians, in order to conceal their evil arts
and to acquire greater admiration among the people.

Next he inveighed against the young man with insults: he said   74
Potitus was leading a wicked life, since his art was conducive to
theft and other evil deeds. The emperor added that these magic
arts usually spawned enmity between a man and his wife, between brothers and between those that were the best of friends,
and conversely produced disgraceful bonds of love between those
who were bitterest enemies. And he added further accusations of

cum adolescens multa mansuetudine respondebat omnia refellens: semper Christum deum id posse, id egisse, quod viderit, neque esse malas artes que bene hominum animos instituant dicebat; 75 proxime de Christi religione disserebat. Sed imperator quo pluries Christi nomen commemorabatur eo vehementius excandescebat:

Quem mihi Christum?, aiebat, quem Jhesum? quas morum novas philosophias? non desines confabulari, porro ito, sacrificato diis patriis. Sat philosophatum est; abigite; pestis hunc tenet.

76 O quam maior pestis illos habet, Antonine, qui iracundiam et iniustitiam secuntur, inquit Potitus. Etenim qui ceteris imperant, sibi quoque imperent necesse est. Seda iracundiam, Antonine; pone odia. Nam cum cetera omnia vitia turpia, tum est maxime iracundia in principe detestanda. Habe gratias Christo deo Jhesu; non sit tibi grave Christi nomen, cuius benefitiam expertus sis, cuius etiam pietatem in dies perspicies.

77 Iterum acclamante Antonino, qui miraculo usque obstupuerant ac reverentia tenebantur puerum tandem rapiunt, orant saluti sue consulat. Nichil ille minus. Ceditur igitur iussu Antonini quam crudelissime fustibus. At dum inter vapulandum iterato ab Antonino rogaretur deorum templa adire mallet quam cedi, Potitus et mente et vultu inmutato non secus atque verbera nullum

this kind, while the young man replied with great gentleness, refuting everything the emperor said. Potitus stated that Christ the Lord was always able to do what the emperor had witnessed, that he had done so on this occasion, and that arts which instructed human minds to do good could not be evil. Then he began to discourse on the Christian religion. But the more he mentioned Christ's name, the more the emperor flew into a violent rage, saying: 75

> Who is this Christ you talk about? Who is this Jesus? What new philosophies of ethics are these? You refuse to stop talking about this, so go now, make sacrifice to the gods of the fatherland. You have philosophized enough; lead him away; he is seized by some terrible sickness.

Potitus replied,   76

> Antoninus, how much more serious is the plague that takes hold of those who are in thrall to anger and injustice; for those who rule over others must also rule themselves. Calm your anger, Antoninus; set aside your hatred. For although all other faults are repellent, anger in a prince is most to be detested. Give thanks to Christ Jesus our Lord; do not let Christ's name be intolerable to you, since you have experienced his benefits, and you will perceive his mercy in the coming days.

But when Antoninus cried out against him once more, those   77 who had been stupefied at the miracle and had been seized with reverence for it, finally grabbed hold of the boy, and begged him to think of his safety. But he thought of anything but that. Thus, on Antoninus' orders the young man was beaten very cruelly with sticks. And while he was being beaten, he was once again asked by the emperor if he preferred to go to the temple of the gods rather than be beaten, but Potitus never altered his mind or his face, as if dolorem intulissent: 'Visne tandem,' inquit, 'deorum tuorum aras aggrediamur? Pareo.'

78   Ergo itur ad templa; proficiscentem puerum hominum fere duo et decem milia comitabantur cupidissimi cum Potitum tum eius miracula visendi. Subit templum Antoninus, deos adit, maximas illis habere gratias dicit ubi obstinatum adolescentem sua cum

79   magia et demone traxerit. Post eum ingressus Potitus Antoninum obstinatum demone captum ostendit, non se. Nam se introeunte omnia deorum simulacra putrefacta et in pulverem collapsa sunt. Hoc spectaculo maiorem in modum mota plebs non tuto succensere imperatorem adolescenti vociferabat, apud quem vel dei vel demonis potestas esset. Nonnulli preterea movebantur oratione adolescentis multa et preclara de dei potentia, de vana gentilium superstitione disserentis.

80   Videns perinde Antoninus passim Potito plebem assentiri, utilius censuit ex hominum oculis exque surgentibus iam iam ad credendum animis adolescentem eripere. Iubet idcirco catenas ponderis maximi Potiti collo alligari, deportari, carcere observari, consignari; talique fortassis oratione ad populum usus est:

81   Etsi nonnullos vestrum, cives, ut quisque pietate et misericordia preditus est commotos esse prospiciam, non tamen verebor hoc ipso tempore apud vos de vestris commodis agere. Satis enim apud vos auctoritate et gratia valere semper Antoni⟨n⟩um intellexi, et perspicuum quidem cum ceteris temporibus fuerit, tum maxime hodierno die vobis, apertissimum esse cupio me pro vostra omnium salute advigilare.

82   Sitis idcirco animis in me facillimis; audite attente que de

the beatings had not inflicted any pain. He said: "Do you now want us to advance on the altars of your gods? I shall obey."

So they went to the temple; as the young man set out, about 78 twelve thousand men accompanied him, very eager to see both Potitus and his miracles. Antoninus went into the temple, approached the altars, and when he had dragged the obstinate youth there with his magic and devils, said he was very thankful to the gods. After this, Potitus went in and showed that it was Antoni- 79 nus, not himself, who was obstinate and possessed by a devil. For as the young man entered, all the statues of the gods crumbled and collapsed into dust. Seeing this spectacle, the people were even more moved and shouted that it was not safe for the emperor to get angry with the young man, since he clearly had the power of a god or the devil. In addition, many were moved by the young man's speech, in which he had mentioned many famous things about the power of God and the vain superstitions of the pagans.

When Antoninus saw that the common people everywhere 80 were being persuaded by Potitus, he thought it better to snatch the young man away from men's eyes and from their minds, which were now inclined to believe him. He therefore ordered chains of maximum weight to be placed around Potitus' neck, commanded that he be led away, kept under surveillance in prison, and bound over; and he addressed the people in a speech that sounded perhaps like this:[19]

Even though I see some of you citizens moved, according to 81 the levels of pity and mercy that each one of us is endowed with, I will not be afraid at this very time to discuss the things that are best for you. I have realized that I, Antoni- nus, have always enjoyed considerable authority and favor from you, and I want it to be very clear that both in other times and especially today I am being vigilant for your safety. So please be accommodating to me; listen carefully to what I 82

horum Christianorum disciplina et genere referam, quos diis genitos imperiti arbitrantur. Ostendam vobis quo instituto hoc hominum genus per orbem discursitet; proxime videbitis quid de novis religionibus censeam.

83 Dico igitur, posteaquam attente que ad vostram salutem attinent vos velle audire prospicio, nullum esse genus hominum abiectius quam eorum, qui omnem vitam otiosam sive industria sive opere ducere constituerint, qui bonas artes, qui rem militarem, qui litteras, qui omne denique reliquum vite 84 ornamentum effugiant, vilipendant, oderint. Hos ipsos esse Christianos scitote abiectissimum hominum genus, desidiosum, ignavum, supinum, nullos labores, nullas artes sectari, nullam civilem disciplinam subire, otio, solitudine, somno languescere didicerunt. Sed huius rei nullos alios testes quam 85 vos ipsos cupio; perspicite ipsi quam vitam ducant. An est vestrum qui illos videat ullis bonis aut publicis aut privatis negotiis operam dare, qui illos armis asciscere, in publicis contionibus esse aut rei publice consulere videat, vel qui verbis, industria aut manu aliqua patriam iuvare uspiam viderit?

86 In abditis congruunt, et quam sibi fortunam eorum ignavia ac inertia turpissimam vilissimamque dedit, hanc magnifice laudant; omnibus rebus dum indigent, pre omnibus se fortunatos dicunt. Per silvas passim aberrant ferarum more, aut per casulas ut fures latitant, hominum cetus omnino fugiunt, et si ob famem quidem ac squalorem sordidissimi ipso aspectu sint, obsceniorem tamen habere animum videntur.

87 Et enim hos, qui talem vitam ducant, nonne tanta vecordia, pigritia notatos esse oportet, ut hominum conspectum merito fugiant, vel etiamne eos tanta immanitate, tantis vitiis abundare oportet ut universo hominum generi se invisos

say about the discipline of these Christians and about what kind of people they are, who are thought by the inexperienced to be descended from gods. I will show you for what purpose these kinds of people roam through the world; after that you will see what I think about new religions.

I say, therefore, observing how you want to listen carefully   83 to those things that concern your wellbeing, that there is no people on earth more abject than those who have decided to live all their life in leisure, rejecting both diligence and hard work. They shun, think little of and even hate military duty, literary study, and any ornamentation of life. You must real-   84 ize that these same Christians are the most worthless race of men: they are lazy, idle, supine; they pursue no labor nor arts, undergo no civic discipline, but have learned to languish in idleness, solitude and sleep. But of this fact I want only you to be witnesses; you see yourselves what kind of life they lead. Is there any among you who sees them working in any   85 public or private affairs, enlisting in the army, making any public speeches or offering advice to the state, or has anyone ever seen them benefiting their fatherland with their words, hard work, or help? They gather together in secret and   86 praise inordinately the most shameful and vile fortune that their laziness and inertia has given them; although they have no material goods, they say they are the most fortunate of men. They wander throughout the woods like packs of wild animals, or hide in huts like thieves; they totally shun all classes of men, and although because of hunger and squalor they are totally sordid to look at, they actually seem to pos- sess an even more obscene mind. For surely people who lead   87 such lives should be blamed for being so foolish and lazy that they rightly avoid the sight of their fellow men, or surely they must abound in such inhumanity and vice that they consider themselves hated by the whole of the human race?

arbitre⟨n⟩tur? Aliter vero cur solitudinem tantopere queritent minime vos intelligere arbitror. At illi dum rogantur se
dicunt suis artibus operam dare, vos reliquos, qui ex labore,
ex industria vivitis, dicunt insanire. Denique que istorum
erit ars? Nempe demonibus imperare, iuventutem seducere,
88   tuto in solitudine, in vitiis esse. O bonas artes. Hen religionem. Colite hos sanctos viros!

   Existimate, cives, me quo vestris pro commodis plurimum
vigilo eo diligentissime ceterorum et maxime huius adolescentis vitam perquisisse. Natus is quidem Serdica urbe claris
parentibus, locupletissimis atque honestissimis civibus. Cum
patre tamen, cui unicus erat filius, a prima ipsa adolescentia
ita vixit ut a patre ob eius vitia repudiatus fuerit. Hen
qualem putatis adolescentem, quibus vitiis abundare, qualem
futurum si vixerit, quem optimus pater omnino alienum
89   immo inimicissimum iudicarit, in exilium pepulerit? Im-
pudicus igitur adolescens cum patris fortune suis lasciviis
minime suppeditarent, ad Christianos, vitiosorum recepta-
culum, vitiorum officinas, accessit, apud quos nihil defuit
quod ad animi sordes contrahendas pertineret. Verum quis
enumerabit in tanto honestissimorum hominum cetu extrema vitia, supremas libidines, nefaria scelera, que Christianos perpetrari adolescens ipse fatetur? Adde his accommodatam turpitudini solitudinem.

90   Sed pudet mehercle recensere que illi impudicissime faciunt, de re enim turpi et scelerata prolixius loqui pudore
prohibeor. Summam esse hanc scitote, Christianos omnibus

Otherwise, I do not think you understand why they seek out solitude so much. When they are asked, they say that they do so in order to devote themselves to their arts, and say that the rest of you who live by your labor and industry are mad. But then what is the art of these people? Clearly to command devils, seduce our youth, to live safely in solitude and vice. What wonderful arts! What a religion! You must worship such holy men as these! 88

Citizens, you have to realize that I who am constantly vigilant for you have thoroughly investigated the lives led by the rest of them and particularly by this young man. He was born in the city of Sofia, of famous parents, of wealthy and very honest citizens. He was his father's only son, but from early adolescence he lived with him in such a way that he was rejected by his father because of his vices. Look, what kind of a young man do you think this is, how many vices does he wallow in, what will he be like if he lives, when his excellent father judged him to be thoroughly alien, or rather a total enemy, and thrust him into exile? So, since his father's wealth did not suffice to procure him his lascivious pleasures, this shameless adolescent went to the Christian community, that receptacle of wicked men and breeding ground of vices; with these men there was everything necessary for defiling the mind. But who among you in this huge crowd of very honest men, will list the extreme vices, the utmost lust, the wicked crimes that this young man himself admits that the Christians perpetrate? Add to this the fact that remote solitude is most conducive to vice. 89

Heavens above! I am ashamed to go into detail about what these most shameless men do, for I am forbidden by modesty to speak at length about something so corrupt and wicked. You should know that this is how things stand: that Christians are covered in all sorts of vices, they are extremely 90

vitiis cohopertos, sordidissimos, inquinatissimosque esse, detestandam nefariamque vitam extra homines sine interpetre ducere. Illic ieiuniis, paupertate hisque talibus ineptiis, suo deo servire se confabulantur. Etenim succedit res. Quidni? Quippe cum deum adventitium stupris, furtis, latibulis, scelere cognoscere nullus libenter optat; at si qui congruunt, perditissimi quoque illi sint necesse est: postremo diis volentibus ex colluvione in publicum exeunt instructi temeritate et audacia loquendi, longum de deo commentum apud vetulas, rusticos, atque imperitos decantant, de moribus, honestate atque omni pietate accuratissime disserentes: inhonestissimi impiissimique ipsi usque adeo sunt, ut nullum avaritie, nullum turpitudinis genus inveniri aut fingi possit, quod ipsum in illis non magnifice sedeat: de virtute itaque aliud opere sentiunt quam verbis loquantur.

Ridiculum mehercle quo eorum verba diffunduntur. Non enim celum, non omnes dii, non orbis terre satis illis ad loquendum videtur, quin etiam ad inferos quoque usque suis fabulis condescendunt; de inferum natura, officio ac regionibus, Superi boni, quam inaudita et terribilia locuntur; denique tametsi pregrandibus verborum ostentis omnes poetas exsuperent, non tamen verentur aperta et inverecunda fronte omnia pro veris asserere. Quae res cum parum successent— non enim ita stulti omnes sumus—itur ad magicas artes, demonem ingredi et egredi suo arbitratu ostendunt, ad multas ostentationes, illusiones, ad multa scelera demonum commercio utuntur. Ac ne tales eorum artes detestabiles abominentur, deum novissimum conflarunt, cuius nomine pietatem coli iubent, publicam amicitiam servari, vitiis

sordid and polluted; without witnesses they lead a detestable, evil existence cut off from the society of other men. There, they say, they worship their God in abstinence and poverty and other such foolish things. This really happens. Why not? Clearly nobody would want to know about a foreign god through tales of rape, robbery, concealment and crime, though if they do, obviously they too must be very wicked. In the end, with the will of the gods, they leave their den of filth and go about in public, trained through their boldness and rashness of speech to recount many lies about their God to old women, country folk, and the inexperienced, although accurately discussing morals, honesty and all kinds of piety. However, they themselves are so dishonest and impious, that no form of avarice or disgraceful behavior can be found or imagined that does not reside spectacularly in them: so they regard virtue differently in deed compared to what they say about it in words.

My goodness, it is ridiculous the way they exaggerate when they speak. The heavens, all the gods, the world itself seem not to be enough for them to talk about; they actually descend to the underworld with their tales. Gods above, what unheard of and terrible things they say about the nature, role and regions of the underworld; lastly, even though they outdo all poets in their extraordinary displays of words,[20] still they are not afraid to assert openly and shamelessly that all these things are true. But since such things will not come to pass—we are not all so stupid—they resort to magic arts, they show that the devil enters and leaves people at their behest, they use their business with devils to organize many displays, illusions and crimes. And so as not to have such hateful arts abhorred by everyone, they have fabricated a totally new God, in whose name they order piety to be cultivated, public friendship to be conserved, and vice to

abstineri; his denique bonis dictis quam sua multa mala facinora obtegere conentur non facile dixerim. Hac paupertatis
professione nebulones quantas imperitorum fortunas dissi-
pant, funditus exedunt! Ut his quoque figmentis homines
capiant, bona extorqueant, quid non pollicentur? Celos do-
nant, stellas, solem ipsum; nam ultra celos etiam possidere
impurissimi narrant.

Sed de scelestissima Christianorum vita satis dictum sit.
Quantum autem rei publice noceat novas religiones admit-
tere apertissime videbitis, cives, si memineritis quantus apud
maiores religionis honos sempiterne sit habitus, qui quidem
viri sine auspiciis, sine religione publica, omnia salutaria minime arbitrabantur. Et erant sane graves et docti, prudentia,
industria rerumque memoria pene divini, sed postponendas
hominum opiniones deorum optimorum consultis et religioni existimabant. An id sine maxima causa a prudentis-
simis illis factum putatis? An ita inconsultos illos fuisse
iudicatis, qui de diis leges promulgarunt, ut sunt fortassis
plerique nostrum? Nonne vetustissima est in urbe lex nullos
posse deos novos admitti nisi quos senatus decreto et sententia publice approbasset? Nonne Marco Emilio principi
sapientissimo, cum Albuernium deum in urbem detulit, senatus auctoritas longum exoranda fuit? Quid secundo bello
punico? Quam acerbissimis edictis novam surgentem religionem extinxere! Quid de Tiberio referam, rerum domino;
nonne cupienti sibi Pilati amicissimi persuasionibus hunc
ipsum Christum in nostra urbe venerari sapientissime,

be avoided; finally, it is not easy to say how many evil deeds
they try to cover up with these fine words. How many are   94
the fortunes of the gullible that are dissipated, totally eaten
up by these cheats despite all this profession of poverty.
What do they not promise in order to take men in with
these figments, and extort their goods from them? They
promise the heavens, the stars, the sun itself, for these most
polluted people claim they own things beyond the heavens.

But we have said enough about the Christians' abominable way of life. You will see very clearly, citizens, how much   95
it damages the state to admit new cults, if you remember
how much the honor of religion has always been important
to our ancestors, men who believed nothing would be safe
without auspices and without public religion. And these
were surely very serious and learned men, almost divine in
their prudence, diligence and memory of history, yet they felt
that the opinions of men should not be placed above the
decisions and religion of the most benign gods. Do you   96
think that this was done by these most prudent of men
without a serious reason? Do you judge them to have been
as ill-advised as most of us are today, when they were the
ones who promulgated the laws about the gods? Is there not
a very ancient law in the city that states that no new gods
can be admitted except those approved by the senate's decree
and public proclamation? Was it not the case that Marcus   97
Aemilius, a very wise leader, had to make a lengthy plea for
the permission of the senate when he brought the god Alburnus into the city? What about during the Second Punic
War? How ferocious were the edicts that extinguished the
new religion? What shall I say about Tiberius, emperor of
the world? Was it not the case that the authority of the senate very wisely, prudently and strongly objected to the worship of this same man Christ in Rome, even though Tiberius

prudentissime fortissimeque obstitit senatus auctoritas?
98 Prudenter id quidem, nam facile rerum novitates sequitur
multitudo, facile seducitur. Verum paucorum hominum temeritate uno aut altero deorum leso, nonne sepe publico
luctu et calamitate universa civitas pependit?

Quid expectatis igitur, cives, ubi hominum numerus deos
patrios spernet, ubi novos demonum ritus superinduxerit?
99 Cavete per deos immortales vetustissimam, sanctissimam ap-
probatissimamque patrum nostrorum religionem fastidire,
deos ledere, vestram iuventutem malis artibus assuefacere.
Mementote bonis disciplinis, non otio et solitudine aut ignavia, sed armis, industria, sudoribus excrevisse orbis impe-
100 rium. Timete postremo deorum iram, vindictam, fulmina.
Existimate me pro vestra omnium salute et gloria advigilare;
ergo parete paternis Antonini consiliis; date operam, vos
Quirites, ut quos nulla exterarum gentium arma, virtus,
multitudo aut bellorum ordo devicerit, ne vos eos Christianorum otia, inertia, fraus decipiant.

101 Hac proterva et stultissima oratione plebs cum in Christi nomen, tum maxime in Potitum odio affecti imperatori palam assentiri, cruciandum, necandum adolescentem profiteri ceperant. Nactus idcirco occasionem qua a Christi religione plebem si parum
oratione divertisset eam atrocissime pene exemplo perterrefaceret,
confestim per precones pronuntiat in amphitheatrum contionem
cogendam, illuc perducendum maleficum iussu populi ultimo

wanted it, thanks to the advice of his close friend Pilate?[21]
Those were prudent actions, for the people easily follow and   98
are seduced by new phenomena. Furthermore, is it not the
case that the whole city has often paid with public disaster
and mourning for the rashness of a few men, or the injuries
done to one or two gods?

What are you waiting for, citizens, when a handful of
men now reject the gods of the fatherland and have brought
in new devilish rites? By the immortal gods, be careful not to   99
spurn the ancient, hallowed religion sanctioned by our fathers, not to hurt the gods, not to make your young people
accustomed to wicked arts! Remember that it was through
good disciplines and not through leisure, solitude and laziness, but through arms, industry and sweat that our rule
over the world expanded. Lastly, be afraid of the anger of the   100
gods, their revenge, their thunderbolts. Bear in mind that I
am ever vigilant for the safety and glory of all of you; so obey
the fatherly advice of Antoninus: Roman citizens, make sure
that those who have not been conquered by the arms,
strength, numbers and order of battle of any external nation,
are not now deceived by the leisure, inertia and fraud of the
Christians.

This arrogant and extremely stupid oration filled the people   101
with hatred both for Christ's name and especially for Potitus: they
openly agreed with the emperor and began to proclaim that the
young man should be tortured and killed. Seizing this opportunity, Antoninus thought that if he had not managed to divert the
common people from the Christian religion through his speech, he
could terrify them by an example of atrocious punishment. The
emperor immediately sent out his heralds to make everyone go to
the amphitheater for an assembly, and ordered that the evildoer
be led there and be punished with the maximum penalty at the

supplicio puniendum. Itur itaque tota ex urbe ad amphitheatrum.
102 Convolant ad Potitum educendum lictores non pauci. Cum autem
ceras et signa integra clausasque carceris valvas comperissent,
aperto carcere, magno impetu corruentes odorata omnia et collus-
trantia comperierunt atque adolescentem catenis liberum intrepide
perambulantem viderunt; paululum idcirco sese continuere. Et
quamquam non hominum manu sed dei iussu catenas discussas
manifestissime intelligerent, nihilo tamen segnius imperatoris iussa
103 execuntur. In amphitheatrum igitur ante tribunal Potitum statuunt, quo loci lex talis indicta est.

> LEX: Deos patrios, Jovem, Phebum, Minervam omnisque
> reliquos, quibus maiores nostri templa, aras publicosque
> honores dedicarunt, vetere urbis ritu publice colito, illis con-
> sueta sacrificia facito. Qui secus faxit, qui repugnet, qui in-
> ficietur capite plectuntor.

104 Accepta igitur lege, negantem id deberi, id velle, Potitum carnifices
appendunt, lampadas facesque ardentes hinc et hinc subigunt, se-
viunt crudelitate atque ira. Non enim sat pene videbatur flammis
tenerum adolescentem urere, quin etiam ungues quoque pedum ac
manuum extirpabant, dislacerabant. Dehinc ubi tantum ira et
ignibus sevissent ut nihil plus ad immanitatem addi posse videre-
105 tur, bestiis adustum adolescentem tradunt. O spectaculum admira-
bile! O preclarum documentum in ferocissimis teterrimisque bel-
luis minus esse crudelitatis quam in ingeniis hominum! Nulla
quidem ferarum innocentem adolescentem non venerari visa est,

command of the people. So from all over the whole city everyone
went off to the amphitheater. Many lictors then rushed to take   102
Potitus from prison. But when they found the wax and seals on
the door unopened and the hinges of the prison door still closed,
they opened the prison and, rushing inside in a great crowd, they
found everything perfumed and shining, and they saw the young
man free of his chains walking about fearlessly. At this they stood
still for a moment. And although they saw very clearly that his
chains had been torn apart not by human hands but by divine
command, nevertheless they quickly carried out the emperor's orders. They placed Potitus in the amphitheater, before the tribunal,   103
where this law was proclaimed:

> LAW: In accordance with the city's ancient ritual, you must
> publicly worship the gods of the fatherland, Jupiter, Apollo,
> Minerva and all the other gods to whom our ancestors dedi-
> cated temples, altars and public honors. Make the usual sac-
> rifices to them. Whoever does otherwise, whoever resists or
> denies this law must be subject to capital punishment.

Once this law had been approved, with Potitus denying his obliga-   104
tion or desire to observe it, the executioners hung him up, and
applied burning torches and flames to him on all sides, then mutilated him in their anger and cruelty. It was not enough punishment for them to see the young man of tender years burning at the
stake, so they also ripped the nails from his hands and feet and
tore his limbs apart.[22] Then after they had angrily tortured him
with flames to such an extent that it seemed that nothing more
could be added to this atrocity, they delivered the young man, now
severely burned, to the beasts. What an astonishing spectacle,   105
what a memorable display of the fact that there is less savagery in
the most ferocious and dangerous animals than in the minds of
men! For all the wild beasts venerated the innocent young man,

corona enim adolescentem cinxere ac spectantes quam familiarissime iacuere bellue.

106   At vero imperator, quamquam superiori crudelitate feras exsuperasset, non recte agi arbitrabatur ni quoque sese crudelitate vinceret. Igitur ex ferarum carcere Potitum educi iubet coramque membratim mutillari, frusta canibus dari. Carnifices tantus habebat ardor exequendi, ut Potitum precidere studentes gravia alter ab altero vulnera acciperet, ille integer servaretur; iterum ad crudelitatem revertentes omnibus viribus deficientibus in terram prolabarentur.

107   Populo hec intuenti multa teneri adolescentis pietas insurgebat, maior etiam in Christi religionem veneratio initiabatur, adeo ut fere duo milia hominum Christi religionem secuti sint. At imperator, ut maiori metu iam iam versos plebis animos revocaret, ferventi oleo adolescentem immergi plumbumque ignitum superfundi
108 iubet. Cum vero tantis tamque atrocissimis suppliciis posset minime adolescentem extinguere, tanta est ira commotus ut pene ad insaniam redigeretur. Iubet igitur dehinc hasta preacuta a capite ad femur usque puerum transfigi. Cumque his omnibus crudelitatibus sibi ipsi parum satisfaceret, fractus indignatione, ira, merore, unaque omnibus reliquis furiis confectus obstupuit, ac multa de utraque religione animo versans indoluit tum se frustra crudelem fuisse, tum precipue suis crudelitatibus populo credendi argu-
109 menta dedisse. Idcirco gravissimo capitis dolore procubuit.

    Hoc loco dicunt forte qua hasta transfixus erat Potitus eadem casu quodam veluti angeli manu Antonini caput fuisse collisum.

surrounded him in a circle and watching over him lay down in a very gentle manner.

But the emperor, although he had outdone the animals in his 106 previous display of cruelty, did not think it was right unless he also outdid himself in barbarity. So he ordered Potitus to be led out from the ring of beasts and to be mutilated bit by bit in his presence, and bits of him to be fed to dogs. The executioners were seized by such zeal for carrying out his order that while trying to be the first to cut pieces off Potitus, they actually wounded each other, whereas the young man remained untouched, and when they went back to their savage attack, all their strength left them and they collapsed on the ground.

When the people saw this, many were filled with great pity for 107 the young man of tender years, and even greater veneration for Christ's religion began to spread, so much so that nearly two thousand people embraced Christianity. But the emperor, seeing the people's minds turning to Christianity, decided to win them back by inculcating even greater fear in them, and ordered the young man to be immersed in burning oil and to have molten lead poured over him. When, however, despite these cruelest of pun- 108 ishments, he saw he could not in any way end the young man's life, he was filled with such anger that he was almost reduced to insanity. So he commanded that the boy should now be pierced by a very sharp spear from his head to his thigh. And when Antoninus could not satisfy himself with all these tortures, he was overcome with indignation, anger and despair and was seized by every other kind of fury. He stood amazed and, pondering many things about both religions in his mind, he grieved both that he had been so vindictive in vain, and particularly that through his cruelties he had given the populace arguments for believing in Christianity. As 109 a result, he crashed to the floor with a terrible pain in his head.

It is said that on this spot Antoninus' head happened to collide, as if guided by an angel's hand, with the spear that had transfixed

Languente quidem Antonino constat Agnetem, eius filiam, patris pietate et miraculorum multitudine motam, Potitum pro Antonini salute exorasse. Potito etiam multa illic de Christi misericordia, de vindicta referente ac pro valetudine Antonini orante, Agnetem ipsam baptizatam esse moxque Antoninum convaluisse constat. Videns subinde Antoninus Potitum palam magno cum populi assensu de Christo contionari, repente illi linguam abscidi iubet. Adsunt carnifices; non modo linguam precidunt, verum etiam oculos obcecant.

111 Magnum dei ministerium! adolescens enim elinguis, nil tamen minus expedite de deo contionabatur, probans necesse unum esse rerum principem, unum Deum, quo cuncta creata sint, quo cuncta moveantur, sine quo nihil sit; Martem, Neptunum, solem minime esse deos, siquidem a deo facta sunt; hominumque animas haud minus divinas esse quam solem ipsum; nam animas immortales esse nemo non stultus dubitat; animorum quidem opus esse verum principium causarum, verum Deum cognoscere suisque operibus, cum universa natura, ita illi deo maximas gratias continuo agere, ut meminerint parata esse meritorum premia et supplicia sempiterna, primam enim corporis vitam brevem, anime autem vitam esse perpetuam et eternam; etenim agitari animos propria ratione et appetitu reliquorum vero etiam celestium corporum, quorum motus et vim sentimus, eosdem omnes certa nature lege subiectos esse. Idcirco nihil esse in rerum natura non finitum, solum hominis peccatum esse infinitum, pro quo luendo Dei filius Jhesus infinitum munus exhibuerit, quandoquidem ut per prophetas perque etiam sibillas erat locutus suo adventu, suo sanguine, patrum nostrorum peccata abluerit, nobis optimam bene vivendi normam

Potitus. All agree that as the emperor lay in pain, his daughter
Agnes, moved by pity for her father and by the many miracles
witnessed, begged Potitus for Antoninus' survival. Potitus then   110
said much about Christ's mercy and about revenge, and while he
prayed for Antoninus' health, Agnes herself was baptized and soon
Antoninus recovered. Then when he saw Potitus preaching about
Christ with the broad consent of the populace, he suddenly ordered his tongue to be cut out. The executioners quickly ran to
obey him: not only did they cut out Potitus' tongue but also
blinded his eyes.

   What a great mystery of God then followed! For the young   111
man, despite not having a tongue, continued preaching about God
as fluently as before, proving that there had to be one ruler of all
things, one God, by whom all things are created and all things are
moved, without whom there is nothing. He said that Mars, Nep-
tune and the Sun were not gods, since they were created by God;
men's souls were no less divine than the Sun itself. For nobody of   112
any intelligence doubted that souls are immortal. The mind's duty
was to recognize the true beginning of things, and the true God,
and to give the greatest thanks constantly, along with the whole of
nature, for his works. This was so that all should remember that
eternal rewards and punishments have been prepared for our
deeds, that the first life, that of the body, is short, but the life of
the soul is perpetual and eternal. He explained that the mind was
moved by its own reason and appetite, and as for the rest of the
heavenly bodies whose motion and strength we perceive, these
were all subject to a fixed law of nature. For this reason there was   113
nothing in nature that was not finite; the only thing that was infinite was man's capacity to sin. He said that Jesus Christ, son of
God, gave us an infinite gift in washing away our sins, since just as
he had spoken through his prophets and also through the Sibyls,
so by his coming down to earth and through his blood he had
absolved all our fathers' sins, and left us an excellent rule for living

114 reliquerit, defunctorum resurrectionem futuram docuerit. Rursus addebat mundi omnia caduca esse, brevem, fragilem hominis vitam, inutiles labores, nocuas voluntates; advigilandum igitur, quoniam sciat nemo diem aut horam; frenandas cupiditates, sedanda odia, quoniam reddenda esset villicationis ratio.

115 His itaque de rebus copiose et eleganter non secus loquebatur ac si dissertissima ex theologorum schola exercitatissima atque in-

116 tegerrima lingua nuper exiisset. Tandem adhuc Christi potentiam, gloriam, divinitatem predicantem non longe a Calabrio fluvio adolescentem decapitarunt. Forte sepulture hoc epigramma Christiani super inscripserunt.

EPIGRAMMA

Hic Potiti Serdici corpus posuimus,
qui famem sitimque exilium solitudinem ultimamque
paupertatem perpeti
gloriam omnesque cruciatus parvifacere
ac mortem ipsam pro Christi religione appetere
omnia hec infra quartum et decimum annum potuit.

[LETTER TO LEONARDO DATI]

Baptista Albertus Leonardo Dato salutem.

1 Eram timida quidem in sententia dum tecum verebar nequid eruditi subdubitarent hanc nostram Potiti istoriam esse fictam aliquam et puerilem fabulam. Memineram enim quam multa in istoria queritent viri non indocti quamve plene rerum causam, rem

well, and taught us that the dead would rise again. Again he added   114
that everything in his world was ephemeral, that man's life was
brief and fragile, his labors were pointless, his will harmful; so one
had to be vigilant, since nobody knows the day or the hour; desires were to be restrained, hatreds to be suppressed, since we have
to give an account of our stewardship.

He discussed such things so copiously and elegantly, just as if   115
he had come out of the most eloquent theology school, with a
well-trained and totally intact tongue. Finally, while he was still   116
preaching about Christ's power, glory and divinity, they decapi-
tated the young man not far from the river Calabrius.[23] The
Christians carved the following inscription on his tomb.

INSCRIPTION

Here we laid the body of Potitus of Sofia,
who bore hunger and thirst, exile, solitude and
extreme poverty,
and he made light of both glory and all forms of torture
and even sought death itself for the sake of the Christian religion.
All this he was able to do before his fourteenth year had passed.[24]

[LETTER TO LEONARDO DATI]

Baptista Alberti to Leonardo Dati: greetings.[25]

I was rather apprehensive, since along with you I worried that   1
learned humanists might suspect that this life of St. Potitus which
I have written was some childish, made-up tale. For I remembered
how many things the erudite demand in a work of history, how
fully they want the cause of events and events themselves to be

gestam, loca, tempora atque personarum dignitatem describi

2 optent. Et videbam quoque apostolorum actus, pontificum martirumque reliquorum vitam dilucide atque plenissime a maioribus descriptam; hanc autem Potiti istoriam ita negligenter traditam, ut facile illam arbitrari potuerim esse ab imperitis non ab illis diligen-

3 tissimis viris editam. Tamen posteaquam Potiti huius singularis adolescentis memoriam apud veteres approbatissimos studiosius percunctari cepi, comperi Potitum quendam non modo sanctum virum sed ne religiosum quidem fuisse. De quo Tacianus vetustissimus et approbatissimus scriptor contra ereses forte de unico rerum principio scribens inquit.

4 TACIANUS. Alii autem sicut ipse Marcion duo esse principia introducit, ex quibus est Potitus et Basiliscus! qui et ipsi secuti sunt Ponticum Lupum.

Hec Tacianus.

5 Comperi praeterea ex quibusdam Lugduniensium epistolis quibus Attali Alexandri ac multorum superiorum martirum interitus narratur fuisse quondam adolescentem annorum XV Antonini Veri temporibus cui nomen Pontico de quo ita recensetur.

6 Ex EPISTOLIS. Sed cum ferarum nulla sanctorum corpora tetigisset, omnibus eos verberum ceterarumque penarum suppliciis cruciatos, ad ultimum in conspectu populi sanctos viros iugulari iubent.

7 Ex EISDEM EPISTOLIS. Baldina rursus cum Pontico annorum fere XV puero iussi aliorum supplicia ut terrerentur aspicere, steterunt. Dehinc iussi per deos iurare iugulantur quoniam

described, not to mention the details of places and times and the merits of the people involved.[26] And I also saw that the acts of the apostles, and the lives of the popes and martyrs were very clearly and fully detailed by our predecessors. But I noticed that this story of Potitus had been so carelessly handed down that I could easily have believed that it had been written by inexperienced people, not by those very precise authors. But after I began to research more diligently the memory of this outstanding young man in the most approved ancient writers, I discovered that there was a certain Potitus who was not only not a saint but was not even religious. Tatian, an ancient and highly approved writer, wrote works against heresies, and when he happened to be writing about the single principle of things, he said:

> TATIAN. Others, such as Marcion himself, introduced the idea of two principles, and among these others are Potitus and Basiliscus! They also followed Ponticus Lupus.

That is what Tatian has to say.[27]

I also discovered from certain epistles written by men of Lyons, which narrate the deaths of Attalus, Alexander and many older martyrs, that there had once been a fifteen-year-old adolescent who lived in the time of Antoninus Verus whose name was Ponticus, and about whom the following is said:

> FROM THE LETTERS. But when none of the beasts touched the bodies of the saints, they ordered the latter to be tortured with all forms of beatings and other punishments before these holy men were finally slaughtered in full view of the populace.

> FROM THE LETTERS. Again Baldina, along with Ponticus, a boy of about fifteen, was ordered to stand and watch the others being tortured in order to terrify them. Then they were told to swear by the gods, but because they strenuously

strenue parere recusassent. Necatorum denique corpora canibus exponunt.

8 Hec itaque ex illis epistolis collegi que tamen illic prolixius numerantur. Habeo igitur hunc Ponticum, cuius etas, res geste, cum Antonini temporibus pulchre convenient. Ille enim epistole Antonini temporibus scripte sunt.

9 Idcirco eorum iudicium minus timeo qui fictam esse historiam arbitrentur. Vel enim sit error in nomine, librariorum negligentia Ponticum pro Potito dixerunt, vel binomius Ponticus Potitus fuerit, constat tamen fuisse adolescentem qui quinto et decimo anno

10 martir sanctissimus fuerit. Adde his, si minus erratum in nomine existimas, quod idibus ianuarii apud Romam ecclesie commemorant.

Ex MARTIROLOGIO. Rome via Lavicana corone militum XL. Pictave civitate Hylarius et metropoli Remigius episcopus . . . vero sanctorum Juliani Celsi Potiti martirum.

Hec ex epitomate martirum qui liber quoque corruptissimus est.

11 Sed de negligentia librariorum aut de nonnullis historiarum
12 scriptoribus quid eruditi existiment alio loco dicetur. Sat nobis sit quantum ex hac nostra librorum inopia colligere potui non erratum esse apud nos in re alia quam in martiris nomine, si persuaderi non potest ulla in re non esse erratum. Vale.

refused to obey, they were executed. Subsequently the bodies of the dead were exposed to the dogs.[28]

This then is what I gathered from those epistles, though they re- 8 count the events in more verbose detail. So I have found this Ponticus, whose age and deeds neatly fit the period of Antoninus. For those epistles were written during Antoninus' reign.

Thus I am less afraid of the verdict of those who think that this 9 is a fictional story. Whether there is an inaccuracy in the boy's name, caused by scribal error, and they call him Ponticus instead of Potitus, or whether he had two names, Ponticus Potitus, there is still agreement at least that there was an adolescent who at the age of fifteen became a holy martyr. In addition to this, if you do 10 not think there is an error in his name, on 13 January the churches in Rome commemorate him.[29]

> FROM THE MARTYROLOGY. Rome, on the Via Labicana, the martyrs' crown for forty soldiers. At Poitiers, Hilarius in the city and Remy the metropolitan bishop . . . and the holy martyrs Julianus, Celsus and Potitus.[30]

This is what I have gleaned from an epitome of the Martyrs' lives, a work whose text is also highly corrupt.

But what learned men think about the negligence of scribes and 11 about certain historians we will discuss in another place. It is 12 enough for me that I have been able to collect this evidence despite the current lack of books; I think it is not erroneous in any aspect except perhaps the martyr's name, although one cannot persuade people that anything is without error.

Farewell.

[LETTER TO MARINO GUADAGNI]

1 Marine, salutem. Dixisti persepius te velle aliquid de meis studiis videre, qua in re tibi satisfacere plurimum cupiebam, sed nimis verebar iudicium tuum elegantissimum ad quem censebam nihil nisi summa arte et lima perfectum atque expolitum dari oportere.

2 Tandem fretus tua facilitate, censui officiosius a me fieri si voluntati tue potius quam verecundie meae obtemperarim. Ea propter volui Potitum hunc nostrum ad te primum venire, ex quo velim non quid ingenio valeam scisciteris, sed Potitum discas unum

3 fuisse in quo laudando aliquid studuerim. Habeo quidem pleraque alia que legentes possint delectare. Verum scias non sine astu hunc a me Potitum permissum fuisse. Scin quare? Certe quia existimo tantum apud te pueri sanctitatem rerumque gestarum admirationem valituram ut plus animo ad Potitum quam ad meam eloquentiam pendeas. Qui quidem cum sua virtute placuerit nihil mihi

4 amplius querendum iudicabo. Amo enim eius laudem in qua amplificanda non nihil diligentie posui ut videbis. Eumque a te pariter ac a ceteris amari vehementer opto quod te facturum existimo si me leges. Lege igitur et Baptistam tuum tibi comendatum habe.

[LETTER TO MARINO GUADAGNI][31]

Dear Marino, greetings. You often said you would like to see 1
something from my studies, and I very much wanted to satisfy you
in this request. But I was too afraid of your very discerning judgment and felt that nothing should be given to you that was not
fully completed and perfected with supreme art and polish. In the 2
end, relying on your affability, I thought it was more my duty to
obey your wishes than to worry about me losing face. For that
reason, I wanted this life of St. Potitus which I have written to
come to you first: in it I would like you to find out, not how impressive my genius is, but how Potitus was one saint in whose
praise I had invested my studies. I actually have many other things 3
which could delight readers. But you must know that this life of
Potitus is being sent by me not without a certain strategy. Do you
know why? Well, because I believe that the holiness of this young
man and admiration for his achievements will make such an im-
pression on you that you will pay more attention to Potitus than
to my eloquence. If you like this man and his virtue, there is nothing more I would want. For I love the praise of Potitus which I 4
have tried to amplify through my diligence. I really want him to be
loved by you and everyone else, which I am sure you will do if you
read me. So read this work and know that Baptista commends
himself to you.

CANIS

1 Erat in more apud maiores nostros, viros omni bonarum artium cognitione et imprimis disciplina morum sanctissimorum et religione prestantissimos, ut bene meritos cives laudibus prosequerentur, clarorumque virorum nomina litteris et, quoad in se esset, immortalitati, summo studio omnique industria commendarent. Id illos ita consuevisse possumus interpretari, partim ut referendis premiis equitate et iustitia uterentur, cui virtuti penitus erant dediti, partim ut iuvenes studiosos ad virtutis cultum, quo patrie utiles et celebres eo pacto apud posteros redderentur, vehementius illicerent et confirmarent, partim etiam ut otium, quo fortassis abundabant, in eo collaudandi munere omnibus grato atque accepto consumerent.

2 Tantumque apud eos et publice et private valuit studium concelebrande laudis hominum probatissimorum, ut non in funeribus modo (quod hac etate, inde accepta consuetudine, fit) publice laudationes haberentur et litterarum monimentis mandarentur, verum etiam eo processit res ut, non contenti humanis laudibus, alii deos effecerint, suis scriptis, eos qui virtute effloruissent, alii preterea fictas et nulla ex parte credendas fabulas ad virtutis illece-

3 bras accomodarint. Hinc Athenis multe a rhetoribus funebres acte orationes. Hinc apud nostros a simili quoque per id tempus vulgata consuetudine sumptaque licentia extitit, ut non modo cives optime de re publica meritos dicendo ornarent, verum et suos

MY DOG

Our elders were men who were outstanding for their complete 1
knowledge of the humanities and particularly for their religion and
disciplined obedience to the most sacred morals.[1] It was their custom to praise citizens who had deserved well of the state and to
entrust the names of famous men to their writings, and, as far as
they could, to exert the utmost zeal and all of their efforts to commend them and guarantee them immortality.[2] We can interpret
this custom of theirs in the following way: it was done partly in
order to confer rewards out of a sense of fairness and justice, virtues to which they were totally dedicated; partly it was done to
encourage young people even more strongly to become enthusias-
tic devotees of the pursuit of virtue and to remain such, in order
that they would become in posterity's view useful to and famous
in their fatherland for that very reason; and lastly it was partly
done in order that they could use even their leisure, which they
probably had plenty of, for that task of praising others, which is
pleasing and acceptable to all.

Their keenness to celebrate the renown of the most upright 2
men both publicly and privately was so strong in them that not
only at funerals (which thanks to their practice is now an accepted
custom) was public praise delivered and committed to writing, but
things went so far that, not content with human praise, some
people in their writings elevated to the status of gods those who
had shone with virtue, while others added fictional and totally
unbelievable fables to the enticements of virtue. Hence at Athens 3
many funeral speeches were pronounced by orators. And hence
among our own Latin people a similar custom was allowed and
became popular in those times, so much so that not only did they
duly make speeches celebrating citizens who had served the state

domesticos publice collaudarint in concione: etenim, ut ceteros omittam, Antonium suam oratione collaudasse matrem in funere, et Fabium Maximum de filii laudibus funebrem habuisse orationem ferunt. Ab hacque denique consuetudine Hercules deus dictus est, addita etiam Hydra et bellua Lerne et eiusdem monstra, que ab re esset et prolixum prosequi.

4   At nobis per istos estivos calores et estus otiosis, cum ipsa sese acerba occasio obtulerit, ut meo mihi admodum innato aliquid continuo agendi aut scriptitandi desiderio honestissime et pene coactus satisfaciam, quid iam est quod promptius exequar quam ut in ea re exercear, in qua officio et, ni fallor, minime improbando 5 desiderio meo conferam? Etenim cum intelligam ita esse ab optima natura ipsa comparatum, ut virtute insignes et eos maxime quibus cari et commendati fuerimus, imprimis diligamus, preter pietatem visum est si hoc amoris officium, quod defuncto cani meo, canum omnium optimo et mei amantissimo debeo, denega- 6 rim. Nam si bonos omnium consensu iuste et pie, quasi virtutum suarum observatores et testificatores, nimirum laudamus, quantum hoc commodius et decentius a me fiet, qui laudare instituerim hunc, quem, apud me educatum, optimis per me disciplinis instructum, ad unguem norim? Qua in re tantam cuperem quidem esse in me dicendi facultatem, ut hac ipsa in funebri oratione maximas illius et incredibiles laudes pro legentium expectatione 7 satis possem recensere. Nam in ea re, quam me acturum prestem, siquid defecerim, ridiculus sim. Sed hoc ad scribendum audentius aggredior quod illius virtus, que iam usque universis orbis

supremely well, but private citizens even praised their own servants in public speeches. For (leaving aside other examples) they say that Antonius praised his own mother at her funeral,[3] and that Fabius Maximus delivered a funeral oration full of the praises of his son.[4] Thanks to this custom Hercules was pronounced a god, and people added in the story of the Lernaean beast and the hydra[5] and of other monsters faced by the same hero, which it would be pointless and simply prolix to go through here.

Now I was at leisure during this boiling summer heat when a sad occasion presented itself which allowed me to satisfy in an honest way—and almost as if forced to do it—my really quite innate desire to always be doing or writing something. What is there that I would more readily do now than to exercise myself in the one activity whereby I could fulfill that duty and desire of mine which (unless I am mistaken) is absolutely not to be criticized. For since I understand that it has been established by that excellent force, nature, that we should primarily love those who are outstanding in virtue, especially those to whom we are dear and have been commended, it seemed to me that it would go against piety to deny the duty of love that I owe to my dead dog, the best dog of all, who loved me so much. For if in everyone's view it is just and pious to praise good men, as though we were the spectators and witnesses of their virtues, how much more appropriately and decently will I be acting if I set out to praise the creature who was brought up in my home and educated by me in the best disciplines and whom I have known thoroughly, down to the tips of his paws? In carrying out this duty I would indeed like to possess so much eloquence that in this funeral oration I could review his vast and incredible merits sufficiently to satisfy the expectations of those who read it. For if I failed in any way in this initiative which I am about to carry out, I would look ridiculous. But I will attempt to write this all the more confidently since the dog's virtue, which by now is widely known and even familiar to all the peoples

terrarum gentibus explorata magna ex parte fuit et cognita, ex se
tanta est, ut cum eloquentie ornamentis minime indigeat, tum esse
illam nobis amplam et rerum dignitate ac varietate elegantem or-
natamque orationem sumministraturam non diffidam.

8   Describam igitur breviter vitam et mores canis mei, ut qui lege-
rit neque prolixitate orationis in fastidium incidat neque nos nimium curiosos et exactos laudatores fuisse iudicet; ac futurum
quidem non vereor ut cum canem ipsum laude dignissimum et in
eo laudando me officium secutum affirment, tum sibi ad voluptatem animi et ad mores bonos plurima apud nos adinvenisse admo-
nimenta non negent, que cum laude sequantur et condigne imitentur.

9   Etenim ortus est canis noster parentibus nobilissimis, patre
Megastomo, cuius in familia vestustissima pene innumerabiles cla-
rissimi principes extitere, ut inter ipsos aliqui ob virtutem in numero sint deorum apud priscas illas sapientissimas Egyptiorum
gentes habiti (qualem, etate hac nostra, medium inter astra fulgen-
tissima, ex eo genere quendam vagari Canem, qui siderum motus
et cursus non ignorant omnes profitentur); matrem autem habuit
pietate insignem ex eadem clarissima et amplissima familia ortam.

10   Qui cum virtute et animi robore et prestantia atque viribus, tum
fide, benivolentia, pietate, observantiaque in eos, a quibus se liberalitate et benefitiis adiutos senserint, ipsos longe homines exupe-
rarint. Ac prolixum quidem esset maiorum suorum omnium facta
dictaque memoratu dignissima recensere. Sed hoc iuvabit aliqua
eorum gesta enumerasse, quo intelligamus hunc nostrum a pris-
11   tina suorum probitate et virtute minime degenerasse. Itaque inter
proavos familie canum memorie traditum est nonnullos tanto
animo et fortitudine preditos extitisse, ut neque leonem quamvis

of the earth, is on its own so great that it does not need the orna-
ments of eloquence at all, and I am confident that his virtue will
supply a speech that will be ample and elegant thanks to the dignity and variety of its topics alone, as well as being eloquent.[6]

I will now describe my dog's life and character briefly so that 8
my readers will not become annoyed with the prolixity of my oration, nor will they judge me to have been too curious and punc-
tilious in my eulogy. I feel sure that while they will affirm that the
dog himself is most worthy of praise and that in praising him I
have carried out my duty, they will also not deny that they have
found in my speech many things that will give their minds pleasure and many incitements to acquiring good morals, incitements
which they can follow with praise and imitate in a worthy fashion.

Now my dog was born from very noble parents: his father was 9
Megastomos,[7] in whose most ancient family were almost countless
famous leaders, so much so that among them were some dogs
who, because of their virtue, were held to be gods by those very
wise ancient peoples of Egypt (all the experts on the movement
and course of the stars say that one of the dogs from that family in
our own time wanders amid the most brightly shining stars).[8] His
mother was distinguished for her piety and was sprung from the
same very famous and prestigious family. These dogs far outdid 10
men themselves both through their virtue, strength of mind, excellence and physical prowess, as well as through their fidelity, benevolence, piety and attention toward those they felt had helped
them with generosity and good deeds. It would indeed take too
long to go through all his ancestors' deeds and sayings, though
they are very worthy of being remembered.[9] But at this point it is
worth listing just some of their achievements, so that we can realize that this dog never degenerated in any way from the pristine
probity and virtue of his forebears. Amongst the ancestors of this 11
family of dogs, tradition has it that some were endowed with such
courage and bravery that they never refused to seek a duel with a

12 acerrimum et ferocissimum, neque elephantum, maximam et valentissimam belluarum, in duellum petere recusarint. Quo ex omnium fortissimorum canum numero ceteri plures et imprimis duo apud Hyarotim Indorum fluvium orti, qui prius sub rege Albanorum, mox sub Alexandro Macedone meruere, celebres notissimique sunt, quos ferunt, cum elephantum aut quanvis belluam morsu comprehendissent, nisi ea prius confecta, neque igni neque ferro ab suscepta dimicatione ac victoria uspiam potuisse avelli.

13 Quanta autem huiusmodi fortissimorum canum extiterit copia, hinc vel maxime perspici potest, quod Caramantum regem suis auspiciis et armis ab exilio in regnum restituerunt, Colophoniosque et Castabalenses, nullis stipendiis acceptis nullaque alia spe lucri proposita, sola benivolentia ducti, primas acies agendo et hostem cedendo sepe a populationibus gravissimis et imminenti

14 servitute vindicarunt. Fuere igitur et perduellionibus et structa in acie fortissimi, atque, quod raro hac etate evenit ut armis fidentes iustitiam et pietatem colant, in hac nobili canum familia sempiterne usque ad hanc diem humanitas, fides et referende gratie studium viguit non minus quam fortitudo.

15 Incredibile dictu est quam illi quidem in servanda fide perpetuo fuerint religiosissimi. Aratus Sycionius, vir et domi et bello clarissimus, capto Acrocorintho, fortissimo provincie aditu, a quo pene omnis patrie salus pendebat, arcem eius loci non fidissimis amicis magis quam canibus quinquaginta tuendam commendavit, quam illi quidem diligentissimis, diu noctuque, excubiis peractis serva-

16 runt. Tantamque, quoquo se loci receperint, omnium gentium in se gratiam et benivolentiam optime agendo semper assecuti sunt,

lion or even an elephant—that biggest and strongest of all animals—no matter how fierce and violent.[10] From this group of all the bravest dogs there were very many, and in particular two, who were born near the river Hyarotis, in India, and who first under the king of the Albani and later under Alexander the Great became famous and very well known.[11] It is said that when they attacked an elephant or any animal, however fierce, with their bites, they could never be torn away from the fight that they had undertaken and from ultimate victory by threat of fire or sword, until the larger animal had been dispatched.

How great a number of this kind of very brave dogs there existed can be seen particularly from this fact, that the king of the Garamantes was restored to his kingdom from exile thanks to the goodwill and protection of some dogs.[12] It was dogs who freed the Colophonians and Castabalenses from terrible depredations and imminent enslavement, yet they did not accept any money, and were not enticed by any hope of profit, but were prompted solely by their generosity and willingness to fight in the front line and slaughter the enemy.[13] They were therefore very brave both in duels and when fighting in the front line, and also—something which only happens very rarely—they cultivated piety and justice while trusting in arms. In this family of noble dogs, right down to our own day, there was always a cult of humanity and loyalty and the display of gratitude no less than bravery.

It is incredible how constant they were in always keeping faith with what they had promised to do. Aratus of Sicyon was a man very famous both in peacetime and in wars, and when Acrocorinth was captured, even though the approach to this province was very strongly fortified, and nearly all of the safety of the fatherland depended on it, he entrusted the protection of its citadel both to his most loyal friends and to fifty dogs who guarded it day and night with the most tireless vigilance.[14] Wherever they went, they gained so much gratitude and goodwill from all people by always

12

13

14

15

16

ut ceteri plerique atque imprimis Xanthippes priscus defunctos canes, quod bene essent meriti, publica impensa honeste humandos censuerit, cuidamque, cuius fidem et amoris constantiam Salamine et in omni sua expeditione esset expertus, in arce apud Athenas sepulchrum quam honorificentissime posuit, locumque nomini eius dicavit qui Cynotaphium nuncuparetur.

17   Quid clarissimo illi fecisset Xanthippes cani, qui Asparagum puerum, cui postea Cyro nomen fuit, crudeliter expositum cum invenisset, motus pietate, ceteris suis posthabitis rebus, summa

18   sollicitudine et inestimabili quadam caritate tutatus est? quive incredibile dictu est quot et quam maximas atque atrocissimas in servando puero contra voraces lupos et istiusmodi fame sevientes feras fortissime, illatis acceptisque vulneribus, dimicationes inierit?

19   Sed ne pietate quidem huic is inferior canis fuit qui, dum a perempti amici cadavere exposito volucres et feras arcendo persisteret, per sitim et famem atque laborem defecerit.

20   Adde his et illum qui, Appio et Plancio consulibus Rome, nulla alia sanctiori necessitudine devinctus nisi quod perdomestice fortassis convivere domumque nonnumquam ex mediis nemoribus raptas ad eum cenas conferre consuesset, familiarem suum hominem quendam tanto officio prosecutus est, ut adversa et calamitosa

21   in fortuna collapsum ne defunctum quidem deseruerit. Nam etsi egenus canis ipse ac pro querendo sibi victu nequicquam esset otiosus, tamen apud familiarem suum carcere publico detentum sese comitem habebat assiduum, ab aliisque amicis rogatum cibum ad hunc miserum hominem in dies deferebat, atque cum miser ille

behaving well, that most people, especially old Xanthippus, declared that dogs who had died after serving the state well should be buried with honor at public expense. For his dog, whose fidelity and constancy of love Xanthippus had witnessed at Salamis and throughout every one of his expeditions, he had a sepulcher of great honor erected in the citadel at Athens, and gave the dog's name to the place calling it the Cynotaph.[15]

What would Xanthippus have given to that other very famous 17 dog who, when he found the boy Asparagus (who was later given the name Cyrus) cruelly exposed, was moved by piety and, setting aside all his own concerns, protected the boy with great solicitude and incredible love?[16] And (this is incredible) he very bravely 18 fought many fierce and violent battles, inflicting and receiving countless wounds, against voracious wolves and other similarly ravenous wild beasts, in order to preserve the child. But in no way 19 inferior in piety was that other dog who, while persisting in fending off wild beasts and birds from the corpse of his friend who had been killed, finally died himself through thirst, hunger and exhaustion.[17]

Add to these also the story of the dog who, not being bound by 20 any other stronger tie, had simply become used to living peacefully with his master in his house and sometimes used to bring dinners for him which he had snatched from the middle of the woods. In the year when Appius and Plancius were consuls in Rome,[18] the dog stayed close to this man who was his friend with such a sense of duty that when the man met his demise, oppressed by a changed and calamitous ill-fortune, the dog did not desert his friend even when the latter died. For even though this dog was needy and was 21 never idle but always seeking food for himself, nevertheless he made himself a constant companion to his friend, now held in the public prison, and he would take food that he had begged from his friends to the poor man every day; and when the wretched prisoner paid the penalty demanded by the Emperor Germanicus,

penas Germanico principi, a quo detineretur, persolvisset, in Ty-
berim eiectum cadaver substentatum summo suo cum periculo
adnatavit.

22   Verum enim siquis velit canum omnium pietatem et fidem
prosequi, tanta et tam multa eorum virtutis exempla ab optimis
auctoribus memorie prodita inveniet, ut quidvis facilius eum posse
existimem quam eadem omnia unum in locum collecta redigere.

23   Que res cum ita sint, nos brevitatis gratia maiorum huius familie laudes pretermittemus atque id quidem ita agemus vel quod de
huius nostri canis laudibus nimium multa et elegantissima ad dicendum suppeditent, vel quod non eo me ingenium preditum
sentiam, ut illorum superiorum preclarissima gesta pro dignitate
queam recensere, vel quod fortassis quibusdam, qui potissimum
canis nostri egregias laudes expectant, ab re esse maiorum hec
24   commemoratio videatur. Preter duos igitur in amicitia singulares,
qui mihi occurrunt et quos ob facti admirationem minime preter-
mittendos duco, ceteros omittemus. Non inter hos quidem illos
commemoro, quorum unus in Epiro amici sui peremptorem, nulla
homicide arma aut minas veritus, presenti animo et acri latratu ac
laniatu in coetu hominum prodidit; quorumve alter pari animi fi-
25   ducia Ganictoris filios Hesiodi occisores indicavit; neque eum, qui
sacrilegum a templo Esculapii sectando obviis peregrinantibus
gestu et nutu monstravit; eumque missum facio canem qui ad
Romanum civem bello civili prostratum adstitit, contra prostrati

who had kept him in prison, and his body was thrown into the Tiber, the dog swam to him and supported the corpse at great risk to himself.[19]

The truth is that if someone wanted to examine the piety and fidelity of all dogs, he will find so many and such noble examples of their virtue handed down to posterity by the best authors, that I think that he would find it very difficult to collect all of these examples in one work.

Since this is the case, for the sake of brevity I shall omit the praises of the ancestors of my dog's family, and I shall do so, either because there are too many wonderful examples to add to the praises of our dog, or because I do not feel that I have the appropriate genius to recount the famous actions of those forebears with the dignity they deserve, or because some people who are expecting particularly praise of the special merits of our dog might think that dwelling so much on his ancestors would seem out of place. So we will omit all the others except for two who come to mind and who provide outstanding examples of friendship and whom I really cannot overlook because of the astonishing nature of their deeds. So among these dogs I will not mention the one who in Epirus showed no fear of the weapons and threats of a murderer. Instead, with great presence of mind and loud barking and tearing at the man the animal betrayed the presence of the person who had murdered the dog's friend.[20] Nor will I talk about the other dog who with similar alacrity of mind revealed the sons of Ganictor as the murderers of Hesiod.[21] Nor will I mention the dog who persistently followed the man who had committed sacrilege in the temple of Aesculapius and revealed the wrongdoer's identity to bypassers through his gestures and by nodding toward him.[22] I will also pass over in silence the dog who stood beside a Roman citizen who had been killed in the civil war: that dog fought against the enemies of the prostrate man with such strength that,

22

23

24

25

inimicos belligerans tantis viribus, ut inimici armati, non nisi prius interfecto cane, abscidere prostrati caput potuerint.

26   Sed hos igitur missos facio, eosque admirabimur, quorum unus, Lysimacho regi amicissimus, cum amicum e vita exisse atque in rogum eius corpus delatum intueretur, pre amici desiderio, ut quem in vita amplius non esset conspecturus morte celebri conse-
27 queretur, sese medias inter flammas funeris iniecit. Alter amici cuiusdam interfecti, cui nomen Iasoni Licio fuerat, tam acerbissime mortem tulit, ut per animi dolorem cibum abhorrens, inedia decesserit. Huiusmodi igitur maiores avi et avorum proavi hac in familia generosissima fuere fortissimi, sanctissimi piissimique.

28   Quos profecto canis hic noster, de quo agimus, omni pietatis modestieque officio maxime imitatus est, nullique pro viribus fuit fortitudinis gloria secundus. Quem cum natura pusillum et ad ferendum immanissimi et prepotentis hostis alicuius impetum haud satis firmum genuisset, tamen, quod sue fuere partes, animo ad rem militarem adeo fuit acri et bellicoso, ut maiores sepe belluas
29 provocatus et iniuriis lacessitus petierit. Qua in re, cum semper maluerit imperatoris laudibus quam militis virtute prestare, idcirco non manus tantum conserendi cupidus, sed ingentis glorie imprimis libidine flagrans, quodcumque in optimis imperatoribus laudi
30 dari animadvertisset, in se recepit: a Fabio enim Maximo maturam illam et prudentissimam cunctandi et continendi militis rationem et cautionem insidiarum; a Marcello et Scipionibus vim et impetum audendi et congrediendi; a Cesare atque ab Alexandro firmitudinem et perseverantiam certandi; ab Hannibale astum et
31 fallendi hostis ingenium et perspicaciam; ac denique, ne in his

although they were armed, they were not able to cut off the man's head until they had first killed the dog.[23]

So we will forget about these examples and admire instead two others, one of whom was a great friend of king Lysimachus: when the dog saw that his friend the king had died and that his body had been placed on the funeral pyre, out of his desire to join his friend whom he would never see again, the animal threw himself into the middle of the flames of the pyre in a famous death.[24] The other dog had a friend who had been killed, one Jason the Lycian, but the animal bore this death so bitterly that the grief in his mind led him to refuse all food, and he died by starvation.[25] So the ancestors and ancestors of ancestors in this most noble family were very brave, religious and pious.

This dog of mine, the subject of my oration today, clearly imitated them, particularly displaying his piety and modesty at every opportunity; and he was second to none in glory for his bravery, as far as was in his power. Since nature had made him rather small and not very resilient in coping with the attack of any huge and arrogant foe, still, as far as was possible, he had a mind so sharp and bellicose in military matters that when he was provoked and goaded by others' attacks he often faced up to beasts that were bigger than him. In this context, since he always preferred to excel in the gifts of a commander rather than in the virtues of a soldier, he was not so keen on hand-to-hand fighting, but burned primarily with the desire for great glory, and developed in himself whatever qualities he noticed were a source of praise in the best commanders. For from Fabius Maximus he adopted that mature and highly prudent rationale of delaying and keeping his soldiers disciplined, and being wary of ambushes;[26] from Marcellus and the Scipios he took their strength and impetuosity in daring and attacking;[27] from Julius Caesar and Alexander the Great he learned firmness and perseverance in battle; and from Hannibal guile and the capacity and cleverness to deceive the enemy. To sum up, and not to

26

27

28

29

30

31

longius vager, a singulis probatissimis imperatoribus singulas deinceps, quibus claruerint, virtutes mihi hac adhibita moderatione
desumpsisse visum est, ut neque in eo laudem poneret quod vali-
dissimum aliquem et efferatum hostem manu armisque, neque
quod perfidia et versutiis fallaces et fedifragos exuperarit; sed quod
acres et feroces fortitudine ac vincendi ratione et consilio anteces-
serit, id sibi ad officium adscribebat, suasque esse partes arbitrabatur perpeti numquam ut laboris aut incommodi atque periculi
32 metu subisse turpitudinem aliquam videretur. Ac pro viribus operam dabat ut laudem et gloriam clarissimis et dignissimis facinori-
bus promeruisse aperte iudicaretur. Tantaque in ceteris rebus fuit
abstinentia et equitate, ut nisi pro iustitia et honestate dimican-
dum uspiam duxerit; ac pro iustitia quidem et libertate tuenda
nullum umquam discrimen recusavit; pro nostrisque subinde rebus servandis fures quamquam armatos et quosvis advenas ignotos
et audaces insultare ac strenue contra infestissimos conclamitare ac
dimicare numquam pertimuerit.

33   Et quod plerique militaris discipline imperiti vituperant, experti
omnes comprobant, nostri erat canis institutum inimicum sibi facere neminem quem viribus et fortune suffragiis superiorem intueretur. Si qui fortassis insolentes et prepotentes ad inimicitiam sese
iniuriis efferebant, lenitate et placabilitate mites et mansuetos ita
reddebat, ut in eo nihil abiectum, nihil assentando aut subsecun-
34 dando humile aut servile fuisse accuses. Denique omni in certamine, ratione quam viribus, amicitia quam armis rem conficere

dwell any longer on these details, my dog seems to me to have taken from each of the most renowned commanders the individual virtues for which they had been famous. At the same time, he never considered it praiseworthy that he overcame the strongest and wildest opponent in arms and manual combat, nor that he outdid in trickery and craftiness others guilty of deception and breaking their word. Instead, he took it on himself as his duty to outdo keen and ferocious enemies in bravery and in his wise strategies for victory, and thought it should be his role never to allow himself to seem as if he had undergone any sort of dishonor through fear of hard work, discomfort or danger. To the best of 32 his abilities he made strenuous efforts so that everyone would judge that he had deserved praise and glory through very famous and very worthy deeds. In other areas he displayed such self-restraint and fairness that he thought he should never fight with anyone unless it was for the sake of justice and honesty. In order to defend justice and freedom he never shied away from any danger; and as a result he was never afraid to jump up even at armed thieves and strangers bent on burglary in order to defend our possessions, and he would strenuously bark and fight against the most hostile of intruders.

As for that tactic that most people inexperienced in military 33 discipline denounce, but those who are experienced in it actually approve, it was our dog's principle never to make anyone an enemy who seemed superior to him in strength and the gifts of fortune. If perhaps some insolent and arrogant enemies got so carried away as to make an enemy of him through their unjust treatment, he would make them gentle and meek through his leniency and desire to placate them, but he would do so in such a way that you could never accuse him of having anything in his behavior that was abject or flattering, or anything groveling or servile in his desire to accommodate them. In short, when fighting he always tried to 34 achieve his goals through reason rather than strength, friendship

semper studuit, hostemque ut prosequeretur nisi fugientem nullis
umquam artibus adduci potuit. Ex quo fiebat ut mature consulendo
semper in tuto esset, et attemperate irrumpendo sepe maxima cum
gloria victor ovans ad me congratulatum rediret, posteaquam
equos omnes, boves hominesque omnes fugientes, Catonis pre-
cepto, magis clamoribus et vocibus quam cedendo aut armis fugas-
set: tanta erat prosequendi arte et peritia, ut nusquam hostem
35 abigendo certationem sibi parasse iniquam penituerit. Itaque sic a
locis, temporibus, ab fortuna denique ipsa prestitam laudis et vic-
torie occasionem negligebat numquam. Ab duro autem certamine
prudentia, non pusillanimitate aut vecordia aliqua precavebat,
semperque (quod meo iudicio sapiens quisque debet) prudentiam
quam vires, modestiamque quam ullam apud se iactantiam valere
ostentabat.

36 Tametsi quis fortitudinem anteponat pietati, fidei, religioni,
quas omnes virtutes esse iustitie partes commemorant? Non ingre-
dior eam disputationem eorum qui dicunt apud quem una sit virtus, eundem omnes alias habere virtutes. Quid? an non iustitia fit
bene merendo ut hostes eque atque nos diligant, aut saltem ne-
37 quicquam oderint. Viri strenui et bellatores, quos fortes nuncupant, in castris intra armorum tumultus versantur, in rapinis, in
cede (si recte interpretamur) consenescunt militando: qua in re
una maxime fortibus istius modi locus est. Iusti in laribus patriis
et domesticis cum Penatibus et caris civibus quietem tranquillita-
temque colunt. Animi audacia et viribus pacem et otium fortasse
queritat miles; per equitatem autem ac leges otio et pace cives bene
morati fruimur.

38 Sed missam faciamus hanc de istiusmodi virtutibus disputationem, siquidem non manus tantum, verum et imprimis ipsum

rather than arms, and could not be persuaded by any means to pursue an enemy unless he fled. All this meant that through his mature reflection he was always safe, and by attacking with great timeliness he often came back to me to receive my congratulations as the triumphant victor bathed in the greatest glory, after he had routed all horses, oxen and humans—even though he did all this more through loud noise than through striking out with his weapons, as Cato recommended.[28] Such was his skill and experience in pursuit that he never had to repent of having set up an unequal fight for himself by chasing after his enemy. Thus he never ne- 35
glected the chance of praise or victory that had been presented to him by the location, the time or by fortune herself. He was very cautious about fierce battles because of his prudence, not through any pusillanimity or folly; and he always proved (as in my view every wise man has to) that prudence was more important than strength, and modesty was better than any showing off.

Yet who would place strength over piety, faith and religion? 36
They say that all these virtues are parts of justice. I will not at this point go into that debate raised by those who say that he who possesses one virtue has all the other virtues as well.[29] What? Is it not a kind of justice to deserve well of others, so that our enemies should love us as much as our friends or at least not hate us? Men 37
of action and fighting men, whom people call brave, spend their time in the camp amid the tumult of arms, and they grow old fighting amid plunder and slaughter (if we interpret this correctly): in this one thing there is a place especially for the brave. The just cultivate peace and tranquility amid the walls of their house and city and alongside their dear fellow citizens. The soldier looks for peace and leisure through his mental daring and his strength; but we well-behaved citizens enjoy our leisure and peace through equity and the laws.

But let us put aside this debate about virtues of this kind, since 38
it is not only in our hands but in particular in our hearts that we

pectus fortitudinis sedem atque domicilium obtinet, ac ne in ferro quidem quantum in animi magnitudine et firmitate fortitudinis gloria collucescit. Ad rem redeamus.

39   Prudens idcirco noster fuit canis, qui ab ineunte etate, spretis armis spretisque istiusmodi (ut quidam fortassis extimant) furoris et immanitatis artibus, sese totum optimis et pacatissimis optima-
40   rum rerum studiis et disciplinis contulit. Nam cum me plurimum litteris delectari et a numero eorum, qui hac etate mediocriter docti habentur, non reiici atque secludi fortassis audisset, illico, neglectis patriis et domesticis delitiis, ad me, animi divitias rebus caducis preferens atque ardua et rarissima expetens, concessit.
41   Cuius ego indolem et decorem forme conspicatus, nimirum amore erga illum affici occepi. Quod ipsum Socrati, cum Alcibiadem formosissimum adolescentem esset conspicatus, accidisse referunt, et negasse Socratem, quoad in se foret, passurum ut, divine adolescentis pulchritudini condigni sanctissimi mores et virtutes non
42   adessent. Erat autem canis noster facie honesta et liberali, liniamentis iis, a quibus Zeusis facile omnem pingendi venustatem et gratiam, ut a virginibus Crotoniatibus sumpsit, excepisset; ore leto et Megastomo patri persimilis, at oculis pietatem atque modestiam
43   matris perquam belle gestiebat. Pectoris quidem amplitudine et ceterorum membrorum dignitate et specie maiorum suorum statuas pulcherrime representabat. Que omnia mirifice ac prope divinitus ad admirabilem adolescentis pulchritudinem convenientia inauditam et incredibilem ingenii et animi vim multo, ut erat, maximam exprimebant.
44   Nam eo fuit quidem singulari et divino ingenio preditus, ut liberales quidem apud me artes ingenuis canibus dignas, inestimabili quadam discendi celeritate, omnes parilis etatis studiosos pau-
45   cis diebus exuperans, integre edidicerit. Memoria fuit maxima—ut

find the seat and headquarters of bravery; and the glory of bravery does not even shine so much in the sword as in the greatness and constancy of one's mind. Let us go back to our topic.

So our dog was prudent since from a very young age, disdaining 39 weapons and the arts (as some people reckon them) of that sort of fury and inhumanity, he gave himself over entirely to the best and most peaceful pursuits and the disciplines of the finest subjects. For perhaps when he heard that I loved literature most of all and 40 that I was not rejected or excluded from the company of those who in our time are considered even moderately learned, at that point he abandoned his family's homely pleasures and came over to join me, preferring the riches of the mind and arduous and very rare pursuits to ephemeral things. When I saw his character and 41 the beauty of his body, not surprisingly, I began to love him. This is what they say happened to Socrates when he saw that most handsome youth Alcibiades: Socrates said he would see to it that, as far as it was in his power to do so, the divine beauty of this youth would be accompanied by appropriately worthy morals and virtues.[30] My dog had an honest, noble face, with those lineaments 42 from which Zeuxis could easily have taken all the beauty and gracefulness for a painting, just as he had done with the virgins of Crotone.[31] He had happy features, very similar to those of Megastomos his father, but in his eyes he displayed the piety and modesty of his mother. In the breadth of his breast and the dig- 43 nity and beauty of his other limbs he most beautifully resembled the statues of his ancestors. All of these qualities wonderfully and almost divinely suited the admirable beauty of this young creature, and magnificently conveyed his unparalleled and incredible strength of mind and considerable intelligence.

For he was so endowed with a unique and almost divine genius 44 that in my company he surpassed all other learners of his age in the incredible speed with which he mastered in just a few days all the liberal arts that are worthy of a wellborn dog. He had an 45

que semel memorie commendarit, nunquam effluxerint, semper ex
tempore atque in promptu affuerint—, neque solum rerum quam
in L. Lucullo fuisse maximam ferunt, sed et verborum, quam
46 Hortensium amplissimam habuisse aiunt. Hinc mirum illud quod,
ne trimatu quidem exacto, latinam grecamque linguam eque atque
47 etruscam tenebat. Ingenio preterea fuit docili et versatili, et ad
quanvis rem apto, et ita accincto, ut brevi adiuncto studio, cuivis
sese rei agende aut arti dedisset, omnem in ea pristinam suam industriam et operam exposuisse diceres.

48   Mente fuit constanti et minime levi aut volubili, ut interdum in
eo illud Catonis dictum subvererer, quo aiebat odisse se puerum
qui precoci esset preditus sapientia. Sed in ea prematuritate nihil
habebat morosi aut fastidiose grave ac nunquam in eo erudiendo
mihi molestum laborem aut stomacum esse suscipiendum sensi.

49 Vita quidem et moribus ea fuit, quam omnes et bene vivendi et
probitatis se propositum habere exemplar faterentur atque con-
gratularentur. Accedebat eo quod, cum esset in omni gestu et
sermone modestus, tum et in omni reliqua vita preter ceteros ut
pecunie sic voluptatum omnium minime cupidus, maxime con-
temptor et esse et haberi studiis omnibus elaborabat: veluti qui a
me sepe auditum meminisset pecunias a vulgo intemperantium et
imperitorum tantopere expeti, quod uni cui sint dediti voluptati
subministrent, et in quo homine longe a voluptate ad virtutem
pendeat animus, non in eo istas opum divitiarumque flagrantes
cadere cupiditates.

50   Fuit igitur pecuniarum omnino gravis et sapiens aspernator.
Una tantum vixit contentus veste. Pes illi ut estate ita et bruma ad

extraordinary memory, so much so that once he had committed
something to memory, he never forgot it, but he was always ready
to recall it if he needed it on the spur of the moment. Nor was his
memory only for things, which they say was what L. Lucullus'
memory was famous for, but he also had a great memory for
words, just like Hortensius.[32] The extraordinary thing is that be-   46
fore he was three he could understand Greek and Latin as much
as Tuscan. In addition, he had a genius that was quick to learn,   47
versatile and suited to any subject: in fact, so ready to learn was he
that once he had added a little application to the study of whatever
subject or art he applied himself to, you would say that he had
spent all his youthful industry and labor in that one area.[33]

He had a mind that was constant and anything but frivolous or   48
voluble, so much so that sometimes I would slightly fear he would
merit Cato's famous reproach when he said that he hated a boy
who was possessed of precocious wisdom.[34] But in that precocity
there was nothing hateful or annoying or heavy, and in educating
him I never sensed that I had taken on an unpleasant task or anything that would not be to my liking. He was such in his life and   49
character that everyone admitted that they held him up as an example of good living and probity, and congratulated me on this. In
addition, he was modest in all his gestures and talk, and in every
other aspect of his life he was above all others in not caring for
either money or any pleasures. He strove to have and to be considered as having the greatest contempt for such things.[35] For he remembered having heard me often say that money was so much
sought after only by the vulgar crowd of intemperate and inexperienced people in order to use it just for their own pleasure, the one
thing they are devoted to; he also knew that the man whose mind
inclines away from pleasure and toward virtue was never con-
sumed by such burning desires for wealth and money.

He was thus a serious and wise despiser of money. He lived   50
content with just the one coat. His paws were bare both in sum-

nives nudus. Somnos non delitie gratia oscitans, sed requiescendi necessitate, sub divo, quovis dabatur loco, modo non turpi atque obscoeno, cum opus esset, capiebat. Vini et pulmentorum abstinentissimus. Itaque in hoc nulla luxuries, nulli sumptus, nullum es

51 alienum, nulla conviviorum libido. Si quem oderat, coram accusabat; in absentes minime unquam maledicus; amicorum secreta nusquam prodidit. Suo contentus, aliena appetivit nunquam. In omnes mitis, affabilis, ad amicitias optimorum pronus et propensus, amicitiasque ipsas obsequiis quam pollicitationibus, re quam ostentatione inibat atque adaugebat; amicitiaque esse per virtutem dignius quam per emolumenta ambicionemque amari cupiebat,

52 tamen dando quam accipiendo in amore progrediebatur. Nulli gravis, nulli durus, preterquam quod ab obscenis, impuris et desidiosis sese alienum et maxime segregatum volebat esse, quos quidem animi quadam generositate ferre nullo modo poterat, atque inprimis eos omnes audaces, qui iniuriam in quempiam inferrent,

53 Herculi similis, summo odio prosequebatur. Amicis meis omnibus obsequens, festivus, officiosus, obtemperans, ut omnes facile eum diligenter et optimam de eo spem susciperent.

54 Crevit igitur una cum fama et rerum notitia, annos et hominum de se opinionem superans, diem nullam otiosam preteriit agendo, omnia cognitu dignissima perscrutando, difficillima, ardua et lau-

55 datissima tentando, nunquam laboribus aut vigiliis parcendo. Denique, ut totum hoc genus laudis brevissime complectar, fuit hoc animi robore atque virtute preditus, ut voluptates imprimis omnes respuendas et aspernandas duceret, otio, desidie, ludis conviviisque ingenuos labores corporis atque animi contentionem ad gloriam

mer and in winter snow.[36] He would sleep not sluggishly or for the sake of pleasure but when it was necessary to rest he would do so anywhere, out in the open, as long as it was not a base or obscene place. He was very sparing with wine and sauces. In short there was no luxury in him, no lavish spending, no debts, no lust for feasting.[37] If he hated anyone, he would accuse them to their face; 51 he would never slander those who were not present; he never betrayed his friends' secrets.[38] Content with his own, he never sought other people's goods. He was gentle and affable with everyone;[39] he was very inclined to make friends with the best kind of people; and he would enter into friendships and increase them through compliance rather than promises, through deeds rather than showing off. In his friendships he desired to be loved more for his virtue than for any rewards or ambition and yet he increased others' love for him by giving rather than receiving. He was not burden- 52 some or harsh to anyone, except that he wanted to be free from and totally segregated from those who were obscene, impure and slothful, and out of a kind of generosity of mind he could not stand such people: like Hercules, he particularly hated all those who rashly attacked someone.[40] With all my friends he was com- 53 pliant, cheerful, dutiful, obedient, so that everybody easily came to love him and entertained the greatest hopes for him.

As his mind grew, so did his reputation and his knowledge of 54 things, going beyond what would be expected of his age and what men hoped for him.[41] He let no day go by without working, without investigating all the things that were most worthy of knowing, attempting the most difficult, arduous and most praiseworthy subjects, never stinting in his labors or studies.[42] In short, in order 55 to embrace briefly all the different elements of praise, he was endowed with such strength of mind and virtue that he believed that all pleasures were to be particularly rejected and despised. He preferred the noble labors of the body and striving of the mind toward glory over leisure, laziness, games and feasting; and

56 preferret, in omnique vite cursu ea minime esse expetenda putaret, que essent a laude et dignitate seiuncta. Seque natum arbitrabatur non ad somnum et delectationem, sed ad virtutem, dignitatem, ad patrie decus et ornamentum, ad studiosorum commoda, ad bonam gratiam, ad famam nominisque claritatem et posteritatem comparandam.

57 Hec igitur illius fuere studia et vite modus: que quidem quasi capita summamque gestorum suorum succincte et presse duxi esse recolligenda. Namque si preclara eius omnia facinora ordine velim recensere, grandis admodum foret et supra meas facultates longe

58 mihi difficillimus susceptus labor; siquidem is omni in laude consequenda studio, industria, opera, assiduitate, diligentia cuivis preclarissimorum hominum concessit nunquam, quin et cum integros dies ad laudem et gloriam summis laboribus et omnibus viribus contendisset, noctu etiam interdum varios canendi modos auribus a concentu sperarum orbis haustos (ne musicam sprevisse

59 et omnino austerus videretur) ad lunam exprimebat. Hocque eo studiosius agebat, quod me disputantem audierat a cognitione earum rerum que turpitudine vacent (modo maiora et digniora studia non pretermittant) minime abhorrere ingenui proprium esse. Namque quis ingenuum se et libere educatum audeat dicere, cum in equo indecenter sedeat, aut palestra turpiter labatur, aut in armis tractandis rudis atque penitus ignarus fuerit? Sed de his alias.

60 Ad canem nostrum redeo. Qui quidem, quo a digno opere nullum vel minimum hore momentum vacaret, cum una mecum—a cuius latere numquam discedebat, apud quem etiam omne tempus perditum arbitrabatur nisi quod discendo consumeret—ad

throughout the course of his life he believed that those things that were devoid of praise and dignity were not to be pursued at all. He believed that he was born not for sleep and pleasure, but for 56 virtue and distinction, and to be the ornament and glory of his fatherland; he was born for the benefit of the scholarly, for the pursuit of good grace, for fame and the acquisition of a reputation that would last for posterity.

These, then, were his pursuits and way of life, which I thought 57 I should gather together in a succinct and brief way as just a list and summary of his deeds. For if I wanted to go through all his famous actions in due order, the labor would really be quite substantial, extremely difficult and far beyond my capacities. For the 58 fact is that this dog, in terms of pursuing all kinds of praise through his efforts, industry, work, assiduity and diligence, never came second to any of the most famous men in history. On the contrary, after whole days devoting his labor and strength to the pursuit of praise and glory, at night he would also sometimes sing to the moon in various musical modes which he drew from the harmony of the spheres, lest he seem to disdain music and appear completely austere.[43] And he did this all the more enthusiastically 59 because he had heard me say that it was right for a noble intellect not to shun knowledge of other disciplines as long as they are free from turpitude and as long as one does not omit greater and more worthy subjects. For who would dare call himself noble and liberally educated if he could not sit appropriately on a horse, or slipped inelegantly in the gymnasium, or was unskilled and totally ignorant in handling arms. But we can talk about such things another time.[44]

Let us return to our dog. In order that he should not spend 60 even a moment of time without doing worthy deeds, he stayed with me and never left my side. In my company he also believed that all time was wasted if it was not spent it in learning something,[45] and would often set off for the gymnasium and the meet-

gymnasium et studiosorum (quod sepe fiebat) conventum proficiscebatur, is letus et quasi ad exspectatissimam voluptatem accersi-
61   tus procedebat. Et quo sibi aliorum vitam, ut aiunt, magistram haberet, et optimos et laudatissimos, selectis spretisque turpibus, imitari commodius posset, quicquid ubique digni ageretur, quid quisque obvius canis saperet doctrinarum, Academiamne, Stoicos an Peripateticos, an Epicuros oleret, sagaci industria scrutabatur, ad meque tantisper mores et ingenium eorum quos tractasset re-
62   ferebat. Bonos comiter consalutabat, segnes ac petulantes castigabat dictis. Denique semper etiam inter eundum erat in officio et cultu virtutis. Cum autem ad gymnasia esset deventum, discendi studio intra coronam disputantium equo et prono animo, cunctis eam rem ferentibus, tacitus atque attentissimus, illud Pythagore observans qui taciturnitatem discipulis imperabat, sese medium
63   continebat. Quod si quem insolentem ostentatorem ingenii sui dicacemque atque nimium arrogantem et immodestum disputatorem offendisset, illico eius ineptias maximis increpationibus coercebat. Nolebat enim eo in loco bonas illas horas male per temeritatem alicuius deperdi.

64   Quibus omnibus in rebus quam assiduus, diligens perseveransque fuerit, quid ergo hoc loco infinita eius exempla connumerem? Quo enim studio, quibus vigiliis ad disciplinas incubuerit, testes sunt scole litteratorum, in quibus persepius summa cum
65   audentium attentione maximis vocibus declamavit. Quo autem morum splendore, qua facilitate, humanitate, affabilitate ornatus fuerit, testes sunt gratia et benivolentia, qua omnes in illum erant, dum vitam ageret, affecti; testis et meror funeris, lacrime bonorum ac desiderium, quo illum omnium etatum omnisque fortune

ing place of scholars: he was happy doing this and felt as if he had been summoned to experience the most longed-for pleasure. And 61 in order that the lives of others, as they say, should be a lesson to himself,[46] and that he could more easily imitate the best and most praised individuals, rejecting and disdaining anyone ignoble, he studied with wise industriousness whatever worthy deed was performed anywhere. He inquired what each dog he met knew of philosophy and whether its views were redolent of the Academy, the Stoics, the Peripatetics or the Epicureans, and he would duly report to me the character and intellect of those he met.[47] He al- 62 ways gave a friendly greeting to good dogs, but would reproach lazy and petulant ones with his sayings. Finally, even when going about his daily rounds, he was always pursuing his duty and cult of virtue. When he went to the gymnasium, out of his love for learning he kept himself in the middle of the crowd of debaters with a fair and well-disposed mind: all the others tolerated this behavior, and he silently and very attentively observed Pythagoras' famous rule that imposed silence on his followers.[48] If he came 63 across anyone insolent showing off his intellect and being sarcastic, or someone too arrogant and immodest as a speaker, he immediately tried to restrain that person's foolishness through his very critical rebukes. For he did not want to waste his precious time in that place because of someone else's rashness.

Why should I list at this point infinite examples to show how 64 assiduous, diligent and persevering he was in all these things? The literature schools bear witness to how much study and concentration he devoted to these disciplines: there he would very often declaim in a loud voice and attract the audience's attention. How 65 endowed he was with splendid morals, how easygoing in his nature, humaneness and affability is evidenced in the gratitude and benevolence with which everyone regarded him while he was alive. Another indication of this was the sadness at his funeral, the tears of good citizens and the way people of all ages and classes missed

66 homines defunctum prosecuti sunt. Quam postremo solida et perfecta et absoluta inter mortales virtute fuerit, quos ego testes alios adducam preter auctoritatem, famam et nominis claritatem, quam magnificis et innumerabilibus suis gestis vivens sibi ipse compara-

67 vit? Quod genus belli in quo non ipse sit cum laude versatus? Maritimis contra anates atque anseres, piratas et fures aquaticos; campestribus contra locustas, ortorum vastatores; murali contra

68 lacertas, alveorum et rerum publicarum perturbatores. Quibus omnibus in rebus, dum corona et triumpho dignus putari quam consequi studuit, omnes eos, qui aut in otio litterarum aut in publico negotio cum laude et auctoritate fuere versati, gloria et claritate antecessit, ut cum in ceteris singulis singulas virtutes singulari aliquo vitio comite et coadiuncto fuisse comperias, in hoc uno omnes fuisse virtutes accumulatas, quovis vel minimo secluso vitio,

69 invenias. Non enim cupidus ut Aristoteles, quem hamo aureo apud inferos pro pisce captum finxere; non lascivus ut Plato, cuius de Stella suo amatorii versus efferuntur; non ambitiosus ut Cicero, qui cum sese laudando pene defessus esset, alios per epistulam oravit ut de laudibus suis librum conscriberent; non crudelis ut Sylla, qui tot civium romanorum milia mactari iussit; non legum et libertatis eversor, non reipublice occupator ut Cesar; non mulierosus ut Cato, qui etiam sua ultima pene etate scribe cuiusdam filiam, amore captus, uxorem petiit; non cupidus ut Crassus, qui, omnium ditissimus, falsa in dies testamenta adiret.

70 Sed quid ego istos omnes prosequar, aut istiusmodi ceteros apud historias celebres cum cane nostro comparem? In illis maxima vitia virtuti applicita aut ad mediocrem probitatem nulla

him and honored him at his death.[49] Finally, to show how un- 66
shakeable, perfect and complete his virtue was among men, what
other witnesses can I call on except the authority, fame and splendor of his name, all things which he achieved on his own with his
countless magnificent deeds during his lifetime? What kind of war 67
is there that he did not engage in and emerge with praise? He
fought on water against ducks and geese, those aquatic pirates and
thieves; he fought land battles against locusts, those destroyers of
gardens; and he fought on walls against lizards, those disturbers of
beehives and the commonwealth of animals. For all these achieve- 68
ments, while he strove simply to be thought worthy of a triumphal
crown, rather than actually to be awarded it,[50] he far outdid in
glory and resounding fame all those who spent their lives acquiring
praise and authority in the leisure of literature or in public office.
Consequently, whereas in each of the others you would find their
virtues accompanied closely by some single vice, in this one dog
you would find all the virtues present with no vice, however slight,
to accompany them. For he was not greedy like Aristotle, who (the 69
story goes) was caught like a fish by a golden hook in the underworld;[51] nor was he lascivious like Plato, whose amatory poems
about his Stella are still read;[52] nor ambitious like Cicero, who
when he was almost exhausted from praising himself, in one of his
letters then asked other people to write a book in his praise;[53] nor
cruel like Sulla, who ordered so many thousands of Roman citizens to be slaughtered; nor was he a subverter of laws and freedom, nor someone who seized the state, like Caesar; nor was he
uxorious like Cato, who even in almost the last phase of his life fell
in love with and asked to marry the daughter of one of his
scribes;[54] nor was he greedy like Crassus, who although he was the
richest man of his time, wrote false testaments day after day.[55]

But why should I rehearse the names of all those people? Or 70
who are the others famous in history that I can compare to my
dog? In them you will find some virtue but it is accompanied by

rerum gestarum preclara monumenta adiecisse invenies. In cane autem hoc nostro maximas et excellentes virtutes, prestantissimum ac pene divinum ingenium, omni vel minima turpitudine et obsce-
71 nitate vacuum, fuisse quisque palam asseverat. Quid est quod in illo optes, aut non longe eum maximis et illustrissimis virtute viris anteponas? qui quidem summa cum fortitudine coniuncta habuit integram iustitiam, incredibili cum animi magnitudine singularem pietatem et religionem, divina cum ingenii flexibilis et versatilis vi firmitudinem et perseverantiam incohatarum et inceptarum rerum, versuta et callida cum natura et mente simplicitatem ac penitus innocuam vite rationem, egregia cum gravitate ac severitate miri-ficam humanitatem ac misericordiam, facilitatem, affabilitatem, grandique ac multiplici cum rerum usu et experientia integram, solidam et absolutam sapientiam.

72 Pro meo idcirco iusto dolore possem incusare fortunam, que optimum illum et sanctissimum nobis acerbo fato eripuerit. Satis quidem ille diu vixit, non nego, qui bene cum virtute ad gloriam vixit. Cuperem tamen ab amicis illum et ab iis, qui suis exemplis
73 in dies meliores et eruditiores reddebantur, minus desiderari. Ete-nim, quis non condoluerit, cum florida etate preter spem et expec-tationem omnium ab invidis atque occultis eum inimicis veneno absumptum meminerit? Quis non merore afficiatur, cum cetus studiosorum eius interitu mestos ac tristes intueatur? Quis non collugeat, cum memorie repetat illius morientis amorem erga me?

74 O noster igitur canis, nostre delitie, decus iuventutis, splendor et ornamentum familie tue, qui et forma et moribus et virtute

the greatest of vices, or they have a mediocre level of uprightness with no famous monuments to their deeds. In my dog everyone openly agrees there was the maximum number of excellent virtues, an outstanding and almost divine intellect which was devoid of even the slightest baseness or obscenity. What is there that you 71 would want him to have had in addition, or why would you not put him far ahead of the men who were greatest and most famous for virtue? This dog possessed a complete sense of justice coupled with maximum fortitude; alongside incredible magnanimity he had a unique form of piety and religion; and he showed strength and perseverance in enterprises he was about to begin or had already begun, coupled with the almost divine strength of his flexible and versatile intellect. He also had a clever and ingenious nature and mind as well as simplicity, and a totally harmless approach to life; alongside his outstanding gravity and severity he possessed a wonderful humaneness and compassion, an approachableness and affability, and in addition to his great and varied experience in practical matters he possessed a solid, complete form of wisdom.

On account of my righteous grief I could blame fortune who 72 bestowed this bitter fate on us and snatched away from us that best and most pious of dogs. I do not deny that anyone who has lived well pursuing glory through virtue has lived long enough. I would, however, like him to be less missed by his friends and by those who were made better and more learned day by day through his examples. For who would not share in our grief when they re- 73 member that in the prime of his life, when he was flourishing more than all of us could have hoped for or expected, he died of poison administered by envious and secret enemies? Who would not be affected with sadness when they see how grief-stricken and bereft all scholars are by his demise? Who would not grieve with us when they remember his love for me as he lay dying?

So, my dog, our source of delight, the glory of our youth, the 74 splendor and ornament of your family: your ancestors were very

nobilissimam, vetustissimam ornatissimamque familiam tuam multo nobilitasti ac longe celeberrimam effecisti, qui iocus et festivitas esse nostra consueveras, quem intuentes iucundum, facetum ac lepidissimum, amenitate, alacritate, hilaritateque quadam af-

75 ficiebantur! Tu cuius presentiam modestie, dignitatis, gratie, humanitatisque refertam studiosi admirabantur; cuius ingenium, doctrinam virtutesque spectando et animo repetendo omnes obstupescebant, suscepto veneno, quasi a complexu amici in longissimam alterius vite peregrinationem discedens, me revisum atque exosculatum moriens, veneno tabidus et confectus, accessisti,

76 atque primo conspectu conlacrimasti. Vale, igitur, canis, atque esto, quantum in me sit, prout tua expetit virtus, immortalis.

Appendix

Leo Baptista—cum ei rhetor quidam, cuius de eloquentia grandis erat apud vulgus opinio, funebrem orationem a se editam ostendisset, quod eam non vehementer comprobaret, succensuit (erat enim ieiuna et enervis)—commotus ea de re, sed quo ostenderet quid intersit accuratum esse an haberi vulgo scriptorem, quove se aliquid ad iudicanda imperitorum opera tenere demonstraret, hanc scribere instituit orationem: in qua illud sibi assumpsit, ut potius emuli oratoris ieiunitatem explicaret, prescrictis [*sc.* prescriptis] et quasi lustratis laudationum et amplificationum locis, quam ut ullam dicendi gloriam captaret.

noble, ancient and laden with honors, but you ennobled that family enormously through your beauty, character and virtue and made them very famous far and wide. You were accustomed to being our source of play and festivity, and when people saw your fun-loving, witty and very clever nature, they were filled with happiness, alacrity and hilarity! Scholars admired your presence, 75 which was full of modesty, dignity, grace and humaneness; they were all astonished as they gazed upon and went through in their minds your genius, erudition, virtues. After you had taken the poison, as though departing from the embrace of your friend as you set out on that very long journey toward another life, you came back to see me and to kiss me even though you were dying, terminally infected with the poison, and at your first sight of me, you wept. Farewell, then, my dog, and may you be — as much as it 76 is in my power to ask for this, and just as your virtue demands — immortal.

Appendix[56]

A certain orator, whose eloquence was very highly thought of among the people, showed Leon Battista a funeral oration he had written, but the orator became angry when the former did not enthusiastically approve of the speech (for it was rather thin and weak). Stirred up by this, Battista decided to write the oration that follows in order to show the man the difference between really being an accurate writer as opposed to just being considered such by the populace,[57] or to prove that he possessed the criteria to judge the works of inexperienced people. In this funeral oration he wanted to show it was more important for him to demonstrate the thinness of the rival orator's work by pointing out and highlighting the places that lent themselves to praise and amplification, rather than aiming at any glory for his own speech.

VITA

1 Omnibus in rebus que ingenuum et libere educatum deceant ita
fuit a pueritia instructus, ut inter primarios etatis sue adolescentes
minime ultimus haberetur. Nam cum arma et equos et musica
instrumenta arte et modo tractare, tum litteris et bonarum artium
studiis rarissimarumque et difficillimarum rerum cognitioni fuit
deditissimus; denique omnia que ad laudem pertinerent studio et
meditatione amplexus est; ut reliqua obmittam, fingendo atque
pingendo nomen quoque adipisci elaboravit; adeo nihil a se fore
pretermissum voluit, quo fieret a bonis approbaretur. Ingenio fuit
versatili, quoad nullam ferme censeas artium bonarum fuisse non
suam. Hinc neque otio aut ignavia tenebatur, neque in agendis
rebus satietate usquam afficiebatur.

2 Solitus fuerat dicere sese in litteris quoque illud animadvertisse
quod aiunt: rerum esse omnium satietatem apud mortales. Sibi
enim litteras, quibus tantopere delectaretur, interdum gemmas
floridas atque odoratissimas videri, adeo ut a libris vix posset fame
aut somno distrahi; interdum autem litteras ipsas suis sub oculis
inglomerari persimiles scorpionibus, ut nihil posset rerum om-
3 nium minus quam libros intueri. A litteris idcirco, si quando sibi
esse illepide occepissent, ad musicam et picturam aut ad membrorum exercitationem sese traducebat. Utebatur pila, iaculo amen-
tato, cursu saltuque luctaque atque imprimis arduo ascensu in
montes delectabatur, quas res omnes valitudini potius quam ludo
4 aut voluptati conferebat. Armorum preludiis adolescens claruit.

MY LIFE

From childhood onward he was so well instructed in every attain- 1
ment that befits a liberally educated gentleman that he occupied
no mean position among the leading young men of his age.[1] For he
was skilled in the art and method of handling weapons, horses,
and musical instruments, and was totally dedicated to literature
and the study of the humanities, as well as to the knowledge of the
most unusual and difficult subjects. In short, with constant study
and reflection he embraced everything that pertained to the acquisition of merit. Leaving aside his other achievements, he strove to
acquire a name for himself also in sculpting and painting, so keen
was he on not omitting anything from his studies that would gain
him approval from good men. He possessed such a versatile mind
that you would think that there was almost none of the humanities that he had not mastered.[2] Hence he was neither held back by
leisure or laziness, nor did he ever tire of doing things.

He used to say that he had also noticed a particular phenome- 2
non in literature mentioned by writers, namely that mortals become weary of everything.[3] For at times literary works, in which he
so delighted, seemed to him to be like flowering, sweet-smelling
buds, so much so that he could not be torn away from his books
by either hunger or sleep; but at other times the letters themselves
seemed to coil up before his eyes like scorpions, so that he could
do anything other than look at a book. As a result, whenever the 3
letters on the page began to be irksome to him, he would turn to
music and painting and physical exercise. He would exercise with
a ball or a thonged javelin, enjoying running, jumping and wres-
tling, and most of all he delighted in climbing steep mountains, all
of which activities he would indulge in more for his health than
for sport or pleasure. As an adolescent he was famous for his feats 4

Pedibus iunctis stantium humeros hominum saltu supra transilibat; cum hasta parem habuit saltantium ferme neminem; sagitta manu contorta thoracis firmissimum ferreum pectus transverberabat. Pede sinistro ab pavimento ad maximi templi parietem adacto, sursum in ethera pomum dirigebat manu, ut fastigia longe supervaderet sublimium tectorum; nummulum argenteum manu tanta vi emittebat, ut qui una secum afforent in templo sonitum celsa convexa tectorum templi ferientis nummi clare exaudirent. Equo insidens, virgula oblonga, altero capite in pedis dorsum constituto et manu ad alterum virge caput adhibita, in omnem partem quadrupedem agitabat, virga ipsa integras, ut volebat, horas immota nusquam: mirum atque rarum in eo, quod ferociores equi et sessorum impatientissimi, cum primum conscendisset, sub eo vehementer contremiscebant atque veluti horrentes subtrepidabant.

5 Musicam nullis preceptoribus tenuit et fuere ipsius opera a doctis musicis approbata; cantu per omnem etatem usus est, sed eo quidem intra privatos parietes aut solus, et presertim rure cum fratre propinquisve tantum. Organis delectabatur et inter primarios musicos in ea re peritus habebatur. Musicos effecit nonnullos eruditiores suis monitis.

6 Cum per etatem coepisset maturescere, ceteris omnibus rebus posthabitis, sese totum dedicavit studiis litterarum. Dedit enim operam iuri pontificio iurique civili annos aliquot, idque tantis vigiliis tantaque assiduitate, ut ex labore studii in gravem corporis valitudinem incideret. In ea quidem egritudine suos perpessus est affines non pios neque humanos. Idcirco consolandi sui gratia,

when training with arms; with his feet joined together he would leap over the shoulders of men standing upright; he had hardly any equal in pole vaulting; an arrow fired by his hand could pierce the strongest iron breastplate. Standing on the ground outside the wall of our biggest church, with his left foot thrust against it, he would throw an apple upward into the air, so that it would go well beyond the topmost part of its lofty roof; inside the cathedral, he would throw a small silver coin with such force that those who were with him there could clearly hear the noise of the coin as it struck the high cupola of the church roof.[4] When he sat on a horse, he would hold an elongated rod, one end of which was placed on the top of his foot and the other he held in his hand, and with this he would guide the horse in every direction, with the stick constantly moving for hours on end, if he wanted. There was something astonishing and very rare in him, namely that as soon as he mounted even the fiercest horses, the ones most impatient of their riders, they would start to shake violently all over and, as if bridling, would tremble beneath him.[5]

Without any teachers he became skilled in the art of music, and $\quad$ 5 his own compositions were appreciated by learned musicians; throughout his life he loved singing, but only on his own or inside the private walls of his house, and especially in the countryside in the presence of only his brother and other relations.[6] He delighted in the organ and he was held by the best performers to be an expert in that discipline. He made several musicians more learned with his advice.

When in the course of time he approached maturity, he put $\quad$ 6 everything else aside and devoted himself to the study of literature. He spent a number of years studying canon and civil law, and he did so with such diligence, reading long into the night, that from the fatigue brought on by studying he became seriously unwell. And it was during that illness that he discovered that his relatives showed him neither sympathy nor humanity.[7] As a result,

intermissis iurium studiis, inter curandum et convalescendum
7 scripsit *Philodoxeos fabulam*, annos natus non plus viginti. Ac, dum
per valitudinem primum licuit, ad coepta deinceps studia et leges
perdiscendas sese restituit; in quibus cum vitam per maximos labores summamque egestatem traheret, iterato gravissima egritu-
8 dine obrutus est. Artus enim debilitatus macritudineque absumpte
vires ac prope totius corporis vigor roburque infractum atque ex-
haustum, eo deventum est gravissima valitudine, ut lectitanti sibi
oculorum illico acies, obortis vertiginibus torminibusque, defecisse
videretur, fragoresque et longa sibila ad inter aures multo reso-
narent.

Has res phisici evenire fessitudine nature statuebant; ea de re
admonebant iterum atque iterum ne in his suis laboriosissimis iu-
9 rium studiis perseveraret. Non paruit, sed cupiditate ediscendi
sese lucubrationibus macerans, cum ex stomaco laborare occepit,
tum et in morbum incidit dignum memoratu. Nomina enim interdum familiarissimorum, cum ex usu id foret futurum, non occur-
rebant (rerum autem que vidisset, quam mirifice fuit tenax). Tandem ex medicorum iussu studia hec, quibus memoria plurimum
10 fatigaretur, prope efflorescens intermisit. Verum, quod sine litteris
esse non posset, annos natus quatuor et viginti ad philosophiam se
atque mathematicas artes contulit: eas enim satis se posse colere
non diffidebat, siquidem in his ingenium magis quam memoriam
exercendam intelligeret.

11 Eo tempore scripsit ad fratrem *De commodis litterarum atque incommodis*, quo in libello, ex re ipsa perdoctus, quidnam de litteris

in order to console himself, he interrupted his legal studies, and in the process of looking after himself and returning to full health, he wrote the comedy *Philodoxeos* when he was not more than twenty years old.[8] As soon as his health permitted, he then went back to the studies he had begun and to a thorough learning of the law; during which process, in the midst of great labor and in total poverty, he was once more overcome by a very serious illness. This time his limbs became debilitated, his strength drained away through loss of weight, and the force and vigor of almost his whole body broke down in a state of exhaustion. This terrible ill health brought him to the point where, as he read, his eyesight at once seemed to fail amid a sudden dizziness and bowel pains, while bangs and long hissing noises resounded loudly in his ears.

The doctors decided that these things were caused by a weakness of nature; and advising him on this subject, they warned him again and again not to persevere in these very laborious legal studies of his. He did not obey them, but grinding himself down with studying because of his love of learning, he began first to have stomach problems, and then fell into an illness that is worthy of note. On occasions the names of his closest relatives and friends would not come to him, even though he regularly frequented them (yet he had an amazingly tenacious memory for things he had seen).[9] In the end, obeying doctors' orders, he abandoned those studies which rely most heavily on memory, just when he was in his prime. However, since he could not live without reading, he turned, at the age of twenty-four, to natural philosophy and mathematics;[10] for he was confident that he could cope with these subjects adequately, since he realized that they demanded more of one's intelligence than of one's memory.

At that time he wrote and dedicated to his brother *De commodis litterarum atque incommodis* (*On the Advantages and Disadvantages of Literature*): in this short work he discussed what views one should hold on literature, based on his own considerable experience.

7

8

9

10

11

12 foret sentiendum disseruit. Scripsitque per ea tempora, animi gratia, complurima opuscula: *Ephebiam, De religione, Deiphiram* et pleraque huiusmodi soluta oratione; tum et versu elegias eglogasque atque cantiones et eiuscemodi amatoria, quibus plane studiosis ad bonos mores imbuendos et ad quietem animi prodesset.

13 Scripsit preterea, et affinium suorum gratia, ut lingue latine ignaris prodesset, patrio sermone, annum ante trigesimum etatis sue, etruscos libros primum, secundum ac tertium *De familia*, quos Rome die nonagesimo quam inchoarat absolvit, sed inelimatos et asperos, neque usquequaque etruscos. Patriam enim linguam, apud exteras nationes per diutinum familie Albertorum exilium educatus, non tenebat, et durum erat hac in lingua scribere eleganter atque nitide, in qua tum primum scribere assuesceret. Sed brevi tempore, multo suo studio, multa industria id assecutus extitit, ut sui cives, qui in senatu se dici eloquentes cuperent, non paucissima ex illius scriptis ad exornandam orationem suam ornamenta in dies suscepisse faterentur.

14 Scripsit et preter hos annum ante trigesimum plerasque *Intercenales*, illas presertim iocosas *Viduam, Defunctum* et istis simillimas, ex quibus, quod non sibi satis mature edite viderentur, tametsi festivissime forent et multos risus excitarent, plures mandavit igni, ne obtrectatoribus suis relinqueret unde se levitatis forte subarguerent.

15 Vituperatoribus rerum quas conscriberet, modo coram sententiam suam depromerent, gratias agebat, in eamque id partem accipiebat, ut se fieri elimatiorem emendatorum admonitu vehementer

Around the same time, in order to amuse himself, he also wrote a 12
number of other short pieces: *Ephebia*, *De religione*, *Deiphira* and
several other works of this sort in prose.[11] In verse he composed
elegies and eclogues and canzoni and other such love poems, with
which he clearly aimed to help scholars to acquire good morals and
reach peace of mind.

In addition, one year before he was thirty, he wrote in the ver- 13
nacular the first three books of *De familia* (*On the Family*) for the
sake of his relatives and in order to benefit those who did not
know Latin: he finished them in Rome, ninety days after starting
the work, but they were unpolished and rather clumsy, and not
fully Tuscan in all places. The fact is that he had not mastered his
native language, since he had been brought up in foreign lands owing to the lengthy exile of the Alberti family, and it was hard for
him to write elegantly and clearly in that language, since he was
only then becoming accustomed to writing in it. Nevertheless, in a
short space of time, through his long study and diligence, he obtained the following outcome: those fellow citizens who wanted to
have a reputation for being eloquent in the senate admitted that
they had lifted no small amount of embellishments from his writings, on a daily basis, in order to adorn their own speeches.

Apart from *De familia* he also composed, before he was thirty, 14
very many *Intercenales* (*Dinner Pieces*), notably the witty *Vidua* (*The
Widow*), *Defunctus* (*The Deceased*) and others in the same vein.[12] A
number of these pieces, however, he decided to burn because they
did not seem to him to have been written with sufficient maturity,
even though they were extremely witty and aroused much laughter: he did this so as not to allow his detractors anything they
might use to accuse him of triviality.[13]

As for those who criticized his writings, he was grateful to 15
them as long as they delivered their verdict in his presence, and he
took it in such good part that he would congratulate himself ex-
ceedingly on being made a more polished writer through their

congratularetur. De re tamen ita sentiebat, omnibus facile persuasum iri posse ut sua plurimum scriptio approbaretur; que, si forte minus quam cuperet delectet, non tamen se inculpandum esse, quandoquidem sibi, secus quam ceteris auctoribus non licuerit.

16 Cuique enim aiebat ab ipsa natura vetitum esse meliora facere sua quam possit facere; demum sat est putandum si quid pro viribus et ingenio muneri satisfecerit.

17 Mores autem suos iterum atque iterum perquam diligentissime cavebat ne a quoquam possent ulla ex parte ne suspitione quidem vituperari, et calumniatores pessimum in vita hominum malum versari aiebat; illos enim didicisse per iocum et voluptatem non minus quam per indignationem et iracundiam famam bonorum sauciare, et posse nullis remediis cicatricem illati eorum perfidia

18 ulceris aboleri. Itaque voluit omni in vita, omni gestu, omni sermone et esse et videri dignus bonorum benivolentia, et cum ceteris in rebus, tum maxime ⟨in⟩ tribus omnem dicebat artem consumendam (sed arti addendam artem, ne quid illic factum arte videatur), dum per urbem obambularis, dum equo veheris, dum loqueris: in his enim omni ex parte circumspiciendum ut nullis non vehementer placeas.

19 Multorum tamen, etsi esset facilis, mitis ac nulli nocuus, sensit iniquissimorum odia occultasque inimicitias sibi incommodas atque nimium graves; ac presertim a suis affinibus acerbissimas iniurias intollerabilesque contumelias pertulit animo constanti.

20 Vixit cum invidis et malivolentissimis tanta modestia et equanimitate, ut obtrectatorum emulorumque nemo, tametsi erga se iratior, apud bonos et graves de se quidpiam nisi plenum laudis et admirationis auderet proloqui; coram, etiam ab ipsis invidis honorifice

criticism. His view on the matter was this: that everyone could easily be persuaded to approve his writings; but if by chance any of his works delighted others less than he might have wished, he should not be blamed, since he could not do differently from other writers. For he used to say that each man was prevented by nature 16 herself from creating anything that was beyond his potential; in the end it was enough if people carried out their tasks in accordance with the strength of their intellect.

He took care again and again to be very diligent in not allowing 17 his own character to be attacked in any respect, avoiding even the suspicion of his morals being criticized, and he said that slanderers were the worst evil in the life of human beings. Such malicious people had learned to wound the reputation of good men as much for fun and pleasure as because of their indignation and anger, and no remedy could heal the scar of the wound that their treachery had inflicted. Consequently, he wanted to be and to be seen to be 18 worthy of the goodwill of upstanding men, in every moment of his life, in every action and in everything he said.[14] He claimed that one should put all one's art into these three areas (though extra art was required if what you did was not to seem artificial): walking through the city, riding a horse, and speaking. One had to take care in every aspect of these activities to be very pleasing to everyone.

However, although he was easygoing and gentle and would 19 harm nobody, he sensed the hatred of many extremely wicked people, and felt that their hidden enmity was a very serious source of discomfort to him; yet with constant equanimity he put up with the bitterest of injuries and intolerable slander particularly from his relatives.[15] He lived amid the envious and the highly ma- 20 levolent with such modesty and equanimity that none of his detractors and rivals, even when they were quite angry with him, dared to utter anything, in the presence of good and serious men, that was not full of praise and admiration. Face to face, he was

accipiebatur; ubi vero aures alicuius levissimi ac sui simillimi paterent, hi maxime, qui pre ceteris diligere simulassent, omnibus ca-
lumniis absentem lacerabant: tam egre ferebant virtute et laudibus
ab eo superari, quem fortuna sibi longe esse inferiorem ipsi omni
21 studio et industria laborassent. Quin et fuere ex necessariis, ut cetera obmittam, qui illius humanitatem, beneficentiam liberalita-
temque experti, intestinum et nefarium in scelus ingratissimi et
crudelissimi coniurarint, servorum audacia in eum excitata, ut vim
22 ferro barbari immeritissimo inferrent. Iniurias istiusmodi ab suis
illatas ferebat equo animo per taciturnitatem, magis quam aut indignatione ad vindictam penderet, aut suorum dedecus et ignomi-
niam iri promulgatum sineret. Suorum enim laudi et nomini plus
satis indulgebat, et quem semel dilexerat, nullis poterat iniuriis
vinci ut odisse inciperet.

23   Sed improbos aiebat maleficiis in bonos inferendis facile superi-
ores futuros (nam satius quidem apud bonos putari sentiebat
iniuriam perpeti quam facere): idcirco nolentibus ledere contra
eos, qui lacessire parati sint, contentionem esse non equam. Itaque
protervorum impetum patientia frangebat, et se ab calamitate,
quoad posset, solo virtutis cultu vendicabat.

24   Bonis et studiosis viris fuit commendatus principibusque non
paucis acceptissimus; sed quod omne ambitionis assentationisque
genus detestaretur, minus multis placuit quam placuisset, si pluri-
bus sese familiarem fecisset. Inter principes tamen italos interque

received with great honor even by the envious themselves; but when he was absent, and there were very frivolous or like-minded people ready to lend their ears, then particularly those who had pretended to love him above all others would destroy his reputation using every form of calumny. They took it very badly that they were outdone in terms of virtue and praise by someone whom they had spent every effort in trying to make vastly inferior to themselves in terms of his worldly fortune. Leaving aside other misdeeds, there were even some of his close relatives, who, having experienced his humanity, good works and generosity, entered most ungratefully and cruelly into a wicked internecine conspiracy, and aroused his servants' boldness against him, so that with barbarous violence they attacked this most undeserving man with a sword. He bore these injuries inflicted on him by his own relations with equanimity and in silence rather than either indignantly deciding on vengeance or allowing his own relatives' evil deed and resulting ignominy to be made public. For he was more than concerned for the good name and praise of his family, and he could not be induced by any injuries to start to hate anyone whom he had once loved.

But he used to say that bad men would easily triumph in the end through their villainous deeds against the good (for he felt that good men believed that it was better to suffer an injury than to inflict one).[16] For that reason he said it was an unequal contest between those who are prepared to provoke and those who refuse to hurt others. So he sought to stifle with his patience the attacks of the arrogant, and to free himself from calamity as best he could, using only his pursuit of virtue.

He was commended by good men and scholars, and he was highly acceptable to no small number of princes; but since he hated all kinds of ambition and flattery, he was liked by fewer than he might have been if he had ingratiated himself with more people. Moreover, amid Italian princes and foreign rulers there were

reges exteros non defuere uni atque item alteri testes et precones
virtutis sue, quorum tamen gratia ad nullius vindictas, cum novis
25 in dies iniuriis irritaretur et plane ulcisci posset, abusus est. Preterea cum tempora incidissent ut his, a quibus graviter esset lesus,
privata sua fortuna valeret pulchre pro meritis referre, beneficio et
omni humanitate maluit quam vindicta efficere, ut scelestos poeni-
teret talem a se virum fuisse lesum.

26 Cum libros *De familia* primum, secundum atque tertium suis
legendos tradidisset, egre tulit eos inter omnes Albertos, alioquin
ociosissimos, vix unum repertum fore, qui titulos librorum per-
legere dignatus sit, cum libri ipsi ab exteris etiam nationibus pete-
rentur; neque potuit non stomachari cum ex suis aliquos intueretur, qui totum illud opus palam et una auctoris ineptissimum
27 institutum irriderent. Eam ob contumeliam decreverat, ni principes aliqui interpellassent, tris eos, quos absolverat, libros igni
perdere; vicit tamen indignationem officio, et post annos tris quam
primos ediderat quartum librum ingratis protulit, 'Hinc si probi
estis,' inquiens, 'me amabitis; sin tandem improbi, vestra vobis
28 improbitas erit odio.' Illis libris illecti, plerique rudes concives stu-
diosissimi litterarum effecti sunt. Eos ceterosque omnes cupidos
litterarum fratrum loco deputabat; illis queque haberet, queque
nosset, queque posset ultro communicavit; suas inventiones dignas
et grandes excercentibus condonavit.

some in both these categories who witnessed and publicized his virtue, but he never abused their favor in order to take revenge on anyone, even though day after day he was irritated by further injuries which he could easily have avenged. In addition, the time 25 eventually came when his private good fortune could have allowed him to pay back nicely in accordance with their deserts those who had seriously harmed him, but he preferred to bestow upon them favors and every act of kindness rather than seek revenge, doing so in order to make the wicked repent of having injured such a man.

When he gave the first, second and third books of On the Family 26 to his relations to read, he was upset that out of all those members of the Alberti clan who in other respects had plenty of leisure, hardly one of them was found who had deigned to read even the titles of those books, even though at that time the dialogue was actually much sought after by foreign nations. Nor could he help being angry when he saw some of his relatives openly mocking the entire work and its author, and calling it a completely inept enterprise. Because of that insult he initially decided that he would 27 burn the three books he had completed, and he would have done so had not some princes intervened. However, he overcame his indignation through his sense of duty, and three years after completing the first three books he produced a fourth book for his ungrateful relatives, saying: "If you are good men, you will love me for this gift; but if you persist in being iniquitous, your disgraceful behavior will make you hated." Several unlearned fellow citizens 28 were so enticed by those books that they became very serious students of literature. He regarded those people, and all others who were fond of literature, as his brothers; he spontaneously shared with them his possessions, his knowledge and his skills. He freely communicated his worthy and important discoveries with people who were active in those spheres.

29   Cum appulisse doctum quemvis audisset, illico sese in illius familiaritatem insinuabat, et a quocumque queque ignorasset ediscebat. A fabris, ab architectis, a naviculariis, ab ipsis sutoribus et sartoribus sciscitabatur, si quidnam forte rarum sua in arte et reconditum quasi peculiare servarent; eadem illico suis civibus volentibus communicabat. Ignarum se multis in rebus simulabat, quo alterius ingenium, mores peritiamque scrutaretur.

30   Itaque rerum, que ad ingenium artesque pertinerent, scrutator fuit assiduus; pecuniarum et questus idem fuit omnino spretor. Pecunias bonaque sua amicis custodienda et usu fruenda dabat; tum apud hos, a quibus se diligi coniectaret, fuit cum rerum sua-

31 rum atque institutorum, tum et secretorum prope futilis. Aliena secreta nusquam prodidit, sed eternum obmutuit. Litteras perfidi cuiusdam, quibus impurissimum ipsum inimicum pessime posset afficere, noluit prodere; sed interea, dum se nequissimus ille convitiator litterarum auctor mordere non desineret, nihilo plus commotus est, quam ut subridens diceret: 'Enimvero, an tu, homo

32 bone, num et scribere litteras meministi?' Ad molestissimum quemdam calumniatorem conversus, arridens, 'Facile,' inquit, 'patiar te quoad voles mentiendo ostendere qualis quisque nostrum sit: tu istiusmodi predicando efficis, ut te isti parum esse modestum sentiant, magis quam me tua istac presenti ignominia vituperes; ego tuas istas ineptias ridendo efficio, ut mecum plus nihil assequaris quam ut, cum frustratus a me discesseris, tum te tui pigeat.'

Whenever he heard that someone learned had arrived, he would 29
immediately work his way into that person's friendship, and would
learn from anyone about any subject of which he was ignorant. He
would inquire of artisans, architects, ship builders and even from
shoemakers and tailors, whether there was perhaps some technique in their craft which was unusual and little known and which
they carefully preserved as something peculiar to their art; and he
immediately explained these same things to his eager fellow citizens.[17] He pretended he was ignorant in many areas so that he
could test the genius, character and expertise of other people.[18]

As a result he was an assiduous researcher into those things 30
that concerned human intelligence and the arts; but he totally
disregarded money and profit. He would give his money and possessions to his friends to look after and use; and with those by
whom he thought he was loved, he was very generous in sharing
his own possessions and projects, as well as his secrets. He never 31
betrayed other people's secrets, but kept permanent silence about
them.[19] He decided not to publish a letter written by a treacherous
man even though with that letter he could have sorely punished
that most evil person who was also one of his own enemies; but
meantime, when this most iniquitous slanderer and author of the
letter would not stop attacking him, he was moved merely to smile
at him and say: "Really, my good man, do you remember writing a
certain letter?" Turning toward another very annoying attacker he 32
smiled at him and said: "I will gladly allow you, as long as you
want to, to show by your lies what kind of man each of us is: by
going around saying such things you don't so much insult me with
that constant calumny of yours as make these men realize that you
are very boastful. I, on the other hand, just laugh at your foolishness which will ensure that you gain nothing more from me than
to have to leave frustrated and ashamed of yourself."

33   Ac fuerat quidem natura ad iracundiam facili⟨s⟩ et animo acri,
sed illico surgentem indignationem reprimebat consilio, atque ex
industria verbosos et pervicaces interdum fugiebat, quod non posset apud eos ad iram non subcalescere, interdum ultro se protervis,
34   quo patientie assuesceret, efferebat. Familiares arcessebat, qui-
buscum de litteris et doctrina suos habebat perpetuos sermones,
illisque excribentibus dictabat opuscula, et una eorum effigies
pingebat aut fingebat cera. Apud Venetias vultus amicorum, qui
Florentie adessent, expressit annum mensesque integros postquam
eos viderat. Solitus erat rogare puerulos eamne imaginem quam
pingeret nossent, et negabat ex arte pictum dici, quod non illico a
pueris usque nosceretur; suos vultus propriumque simulacrum
emulatus, ut ex picta fictaque effigie ignotis ad se appellentibus
fieret notior.

35   Scripsit libellos *De pictura*; tum et opera ex ipsa arte pingendi
effecit inaudita et spectatoribus incredibilia, que quidem parva in
capsa conclusa pusillum per foramen ostenderet: vidisses illic
montes maximos vastasque provincias sinum immane⟨m⟩ maris
ambientes, tum e conspectu longe sepositas regiones, usque adeo
remotissimas, ut visenti acies deficeret. Has res 'demonstrationes'
appellabat, et erant eiusmodi, ut periti imperitique non pictas,
36   sed veras ipsas res nature intueri decernerent. Demonstratio-
num erant duo genera, unum quod diurnum, alterum quod noc-
turnum nuncuparet. Nocturnis demonstrationibus vides Artu-
rum, Pleiades, Oriona et istiusmodi signa micantia, illucescitque
excelso a rupium et verrucarum vertice surgens luna ardentque

However, he was of a nature that was quick to anger, and had a   33
sharp temper, though he would immediately use his better judgment to suppress his rising indignation. Meanwhile he would
avoid argumentative and obstinate people on purpose, because he
could not help becoming rather heated and angry in their company; on other occasions he would deliberately frequent the impudent so that he could accustom himself to patience. He would   34
regularly summon his friends, with whom he would hold endless
discussions about literature and learning, and he would dictate
brief works for them to write down, and in their presence he
would paint their likeness or make wax models of them.[20] In Venice he reproduced the features of his friends who were still in Florence, a year and several months after seeing them.[21] He used to ask
young boys whether they recognized whose likeness he was painting, and he used to deny that anything could be said to have been
painted artistically that could not instantly be recognized by children. He would strive to reproduce his own features and image so
that through these painted or sculpted likenesses he would become better known to any strangers who wanted to approach him.

He wrote a treatise *On Painting* in three short books,[22] and he   35
also made paintings that were totally original and seemed incredible to those who saw them, works which were enclosed in a small
casket and viewed through a tiny hole.[23] There you could see very
high mountains and enormous stretches of land enclosing a huge
gulf of the sea, and also regions that were far removed from one's
sight, so remote in fact that the spectator's eyesight failed in trying
to glimpse them. These things he called his "demonstrations" and
they were of such a kind that both the expert and the amateur
would decide that what they were seeing seemed actual natural
phenomena and not just painted images. These displays were of   36
two kinds: one he called diurnal, the other nocturnal. In the night-
time demonstrations you could see Arcturus, the Pleiades, Orion
and similar bright stars, while the moon rising up from a lofty

37 antelucana sidera. Diurnis in demonstrationibus splendor passim
lateque irradiat immensum terrarum orbem is, qui post irigeniam,

38 uti ait Homerus, Auroram fulget. Quosdam Grecorum proceres,
quibus mare foret percognitum, in sui admirationem pellexit. Nam
cum illis mundi hanc fictam molem per pusillum, ut dixi, foramen
ostenderet ac rogaret et quidnam vidissent, 'Eia,' inquiunt illi, 'classem navium in mediis undis intuemur; eam ante meridiem apud
nos habebimus, ni istic, qui ad orientem solem nimbus atque atrox
tempestas properat, offenderit; tum et mare inhorruisse intuemur
periculique signa sunt, quod a sole nimium acres mare advorsum
iactat radios.'

39 Huiusmodi rebus investigandis opere plus adhibuit quam pro-
mulgandis; nam plus ingenio quam glorie inserviebat. Numquam
vacabat animo a meditatione et commentatione; raro se domi ex
publico recipiebat non aliquid commentatus, tum et inter coenas
commentando. Hinc fiebat ut esset admodum taciturnus et solita-
rius aspectuque subtristis, sed moribus minime difficilis, quin inter familiares, etiam cum de rebus seriis disputaret, semper sese
exibebat iocundum et, servata dignitate, festivum.

40 Fuerunt qui eius dicta et seria et ridicula complurima collige-
rent, que quidem ille ex tempore atque e vestigio celerius ediderit
ferme quam premeditarit. Ex multis pauca exempli gratia referemus.

41 De quodam, qui diutius inter disserendum ostentande memorie
gratia nimium multa nullo cum ordine esset prolocutus, cum rogaretur qualis sibi disputator esset visus, respondit eam sibi peram
libris laceris et disvolutis refertam videri.

peak of rocks and hills began to shine as the predawn stars glowed. In the daytime demonstrations you would see that light which shines after "dawn, the child of morning," as Homer says,[24] as it radiates far and wide over the immense world. He managed to make some Greek experts, who knew the sea thoroughly, admirers of his. For when he showed them this fictional mass of the world through the tiny hole I mentioned, and asked them what they saw, they replied: "Oh, we see a fleet of ships in the midst of the waves; we will have them here with us before noon, unless that cloud and fierce storm scurrying eastward toward the rising sun overtakes them first; we also observe that the sea has become stormy and these are signs of danger because the sea's surface is reflecting the sun's rays too sharply."

He spent more time researching these things than in publicizing them, for he was in thrall more to his intelligence than to fame. His mind never stopped meditating and commenting on things; it was a rare event if he went home from the city without having pondered on some problem, and he would also reflect on various subjects over dinner.[25] Hence he became quite taciturn and solitary and with a slightly melancholy look, but he was certainly not difficult in character: in fact, among his close friends, even when discussing serious topics, he would always be humorous and amusing, though staying within the bounds of dignity.[26]

There were some people who collected his many serious and witty sayings: in fact he would come out with these off-the-cuff remarks and would produce them so quickly that he could not have had time to think them up in advance. From his many sayings we will select a few, for the sake of example.[27]

A certain man had spoken for rather a long time in a debate, and in order to show off his memory said far too much in a disorganized speech: when asked his opinion of this debater, he replied that he seemed to him like a satchel packed with books that were disordered and torn.

37

38

39

40

41

42   Domum vetustam, obscuram et male edificatam in qua divertisset, tritavam atque idcirco nobilissimam edium appellabat, siquidem ceca et incurva esset.

43   Peregrino roganti quanam foret via eundum sibi eo versus, ubi
ius redderetur, 'Non equidem, mi hospes,' inquit, 'novi'; tum
concives qui aderant: 'Ne vero non id novisti,' inquiunt, 'preto-
rium?' 'Non equidem,' inquit, 'ius ipsum istic habitasse, o cives,
memineram.'

44   Roganti ambitioso purpurane decenter uteretur: 'Pulchre,' inquit, 'ea, modo pectus tegat.'

45   Otiosum quendam garrulum scurram increpans, 'Eia,' inquit, 'ut
apte carioso in trunco evigilans considet rana!'

46   Cum familiarem admoneret ut a maledici consuetudine sese
abdicaret, 'Crabrones,' dicebat, 'non recipiendos sinu.' Cumque sibi
contra a mathematico improperaretur quod bilinguem et versipel-
lem hospitem detinuisset, 'Num tu,' inquit, 'nosti nisi in puncto
equam superficiem attingat globum?'

47   Levitatem et inconstantiam a natura esse datam mulieribus
dicebat, in remedium earum perfidie et nequitie; quod, si perseveraret mulier suis incoeptis, fore ut omnes bonas hominum res suis
flagitiis funditus perderet.

48   Amicum paulo celeriorem et concitatiorem animis quam optas-
set offendens, 'Heus tu,' inquit, 'cave ne ad currendum currendo
ruas.'

49   Dicebat invidiam cecam esse pestem et omnium insidiosissi-
mam: eam enim per aures, per oculos, per nares, per os denique,
ipsas etiam per unguiculas ad animum ingredi et cecis flammis

When he stopped by an old, dark and badly built house, he   42
called it a remote ancestor of a house and therefore a very noble
building for it was blind and crooked.

A foreigner asked him which was the way to the palace of jus-   43
tice, and he replied: "I don't know, stranger." Then some fellow
citizens standing by said: "Are you really saying you don't know
that this building here is the court?" He replied: "Fellow citizens,
I had no recollection of justice ever having been in those prem-
ises."

An ambitious man asked him whether he could decently wear   44
purple, and he replied: "Yes, it will be beautiful on you, as long as
it conceals what's in your breast."

He upbraided a lazy, talkative villain with the words: "Oh, how   45
fitting it is that a croaking frog sits awake on a rotten trunk."

When advising a friend to abstain from the company of a foul-   46
mouthed man, he said: "Hornets should not be welcomed into the
bosom." And when he was being reproached by a mathematician
because he had entertained a double-tongued, double-crossing
guest, he replied: "Surely you must know that a sphere touches an
even surface only at one point."

He said that superficiality and inconstancy had been given to   47
women by nature in order to thwart their treachery and wickedness; for if a woman continued what she had begun, she would
totally destroy with her misdeeds all the good things found by
man.[28]

When he came across a friend who moved faster and was more   48
excitable than he would have wished, he said to him: "Watch out,
be careful that by running just in order to keep going, you don't
collapse on the ground."

He said that envy was a blind plague, the most insidious of all: 49
for it creeps into one's mind through the ears, eyes, nose, mouth,
and finally even through the fingernails, burning with invisible

inurere, ut etiam qui se sanos putent isthac ipsa peste contabescant.

50 Aurum dicebat laboris dominum, laborem ipsum voluptatis servum esse.

51 Ceteris in rebus mediocritatem approbabat; unam excipiebat patientiam, quam aut nimis servandam, aut nihil suscipiendam statuebat, aiebatque persepius graviora ob patientiam tollerari quam ob vehementem acrimoniam tulissemus.

52 Ut morbos, sic et protervorum audaciam aiebat interdum non aliter quam periculosis curandi rationibus posse tolli. Sat eum dicebat hominem sapere, qui saperet que saperet, satisque posse, qui posset ⟨que posset⟩, satisque habere ipsum hunc, qui que haberet eadem haberet.

53 In iurisconsultum perfidum, qui altero humero depresso, altero sublato deformis incederet, 'Equa,' inquit, 'istic nimirum iniqua sunt, ubi lances in libra non eque pendeant.'

54 Dicebat omnem splendorem vim habere igneam: non idcirco mirandum, si nimium splendidi cives de se in animis hominum invidiam succenderent.

55 Tuta ab hostium iniuriis civitate, cum facinorosorum concivium coepta esset ratio, 'Nonne,' inquit, 'istuc fit percommode, ut imbre sedato tecta resarciantur?'

56 Rogatus quinam essent hominum pessimi, respondit: 'Qui se optimos videri velint, cum mali sint.' Iterum rogatus quisnam esset civium optimus, respondit: 'Qui nulla in re mentiri instituerit.'

flames, so that even those who think themselves healthy are actually wasting away with this disease.

He said that gold was the boss of labor, and labor itself was the slave of pleasure. 50

In everything else he approved of moderation, with one exception: patience. About patience he felt either one ought to have an enormous amount of it, or not have it at all, saying also that through patience we often put up with things that are more unbearable than those we would have tolerated in a very bitter dispute. 51

He said that the boldness of the impudent was like a disease, that sometimes it could only be removed by very dangerous remedies. He said that the person who knew what he knew had sufficient knowledge, and that he who could do what he was able to do had sufficient power, and that the man who had what he possessed was sufficiently wealthy. 52

He said of a perfidious lawyer who walked along in a deformed fashion with one shoulder down and the other raised up, "No wonder what is fair can seem unfair, when the scales on someone's balance don't hang evenly." 53

He said that all things that shone had a fiery force, so it was no wonder if very brilliant citizens kindled envy of themselves in the minds of men. 54

After the city was made safe from its enemies' attacks, some criminal citizens were called to account. When this happened, he said: "Surely this is perfect timing, so that the roof can be repaired now that the shower has stopped." 55

When asked who were the worst kind of men, he replied: "Those who want to seem the best though they are in fact the worst." Again, when asked who was the best citizen, he replied: "He who has learned not to lie in anything." 56

57   Aiebat nihil esse tam proprium insitumve atque innatum mulieribus, quam ut eas rerum omnium que egerint dixerintve illico poeniteat.

58   Latum anulum affluenti fortune simillimum sibi videri predicabat, qui quidem ni alligata stuppa arctior reddatur, perfacile e digito decidat.

59   Rogatus quid esset maximum rerum omnium apud mortales, respondit: 'Spes'; quid minimum, inquit: 'Quod inter hominem est atque cadaver'; rerum omnium suavissimum: 'Amari'; liberale? 'Tempus.'

60   Paupertatem in vita hominum aiebat eiusmodi esse ac si via sallebrosa nudis tibi sit pedibus eundum: nam usu callus superinducitur, eo quod fit ut minus in dies tibi reddatur aspera.

61   De cive insolentissimo et omnium importuno, cum audisset missum in exilium, 'Numquid non predixeram,' inquit, 'homini huic, qui quidem, sublato mento, assiduo nebularum olfatu delectabatur, cavendum ne quid offenderet, quo sibi illiso pede esset ruendum?'

62   Fortunatos assimilabat his qui sitienti in flumine navigarent; namque, ni levigato navigio contis laborent, hereant.

63   In concivem quendam maleficum, cum ad magistratum se vocatum congratularetur, 'Memento,' inquit, 'olim te iterum futurum privatum, aut in magistratu emoriturum.'

64   Petierat a quodam, qui sese in republica administranda principem gloriaretur, pluresne essent ii qui scalas edium publicarum conscenderent, quam qui descenderent; cumque ille respondisset parem ferme utrimque sibi videri numerum, iterato quesivit pluresne essent qui per fenestras ingrederentur, quam qui egrederentur.

65   ⟨In quendam⟩ rebus puerilibus et levissimis plurimam operam perdentem, dixit: 'Hunc annos Nestoris multo superaturum'; rogatus quid ita, 'Quoniam,' inquit, 'quadragenarium puerum intueor.'

He would say that there was nothing so proper to women, so 57
intrinsic and innate to them, as their immediate regret at whatever
they had done or said.

He said a broad ring was very like good fortune since it easily 58
fell off the finger unless it was tightened by tying a cord round it.

When asked what the greatest thing was for mankind, he re- 59
plied: "Hope"; when asked what was the smallest thing, he said:
"The difference between a man and his corpse"; the sweetest
thing: "To be loved"; the most copious thing? "Time."29

He said that poverty in the life of men was like having to go 60
along a rough road with bare feet: for a blister develops through
wear, which is why the road becomes less rough every day.

When he heard that a very insolent citizen, the most obstinate 61
man of all, had been sent into exile, he said: "Didn't I warn this
man that he had to be careful, since someone who held his chin up
and delighted in constantly sniffing the clouds should beware in
case his feet stumble on something and he falls down?"

He likened lucky men to people on a boat in a stream that was 62
drying up; for unless they lightened the ship and worked hard
with their poles, they would get stuck.

When an evil citizen was congratulating himself on being called 63
to public office, he said: "Remember that either you will eventually
become a private citizen again, or you will die in office."

He asked someone who was boasting of being the chief person 64
in the republic whether more people climbed the stairs of public
office than descended them; and when the former replied that it
seemed to him that the number was more or less the same on both
sides, he then asked whether more people came in through the
windows than were forced out of them.30

When he saw someone wasting a lot of his time with childish 65
and trivial things, he said: "This man will far outdo Nestor in
longevity," and when asked why so, he replied: "Because what I see
is a forty-year-old who is still a boy."31

66
67
68 Presentibus utendum ut presentibus; doctas amicorum aures scriptorum limam dictitabat; obtrectatores, fallaces, ambiguos et omnes denique mendaces ut sacrilegos et capitales fures aiebat esse plectendos, quod veritatem iuditiumque, religiosissimas ac multo rarissimas res, e medio involent.

69 Cum iniquos affines multis beneficiis et omni officio sepius sibi reconciliasset, solitus erat dicere meminisse quidem se fenum putridum nodo non teneri.

70 Ditissimi et fortunatissimi cuiusdam edes procul fugiendas admonebat; nam solere quidem aiebat, ubi nimium oppleta sint vasa, omnia effundere.

71 Cum intueretur levissimos et ambitiosos aliquos, qui se philosophari profiterentur, per urbem vagari et se oculis multitudinis ostentare, 'Eccum nostros caprificos,' aiebat 'qui quidem infructuosissimam et superbam istanc solitudinem adamarint, que publica sit.'

72 Petitus arbiter ad dirimendam litem nonnullos inter pervicaces et importunos, munus id suscipere recusavit, atque amicis rogantibus quid ita preter officium et pristinam suam facilitatem ageret, 'Lyram,' inquit, 'fractam et penitus discordem ad pueros fore atque ad stultos reiciendam.'

73 De cive rus, facile mortales reddi locupletes aiebat, si ea que paupertas cogat sponte exequantur; atque profligari quidem paupertatem cedendo.

74 Ambitiosi domum spectans, 'Turgida,' inquit, 'domus hec propediem efflabit erum'; ut evenit quidem: nam ob alienum es ipsa-
75 rum edium fortunatissimus dominus in exilium secessit. Cuidam prodigo et insolenti, qui se dictis morderet, cum satis obticuisset,

He said present things had to be used for what they were, since 66
they were present only then; he claimed that the learned ears of 67
friends were the writer's polishing tool; he said that detractors, the 68
deceitful, the untrustworthy and in short all liars were to be punished as if they had committed sacrilege or capital theft, since they
stole from public view those extremely sacred and rare things,
truth and judgment.

After he had reconciled his wicked relatives through his many 69
good acts and all sorts of duties toward them, he used to say that
he remembered that one cannot tie rotten hay.[32]

He warned that people should shun the house of an extremely 70
rich and fortunate man, for—he said—where the vases are too
full, everything tends to overflow.

When he saw some superficial and ambitious men who claimed 71
to be philosophers wandering through the city and showing off in
front of the crowds, he said: "Here are our wild figs: for they delight in this most infertile and proud solitude where the public
gather."[33]

When he was asked to arbitrate in a dispute between some ob- 72
stinate and importunate people, he refused to undertake this task,
and when his friends asked why he was behaving in a manner so
inconsistent with his sense of duty and earlier affability, he replied:
"A lyre that is broken and completely out of tune should be
thrown to children and fools."

Of a citizen going off to the countryside he said: "It is easy for 73
men to be made rich if they carry out of their own accord what
poverty forces other men to do, and it is easy for poverty to be
conquered by giving way."

Looking at the house of an ambitious man, he remarked: "This 74
heaving house will soon spew out its owner"; as indeed happened,
for its very wealthy owner had to go into exile because of the debts
contracted in buying that same house. When a wasteful and inso- 75
lent person attacked him, he was silent for a long time, then said:

'Non tecum,' inquit, 'o beate, contendam, quem respublica suo sit hospitio acceptura.' Horum verborum mordax ille, cum carceribus
76 detentus diem obiret, meminit. Ferrariensibus, ante edem qua per Nicolai Estensis tyranni tempora maxima iuventutis pars eius urbis deleta est, 'O amici,' inquit 'quam lubrica erunt proximam per estatem pavimenta hec, quando sub his tectis multe impluent gutte!'

77   Etenim predicendis rebus futuris prudentiam doctrine et ingenium artibus divinationum coniungebat. Extant eius epistole ad Paulum phisicum, in quibus futuros casus patrie annos integros ante prescripserat; tum et pontificum fortunas, que ad annum usque duodecimum essent affuture predixerat, multarumque reliquarum urbium et principum motus ab illo fuisse enunciatos
78 amici et familiares sui memorie prodiderunt. Habebat pectore radium, quo benivolentias et odia hominum erga se presentisceret; ex solo intuitu plurima cuiusque presentis vitia ediscebat. Omnibus argumentis maximoque opere, sed frustra, elaboravit aliquos erga se mansuetiores reddere, quos futuros infensos ex ipso aspectu sensisset. Eorum tamen inimicitias quasi fatalem quandam necessitatem mediocriter ferebat, in omnique contentione moderatius sibi fore contendendum indicebat, quam fortassis licuisset, preterquam in reddenda mutui beneficii gratia.

79   Vix poterat perpeti pre se quemquam superiorem videri benivolentia, seclusa ambitione, a qua tam longe abfuit, ut etiam quas ipse gesserit res dignas memoratu, suis eas maioribus in libris *De familia* adscripserit. Tum suis in opusculis aliorum titulos apposuit, et integra opera amicorum fame elargitus extitit.

"You lucky man, I will not argue with you since the state will soon take you into its care." That sarcastic man remembered these words on the day he was about to die in prison. Standing in front of the building in Ferrara where in the time of the tyrant Niccolò d'Este most of the city's youth had been killed, he said: "Friends, how slippery will these floors be next summer when many drops will rain down from this roof."[34]   76

He also combined the foresight that came from his learning and genius with the arts of divination in foretelling future events.[35] There are letters of his extant, to Paolo dal Pozzo Toscanelli, the natural scientist,[36] in which he wrote down—whole years before they took place—things that would happen to his country in the future. He also foretold the fortunes of the papacy, up to twelve years before those events came about; and his friends and family have testified that the upheavals that affected many other cities and princes had been previously foretold by him.[37] He had in his breast a kind of ray that allowed him to sense in advance the good-will or hatred of men toward himself; just from a glance he could learn the many vices of anyone in his presence.[38] He would try all methods and expend huge efforts, even though in vain, in order to make others gentler toward himself when he had sensed, just from their look, that they would be hostile to him. However, he tolerated their enmity with moderation, as a kind of necessity of fate, and he claimed that when it came to competing with others he would contend more moderately perhaps than was allowed, apart from when it came to returning thanks for a favor.   77   78

He could hardly stand to see someone seeming to outdo himself in benevolence, and he suppressed his ambition, a flaw from which he was so distant that in the books De familia he would attribute to his ancestors even memorable actions carried out by himself. Also in some of his writings he would insert a title page that ascribed them to others, and made a present of whole works to the fame of his friends.[39]   79

80   Doloris etiam et frigoris et estus fuit patiens. Cum accepisset grave in pedem vulnus, annos natus non integros quindecim, et a medico disducte pedis partes pro more et arte consuerentur, ducta per cutem acu, ⟨et⟩ adnodarentur, emisit gemitum penitus nullum; propriis etiam in tanto dolore manibus curanti medico submini-
81 stravit vulnusque ipsum tractavit. Febribus flagrans et ob laterum dolores frigidas totis temporibus undas desudans, accitis musicis horas ferme duas vim mali et doloris molestiam canendo superare
82 innitebatur. Caput habebat a natura frigoris aureque penitus impatientissimum; id effecit ferendo et sensim per estatem perducta consuetudine, ut bruma et quovis perflante vento nullis capite
83 vestibus operto obequitaret. Allia atque imprimis mel, nature quodam vitio, fastidibat, adeo ut solo intuitu, si quando casu ea sibi fuissent oblata, bilis a stomaco sibi excitaretur. Vicit sese ipsum usu spectandi tractandique ingrata, quoad eo pervenit ut minus offenderent, et exemplum prebuit posse homines de se omnia, ut velint.

84   Animi gratia e domo in publicum exiens, cum artifices omnes assiduos in tabernis versari ad opus intueretur, quasi gravissimo aliquo abs censore commonefactus, sepe domum repetebat, 'Et nos
85 quoque pro suscepto officio' inquiens 'exercebimur.' Vere novo cum rura et colles efflorescentes intueretur, arbustaque et plantas omnes maximam pre se fructuum spem ferre animadverteret, vehementer tristis animus reddebatur hisque sese castigabat dictis: 'Nunc te quoque, o Baptista, tuis de studiis quidpiam fructuum generi

He was also patient when suffering from pain, cold or heat.[40]   80
Before he was fifteen, he seriously injured his foot and when the
two bits which had been torn apart were being sewn together by
the doctors with a needle through his skin, according to the rules
of their art, and then joined together, he did not let out a single
groan; despite being in such pain, he even used his own hands to
help the doctor who was looking after him and treated his own
wound himself. He suffered much from fevers, and because of   81
pains in his sides he would constantly be subject to cold sweats, so
he would summon musicians and would strive to overcome this
serious illness and the unpleasantness of the pain by singing for
nearly two hours on end. By nature his head was very intolerant of   82
the cold and drafts; but by putting up with these things and training himself to ride bareheaded throughout the summer he managed to go on horseback in winter without any covering for his
head, no matter how biting a wind was blowing.[41] By a curious   83
defect of nature he could not stand garlic or especially honey, so
much so that even the sight of them, if by chance they were offered to him, caused bile to rise up in his stomach. He overcame
his weakness by getting into the habit of looking at and handling
these things he disliked, until he reached the point where they
gave him less trouble, and thus he provided a lesson, proving that
men can do everything in their lives as long as they want to.[42]

To relax his mind he would leave his house and go outside, and   84
when he saw artisans assiduously going about their business in
their shops, he would often hurry home, as though he had been
warned by some rigorous censor, saying to himself: "And we too
must exercise ourselves in the task we have undertaken." When   85
spring came and he saw the countryside and hillsides blooming,
and noticed that all the bushes and plants were showing abundant
promise of fruit, his mind would become very sad and he would
castigate himself with these words: "Now you too, Battista, must
promise some fruit from your studies for human kind."[43]

86   hominum polliceri oportet!' Cum autem agros messibus graves et
in arboribus vim pomorum per autunnum pendere conspicaretur,
ita afficiebatur moerore, ut sint qui illum viderint pre animi dolore
interdum collacrimasse, eiusque immurmurantis verba exaudierint:
'En Leo, ut undique testes atque accusatores nostre inertie cir-
cumstant! Et quidnam usquam est, quod integro in anno multam
de se mortalibus utilitatem non attulerit? At tu et quidnam habes,
quod in medium tuo pro officio abs te perfectum efferas?'

87   Precipuam et singularem voluptatem capiebat spectandis rebus,
in quibus aliquod esset specimen forme ac decus. Senes preditos
dignitate aspectu et integros atque valentes iterum atque iterum
demirabatur, delitiasque nature sese venerari predicabat. Quadru-
pedes, aves ceterasque animantes forma prestantes dicebat dignas
benivolentia, quod egregia essent ab ipsa natura dignate gratia.
Lepidissimo cani suo defuncto funebrem scripsit orationem.

88   Quicquid ingenio esset hominum cum quadam effectum elegantia, id prope divinum ducebat, et in quavis re expositam industriam ⟨tanti⟩ faciebat, ut etiam malos scriptores dignos laude as-
severaret. Gemmis, floribus ac locis presertim amenis visendis
nonnumquam ab egritudine in bonam valitudinem rediit.

89   Ore porrecto et subafflicto quidam incedebat: 'Huic,' inquit, 'sua
olet barba.'

90   In insolentem et irridentem: 'Heus tu,' inquit, 'ut solent quidem
apte flere, qui rideant inepte!'

91   In eum qui sua prolixa gloriaretur barba: 'Sordes,' inquit, 'pectoris perquam belle subintegit.'

And when he saw in autumn the fields laden with crops and quan- 86
tities of fruit hanging on the trees, he was so overcome with un-
happiness that there were some people who saw him weep sometimes because of the sadness in his mind, and overheard him
murmur these words to himself: "Behold, Leon, how we are surrounded everywhere by the witnesses and accusers of our laziness!
And what is there anywhere in the world that in a whole year does
not bring great usefulness to men? But you—what thing can *you*
bring before the public that you have finished, as your duty demands?"[44]

He took enormous and special pleasure in looking at things in 87
which there was some model image of beauty and loveliness. He
would gaze in wonder again and again at old men who still conserved a dignified look and were well and strong, and he used to
proclaim that he venerated the delights of nature. He said that
quadrupeds, birds, and other animals that were outstandingly
beautiful deserved our goodwill, since they had been dignified
with exceptional grace by nature herself. When his very charming
dog died, he wrote a funeral oration in its honor.[45]

He regarded as something almost divine whatever man's intel- 88
ligence had created with any elegance, and he thought so highly of
any account that diligently set out any subject, that he would
maintain that even bad writers deserved praise.[46] On several occasions he would return from sickness to good health just by gazing
on buds, flowers and especially beautiful places.

When he saw a man walking along with his mouth thrust for- 89
ward and a rather afflicted look, he said "This man's beard must
stink."

To an insolent and mocking man he retorted: "You should be- 90
ware that those who laugh without reason usually end up weeping
with reason."

Of a man who gloried in his lengthy beard, he said: "How clev- 91
erly he covers the filth in his breast."

92   Ex verbosi ore teter flatus in eius os effundebatur; ille se finxit casu starnutaturum atque: 'Et quidnam cause est,' inquit, 'quod solem starnutabundi aspicimus?' Risere amici, et disputatione hac iocosa verbosi historiam interrupere.

93   Roganti levissimo cuidam quid ita simulacrum finxisset ore aperto: 'Ut cantet,' inquit, 'ubi ipse saltaveris.'

94   Cum laudaretur quidam, quod diligens animadversor esset et scriptorum errores perquam severe colligeret: 'Nunc,' inquit, 'hunc video, unde sit erroribus refertissimus.'

95   Helluonem conspicatus, qui quidem esset ad egestatem reductus: 'Non,' inquit, 'hoc phisici novere, homines ex crapula famescere.'

96   Tumidum quendam et plane morosum despectans, dixit: bonum hunc sibi videri musicum, qui quidem ex vestigii compressione excitatam armoniam parvis auribus gradiendo capesceret.

97   Cuidam procaciori cui esset pollicitus nummos, cum aureos rogaret, undecim connumeratis nummis: 'Alium,' inquit, 'si addidero, solidum dedero, qui nummos promisi.'

98   In quendam pinguem, qui esset multo ere alieno astrictus: 'Sic,' inquit, 'et saccus quidem isthoc pacto fieret turgidus, multa capiens et nihil reddens.'

99   In invidum et maledicum: 'At enim,' inquit, 'horrendum canit noctua.'

100   Cuidam qui sue superbiam uxoris detestaretur: 'Neque irasci,' inquit, 'nosti, neque irridere.'

101   In familiarem inertem et somniculosum rogantem quid ita esset, quod suis in edibus hirundines non nidificarent: 'Minime,' inquit, 'mirum; nam istic algent homines.'

When one verbose man's awful breath was being blown in his 92
face, he pretended that he was about to sneeze, adding: "And what
is the reason that when we are about to sneeze we look at the
sun?"[47] His friends laughed, and with this witty exchange they
interrupted the wordy man's chatter.

When some frivolous man asked him why he made a likeness 93
with its mouth open, he replied: "So that he can sing when you
dance."

When someone was being praised because he was a diligent 94
critic, one who very strictly listed writers' mistakes, he said: "Now
I see why this man is so stuffed with errors."

When he saw a spendthrift reduced to poverty, he remarked: 95
"Physicians did not know this, that after excessive feasting men are
hungry."

He looked down on a pompous and clearly difficult man and 96
said: "This man thinks he is a good musician, since with his little
ears he tries to catch the harmony caused by the sound of his own
footsteps."

He once promised money to someone who was quite brash, so 97
when the latter asked for gold, he counted out eleven coins, saying: "If I give you another coin, I would be giving you a gold shil-
ling when I promised you pence."

Of someone fat who was burdened with considerable debt he 98
said: "That is how a sack too would get swollen, by taking much
and not giving anything back."

To a jealous man who was always slandering others he said: 99
"Yes, the song of the night owl is dreadful."[48]

To someone who hated his wife's arrogance, he said: "You don't 100
know how to get angry or to mock."

When a friend of his who was lazy and sleepy asked why was it 101
that swallows did not nest in his house, he replied: "It's no wonder: for in that house men are cold."[49]

102   Ex gibbosi cuiusdam delatoris dorso ab se proficiscentis talpam iam tum surgentem affuturam dixit.

103   Quosdam ex magistratibus improbos a porta propere exeuntes conspicatus, 'Bene,' inquit, 'sese res habet, quandoquidem isti effugiant!'

104   Macie confectum hominem quendam salutans, 'Salve,' inquit, 'salus!'

105   Importuno et plurima petenti: 'O,' inquit, 'mi homo, quantam attulisti negandi facultatem!'

106   Patere aiebat Bononie vicos, quod esset illa quidem pinguis civitas, sed insulsa.

107   In eum qui esset claudus: 'Poplitem is,' inquit, 'perquam belle scalpit.'

When some hunchbacked informer left him, he said he could   102
see the mole rising from his back.

When he saw some corrupt magistrates rushing out of a door,   103
he said: "Things are in a good state if these men are fleeing."

On greeting a man who was thin and wasting away, he said: 104
"God save . . . your health."

To an insistent person who was making a lot of requests, he   105
said: "Oh, my good man, what a lot of opportunities you have
given me . . . to say no!"[50]

He said that the streets of Bologna were wide because it was a   106
rich but insipid city.[51]

Of a man who limped, he said: "How elegantly this man   107
scratches his knee."

MUSCA

Leo Baptista Albertus Landino s.p. dicit.

Incideram in febriculam et languore affectus per meridiem accubabam, amicis aliquot astantibus, cum ad nos littere Guarini allate sunt et cum his *Musca* Luciani, quam meo nomini latinam effecerat. Litteris igitur et *Musca* perlectis facti illariores, 'Utrum,' inquam, 'vestrum est quispiam, qui pro nostro more velit, me dictitante, scribere?' Cum illico sumpsissent calamos, paulo premeditatus hanc edidi *Muscam* tanto cum cachinno, ut ex ea hora febris tedium, levi sudore evaporato, solveretur. Postridie Marcus noster petiit eam ad te mitterem, quo et tu rideres. Congratulor et habeo gratias muscis, quarum ope convalui.

1 Philosophum nescio quem celebrem ferunt solitum admirari ineptias hominum, quod res plerasque in medium expositas et cognitu perfaciles negligant, res vero a conspectu abditas natura et in obscurum retrusas omni studio et omni opere perscrutentur, et eam
2 rem sic expostulasse aiunt: 'Caeline ambitum et siderum motus et huiusmodi reliqua vix ipsi nature satis cognita inepti mortales odiosa nostra curiositate disquirere non cessabimus? Quid vero animans animanti prestet, quidve hi maxime quibus cum vitam degimus ad bene beateque vivendum emolumenti possint afferre,

THE FLY

Leon Battista Alberti to Cristoforo Landino: Greetings.[1]

I had fallen victim to a slight fever and, feeling rather listless, I had lain down about midday, with some friends standing around, when Guarino's letter was brought to me and along with it Lucian's *Musca*, which he had translated into Latin and dedicated to me.[2] When I read both the letter and the *Musca* I cheered up and said: "Is there any one of you who would like to write while I dictate something, as is our custom?" When they immediately took up their pens, I thought about the subject briefly, then composed this version of the *Musca* with such laughter that from that moment onward, once the slight sweat had evaporated, the nausea of the fever vanished too. The next day our Marco asked me to send it to you so that you too could laugh.[3] I congratulate and give thanks to the flies through whose help I recovered.

They say that a famous philosopher used to be amazed at the 1
foolishness of men, because they mostly ignore things that are right in front of their eyes and are very easy to understand, but instead, deploying all their scholarly efforts, they study intensely matters that are hidden from view by nature and concealed in obscurity.[4] People claim that the philosopher expostulated on this fact in the following words: "Will we mortals never cease from 2
being driven by our hateful curiosity to inquire into the circle of the heavens, the movement of the stars and all other such things that are scarcely known even to nature herself? Will we never have any interest in why one animal is superior to another, or what benefit toward leading the good and blessed existence can be brought to us especially by the creatures with whom we spend our

nobis erit penitus nihil cure? Quotus enim quisque est a quo domestica hec si postules (sino maiora), ut quenam ex bove aut iumento in vita hominum commoda suscipiantur, satis id explicite queat pro sua prudentia dicere? An adeo id inter homines vitium est aliunde nisi quod, spretis his rebus que ob oculos vagentur, quasi fastidio quodam acti, commodissima dispicimus et ea demum sectamur que quidem humanis ingenii viribus et studiis nequicquam assequi pro desiderio liceat?'

3   Quod si idcirco ita statuisse oportet studiosos et rerum optimarum cognitioni deditos versari percommode in hiis domesticis et familiaribus rebus dinoscendis, quarum exemplis suas in vita rationes meliores reddant, quis erit qui nostram improbet diligentiam, si in minutorum animantium natura et moribus recensendis aliquid per otium et animi causa opere consumpserimus? Ac, meo quidem iudicio, erimus apud cupidos litterarum non omnino aspernandi, quandoquidem nos qui legerint ita intelligent esse compertum natura, ut voluerit bonas vivendi artes passim, vel a quovis infimo animante, medium inter hominum usum exstare—tametsi ipsa, de qua brevissime dicturi sumus, musca, inter alites una familie nobilitate et prisca maiorum gloria plurimum prestet, ut nequeam et ipse non admirari veteres poetas in laudandis apibus,

4   spreta musca, tantum posuisse opere et diligentie. Quarum quidem seu stirpis generositatem, seu mores omnemque denique vitam compares, multo precellere splendoreque multo muscas quam apes esse illustriores comperias: ex Inaci quidem filia apes ortas non inficior, modo et poete ipsi fateantur muscas ex Centaurorum genere progenitas, ut linteis annalium libris testari fama est.

life? How many people are there who, if you ask them these domestic questions (never mind anything more serious), such as what benefits toward human life can man find in the ox or a horse, can answer clearly enough, relying on their own knowledge? Does this vice among men stem from any other source than the fact that we disdain those things that are before our eyes and are driven by some sort of fastidiousness to despise what is really easy for us to understand? As a result, we end up using the strength and efforts of our human intellect to pursue only those things which we are not permitted to know as much as we would like?"

If then we must decide that scholars and those who are devoted 3 to the knowledge of the finest subjects should spend their time comfortably acquiring understanding of these domestic and familiar matters, by whose example they can improve their rationale for living, who will rebuke our diligence if in our leisure and in order to relax our minds we spend some time in reviewing the nature and character of the tiniest of living things? And in my view, we will not be totally despised by those who love literature, since those who read us will in this way realize that nature has organized things in such a way that she has wanted the fine arts of living to be available everywhere for man's everyday use and wants these to be learned even from the humblest of animals. Yet the fly, about which we are going to talk very briefly, alone among winged creatures is far superior to others in the nobility of its family and in the ancient glory of its ancestors, so much so that I myself cannot but be amazed that the ancient poets rejected the fly and devoted so much work and diligence to praising bees.[5] If you com 4 pare the nobility of its race, or its morals and its whole way of life, you will find that flies far outdo bees and with their splendid achievements are far more illustrious than them. I will not deny that bees sprang from the daughter of Inachus, as long as poets themselves admit that flies are born from the race of Centaurs, as is reportedly stated in the ancient linen books of annals.[6]

5   Et profecto de muscarum prole ita duco esse statuendum, ut quarum intuear vitam pro innato sibi more esse multa ex parte non aliunde quam ex optima, vetere et probatissima disciplina militari, earum aut a Bellona stirpem aut a bellicosissima aliqua

6 invictissimaque gente deductam opinemur. Nam cum, uti aiunt, in re militari hec prima sunt: exercitum instruere ut volens ac lubens pareat; proximum, falangem per tuta sensim deducere; tertium, apto habere loco militem ad urgendum hostem, ad ferendum adversos omnes casus, quis erit qui omnibus his in rebus muscas prescripta veteris familie muscarum disciplina egregie instructas

7 neget? Principio quidem nulla muscarum est, que non veterani militis officium et expertissimi imperatoris munus, nullis aliunde quam a sua solertia et acri perspicacia atque a temporum locorumque occasione captis imperiis exsequatur. Ex quo fit ut non rege et castigatore, veluti tironum greges apium, cohercende sint, sed libero quodam militandi ordine modo pabulatum vagantur, modo in manipulos, modo in maiores turmas pretoriasque cohortes hostem illudendo, in insidias illiciendo atque miris artibus fallendo conveniunt.

8   Getis quidem, quod muscas imitari conati sint, apud claros veteres scriptores ad egregiam laudem adscribitur. Quanta idcirco erit muscarum gloria, que quidem mirifice atque unice genus hoc ipsum militandi norunt? Sole musce ob earum assiduum et inveteratum armorum usum militari gloria celebrande sunt. An fuere unquam seu maiora seu minora ex hibernis mota per omnem hominum memoriam castra, in quibus non ingens muscarum manus

9 inter equestres ordines commilitarit? Nulla uspiam facta preda pecoris qua non participes musce fuerint; agrorum incendia tectorumque ruinas, quod immanitatem saperent, musce nusquam

Indeed I think that as far as the flies' lineage is concerned, we 5
should believe that those whose way of life derives to a large extent
from nothing other than their excellent old military discipline,
which has been tried and tested (as can be seen from their innate
habits), must surely trace their ancestry back to either Bellona or
to some bellicose and invincible race.[7] As is said, the first things in 6
military life are these: to draw up an army so that it is willing and
happy to obey; second, to lead the phalanxes carefully through safe
places; thirdly, to place your soldiers in an appropriate place to attack the enemy, and to bear all adverse fortunes. Since this is the
case, who is there who would deny that flies have been educated
magnificently and according to the ancient discipline of the whole
family of flies? For a start there is no fly who does not know how 7
to carry out the duties of a veteran soldier and the duty of a most
expert leader, relying on nothing but its cleverness, sharp perspi-
cacity and the authority it has gained from tactical opportunities
of time and place. As a result, flies do not need a king or chastiser
to keep them in order, like the swarms of young bee recruits, but
rather they roam sometimes in free formation, wandering around
looking for food, sometimes gathering together in companies, or at
other times in larger swarms and praetorian cohorts, deceiving
their enemy, enticing him into traps, and tricking him with wonderful artistry.[8]

The Getae are egregiously praised by famous old writers be- 8
cause they tried to imitate flies.[9] So how great will the glory of
flies be, since they alone know wonderfully well this style of sol-
diering? Only flies are to be celebrated with military glory for their
assiduous and inveterate use of arms. Has any army in human
memory ever moved camp, big or small, from winter quarters
without a huge company of flies marching alongside the ranks of
knights? There was never any rounding up of animals in which 9
flies did not participate. But these insects have never approved of
the burning of fields or the destruction of house roofs since such

255

probavere, ut facile muscas intelligas cum omnem etatem assidua
militia contrivisse, tum et ipsis victricibus in armis semper humanitatis fuisse et pietatis memores.

10   Illud etiam ex vetere disciplina apud muscas observatur, ut
noctu castris tutissima in edium parte positis congruant caveant-
que ne cum natura irata advorsum, neve cum tempestatibus, al-
gore, siti, neve cum hoste infesto aliquo sibi sit iniquo Marte de-
certandum. Qua quidem in re muscarum prudentiam et belli
peritiam quis satis aut ut merentur laudarit, aut imitabitur ut par
est? Nusquam enim musca castra meditabitur, nusquam assidebit
loco, ni prius terque quaterque tutone illic sibi consedisse liceat
pertentarit, quod ipsum ex primis esse militie laudibus Agesilaus
Pirrhus Fabiusque asserebant.

11   Sed quid multa? Quales tu eas putas publicis futuras in expeditionibus, quas quidem privatis quibusque suis in profectionibus
continuo classicum aliquid pro more canere et ad quoscumque
bellorum usus singula premeditari animadvertas? Timotheum musicum ferunt solitum phidibus et cantu principum animos e convi-
vio in arma et ab acie in convivium revocare: at musca procul voce
canora e regione volitans ipsum in bella ciet Martem, ut arbitrer
Lacenas hinc suum traxisse morem ad tibiam coequatis exercitum
gradibus ductitandi.

12   Accedit his, que hactenus recensui, habitus atque ornatus, quo
quidem maiores nostri heroum statuas et magnorum deorum si-
mulachra adornatas in templis theatrisque ponebant. Aureo enim
et discolori ere thoraca et ab humeris pendulis alis pro tua, o

actions smack of infamy, so you can easily understand that, although flies have spent all their time in assiduous military duty, at the same time they have always been mindful of humanity and mercy even when victorious in arms.

Another thing to be noticed in flies that comes from their ancient military discipline is that at night they gather together, having set up camp in the safest part of the building, and are careful not to fight an unequal battle outside against nature when she is angry, nor against storms, cold, thirst, nor against a hostile enemy. In this context, who has ever praised flies' prudence and experience of war enough or as much as they actually deserve, or has imitated them as they should? For flies will never plan the site of their camp, will never settle in any place, unless they have first ascertained three or four times whether they can settle there safely; and leaders like Agesilaus, Pyrrhus and Fabius asserted that this kind of attentiveness was one of the first things to be praised in soldiery.[10]

But why go on? What do you think they will be like in future expeditions when in each of their private excursions they have the custom of immediately sounding a kind of military horn, and you see them meditating in advance on each aspect of the habits of war? They say that Timotheus the musician used to employ the lyre and songs to lead the minds of princes from feasting to arms, and would also use the same means to call them back from battle to the symposium.[11] But the fly, even from afar, could with its melodious voice rouse Mars himself to war, so that I would think it was from flies that the Spartans derived their custom of leading the army with equal steps to the sound of the flute.[12]

In addition to these things that I have just recounted, flies have the ornate clothes and adornments with which our ancestors decorated the statues of heroes and the images of the great gods in their temples and theaters. For the fly uses a breastplate with varied colors of gold and bronze, and it has wings that hang from its

Romane, toga utitur musca, tantique apud ingenuum muscarum genus a maioribus usque deducta consuetudo fit, ut ne in provincia quidem novos unquam susceperint habitus, quin et virgines matroneque adulte Amazonum more nudis ere pectoribus vagari non novere; et, quod magis mirere, earum vultus si spectes, humanitatemne atque mansuetudinem magis an acrimoniam et iniuriarum quandam militarem intolerantiam pre se ferant musce non

13 satis discernas. Neque id in musca evenit quod in ceteris plerisque militaribus, tum et maxime in milvo, vituperatur, ut supercilio aspero et naso adunco et preacutis falcibus sese sublimem ostentans perduellio atrocissimus haberi velit, acie vero et belli expeditionibus longe effeminatior sit quam secundo esse Gallos impetu re-

14 ferant historici. Quibus demum predita viribus sit musca, cum aliunde tum vel hinc perspicuum est, quod elephantum a musca prostratum se posteritas vidisse litterarum monumentis tradidit. At nos quotiens firmissimum bovem tota exagitatum silva vidimus musca urgente?

15 Que tamen cum et vi et viribus et disciplina maiorem in modum ad omnem armorum usum valeant, hanc sibi primam et precipuam laudem iam tum pridem vendicasse gloriantur, ut cum ceteris virtutibus, tum presertim innocentia maiorum suorum mi-

16 rificas laudes exsuperarint. Sunt qui vulturem egregie commendent auspicatissimumque esse alitem asseverent, quod unum hoc ipsum animal penitus innocuum nullos lacessere, omnibus parcere nature operibus assueverit. At musca nullum flagitium in vita, nullum furtum, nullas rapinas exercet; non floribus celitus noctu demissos hyacinthos, smaragdos, succinos, uniones et eiusmodi gemmas

shoulders like a Roman's toga. In this noble race of flies the tradition deriving from its elders has so taken root that not even in the
provinces did they ever don other clothes: why even maidens and
adult matrons have never learned to fly around without their
breasts covered in bronze like Amazons. What will amaze you
more, if you look at their faces, is that you will not be able to discern clearly whether they show more humaneness and gentleness
or acrimony and a kind of military intolerance of injuries. Nor 13
does one find in the fly a flaw that is criticized in most other warlike creatures, especially in the kite: for that bird with its harsh
brow, pointed nose and ferociously sharp claws, shows itself aloft
in the air and wants to be seen as very fierce in a fight, but when it
comes to an actual battle or expedition, it is much more effeminate
than the Gauls were at the second charge, according to the historians.[13] And finally, the strength the creature is endowed with can 14
be seen from other things but especially from this, that the monuments of literature have handed down to posterity the fact that it
has even been known for an elephant to be laid low by a fly.[14]
How often have we ourselves seen a very strong bull driven
through a whole forest with a fly stinging it?

Yet although flies are more suited to all uses of arms through 15
their strength and power and discipline, they boast of having
achieved another first and most outstanding source of praise a
long time ago, namely that through all their other virtues but especially through their innocence they have outdone the magnificent
merits of their ancestors. There are those who commend the vul- 16
ture in superlative terms and claim that it is the most auspicious
bird, because this one thoroughly innocuous animal never pro-
vokes any other creature and has become accustomed to sparing all
of nature's works.[15] But the fly does not commit any outrage when
it is alive, or carry out any theft or robbery; nor does it pluck from
flowers the amethysts, emeralds, amber, pearls or other such gems
that have fallen from the sky during the night;[16] nor does it, like

decerpit; non in abditum, ut apes, sibi immodicam divitiarum vim
17 congerit. In luce musca, inter hominum frequentiam, in orbis terrarum, ut ita loquar, theatro vitam degit, nullis gravem, sibi quie-
tam, aliis non invisam, suaque studet esse omnia gesta nusquam
vacua interpetre et spectatore. In propatulo convivatur, spatiatur,
dormitat, ut a musca veterem illum Lacedemoniorum morem in
18 publico cenandi institutum arbitrer. Paucis minimisque contenta
musca est, non ambitione, non invidia, non ceteris aliis seditionum
seminariis et discordiarum inritamentis exercetur musca, non tu-
met fastu: eque enim principem atque plebeium, eque divitem
atque egenum amplexatur, exosculatur, confovet alis atque applau-
det.

19   Verum o dignam muscarum vitam! Una epulantur, una alacres,
coactis in unum frontibus, amoris signum, ebibunt, docte quod
aiunt convivium esse alumnum amicitie. Sed quid in his commo-
rer? Utrumne qua inter se pietate et gratia convivant palam et in
promptu parum est, quando fessas muscas ab amica submissis
humeris toto portari ethere intueamur, quo uno solo pietatis me-
20 rito effecit vates ut se Eneas supra sidera notum gloriaretur? Tantaque preterea musce inter se quiete convivunt, tanta et animi
tranquillitate, ut nusquam ex omni historia invenias a musca ferro
aut veneno aut laqueo aut huiusmodi nefario aliquo scelere esse
peremptam muscam, non dolo, non fraude male affectam; non
hanc usque in diem fuere inter muscas odia, simultates, discidia.
Non, ut apes, vatum inmerite delitie, civilia exercent inter se bella;
non ira concitatam detestabile aliquod uspiam facinus muscam se
21 admisisse ex omni memoria comperies. Cetera ferme omnia animantia mortalibus pestem olim atque perniciem attulere: ut cetera

bees, hoard away in a hidden place an excessive amount of riches for itself. This insect spends its life in broad daylight amid crowds 17 of humans, in the world's theater, as it were, not being a burden to anyone, but a quiet creature keeping itself to itself. It is not hated by others, and it tries to make all its deeds have witnesses and spectators. It banquets in company in an open space, it moves around and sleeps in the open, so much so that I believe that the ancient Spartan custom of feasting in public was derived from the fly's behavior.[17] This creature is content with very few and very 18 small things, and is not bothered by ambition or envy or any of the other seeds of dissatisfaction and discord. It does not swell up with pomp: it embraces and kisses both the prince and the pauper equally, cherishing them with its wings and applauding them.

Truly, what a worthy life is that of the fly! They feast together 19 and they drink with alacrity in each other's company, with their foreheads locked together as a sign of love, since they know the learned saying that banquets nourish friendship.[18] But why do I dwell on these things? Is it not obvious and plain to see what piety and grace they exhibit in living together, when we catch sight of one tired fly being borne over the sky by a friendly fellow fly which puts its shoulders under the tired one? With this one virtue of piety the poet managed to ensure that Aeneas could boast that his fame rose above the stars.[19] Moreover flies live among themselves 20 with such peacefulness, such tranquility of mind, that nowhere throughout history will you find one of them having been killed by another fly with the sword, poison, the noose or any such wicked weapons; nor will you find a fly affected badly by deceit or fraud; and there has never been to this day any hatred, arguments or discord among flies. Unlike bees, those unworthy favorites of the poets, they do not engage in civil war;[20] nor will you find in living memory a fly moved by anger to commit any detestable deed. By 21 contrast, almost all other living creatures have brought plagues and perdition at some time to mortal men. Leaving all other examples omittam, locustas legimus agros vastasse, populasse, inediamque et malam pestem reliquisse; formicas item legimus fuisse urbibus exitio; mitem, pacatam equabilemque vitam ipsi homines utinam ducerent persimilem muscis! Non enim plures hominum manu quam omni reliquo calamitatis genere homines periissent; non Transimenus, non Canne hominum cruore maduissent; non flumina cadaveribus coercita constitissent, non ferro flammis et tristi favilla, uti ait poeta, tam multa immersa iacerent; non sic se Cesar plus quatrigenta millia hominum e vita sustulisse gloriaretur. Sed de his alias.

22   Quam vero reliquis omnibus animi laudibus musca egregie exculta sit, quis satis pro dignitate queat recensere? Omnium profecto philosophorum scholas bonos edocuisse mores et bonis instruxisse artibus muscam, si satis eam novi, posse me affirmare non negarim. Missam facio innocentiam, mansuetudinem, mitem animum, simplex pacatumque ingenium, tranquillam et equabilem vite rationem, quibus in rebus muscam longe precellere edocuimus, quas item res in pectoribus militaribus perquam rarissime comperies, ut qui vi et viribus prepotens sit et quoad velit tuto esse contumax queat, idem equitate et mansuetudine diligi quam for-
23   tuna et secundis suis rebus metui ducat antiquius. Maiora enim hec sunt quam ut pro nostris eloquentie viribus condigne possint hoc loco dicendo exornari. Ceterum quanta sint religione imbute musce, quis est quem lateat? An uspiam fuere dapes diis exposite an factum unquam sacrificium, cui non, quoad licuerit, musca

aside, we read how locusts have destroyed and ravaged fields, leaving behind them famine and a terrible plague;[21] likewise we read that ants have destroyed cities.[22] If only men themselves could live a peaceful and calm life, a life very similar to that of the fly! For then it would no longer be the case that more men have perished at the hands of other men than through all other kinds of calamity. Lake Trasimene and the battlefield at Cannae would not have been swollen with the gore of slaughtered soldiers;[23] the rivers would not have become congested with corpses; and so many others would not have lain buried by sword, fire and sad ash, as the poet says;[24] and Caesar would not have boasted about having taken the life of over four hundred thousand men.[25] But more of this at some other time.

Who could recount in a manner worthy of its dignity how exquisitely refined the fly is in all the other topics of praise that have to do with the mind? I can confidently affirm that, if I know the fly well, it has taught fine morals to the schools of all philosophers and instructed them in the good arts. Let me leave aside its innocence, gentleness, its mild manner, its simple and peaceful intelligence, its calm and equable tenor of life, in all of which things we have learned that the fly far outstrips other animals, and these same qualities you will only find very rarely in military breasts. As a result, although it is all-powerful in strength and power, and could be insolent without risk as long as it wants, this same creature thinks it is preferable to be loved for fairness and clemency than to be feared for its good fortune and success. These are matters that are too great to be enhanced appropriately at this point, given my own rhetorical abilities. But who is there who does not see to what extent flies are endowed with religion? Were there ever feasts set out for the gods, or was there ever a sacrifice made where flies were not also present as much as was permitted? They are the

22

23

interfuerit? Prime libant, postreme ab aris decedunt, assidue ad sacrum coherent, noctu ipsis cum diis lucubrantur.

24 Prudentia sunt penitus admirabili: quid enim prudentem magis decet quam ipsum sese nosse ad quam sit potissimum rem peragendam natus? Quid est quod ex bene consulti officio magis conveniat quam ei sese rei totum tradere et id ipsum omni studio et diligentia exsequi, quod te non invita, uti aiunt, Minerva susce-

25 pisse intelligas? Musca quidem, cum se ad rerum investigationem et cognitionem ortam animadverteret, cum a natura ita se adornatam oculis pregrandibus senserit, ut que trans celum, que imo sub profundo queve omnem ultra regionis limbum atque ultimum horizontem latitent facile discernat, quonam in opere commodius, duce natura, comite solertia, exercebitur quam in eo quidem quo flagranti suo studio assequatur, ut nulle se rerum occultarum latebre indagantem lateant? Quod si hominem, cuius ocelli ne vigesima quidem capitis sui pars, ex Pireo Carthaginensium classem a portu progredientem vidisse ferunt, quid erit quod suis turgidissimis oculis non videat musca, quid erit quod suam fugiat curiosita-

26 tem? Ac novit quidem musca quas offas Circe, suos ut in monstra hospites converteret, exposuerit; novit quonam loco diu quesitus Osiris latitet; novit et quenam in natibus adsint vitia Helene, tum et Ganimedis occulta omnia attrectavit; Andromache quoque pendulas vietasque mammas quid austerum saperent iterum atque iterum applicans sensit; denique cum nullas penitus rerum occultarum musca non noverit, o admirabilem inauditamque virtutem!

first to taste and the last to leave the food-laden altars; they assiduously stick close to the sacred meals, and at night they study with
the gods themselves.

They are admirably prudent. For what is more fitting for a pru- 24
dent being than to know by itself what particular task it has been
born to carry out? Is there a better philosophy of life than to devote yourself to the one thing that you know you have undertaken
with the inspiration of Minerva, as they say, and to follow that
through with all diligence and zeal?[26] The fly knows that it has 25
been born to pursue the investigation and knowledge of things. It
recognizes that it has been endowed by nature with such enormous eyes that they can easily discover what lies hidden beyond
the heavens, or below the bottom-most depths of the earth or
outside the borders of its own region and indeed beyond the last
horizon. As a result, one wonders in what operation could the
fly be more appropriately occupied—guided as it is by nature,
and accompanied by its own wisdom—than in that very pursuit
whereby, thanks to its zealous study, nothing that is hidden es-
capes its researches? For if, as they say, a man, whose tiny eyes
occupy not even a twentieth of his head, can see from the Piraeus
the Carthaginian fleet proceeding from its port, what is there that
the fly cannot see with its gigantic eyes and what can escape its
curiosity?[27] The fly actually knows which cakes Circe laid out in 26
order to turn her guests into monsters;[28] it has learned where the
long sought after Osiris lies hidden;[29] it even knows what blemishes Helen of Troy has on her bottom,[30] has fondled all of Ganymede's hidden parts, and knows by constantly landing on them
how bitter is the taste of Andromache's ancient, sagging breasts.[31]
Lastly, since there is nothing that is so deeply hidden that the fly
does not know about it, we can only say what admirable and unheard of virtue it possesses!

27   Pompeium fuisse taciturnum ferunt, et alios ne tormentis quidem adduci potuisse ut conscios facinoris propalarent; hancque
virtutem prope divinis laudibus extollunt. Quid musca, que omnium conscia, nullius tamen unquam dicta aut facta revelavit?
Eam nos quibus laudibus prosequemur? Remne unquam tam se-

28 crete fecimus, ut musca interpres consciaque non fuerit? An musce
lingua tibi esse ullum importatum damnum meministi? A nulla
tantum re abhorrere muscas quam a delatoris perfidia et scelere,
quandoquidem, ex tanto hominum numero, ex tam assidua pecca-
torum exuberantia, que teste musca perpetrantur per omne evum,
musca nullius preter unius tantum Domitiani flagitium et immanitatem, atrocitate iniurie permota, vindicte causa, promulgavit:
scelestissimum enim principem, nimiis in muscarum familiam
odiis delirantem et domesticas familiaresque atque sue solitudinis
comites muscas detestabili crudelitate prosequentem, ut par fuit,

29 inimicum effecit. Etenim quis hunc, qui se preacuto stilo veluti
hostem patrie et iuris publici atque dignitatis perturbatorem
prosequeretur, ferre diutius quivisset? Igitur qua una re sola principum iniurias privati ulciscimur, quamve unam rem solam principes ipsi non metuere non didicere, ea sibi musca penas a consce-
leratissimo desumere iusque fasque exprobatissimorum consensu

30 et opinione duxit: infamia. Nam eius nefarium facinus, diram et
tetram mentem, ut omnibus paterent, ut esset orbi terrarum sua
infamia odio, promulgavit. Neque id quidem sponte, sed coacta:
nam tantis satellitibus armatum ulcisci principem non linquebatur

They say that Pompey was a taciturn man, and that there were   27
others too who could not be induced even by torture to reveal the
names of others in a conspiracy;[32] and people celebrate this kind
of virtue with almost divine eulogies. What about the fly, who
is aware of everything yet has never revealed anyone's deeds or
words? What compliments should we use to praise it? Have we
ever done any deed so secretly that the fly has not been a spectator
and witness of it? Do you ever remember the fly's tongue causing   28
you harm? Flies abhor nothing so much as the perfidy and wickedness of the informer. The fact is that despite the huge number
of such people and the constant, even excessive amounts of such
crimes, which the fly has witnessed everywhere and in every age,
this insect has never broadcast any wicked deed except the outrageous criminal action of one person, the emperor Domitian.[33]
Flies were moved by the atrocity of his attack on them and driven
to revenge. The truth is that the rage of this most nefarious ruler,
his excessive hatred for the whole family of flies, and his persecu-
tion and detestable cruelty against these domestic and friendly
creatures, the sharers of his solitude, made them declare him an
enemy, as was only right. For what being could have put up any   29
longer with this man who attacked him with a very sharp dagger
as though he was the enemy of the fatherland and the subverter of
public right and dignity? Thus using the one thing with which as
private individuals we take revenge for the injuries done to us by a
prince, and the one thing that princes have never learned not to
fear, namely an evil reputation, the fly thought it was both a human and divine right to exact punishment on this most wicked
man with the consensus and approval of the most upright people.
For the fly publicized his outrageous deed and his monstrous   30
mind so that they should be obvious to everyone, and that he
should be hated by the whole world for his infamy. Nor did it do
so of its own volition, but because it was forced to: for it was not
possible to take revenge on an emperor protected by so many

et tantas tamque atroces iniurias non sentire non licebat. Quis igitur inculparit si graves musca iniurias quoquo potuit pacto occulti sceleris promulgatione vindicavit?

31   Aliorum ineptias et iracundas in se manus modice et modeste pro sua semper facilitate pertulit; conviciis, obtrectationibus, maledictis calumniisque improborum ab officio nusquam discessit. Nescio quem laudent philosophum eodem semper domum rediisse vultu quo abierat; at ego sic de musca deierarim: unum hoc animal tanta frui equanimitate, ut ne ridere neve flere neve supercilium contraxisse neve frontem laxasse in adversis prosperisve rebus uspiam visa sit. Una atque eadem privata in domo et in publicis locis forma oris sempiterne sese musca exhibet.

32   Quid de cultu ingenii, de studiis bonarum rerum, quibus se exercent musce, dixerim? Veteres Pythagoreos optimas plerasque artes muscarum gens edocuit: vocum rationem et canendi modos, qua maiorem in modum delectantur Pythagorici, a musca musicam nuncupavere, quo eos memores accepti beneficii posteritas
33 fuisse intelligeret. Nam, cum ex gutrullo oleario exque mitreta vinaria profundum intonans primas illas graves apud musicos notissimas voces *ut* atque *re* in usum produxisset, acutas *sol* et *la* canoris vocibus preter propter volitando ipso ex ethere applausisset, medias voces *mi* et *fa*, quod subexstincte et lugubres sint, telis aranearum implicita effinxit: ergo merito hanc Pythagoras muscarum generi gratiam retulit, ut tam preclare artis auctoris nomen eo
34 pacto posteritati commendaret. At mathematicos quis negarit

guards and yet it was impossible not to be provoked by so many and such atrocious injuries. Who will blame the fly if it took revenge for so many serious injustices in the only way it could, namely by broadcasting openly his secret crime?

The fly has always borne foolishness and angry hands laid upon 31 it with moderation and modesty in accordance with its good nature. It has never abandoned its duty despite the insults, violence, curses and calumnies of the wicked. Let people praise that philosopher, whoever it was, who, it was said, always came back home with the same expression with which he had gone out.[34] But I would praise the fly in the same way and swear that this one creature enjoys so much equanimity that it has never been seen to laugh or cry, never been seen to let his brow relax or frown in prosperous or adverse times. The fly's face is always the same both when it is in private in its house and in public places, and it always shows itself to be of the same demeanor.

What should I say about its sophisticated intelligence and its 32 studies in the best disciplines to which it constantly devotes itself? It was the race of flies that taught the ancient Pythagoreans most of the finest arts. The Pythagoreans invented the name music (*musica*) from the fly (*musca*)[35] and applied it to the rules for the voice and the different ways of singing, in which those philosophers delighted, so that posterity would understand that they had been mindful of the gift they had received from the insect. For the fly 33 intoned from an oil jar and a wine container a deep tone and gave out the first bass notes, sounds very well known to musicians, and put *do* and *re* into use, and then it produced the high note *so* and the melodious sound *la*, as it flew back and forth, applauding from the air with its wings, and finally, when it was caught up in spiders' webs, it produced the middle sounds of *mi* and *fa*, which are almost faint and lugubrious.[36] So Pythagoras rightly gave thanks to the race of flies in order that he could commend their name to posterity as the authors of that famous musical art. Who will deny 34

muscarum alis celum sideraque ipsa conscendisse? Beryllo enim adamanteque contextis alis muscarum geometre omnium dimensionum conscriptiones adinvenere; quin et mundi picturam Ptolomeum mathematicum illinc aiunt desumpsisse: nam et ferunt alis muscarum Gangem, Histrum, Nilum et eiusmodi, quibus a montibus in mare perfluat quasve inundet gentes pulchre expictas exstare: sunt et qui affirment illic Egyptias pyramides Eleusinumque templum conspici: tantas me res fateor non illic satis recognovisse: Caspium mare Meotimque paludem atque Elicona, crispantibus

35 sub radio undis, me interdum despectasse illic non infitior. Illud preterea facile assentiar ac mihi fit quidem verisimile quod fama in primis fertur, Pythagoram non, ut ineruditi librarii exscribunt, musis, sed muscis hecatomben, muscis inquam, hecatomben sacrificium fecisse, in earum alis geometrica illa altimetra omnium admirabili figura adinventa.

36   Tam multe dicenti mihi muscarum accurrunt in mentem laudes, tam varie, tam inaudite, ut sentiam longe maiore quam mea sit eloquentia ad eas recensendas esse opus. Preterea multitudini imperitorum tam sunt musce invise, ut verear ne, si diligentius muscarum singulas laudes fuero pro nostri ingenii viribus prosecutus, omnium in me unum invidorum odia provocem. Ac novi quidem, non sine mearum rerum iactura, quid ipsa possit invidia, malorum inter mortales culmen; idcirco multa, cum de meo ingenio diffisus, tum invidiam veritus, consulto mihi fore pretereunda statuo.

37 Illud non negligendum pro rei indignitate censeo, quod plerique

that it was on the wings of flies that mathematicians ascended to the heavens and the stars themselves? Since the fly's wings are woven with beryl and diamonds, it was there that geometers discovered how to write about all systems of measurements. Indeed, it was from that source that, they say, Ptolemy the mathematician derived the image of the world, for it is said that on the fly's wings are beautifully depicted the Ganges, the Danube, the Nile and similar rivers, as well as the mountains from which each of them flows down to the sea and the countries that they flood. There are also those who affirm that there too one can see the Egyptian pyramids and the temple of Eleusis. I must admit that I have not recognized quite so many things there, though I do not deny that I have sometimes seen on their wings the Caspian sea, the marsh of Maeotis and mount Helicon with the waves rising up under the rays of the sun.[37] But I would willingly agree, and it seems probable, as it was famously first reported, that Pythagoras did not, as the careless copyists wrote, sacrifice a hecatomb to the Muses (*musis*) but to the flies (*muscis*). And I say that he sacrificed a hecatomb to the flies, since in their wings he had discovered that amazing geometric figure which allows us to measure height.[38]   35

So many varied and unheard of praises of the fly come into my mind as I am speaking that I feel that one needs much greater eloquence than I possess in order to go through them all. Besides, flies are so hated by the multitude of ignorant people that I fear that if I diligently go through the individual praises of this insect, as far as my intelligence will allow me, I will arouse the hatred of all envious people against myself. And I myself know, not without loss to my own affairs, just how powerful envy itself is, that worst of all evils among men. For that reason I have decided that I must deliberately pass over many of their achievements, both because I distrust my own ability and because I am afraid of provoking envy. But one thing I believe should not be neglected, since it is so shameful, is what their many detractors say of them at street   36

  37

obtrectatores annuente plebe in triviis obloquuntur: muscas hiulcum esse animal, procacem, inconsultam; nihil esse quod prima non sorbeat, ipso in poculo ob voracitatem animam soffocasse, reges deosque ipsos lacessere assuesse, sed penas pendere sceleris aranea vindice: has nos calumnias non dicendi artibus—nam incompta et subinculta nostra hec est oratio—sed veritate ipsa abolebimus; et, queso, eadem qua huc usque voluptate, o studiosi, quam belle et succinte rem ipsam transigam perlegite.

38   Vos, o iniqui obtrectatores, utrumne tam imprudenter quod summis viris a doctis quibusque datur laudi, id vos vituperio ascribetis muscis? Laudatur Plato, laudantur et alii non paucissimi viri litteris et rerum cognitioni dediti, quod longas obierint peregrinationes nullas res ignorandi gratia, quas quidem mortales quovis loco tenuissent: vosne solertiam muscarum odistis, improbi atque inertissimi, quod pro suo philosophandi instituto vos esse non

39   usquequaque otiosos velint? O segnes et tardissimi, quos vix stimulis ipsis ad opus musca excitet, discite bonos mores a prompta virtutis instructrice musca! Nusquam quidem otiosa est, desidesque pro officio, quoad in se est, acrius exercet. Peniteat aliquando per ignaviam somno sepultam vitam degere, et imitasse quidem muscam decet, que cum interdiu nusquam a cultu virtutis cesset, tum et noctem a forensi opere vacua in meditatione rerum maiorum magna ex parte insomnem ducit, et, noctem ipsam ut commodius per vigilias trahat, pedibus a lacunari aut a camini labro

40   resupine adacta dependet. Neque pigeat eas imitari, quas et summi viri imitati sunt. Aristotelem philosophum memorie proditum est solitum quidpiam supra pelvim manu protensa substinere, cuius

corners with the common crowd all nodding in assent: namely that the fly is a greedy, insolent, unwise animal; that there is no liquid that this insect is not the first to suck up, and because of its greed it often drowns in the glass itself; that the fly has become accustomed to attacking even kings and gods, but it pays the penalty thanks to the vengeance of the spider. We will dispel such calumnies not with the arts of rhetoric — for this is an unpolished and not very cultured oration — but with the truth itself, and I pray you scholars to continue reading with the same pleasure as you have done hitherto and see how finely and succinctly I will conclude this subject.[39]

You wicked detractors, will you be so imprudent as to ascribe as an insult to the fly something that is praised in the greatest men by all the learned? Plato is lauded, along with many others who have devoted themselves to literature and the knowledge of things, because they went on very long journeys in order not to be ignorant of anything that mortals have philosophized about.[40] Do you reprobates and lazy people hate the diligence of flies who, because of their philosophical principles, do not want you always to be idle? You sluggish and tardy people, who are not roused even by the fly's stings into doing some work, learn good morals from that ready instructor in virtue, the fly. For it is never idle; on the contrary, to the best of its ability it energetically encourages the lazy to action, as is its duty. You should finally repent of leading your lives buried in sleep, and should rather imitate the fly, which never rests from the pursuit of virtue by day, and it also spends most of the night not sleeping but, freed from its active duties, meditating on more serious questions. And in order to spend the night awake more usefully, it hangs upside down with its feet on the ceiling or on the edge of the fireplace looking at the sky. Nor should we be ashamed to imitate those whom even the greatest men have imitated. Tradition has it that the philosopher Aristotle used to hold something in his outstretched hand above a basin so that when he

38

39

40

cadentis strepitu obdormiscens resipisceret. Preclara musce laus, quam summi viri imitentur!

41   Hiulcam atque voracem dicunt esse muscam: dispeream, si quod intra mortales animans aliud viget, cui sit omni parsimonia astrictior gula! et vescitur crudis oleribus eque musca atque decoctis, neque muscam memini unquam cum lixa aut coco fecisse iurgium. At poculo enectam vituperant: longum esset eos referre qui inter cenas defecere; multi enumerantur patritii, pretorii, consulares et eiusmodi viri probi et modesti inter offas et calices defe-

42   cisse. Sed quid agimus? Parumne intelligimus hanc precipuam et prope divinam esse muscarum naturam et morem ut, quo assiduo philosophantur et rerum secreta sedulo rimantur, eo interdum

43   queritandi gratia et dinoscendi studio in periculum incidant? Sapientiam aiebat Afranius memorie et usus esse filiam. Multa nimirum scrutetur oportet qui se a multitudinis grege ad cultum sapientie dedicarit: Plinium doctum illum, qui omnem rerum naturam sua in historia complexus est, legimus ob suam investigandi curiositatem ab estu erumpentis Etne absorptum et in profundum vastumque montis hiatum summo a vertice corruisse; non tamen vituperatur vir diligens, agens, discendique studio magis flagrans quam ipse Etne mons; muscam quod discendi voluptate detinea-

44   tur, vituperant. Dicunt phisici lac esse cruorem non decoctum, et vinum esse terre sanguinem scripsit Androcides clarus sapiens; id ita ne sit musca pitissando ediscit, quidve in unum congestus atque confusus multorum florum desudans chymus sapiat

started to doze the noise of the object falling would waken him up.[41] So the praise of the fly is second to none, since the greatest men imitate it!

They say the fly is greedy and gluttonous. I'll be damned if there were another creature whose throat was narrower thanks to its constant parsimony! The fly eats both raw and cooked vegetables, and I never knew a fly that quarreled with a servant or a cook. But people blame the insect because it meets its death in a wineglass. It would take a long time to list all those who have died during a dinner: there are many patricians, ex-praetors, consuls and other upright and modest men of that kind who have passed away while eating food and drinking wine.[42] But what can we do? Do we not realize that this is the special, almost divine nature and habit of flies that they are assiduous philosophers and are constantly exploring the secrets of nature, so it is inevitable that sometimes in their pursuit of research and their zeal for knowledge they fall into danger? Afranius used to say that wisdom was the daughter of memory and practice.[43] There is no doubt that the person who separates himself from the crowd and dedicates himself to wisdom will have to scrutinize many things. We read that that learned man Pliny, who encompassed the whole of nature in his history, because of his curiosity for investigating things was sucked into the roaring heat of Etna when it was erupting. He plummeted down from the top of the mountain into the depths of the vast abyss of the volcano.[44] But that diligent, active man, who blazed with the love of learning more than the mountain of Etna itself, is not criticized for this. Yet people vituperate the fly because it becomes obsessed with the pleasure it takes in discovering things. The physicians say that milk is blood that has not been properly absorbed,[45] and the famous wise man Androcydes wrote that wine is the blood of the earth.[46] The fly learns whether this is so by sipping it, or it very diligently tastes what flavor the chyme of many flowers has when it is pressed together and mingled. People

41

42

43

44

diligentius degustat. Archimedem mathematicum Syracusis ne tumultu quidem hostili et fragore ruentis patrie ab rerum occultarum investigatione potuisse abvelli commendant; muscam ita odere, ut meritas diis poenas dicant pendere, quod in pervestigandi opere detineatur quodve aranee laqueis intercepta pereat in servitute. Servi fuere et summi complures philosophi et nonnulli poete. Vel quisnam est qui se liberum tum audeat dicere, ni tantum is qui nulli serviat turpitudini? Sed de his alias.

45   Ego sic statuo—dicant improbi contra quid velint: a flagranti studio virtutis imminere muscis quot quot immineant pericula. Cupit musca uti ceteras nosse res, ita et quid sibi in propatulo extensa illa aranee velint opera. Quid mirum igitur si, incauta et animis ad cultum virtutis occupata, musca insidiis vafre et omnibus militie artibus callentis aranee iniquam in decertationem collapsa capitur, quasi non multi etiam fortissimorum imperatorum

46   insidiis subcubuerint. Sed suo in miserabili casu an non tu id muscis ad summam laudem deputes? Prelongis utitur aranea sabinis hastis, et, laquea iactare edocta melius quam Alanus is qui in acie Tiriadem, Armenie regem, laqueo comprehendit, non tamen audet latitans prius paratum ad duellum erumpere quam complicitum et penitus obstrictum hostem e castris intueatur. Atque tanta erga innocuum muscarum genus crudelitate bellua ipsa sevire crassarique assuevit, ut facere captivam missam nullis unquam flecti precibus potuerit. Pisces Arion, immitissima et immansuetissima

47   animantia, cantu ad sui misericordiam traxit, pisciumque opera salutem adeptus exstitit. Musca, vocum cantusque inventrix, apud

commend Archimedes the mathematician because he could not be torn away from his investigation of hidden things, not even by the hostile tumult and clamor of his collapsing fatherland of Syracuse.[47] People hate flies so much that they say they undergo a deserved punishment when they are captured while investigating things, or because they become entangled in the spider's webs and perish in slavery. But several major philosophers and a number of poets were enslaved.[48] And who would then dare to call himself free, except the person who is not a slave to any base action? But more of this another time.

What I believe is this: the wicked can say what they want against the fly, but all the many dangers that hang over it come from its burning love of virtue. The fly loves to know both many other things and also what the spider's extensive web spread out before him really means. What wonder, then, if incautiously and with its mind preoccupied with the cultivation of virtue, the fly gets caught in the snare set by the crafty spider, which is so skilled in all the military arts? This insect becomes involved in an unequal struggle which ends with it falling into the trap and being captured?[49] As if many of even the bravest commanders have not fallen into traps! But do you not consider its pitiable fall as actually part of its highest praise? The spider uses very long Sabine spears,[50] and is more skilled in throwing a lasso than that Alanus, who caught with his rope Tiriades the king of Armenia who was in the front line.[51] The spider hides and never comes out to the duel he has already prepared for in advance until he sees from the safety of his camp that his enemy, the fly, is caught up and totally impeded from movement by his web. But that wild beast the spider rages and attacks the innocent race of flies with such cruelty that it has never been swayed by prayers to let his captive go. Through his singing Arion drew those very cruel and inhumane animals, the fishes, to take pity on him, and thanks to the fishes' operations he reached safety and survived.[52] But even though the

45

46

47

immanissimam Arachnem, fibras precordiorum canendo rumpens, nullam potest adinvenisse misericordiam. Quod si una tantum ullis unquam temporibus postliminio reversa suos accepte iniurie potuisset reddere certiores, testor patrios muscarum deos superos et inferos, quot habet terrarum orbis muscas, tot experta non sine maximo suo malo fuisset aranea Scipiones atque Cesares.

48 Sed iam satis multa mihi videor de muscarum laudibus dixisse. Dixi qua sint forma egregia predite, quo ingenio, qua disciplina, quibus animi virtutibus imbute atque ornate. Possent et pleraque adduci muscarum dicta factaque digna memoratu; tum et de muscarum natura et viribus, admirabili ad res varias agendas, multa fortassis essent edisserenda, veluti, si id instituat, muscarum familia queatne ad oras usque Oceani et tenus columnas Herculis Rhodium colossum trahere, quod optimi architecti posse muscas

49 asseverant. Ac compertum quidem apud me est, qui talibus non nihil delector, Caucasum montem Taurumque montem Casiumque montem a musca supra Baleares insulas posse, ni tempus vitaque desit, transferri; quod opus nature infensum ne faciant, Proserpina generi muscarum properam atque immaturam dedit mortem.

50 Uterer epilogo et in eo presertim grandi vagarer commiseratione—nam amplificatione pro rerum magnitudine non liceret; sed ingens muscarum copia suorum meritorum conscriptori congratulatum confluens id ne exequar crebris osculis interpellant.

Scripsimus hec ridendo et vos ridete.

fly is the inventor of song and music, and breaks its heart singing for mercy, it cannot find any clemency in the cruel spider. If the fly should return just once, someday, to its own people, and could tell them about the injuries it has suffered, I swear by the gods of the flies in the heavens and down below that spiders would have to face an army of the enormous number of flies that inhabit the earth and would endure total destruction, just as if it were confronted by so many Scipios and Caesars.

But it seems to me that I have said quite enough in praise of flies. I have spoken about how outstanding a body they have, what genius and discipline they possess, and what virtues of the mind they are adorned and imbued with. One could also adduce the flies' many memorable deeds and sayings.[53] Then one could say much about their admirable nature and strength which they use for their various achievements: for instance, the family of flies might, if it wanted to, be able to drag the colossus of Rhodes as far as the shores of the Ocean and the pillars of Hercules, something that the best architects claim flies can do. But what I, who take great delight in such things, have certainly found out is that the Caucasian mountain range and Mount Taurus and the Casian mountain could be transported by the fly, if it had enough time and life left, to above the Balearic Islands;[54] but in order that they do not carry out that operation which would be offensive to nature, Proserpina gave a quick and early death to the race of flies.

I would at this point deploy an epilogue and in it I would especially indulge in evoking great commiseration for them, for I would not be allowed to use rhetorical amplification given the size of this subject, but a huge swarm of flies has flown in to congratulate the person who has written about their merits and with their constant kisses they prevent me from carrying this out.

We wrote the above laughing, and you too should laugh.

Note on the Texts

⚸§¿⚸

With the exception of *On the Advantages*, the texts of the Latin works in this volume are those established by Roberto Cardini and his colleagues in Leon Battista Alberti, *Opere latine*, ed. Roberto Cardini (Rome: Istituto Poligrafico e Zecca dello Stato, 2010), henceforth, "Cardini 2010." The Latin text of *On the Advantages* follows that prepared by Mariangela Regoliosi for the Edizione Nazionale delle Opere di Leon Battista Alberti: Leon Battista Alberti, *De commodis litterarum atque incommodis*, ed. Mariangela Regoliosi (Florence: Polistampa, 2021). I have also followed the punctuation and the paragraph numbering of those editions.

In this Note on the Texts I summarize the main witnesses for each of the five works. After that, in the Notes to the Texts, I mention some of the more significant textual variants.

ON THE ADVANTAGES AND DISADVANTAGES OF LITERATURE

Full details of manuscripts and early printed editions are to be found in Mariangela Regoliosi's recent edition of the *De commodis* mentioned above (1:39–62). There are three witnesses (two manuscripts and one incunabulum):

C   Chicago, Newberry Library, Case MS 102 (olim 44), fols. 1r–24v

G   Genoa, Biblioteca Universitaria, MS G IV 29, fols. 4v–27v

I   Leon Battista Alberti, *Opera*, ed. Girolamo Massaini (Florence: Bartolomeo de' Libri, ca. 1499), fols. 4v–28v

Regoliosi's text is based on a new collation of the three witnesses. She notes that G is a later redaction than C and that the scribe of *De commodis* in G is the same as the scribe of the last section (fols. 221–37) of the important Oxford manuscript of Alberti's works:

O   Bodleian Library, MS Canon. misc. 172

Initially, these sections of G and O were part of the same manuscript. Regoliosi's edition follows G except for obvious errors.

THE LIFE OF ST. POTITUS

Full details of the manuscript are to be found in Elena Giannarelli, "Nota al testo della *Vita S. Potiti*" (Cardini 2010, 155–56), and in her "Testi di accompagnamento alla *Vita Sancti Potiti*" (ibid., 157–64). Her Latin text is on pp. 125–36. Also useful is her translation with footnotes (ibid., 137–54) and her edition and notes to the three paratextual letters (ibid., 157–64).

There is just one manuscript:

F   Florence, Biblioteca Riccardiana, MS Ricc. 767, fols. 34r–40r

There are autograph corrections to the text, and the three paratextual letters that follow the text of the *Vita* are all autograph:

40v–41r: "Prohemium" to Biagio Molin
41r: Letter to Marino Guadagni
42r–v: Letter to Leonardo Dati

On fol. 40v, Alberti's marginal note regarding the letter to Molin ("ponatur ante vitam") shows that he wanted the letter to Biagio Molin to precede the biography; and his note on 42r ("ponatur hec epistola in fine vite") confirms that he wanted the letter to his friend and fellow humanist, Leonardo Dati, to come after the end of the *Vita*. Alberti provided no indication as to where the letter to Marino Guadagni should be placed, though Coppini argues that it probably accompanied the text of *The Life of St. Potitus* when it was sent to Guadagni and that the letter to Molin was written some time before the biography was composed, since at that stage Molin had not decided which saint's life he wanted Alberti to work on. See Donatella Coppini, "Leon Battista Alberti si corregge. Il caso della *Mosca* Riccardiana," in *Leon Battista Alberti. La biblioteca di un umanista*, ed. Roberto Cardini et al., 51–56, esp. 55–56. See also Elisabetta Arfanotti, "Scheda 20," in *Leon Battista Alberti. La biblioteca di un umanista*, 295–97.

MY DOG

Full details of manuscripts and early printed editions are to be found in Mariangela Regoliosi, "Nota al testo del *Canis*" (Cardini 2010, 983–86). See also Mariangela Regoliosi, "Linee di filologia albertiana: il *De commodis litterarum atque incommodis* e il *Canis*," in *Leon Battista Alberti umanista e scrittore*, 1:221–44. The main witnesses for the *Canis* are one incunable and sixteen manuscripts. For the sixteen manuscripts, see Regoliosi's list in Cardini 2010, 983. The incunable is: Alberti, *Opera*, ed. Girolamo Massaini (Florence: Bartolomeo de' Libri, ca. 1499).

Grayson's 1983 edition is based only on Massaini's incunable. Rosario Contarino's edition is based on Massaini's text, the Oxford manuscript (O, fols. 2r–8r), and the Rimini codex:

Ri   Rimini, Biblioteca Gambalunga, MS 22

As often, O contains the final redaction of the work, and Regoliosi's text is based on O.

MY LIFE

Full details of manuscripts and early printed editions are to be found in Roberto Cardini (with the collaboration of Mariangela Regoliosi), "Nota al testo dell'*Autobiografia*" (Cardini 2010, 1011–14). In addition to G, fols. 58r–67v, there are also two other manuscripts:

F_1 Florence, Biblioteca Nazionale Centrale, MS Naz. II IV 48, fols. 222v–228v

F_2 Florence, Biblioteca Nazionale Centrale, MS Magl. VIII 1490, insert IV

G is the most authoritative manuscript. Cardini's text follows broadly the modern edition established by Riccardo Fubini and Anna Menci Gallorini, "L'autobiografia di Leon Battista Alberti: Studio e edizione," *Rinascimento*, ser. 2, 12 (1972): 21–78, but with some radical changes in the adopted readings based on an analysis of all the manuscripts.

THE FLY

Full details of manuscripts and early printed editions are to be found in
M. Bracciali Magnini and Donatella Coppini, "Nota al testo della *Musca*"
(Cardini 2010, 1036–38). There are three manuscripts: F, fols. 43r–47r
(with autograph corrections); O, fols. 14v–20v; and

A   Rimini, Biblioteca Civica Gambalunga, MS D IV 208

Alberti's dedicatory letter to Cristoforo Landino precedes *Musca* only in
the Oxford manuscript (O). Grayson (in his 1954 edition) thought that
O was written later than the corrections in F, so he adopted O as his
main text. However, although O usually presents the latest redactions of
Alberti's Latin works, Coppini believes that, for the *Musca*, O seems to
represent a separate correction campaign that sometimes leaves out earlier corrections by the author himself in F. The text prepared by Coppini
is largely based on F and incorporates the autograph corrections. For
details, see Donatella Coppini, "Leon Battista Alberti si corregge. Il caso
della *Mosca* Riccardiana," in *Leon Battista Alberti. La biblioteca di un umanista*, 51–56.

Notes to the Texts

✿✿✿

THE ADVANTAGES AND
DISADVANTAGES OF LITERATURE

4.210. levis: lenis *other witnesses. See note 18 to the translation.*

MY DOG

3. Antonium: Marcum Antonium *other mss. Regoliosi adopts O's reading. See note 3 to the translation.*

17. Asparagum puerum: Sparagum, Spargum *other witnesses. Regoliosi adopts O's reading as it is a later redaction. See note 16 to the translation.*

50. nulla conviviorum libido: nulla, uti aiunt, conviviorum libido *other mss. See note 37 to the translation.*

App. Leo Baptista . . . gloriam captaret: *this note is found only in the authoritative Oxford manuscript (Bodleian Library, Canon. misc. 172, 8r) after the* Canis. *See note 56 to the translation.*

MY LIFE

10. philosophiam: phisicam *Fubini-Menci Gallorini*

48. celeriorem: clariorem *Fubini-Menci Gallorini*

50. dominum: animum *Fubini-Menci Gallorini*

59. rerum omnium suavissimum: 'Amari'; liberale? 'Tempus.' *On this vexed passage, see note 29 to the translation.*

61. mento: merito *Fubini-Menci Gallorini*

69. fenum: forum *Fubini-Menci Gallorini. See note 32 to the translation.*

88. industriam: historiam *Fubini-Menci Gallorini. G reads "melustoram," which makes no sense. "Historiam" seems to make more sense than "industriam," though Alberti is fond of both words.*

THE FLY

8. Getis quidem, quod muscas imitari conati sint: Mavorti quidem genti, Getis, quod muscas imitari conata sit O. *See note 9 to the translation.*

13. preacutis falcibus: preacutis falcibus ferreisque unguibus O. See Donatella Coppini, "Leon Battista Alberti si corregge. Il caso della *Mosca Riccardiana,*" in *Leon Battista Alberti. La biblioteca di un umanista,* 53.

49. Casiumque montem: Caspiumque montem O. *See note 54 to the translation.*

Notes to the Translations

ON THE ADVANTAGES AND
DISADVANTAGES OF LITERATURE

1. Here in Alberti's first major Latin treatise, just as in his first substantial vernacular work, *De familia*, homage is paid to Battista's father, Lorenzo di Benedetto degli Alberti, who died in 1421. This work is dedicated to Battista's younger brother Carlo, who like his older brother was born illegitimate: for details of his life, see Carlo Alberti, *Tutti gli scritti*, ed. Alberto Martelli (Florence: Polistampa, 2015), 47–56.

2. Alberti's phrase about never letting a day go by without reading or writing something is the first of many intertextual allusions in the treatise: in their editions, Goggi Carotti (p. 38 n. 3) and Regoliosi (p. 272) cite as the source Cicero, *Brutus* 88.302–89.305. These editions contain a full list of Alberti's allusions to this and other texts in this treatise, so I will not repeat them here. The *Brutus* is a likely source for many of Alberti's ideas and phrasing since he possessed his own copy of Cicero's dialogue, now in Venice, Biblioteca Nazionale Marciana, MS Lat. XI 67 (3859): see Maria Luisa Tanganelli, "Scheda 62," in *Leon Battista Alberti: La biblioteca di un umanista*, 404–5. (Full references for short-title citations in the Notes to the Translations may be found in the Bibliography.) There is also discussion of Alberti's debts to Cicero in this and other works in Farris' edition of the *De commodis*, 23–36. Given that these critics have noted most such allusions, I will not list the many references to Cicero and other Latin authors (nor those to Greek writers such as Isocrates, Lucian, and Plutarch), but simply note here the extremely wide range of them — from Cicero and Quintilian to Martial and Plautus — in what is a very early treatise.

3. Alberti's reference to the "ill fortune" that oppressed him is one of many allusions to his quarrels with his family, who after Battista's father's death in 1421 refused to pass on to his two illegitimate sons, Battista and Carlo, the legacy their father had left them in his will.

4. Goggi Carotti and Regoliosi note that the decision to write something however inadequate rather than remaining silent was a motif already present in Bruni's preface to his *History of the Florentine People*, which was already circulating in 1416: "I came to feel that, on the whole, any plan for writing was better than silence and idleness" (Leonardo Bruni, *History of the Florentine People*, vol. 1: Books I–IV, ed. and trans. James Hankins, I Tatti Renaissance Library 3 [Cambridge, MA: Harvard University Press, 2001], 5).

5. Goggi Carotti and Regoliosi point out that according to Quintilian (*On the Training of an Orator* 2.17.4), another of Alberti's favorite authors, it was Polycrates, not Isocrates, who composed these two paradoxical works, which were standard rhetorical exercises; but they note that Alberti mistakenly attributes these works to Isocrates, possibly because of a phrase in Servius' commentary on Virgil, *Georgics* 3.5, which says it was Isocrates who wrote the encomium of Busiris. Isocrates did indeed write a work entitled *Busiris*, which begins (*Busiris* 4) with a mention of Polycrates' *Defense of Busiris* and *Accusation of Socrates*, but then proceeds to show Polycrates how he should have defended the Egyptian tyrant.

6. Alberti seems to be thinking of humanists of the preceding generation, such as Leonardo Bruni, who had begun his major work *History of the Florentine People* in 1415, and Pier Paolo Vergerio, who had written a highly praised educational treatise, *The Character and Studies Befitting a Freeborn Youth* (1400–1402). Both works are available in this I Tatti Renaissance Library.

7. Despite the many debts to Cicero in this treatise, the choice of the key words *commoda* and *incommoda* in Alberti's title may derive from an important passage in Seneca that repeats the words several times in a much-read letter on the good life: "There are in life things which are advantageous and disadvantageous (*commoda et incommoda*), — both beyond our control. If a good man, in spite of being weighed down by all kinds of disadvantages, is not wretched, how is he not supremely happy, no matter if he does lack certain advantages? For as he is not weighted down to wretchedness by his burden of disadvantages, so he is not withdrawn from supreme happiness through lack of any advantages; nay, he is just as supremely happy without the advantages as he is free from wretchedness

though under the load of his disadvantages." Seneca, *To Lucilius* 92.16; translation from Seneca, *Epistles 66–92*, trans. Richard M. Gummere (Cambridge, MA: Harvard University Press, 1920), 457.

8. Carlo Alberti's *Ephebia* was written by January 1, 1432: see Roberto Cardini, "Quando e dove l'Alberti conobbe il nuovo Plauto (e qual è la cronologia del *De commodis* e dell'*Ecatonfilea*)," in *Itinerari del testo. Per Stefano Pittaluga*, ed. Cristina Cocco et al. (Genoa: Università degli Studî: Da.Fi.St. / D.Ar.Fi.Cl.eT., 2018), 141–94, esp. 160–61. For the edition of the *Ephebia*, see Carlo Alberti, *Tutti gli scritti*, 143–69. Goggi Carotti notes that the phrase about emending the work appears not in the *Ephebia* itself, but in Carlo's accompanying letter to Francesco Alberti: see Carlo Alberti, *Tutti gli scritti*, 144.

9. These three topics (pleasure, wealth, honors) will be dealt with respectively in the three sections (III, IV, V) that follow this one.

10. This section (2.24–25) sets out Alberti's stylistic ideals of brevity and plain speech, though such declarations are clearly a topos since this work is not very brief and is not without rhetorical embellishment. He repeats such claims both in this work (see 4.15, 4.106, 4.134, 4.209–10, 5.75, 6.3–5) and in many others.

11. This is the first indication of Alberti's interest in architecture, both in its aesthetic and its military dimensions.

12. Goggi Carotti and Regoliosi point out that the unusual adjective "pertricosus" (complex) is used only in Martial, *Epigrams* 3.63.14 (of a handsome man); see also David Marsh, "*Lvdens cvm leone*: Echoes of Martial in Alberti's Works," in *Alberti Lvdens* 23.2 (2020): 225–38, esp. 226.

13. Alberti went to Bologna to study canon and civil law in 1421, after his father died. His father's death was a tragic event also because, as noted above, his relatives refused to give him the money left to the two brothers by their father in his will. The father's last few days are the setting for the beginning of Book 1 of *De familia*. There is little documentation on Alberti's Bologna years, but it seems he finished studying law there around 1428: see Boschetto, *Leon Battista Alberti e Firenze*, 71–77; David A. Lines, "Leon Battista Alberti e lo Studio di Bologna negli anni Venti," in *La vita*

e il mondo di Leon Battista Alberti. Atti dei Convegni internazionali del Comitato Nazionale VI centenario della nascita di Leon Battista Alberti (Genova, 19–21 febbraio 2004) (Florence: Olschki, 2008), 377–95.

14. The mention of the two orators' different rhetorical talents seems to derive from Cicero, *Academica* 2.1.2, which notes Lucullus' wonderful memory of things and Hortensius' greater memory of words. The distinction recurs in *My Dog*: see McLaughlin, "Alberti's *Canis*," 65; see also note 32 in the translation of *My Dog*.

15. Alberti will devote a lot of attention to the dangers of infected air in *De re aedificatoria* (*On the Art of Building*), Book 1, chap. 3.

16. Goggi Carotti and Regoliosi note that the emperor in question was Augustus (Suetonius, *Augustus* 25): Suetonius explains that no catch would ever compensate for the loss of such a hook. The former critic also claims that the mention in *My Dog* of Aristotle being caught like a fish with a golden hook is more obscure, but actually the source is Lucian, *The Dead Come to Life, or the Fisherman* 50–51: see McLaughlin, "Alberti's *Canis*," 64; and also note 51 to *My Dog*.

17. Alberti's misogyny will recur in this and other works, whether in Latin or the vernacular.

18. There is a textual doubt about the second adjective that Alberti uses here to describe his style (*levis*) since other witnesses have *lenis* (mild) rather than *levis* (light). Goggi Carotti opts for *lenis*, since that is what Alberti would have found in texts he definitely read: Cicero, *On the Orator* 2.43.183; *Brutus* 92.317; *On Duties* 1.37.134. Regoliosi prefers *levis*, noting Alberti could have read the adjective in Cicero, *Orator* 5.20, and justifies her choice in her introduction (pp. 144–45).

19. Regoliosi (pp. 424–28) notes that this whole critique of the knights is connected with Leonardo Bruni's *De militia* (1421), a work on knighthood whose ideas Alberti sometimes follows and sometimes critiques. For Bruni's text, see Leonardo Bruni, *Opere letterarie e politiche*, ed. Paolo Viti (Turin: UTET, 1996), 649–702. (For an English translation, see *The Humanism of Leonardo Bruni* [Binghampton NY: MRTS, 1987], 127–45). Here, Alberti seems to align himself with Bruni, who criticizes knights in their fancy clothes and calls for them to dress simply. The reference to

gold here is probably a synecdoche for the Roman knight's golden ring (*anulus aureus*), and the mention in the next sentence of his "jewels and gold" hints at the excessively splendid dress of these knights: on all this, see James Hankins, *Virtue Politics: Soulcraft and Statecraft in Renaissance Italy* (Cambridge, MA-London: Belknap Press of Harvard University Press, 2019), 238–53, esp. 250. Hankins points out that this is another Renaissance *paragone*, this time of the *litteratus* versus the *miles*.

20. Regoliosi (429–30) suggests that Alberti's mention here of "maidens, destitute and defenseless widows and wards" refers to Bruni's allusion to the knight's duty to act in defense when he sees "widows being harrassed, and wards being robbed" (*Opere*, ed. Viti, 686). She notes, however, that Alberti does not share Bruni's view of the uninterrupted tradition of knighthood from classical *equites* to the medieval knights and the *milites* of Bruni's time.

21. Regoliosi observes that Alberti here makes the wealthy reverse Cicero's hexameter verse that he quotes at *On Duties* 1.22.77: "Yield, ye arms, to the toga; to civic praises, ye laurels (*cedant arma togae, concedat laurea laudi*)"—though the laurels in Cicero's verse are those of a conquering general, not a poet. Alberti here echoes a common humanist theme, that city governments pay far too much respect to the wealthy and far too little to the educated. He shows us here how literati appear in the eyes of the mercantile classes, thus enlarging the *paragone* to embrace merchants as well as knights and literati.

22. The "rest of the common people" are ordinary, nonelite citizens (*plebs*): not wealthy, educated, or deriving status from ancestry or military occupations. Alberti is going class by class through the entire city, saying how little each class is going to respect literati.

23. It is clear from this passage that Alberti had been in Tuscany for some time, presumably after 1428, when the ban of exile on the Albertis was lifted. Lorenz Böninger, "Leon Battista Alberti as a Student of the Florentine University and the Priory of San Martino a Gangalandi (1429–1430)," in *Renaissance Politics and Culture. Essays in Honour of Robert Black*, ed. Jonathan Davies and John Monfasani (Leiden-Boston: E. J. Brill, 2021), 141–54, has recently shown that Alberti was definitely in

Florence in 1429–30, continuing his law studies at the Florentine Studium.

24. Regoliosi (p. 452) suggests that Alberti's wording here about the seven planets, wandering stars, the sun, and the moon reflects a passage in a work of Cicero that Alberti knew well and that mentions the wise man's pleasure in contemplating the fixed stars and the seven wandering planets (*Tusculan Disputations* 5.24.69–70). He seems to be taking here a more Poggian attitude that tries to present literary study in modern times, owing to corruption, as the sphere of the *privatus*, while public life is intrinsically corrupting; see Hankins, *Virtue Politics*, 319–25. But the real attitude of both Poggio and Alberti here may be distorted or exaggerated by their rhetorical forms — Poggio defending Niccoli's position in his *De infelicitate principum*, and Alberti trying to make a point in this invective. As he was illegitimate, Alberti could not hold office in Florence, which may help explain his attitude.

25. There is a real contrast here with Bruni, in that the latter wants to harness the humanities to reform the state, like most humanists, while Alberti falls into the group discussed by Davide Canfora (Traversari, Niccoli as presented by Poggio), who want to keep the humanities unspotted by the world: see Davide Canfora, *Prima di Machiavelli. Politica e cultura in età umanistica* (Rome-Bari: Laterza, 2005), 42–43, which discusses this passage. Here, Alberti argues that the desire of literati for public office will destroy literature.

26. The shipwreck metaphor was ubiquitous among humanists. It was used famously by Bruni to describe the "shipwreck of classical learning" in his own times: see his *Dialogues for Pierpaolo Vergerio* Book 1, in Bruni, *Opere*, ed. Viti, 96. It was deployed by other humanists of the time, including Alberti: see Caspar Pearson, "The Return of the Giants: Reflections on Technical Mastery and Moral Jeopardy in Leon Battista Alberti's Letter to Filippo Brunelleschi," *Journal of the Warburg and Courtauld Institutes* 82 (2019): 113–41 (esp. 134–40). Alberti uses the image at the beginning of Book 6 of *On the Art of Building* where he describes Vitruvius as "almost the sole survivor of this vast shipwreck": see Leon Battista Alberti, *On the Art of Building in Ten Books*, trans. J. Rykwert, N. Leach, R. Tavernor (Cambridge, MA-London: MIT Press, 1988), 154.

27. The phrase Alberti cites for "greedy people" (*hiulca gens*) looks like a direct allusion to the use of the phrase in Plautus, *Trinummus* 285–86, one of the new Plautus plays brought to Italy in 1429. But Goggi Carotti doubts this, as do Cardini and Regoliosi, all three of whom believe that there must be a now lost indirect source for Alberti's knowledge of the rare adjective *hiulca* in this unusual meaning of "greedy": see Cardini, "Quando e dove l'Alberti conobbe il nuovo Plauto," 180–84; and Regoliosi's commentary in her edition, p. 466.

28. Alberti was fond of the contrast between seeming and being, a topic that went back to classical rhetoric (and philosophy, beginning with Plato); for its use in *De familia*, see Martin McLaughlin, "Unità tematica e strutturale nel *De familia*," in Id., *Leon Battista Alberti. La vita, l'umanesimo, le opere letterarie*, 99–123, esp. 104–5. See also note 35 to the translation of *My Dog*. Usually we are dealing with a *contrast* between being and seeming: *esse, non videri* (be really good, don't just pretend), but here Alberti is talking about people who want *both* to seem *and* to be.

THE LIFE OF ST. POTITUS

1. This first paratext, entitled "Prohemium," is a letter dedicated to Alberti's patron in the papal chancery in the early 1430s, Biagio Molin. *The Life of St. Potitus* was written between the end of 1432 and March 1434: for the dating, see Paolo Viti, "Leon Battista Alberti e la politica culturale fiorentina premedicea," in his *Forme letterarie umanistiche. Studi e ricerche* (Lecce: Conte, 1999), 9–27, esp. 20. It is clear from section 6 of this letter that Molin had not yet chosen St. Potitus as the first life he wanted Alberti to write, whereas the letter to Marino Guadagni mentions specifically St. Potitus, so the letter to Molin was composed before the one to Guadagni. For further details on the paratexts, see the Note on the Texts.

2. For the opening greeting, Grayson (*Opuscoli inediti*, 63) cites Rufinus' Latin version of Eusebius, *History of the Church* 5.1.3, which quotes the letter about persecutions sent from the churches of Lyons and Vienne to the churches in Asia and Phrygia, a letter that begins: "Pax vobis et gratia et gloria a Deo patre et Christo Jhesu Domino nostro," the same greeting

used by Alberti to Molin. Grayson's edition and Elena Giannarelli's translation in Cardini 2010, 137–63, both provide the main sources that Alberti's *The Life of St. Potitus* draws on, so these will not be repeated here. On the Christian sources of the biography, see Elena Giannarelli's helpful articles: "Alberti, i padri della Chiesa e la letteratura cristiana antica: Linee di un problema," in *Leon Battista Alberti e la tradizione*, 2:425–57; and "San Potito: chi era costui? I 'misteri' dell'Alberti agiografo" in *Leon Battista Alberti umanista e scrittore*, 1:245–65.

3. Giannarelli points out here (Cardini 2010, 137 n. 4) that the Latin name of the town, Serdica (which usually meant the town of Sofia), had an alternative form, Sardica, so Potitus was sometimes claimed as a Sardinian saint; others say he was born in Puglia. On such questions I am grateful to Bryan Ward-Perkins for directing me to the database of *The Cult of Saints in Late Antiquity* (up to 700 CE), where Matthieu Pignot wrote the entry on Potitus, which links the saint with Puglia: http://csla .history.ox.ac.uk/record.php?recid=E01983. The brilliance of the young saint, his modesty and the rays he emanated are motifs that will be picked up in Alberti's own self-portrait in his autobiography: see Introduction.

4. Hylas was also the name of Hercules' lover, but more significant here is the fact that the name of Potitus' pagan father was associated with *hyle*, the Greek word for "matter" as opposed to "spirit."

5. The word for "high-minded" here (*ingenuum*) is much used by Alberti, often of himself. It appears several times in *On the Advantages*, twice in *The Life of St. Potitus* (here and section 50), three times in *My Dog* (sections 44, 55, 59), once in *The Fly* (section 12), and also in the opening sentence of the autobiography (*My Life* 1).

6. Here, after Potitus' direct speech (sections 10–16), Alberti varies the account with, first, Hylas' speech recounted in indirect speech (sections 20–22), then Potitus' reply, also in indirect speech (sections 23–24). This alternation between direct and indirect speech was part of the rhetorical rules of variation, and Alberti uses the technique in other works, such as *Uxoria* and *Naufragus*, two of his *Intercenales*: see Martin McLaughlin, "Alberti traduttore di se stesso: *Uxoria* e *Naufragus*," in Marcial Rubio

Árquez and Nicola D'Antuono, eds., *Autotraduzione: Teoria ed esempi fra Italia e Spagna (e oltre)* (Milan: LED Edizioni, 2012), 77–106, esp. 87–88, 100–101.

7. Giannarelli (Cardini 2010, 139 n. 15) sees an allusion here to Luke 2:51, where after the episode in the Temple, Christ submits to his parents' authority.

8. Giannarelli (Cardini 2010, 140 n. 18) notes that in antiquity Epirus was famous as a harsh mountainous region.

9. Rinaldo Rinaldi, "Un travestimento agiografico: *La Vita S. Potiti*," in his *"Melancholia christiana": Studi delle fonti di L. B. Alberti* (Florence: Olschki, 2002), 87–110, esp. 87–91, points out that Alberti's ambivalent ideas concerning the virtues of the earthly existence are proposed three times in this work: first, in the devil's speech here; later, in the eunuch Jacintus' words to Potitus; and, finally, in the emperor Antoninus' oration. Alberti's apparent ambiguity here has exercised critics from the time of Grayson's edition onward: Eugenio Garin, "Studi su Leon Battista Alberti," sees it as one of Alberti's many paradoxes (p. 174); Paolo Marolda, *Crisi e conflitto in Leon Battista Alberti* (Rome: Bonacci, 1988), 73–78, takes a similar view. See also Kircher, *Living Well in Renaissance Italy*, 24–34; Giannarelli, "Alberti, i padri della Chiesa." On the later speech by the emperor, see Anthony Grafton, "*Historia* and *Istoria*: Alberti's Terminology in Context," in *I Tatti Studies in the Italian Renaissance* 8 (1999): 37–68, esp. 52. At other times, for instance in the *Theogenius* and *Momus*, Alberti seems to suggest it is better to flee politics altogether: for this technique of "double focus," see also the Introduction in this volume. On humanist attitudes to political involvement, see Davide Canfora, *Prima di Machiavelli*, 55–62; and James Hankins, "Leon Battista Alberti on Corrupt Princes and Virtuous Oligarchs," in Id., *Virtue Politics: Soulcraft and Statecraft in Renaissance Italy*, 318–34.

10. The idea that humans were born for their fellow humans ultimately derived from Plato, though it is likely Alberti would have read the phrase in Cicero, *On Duties* 1.7.22. In any case, he was fond of the notion and repeated it in several works, including his vernacular dialogues *De familia* and *Theogenius*.

11. Giannarelli (Cardini 2010, 141 n. 21) notes the echoes of Cicero's *On Duties* in this speech and refers to Roberto Cardini, *Mosaici*, 25, 51–52, 54.

12. Alberti's interest in visual images (*picturae*) also emerges in these paragraphs, though it is of course another allegorical reading, this time of the phantom's monstrous height: the monster is enormous, but his heel leaves no trace.

13. The phrase "aereum corpus" (aery body) was often used in discussions of the devil in the Church Fathers.

14. Giannarelli (Cardini 2010, 143 n. 28) notes that in Jerome, *Tractatus in Psalmos CXLIII*, 14, the ox stands for the teachers of heretics who instruct their pupils to desire earthly goods. She also refers to Rinaldi, "*Melancholia christiana*," 94–95, who sees an allusion to the biblical golden calf here, since the yellow color of the ox recalls the color of gold.

15. Alberti's interest in pictures and images is again evident here. Giannarelli (Cardini 2010, 144 n. 32) points out links with *Picture*, one of Alberti's *Intercenales*, and refers us to Cardini, *Mosaici*, 31–33.

16. Again we see Alberti's interest in *ars* and *ingenium*, key words in the autobiography.

17. The famous story of how Pope Sylvester cured the emperor Constantine of leprosy was well known in the Middle Ages. Constantine's conversion in 312 CE was followed by his decision to leave all earthly power in the West to the pope, according to the forged *Donation of Constantine*.

18. Once more, rhetorical variation is in evidence: after the direct speech used for the conversation between Jacintus and Potitus (50–55), the emperor's words and Potitus' reply are given in indirect speech (sections 69–74), then their further conversation is in direct speech (75–76).

19. The final oration by Antoninus is the longest in the biography and is given in direct speech (sections 81–100). It is structured like a classical *oratio* and is much longer than the brief remarks made by the emperor to Potitus in what was probably one of Alberti's sources, namely the early medieval *Passio S. Potiti* (most manuscripts are from the eighth to the fourteenth centuries): see Victor Saxer, "San Potito tra storia e leggenda: Dati dei codici, dei martirologi e dell'epigrafia," *Atti della Pontificia Acca-*

demia Romana di Archeologia 73 (2000–2001): 63–100 (edition on pp. 85–100). The invented oration attributed to a leader, typical of Greco-Roman historiography, seems also to be part of Alberti's plan to write a biography that met the new humanist rules for writing historical works.

20. The Latin original seems to echo Cicero's condemnation of soothsayers' monstrous words in his *On the Nature of the Gods* 2.3.7.

21. In the first example in section 97, the Latin text uses the form "Albuernius," but it should be "Alburnus," as we find in Tertullian, *Apology*, 1.5.1–2, Alberti's ultimate source here. As Giannarelli points out (Cardini 2010, 151 n. 54), Alberti probably read Tertullian's passage in Eusebius, *History of the Church* 2.2.5, which mentions Marcus Aemilius (Scaurus) and Tiberius. See also Giannarelli, "Alberti, i padri della Chiesa," 436–39. So the first and third of Alberti's examples in this section, Marcus Aemilius Scaurus (consul in 115 BCE) and the emperor Tiberius, come from Tertullian. But in between these two, Alberti alludes vaguely to ferocious edicts against new religions in the Second Punic War. This middle example probably derives from a secular author, Livy (25.1.11), who says that in 216 BCE the senate entrusted Marcus Aemilius Lepidus, the praetor, with the task of ridding the populace of the new religions that had sprung up during the Second Punic War. This book of Livy's history was one Alberti knew well, since elsewhere he cites from it the famous capture of Syracuse and death of Archimedes (25.31.9). The Archimedes episode is cited both in *The Fly* and in the vernacular dialogue *Profugiorum ab aerumna libri*: see the English translation of *The Fly*, below, note 47. In addition, we find here the same "splicing" of sources (the Livy episode is inserted between the two from Tertullian/Eusebius) as in *My Dog*: see McLaughlin, "Alberti's *Canis*," 72–74. In any case, Livy was one of Alberti's favorite authors and is mentioned in the first book of *De familia* as being essential reading for the young: see Leon Battista Alberti, *I libri della famiglia*, ed. Ruggiero Romano, Alberto Tenenti, Francesco Furlan (Turin: Einaudi, 1994), 87–88.

22. The detail of Potitus' feet being torn apart bears a slight resemblance to Alberti's decription of his own bravery when having his foot sewn together again by surgeons (see below, *My Life* 80).

23. Giannarelli (Cardini 2010, 154 n. 64) suggests that this river Calabrius was in the Salento area of Puglia: "Calabri" were the inhabitants of today's Puglia, not Calabria. See, for example, the phrase in Vergil's famous epitaph, which says "Calabri rapuere," referring to his death in Brindisi.

24. Giannarelli (Cardini 2010, 154 n. 65) quotes Cardini as having pointed out that in *De re aedificatoria* (*On the Art of Building*) 8.4, Alberti quotes Plato, *Laws* 12.958E, who says that the ideal length of a funerary epitaph is four verses (though here there are five). She also observes that the Latin inscription cited by Alberti is not in the traditional hexameter form, but although it reads like prose, it does contain assonance and internal rhymes as well as a liturgical rhythm.

25. Leonardo Dati (1408–72) was a fellow humanist and close friend of Alberti, who also wrote in both Latin and the vernacular, participated in the Certame Coronario (1441), Alberti's initiative on behalf of the *volgare*, and offered him linguistic advice on his vernacular dialogue *De familia*.

26. Alberti's words here about the causes, topography, and chronology of events as well as the standing of the people involved echo a much-quoted passage from Cicero on the rules for writing history (*De oratore* 2.15.62–63). Cicero's passage sparked a number of debates in humanist circles about the *ars historica*: see Girolamo Cotroneo, *I trattatisti dell'*ars historica (Naples: Giannini, 1971); Robert Black, "The New Laws of History," *Renaissance Studies* 1 (1987): 126–56; Mariangela Regoliosi, "Riflessioni umanistiche sullo 'scrivere storia,'" *Rinascimento*, ser. 2, 31 (1991): 3–37; Ead., "Lorenzo Valla e la concezione della storia," in *La storiografia umanistica: Convegno internazionale dell'Associazione per il Medio Evo e l'Umanesimo latini* (Messina, 22–25 ottobre 1987) (Messina: Sicania, 1994), 1.2:549–71; Anthony Grafton, *What Was History? The Art of History in Early Modern Europe* (Cambridge: Cambridge University Press, 2007); and Grafton, "*Historia* and *Istoria*: Alberti's Terminology in Context," 51–53. On the humanist elements in the letter to Dati, see Anthony Grafton, "The 2019 Josephine Waters Bennett Lecture: The Winged Eye at Work," *Renaissance Quarterly* 73 (2020): 1137–78, esp. 1159–67; Marta Celati, *Conspiracy Literature in Early Renaissance Italy: Historiography and Princely Ideology* (Oxford: Oxford University Press, 2021), 83–89.

27. Giannarelli (Cardini 2010, 163–64) and Rinaldi (*"Melancholia christiana,"* 92–93) note that the quotation is not from Tatian himself but from Eusebius (*History of the Church* 5.13.1–4): in that passage Eusebius quotes a work by Rhodo, a pupil of Tatian, which attacks the heresy of Marcion but says that the latter's idea of the two principles governing the world was followed by "Potitus and Basilicus." The quotation is attributed by Alberti to Tatian, possibly because he was more famous than his pupil Rhodo, but curiously Alberti does not mention his main source, Eusebius, on which he had drawn in his opening letter to Biagio Molin: see above, note 2.

28. For the quotations from these Letters, Giannarelli (Cardini 2010, 164) points out that Alberti turns again to the same Book 5 of Eusebius that he had quoted at the opening of his letter to Molin. At *Historia Ecclesiastica* 5.1.40–42 we are told that the martyr Blandina (her name was Baldina in Alberti's copy) was tortured in the amphitheater, but when the beasts would not harm her, more punishments were prepared for her and the other martyrs (the first quotation); a few paragraphs later we read that she was then accompanied to the arena by "Ponticus, a boy about fifteen years old" (5.1.53), who was martyred alongside her (the second quotation here).

29. Rinaldi, *"Melancholia christiana,"* 96–98 and 106–10, suggests that *The Life of St. Potitus* could be read in autobiographical terms, in particular as an allusion to the young Battista's entry into the papal chancery, especially as the saint's feast day, January 13, is also the date of the baptism of Christ, so Battista's "name-day."

30. Giannarelli says that the first part of the quotation is from the *Martyrologium Romanum* for January 13, and there are mentions of Julianus, Celsus and Potitus on this and other January dates in different editions. Alberti's direct quotations from Tatian, from the bishops' letters, and from the Martyrology show him grappling with writing a historical work that met the new standards of humanist historiography by citing reliable sources: see the bibliography cited at note 26, above.

31. Rinaldi, *"Melancholia christiana,"* 98–103, sheds light on Marino Guadagni's political background: his family were allies of Rinaldo degli Al-

bizzi, thus on the opposite side to the Alberti in Florence; and the scene of Potitus' suffering, according to Rinaldi, might have reminded Guadagni of the sufferings of Cosimo de' Medici when he was imprisoned and then exiled in 1433.

MY DOG

1. Bracciali Magnini (Cardini 2010, 971 n. 1) suggests that the solemn opening of the work may have derived from Cicero, *On Laws* 2.16.40, which talks of the religion habitually practiced by his ancestors. This is likely since Alberti possessed his own copy of Cicero's work: see Maria Luisa Tanganelli and Sara Donegà, "Scheda 60," in *Leon Battista Alberti: La biblioteca di un umanista*, 396–402.

2. Contarino's edition (see Bibliography), 142 n. 1, points out that Alberti continued to be interested in funeral orations when he wrote in the *De iciarchia* (ca. 1465) that in their "funerali collaudazioni" eloquent men listed the dead person's virtues, among which were "their expertise and knowledge of things including the humanities": see Alberti, *Opere volgari*, ed. Grayson, 2:220.

3. Bracciali Magnini (Cardini 2010, 971 n. 3) suggests that this was Mark Antony the triumvir, whose mother, Julia (of Caesar's family), was married to M. Antonius Creticus, and she cites Cicero, *Philippics* 2.84ff. (possibly she was thinking of 2.24.58, which mentions Antony's mother but not a funeral oration for her). However, the authoritative Oxford manuscript of most of Alberti's Latin works (O) reads just "Antonium," not "Marcum Antonium," so (as I have argued elsewhere) in fact the Antonius referred to here could well be Mark Antony's grandfather, though there is no mention of him having composed a funeral speech for his mother. This Antonius was an interlocutor in another of Alberti's favorite Cicero dialogues, *On the Orator*, where he says to Catulus that he, Catulus, wrote the funeral oration for his mother, Popilia, the first one in Roman history (2.11.44). So perhaps Alberti misunderstood Cicero's text, or the text he read was corrupt and led him to believe that it was Antonius who wrote a funeral oration for his own mother. In fact, one of the manuscripts of Cicero's dialogue has "mater nostra" instead of "mater

vestra," which would suggest that it might have been Antonius' own mother who first had this honor of having a funeral oration composed by her son. For details, see McLaughlin, "Alberti's *Canis*," 68–70. Alternatively, the allusion might be a misremembering of Plutarch, *Life of Julius Caesar* 5.1–4, which mentions Caesar's funeral orations for his aunt (Julia) and his wife (Cornelia); one final possibility is a confused memory of Suetonius, *Augustus* 8.1, which talks of Augustus' funeral speech for his grandmother. For the latter two possible sources (Plutarch and Suetonius), I am grateful to Christopher Pelling.

4. Alberti could have read about this either in Plutarch (*Life of Fabius Maximus* 1.5) or in Cicero (*On Old Age* 4.12).

5. Bracciali Magnini (Cardini 2010, 972 n. 5) points out that Alberti mistakenly doubles Hercules' second labor here, the killing of the Lernaean Hydra, into the defeat of two monsters, the beast of Lerna and the Hydra. She points out that he makes the same mistake in one of the *Intercenales*, *Nebule* (Cardini 2010, 479), and in *De re aedificatoria* (*On the Art of Building*) 7.16.

6. This topos—of a work not needing rhetorical embellishments since the subject alone is so important—is regularly used by Alberti: see, for instance, the English translation of *On the Advantages* above, section 2.24, and note 10.

7. A Greek name meaning Great Mouth or Great Jaws. Bracciali Magnini (Cardini 2010, 972 n. 6) notes that it is also the name of a dog belonging to Piero di Bartolomeo degli Alberti, in *De familia*, Book 4: see Leon Battista Alberti, *I libri della famiglia*, ed. Ruggiero Romano, Alberto Tenenti, Francesco Furlan (Turin: Einaudi, 1994), 339.

8. According to Bracciali Magnini (Cardini 2010, 972 n. 7), the allusion is probably to the Dog-Star Sirius, Canis Maior, the brightest star in the night sky, though Contarino (146 n. 7) argues for Canis Minor. Some critics argue from this that Alberti wrote *My Dog* during the hot summer "dog days": see Marco Dezzi Bardeschi, "L'occhio profondo: Il dettaglio e l'intreccio. Cosmologia ed ermetismo nella cultura di Leon Battista Alberti: il *Canis*," *Arte Lombarda* 110–11.3–4 (1994): 24–28.

9. This mention of his dog's ancestors' famous sayings portrays them as philosophers, since many of the biographies in Diogenes Laertius' *Lives of the Eminent Philosophers* end with a list of the philosopher's celebrated maxims.

10. As noted in the Introduction, Alberti's main sources for legendary dogs were Pliny, *Natural History* 8.61.142–50, and Plutarch, *On the Cleverness of Animals* 969B–971A, though Magnini Bracciali has doubts about whether Alberti could have had access to that whole section of Plutarch's text ("L. B. Alberti, *Canis* 10–27," 2:778). Solinus, *Memorabilia* 15.6, is also another possible source, though the latter mostly recycles examples from Pliny.

11. Interestingly, for this first example of canine bravery, Alberti conflates details from the final example in the lists of both Pliny and Plutarch, but the geographical detail about the Indian river Hyarotis comes from Quintus Curtius, *History of Alexander the Great* 9.1.12 and 9. 1.31–34: see McLaughlin, "Alberti's *Canis*," 66–68. Bracciali Magnini (Cardini 2010, 973 n. 10) says that the Albani were a Caucasian tribe living near the Caspian Sea: see Pliny, *Natural History* 6.15.38.

12. The Garamantes were a North African tribe (Bracciali Magnini. in Cardini 2010, 973 n. 11). This was Pliny's third example: for Alberti's deliberate alternation of allusions from the end and from the beginning of the classical source, as well as for his technique of "splicing" two sources, see McLaughlin, "Alberti's *Canis*," 72–74. Here Pliny says a team of two hundred dogs escorted the king back to his kingdom (*Natural History* 8.61.143).

13. According to Bracciali Magnini (Cardini 2010, 973 n. 12), in 299 BCE the Colophonians were besieged by Lysimachus, king of Thrace; and Castabala was in Cilicia or Cappadocia. The story was the fourth in Pliny's list, so—as in Alberti's list—it comes immediately after that of the king of the Garamantes. Pliny says they had whole cohorts of dogs who fought in the front rank, were totally dependable, and did not want any pay (*Natural History* 8.61.143).

14. Acrocorinth was captured in 243 BCE by Aratus, who was head of the Achaean League: Bracciali Magnini (Cardini 2010, 973 n. 14) gives Al-

berti's source here as Plutarch, *Life of Aratus* 24.1. In her article, "L. B. Alberti, *Canis* 10–27," 804, she suggests that Alberti was particularly interested in Plutarch's *Life of Aratus* because it is itself almost a funeral oration, and Aratus too died of poisoning, like Alberti's dog.

15. Xanthippus was the father of Pericles. At the battle of Salamis the dog could not get on board the Athenians' ships, so it swam after them but died in his attempt to keep up with them. Alberti either invents the word *Cynotaphium* (dog's tomb) on the model of the word *Cenotaphium* (empty tomb), or as Magnini Bracciali suggests, he took the word from Francesco Barbaro's translation of Plutarch's *Life of Cato the Elder* ("L. B. Alberti, *Canis* 10–27. Fonti e problemi," 806). In any case, the source here is Plutarch, *Themistocles* 10.6 (Bracciali Magnini in Cardini 2010, 974 n. 15).

16. The story of the boy called Asparagus (or Spargos or Spargus in some witnesses), who later became Cyrus the Great, king of the Persians, ultimately derived from Herodotus (*Histories* 1.110, 1.122). However, there is some confusion over the name. Herodotus (*Histories* 1.110) says that the herdsman's wife who took in the child was called Kyno in Greek, and Spako in the Median language, both of which names meant "dog," hence the myth that Cyrus had been raised by a dog (*Histories* 1.122). Alberti probably read the story not in the original Greek but in an indirect Latin source, Justinus' *Epitome of Trogus* (1.4), which says that the herdsman handed the child over to a nurse called Spargos, which is closer to the form in Alberti's text than Herodotus' Spako: see McLaughlin, "Alberti's *Canis*," 65–66. On the whole episode, see Magnini Bracciali, "L. B. Alberti, *Canis* 10–27," 806–10.

17. This unnamed dog is Pliny's first example (*Natural History* 8.61.142). Magnini Bracciali, "L. B. Alberti, *Canis* 10–27," 803, notes how this and the following examples stress less the bellicose qualities of dogs and more the peaceful virtues, such as *fides* and *pietas*.

18. The source here is Pliny, *Natural History* 8.61.145, the penultimate example in Pliny, who says that the man's name was Titius Sabinus. For the date, Pliny says, "When Appius Junius and P. Silius were consuls," but Alberti or his manuscript of Pliny seems to have mistaken the name

of the second consul, since the consuls were Appius Junius Silanus and Publius (not Plancius) Silius Nerva. These two men were consuls in 28 CE.

19. Bracciali Magnini (Cardini 2010, 974 n. 18) points out that if the source here is Pliny, *Natural History* 8.61.145, Alberti has misunderstood his source: Germanicus, son of Drusus, was himself put to death by the emperor Tiberius. On the whole passage and its problems, see also Magnini Bracciali, "L. B. Alberti, *Canis* 10–27," 810–16.

20. This is probably based on Plutarch's second example of the courage of dogs (*On the Cleverness of Animals* 969D).

21. Bracciali Magnini (Cardini 2010, 975 n. 20) says that the legend of the killing of the poet Hesiod was filtered through the Byzantine sources, John Tzetzes and the *Souda*. But it is also Plutarch's third example, *On the Cleverness of Animals* 969E.

22. Plutarch's fourth example, *On the Cleverness of Animals* 969E–F.

23. Plutarch's first example, *On the Cleverness of Animals* 969C.

24. Bracciali Magnini (Cardini 2010, 975 n. 21) says this Lysimachus was Alexander the Great's general who then became king of Thracia. This was Plutarch's fifth example (*On the Cleverness of Animals* 970C), and Pliny's seventh.

25. This is Pliny's sixth example.

26. The reference is to Quintus Fabius Maximus Verrucosus, nicknamed Cunctator, or the Delayer, because of the successful delaying tactics he deployed in the Second Punic War, especially in his battles with Hannibal, the Carthaginian leader.

27. According to Bracciali Magnini (Cardini 2010, 975 n. 22), the Marcellus concerned was probably Marcus Claudius Marcellus, one of the greatest Roman generals in the First and Second Punic Wars. The fact that Plutarch also wrote a life of this Marcellus would tend to confirm this.

28. Contarino (154 n. 13) and Bracciali Magnini (Cardini 2010, 976 n. 24) suggest that the source is Plutarch, *The Apophthegms of Cato the El-*

der 23, but perhaps a more obvious source was Plutarch, *Life of Cato the Elder* 1.6: see McLaughlin, "Alberti's *Canis*," 64 n. 37. Francesco Barbaro's Latin versions of the lives of Aristides and Cato (1415–16) were much in demand: see Marianne Pade, *The Reception of Plutarch's Lives in Fifteenth-Century Italy* (Copenhagen: Museum Tusculanum Press, 2007), 1:191–201; 2:84–85.

29. Contarino (156 n. 14) suggests that this refers to a Stoic concept mentioned in Plutarch, *The Fortune or Virtue of Alexander the Great* 1.11, "that principle of the Stoics which declares that every act which a wise man performs is an activity in accord with every virtue": Plutarch, *Moralia*, trans. Frank Cole Babbitt and others, 16 vols. (Cambridge, MA: Harvard University Press, 1927–2004), 4:415.

30. Bracciali Magnini (Cardini 2010, 977 n. 25) says the source is Plutarch, *Life of Alcibiades* 4.1. See McLaughlin, "Alberti's *Canis*," 70.

31. Alberti is alluding to the famous anecdote about Zeuxis choosing the most beautiful virgins of a town in order to make his painting of Helen of Troy for the temple of Juno in Crotone (Cicero, *On Invention* 2.1–3); but Pliny says it was for the temple of Juno in Agrigento (Pliny, *Natural History* 35.36.64). However, since Alberti says that the place was Crotone, and his phrase "venustatem et gratiam" (beauty and grace) is an expansion of Cicero's word "venustatem" (*On Invention* 2.3), which Pliny does not mention, we can deduce that Alberti was recalling Cicero's account, not Pliny's. He was fond of the anecdote and alludes to it in *De pictura* 3.56: see *Opere volgari*, ed. Grayson, 3:96–97; or Leon Battista Alberti, *De pictura (redazione volgare)*, ed. Lucia Bertolini (Florence: Polistampa, 2011), 308–9.

32. Bracciali Magnini (Cardini 2010, 978 n. 27) suggests Cicero, *Tusculan Disputations* 1.26.65, as the source, while Contarino points to Cicero, *Brutus* 88.301, but in both cases only Hortensius' memory is praised. However, the mention of both Lucullus and Hortensius as having great memories for things and words, respectively, confirms that the precise source is Cicero, *Academica* 2.1.2: see McLaughlin, "Alberti's *Canis*," 64–65; and note 14 to the translation of *On the Advantages*, above; see also the translation of *My Life*, note 9, below.

33. The idea of someone's versatility being such that they seem to have mastered all the arts derives ultimately from Livy's portrait (39.40) of Cato the Elder, so if Cato was in Alberti's mind here, it is not surprising that he mentions him in the next sentence. The Livy passage is the subtext behind the opening paragraph of Alberti's autobiography.

34. Contarino (158 n. 21) suggests Pliny, *Natural History* 7.51.171, as the source; but David Marsh says that in Apuleius, *Apologia* 85, the phrase about precocious boys is quoted but attributed to an unnamed poet: see David Marsh, "Alberti and Apuleius. Comic Violence and Vehemence in the *Intercenales* and *Momus*," in *Leon Battista Alberti: Actes du Congrès international de Paris (Sorbonne-Institut de France-Institut Culturel italien-Collège de France, 10–15 avril 1995)*, ed. F. Furlan, P. Laurens, S. Matton (Paris: J. Vrin; Turin: Aragno, 2000), 1:405–26, esp. 408, 422 n. 28. Interestingly, Alberti attributes the phrase not to a poet but to one of his favorite ancient personages, Cato: see McLaughlin, "Alberti's *Canis*," 57 n. 7.

35. Bracciali Magnini (Cardini 2010, 978 n. 30) points out that the contrast between seeming and being, which goes back to classical times, occurs often in Alberti: see the translation of *On the Advantages*, note 28.

36. A similar motif will be found in *My Life* when Alberti says that he would ride horseback with his head uncovered in summer and in winter (*My Life* 82).

37. Alberti's formula here, about no luxury, no spending, and so on, derives from Cicero, *Pro Caelio* 19.44: see McLaughlin, "Alberti's *Canis*," 71. In fact, in some manuscripts Alberti's phrase reads "nulla, uti aiunt, conviviorum libido" (no lust for feasting, as they say), which explicitly alludes to the fact that it is a quotation. Here as elsewhere, Alberti shows appreciation for the ancient Greek tradition of Cynicism: Alberti's dog is as contemptuous of ordinary human needs here as Diogenes of Sinope, the founder of the sect.

38. Contarino (160 n. 23) notes that this phrase in *My Dog* about never betraying secrets is repeated almost verbatim in the autobiography (*My Life* 31).

39. Contarino (160 n. 24) says that this phrase about his gentleness and affability recurs in the autobiography (*My Life* 19). He also sees a parallel

in Landino's description of Alberti in one of his poems (*Xandra*, 1.13.24) as indulgent to all and severe with none: see Cristoforo Landino, *Poems*, trans. Mary P. Chatfield, I Tatti Renaissance Library 35 (Cambridge, MA: Harvard University Press, 2008), 26–27. Gabriella Albanese, "Leon Battista Alberti nella storiografia letteraria e artistica dell'Umanesimo e del Rinascimento," *Rinascimento* ser. 2, 47 (2007): 49–91 (esp. 56, 74–80), notes the way certain phrases of Alberti about himself were quickly adopted by fellow humanists such as Lapo da Castiglionchio and Landino. The latter's poem also mentions Alberti's "witty, clever *Fly*" (verse 34 of poem 1.13): see Landino, *Poems*, ed. Chatfield, 26.

40. The precise allusion here is not clear, but many of Hercules' labors involved conquering ferocious animals, for instance, his revenge on the violent centaur Cacus (Vergil, *Aeneid* 8.184–305).

41. Magnini Bracciali, "L. B. Alberti, *Canis* 10–27," 822–23, says that Alberti's phrasing here about exceeding the expectations of others recalls the words spoken by Laelius in another favorite Ciceronian work (*On Friendship* 3.11).

42. Once more, this seems to draw on Cicero's praise of the orator's work ethic in *Brutus* 88.302–89.305: see *On the Advantages*, note 2.

43. The phrase for "various musical modes" in the original Latin text ("varios canendi modos") no doubt includes a pun on the Latin for dog, "canis." A similar pun occurs in *The Fly*: see note 35. Contarino (162 n. 25) notes that there is an analogous emphasis on Alberti's own musical achievements in the autobiography (*My Life* 1, 3, 5, 81).

44. Alberti does indeed deal with these skills another time since they are attributed to himself in *My Life*. Again, the original phrasing here is picked up in the opening sentence of the autobiography (*My Life* 1).

45. Contarino (162–64 n. 27) points out that this phrase and concept are close to a motif in Pliny the Younger's portrait of his uncle, Pliny the Elder (Pliny the Younger, *Letters* 3.5.16).

46. Alberti's wording here is similar to the praise of philosophy as "magistra vitae" in Cicero, *Tusculan Disputations* 2.6.16: see McLaughlin, "Alberti's *Canis*," 71; and it also seems close to the famous passage about history being a "magistra vitae" in Cicero, *On the Orator* 2.9.36.

47. Bracciali Magnini (Cardini 2010, 978 n. 33) notes that the verb Alberti uses here, *oleret*, is also used by Cicero, *On the Nature of the Gods* 1.26.72, where Epicurus is said not to be redolent of Plato's Academy or of the philosophy of the Lyceum (the Peripatetic school); but there is also the play on the other meaning of *olere*, i.e., to smell, alluding to all dogs' propensity to smell other dogs.

48. Bracciali Magnini (Cardini 2010, 978 n. 34) and Contarino (164 n. 29) point to Aulus Gellius, *Attic Nights* 1.9.3–4, for Pythagoras' two-year vow of silence that he imposed on his followers; or to Apuleius, *Florida* 15, for a five-year ban. But Contarino also refers to one of Alberti's favorite Greek sources, Diogenes Laertius, *Lives of the Eminent Philosophers* 8.8, translated into Latin in 1431 by Ambrogio Traversari and often used by Alberti as a source.

49. Magnini Bracciali, "L. B. Alberti, *Canis* 10–27," 823, observes that Alberti's syntagma here about people's sadness over his funeral echoes the same phrase in a Cicero dialogue that was hugely influential on our author (*On Friendship*, 3.11): clearly a passage with which he was very familiar, since another phrase from the same paragraph was alluded to earlier on (see note 41 above).

50. Alberti's phrase here reminds us that also in one of his humorous *Apologi centum* (no. 93) he attributes to the lion this same motif of wanting simply to be thought worthy of the reward of a place in the heavens, not actually to be given it (Cardini 2010, 937).

51. Bracciali Magnini (Cardini 2010, 981 n. 35) notes that Lucian, *The Dead Come to Life, or The Fisherman* 50–51, offers some parallels to this story but also some discrepancies. In any case, there were other anecdotes about Aristotle's avarice, for instance that he sold the oil he had cleansed himself with: see Diogenes Laertius, *Lives of the Eminent Philosophers* 5.1.16. Alberti quotes this anecdote in *Profugiorum ab aerumna libri*, Book 1 (*Opere volgari*, ed. Grayson, 2:116 = Leon Battista Alberti, *Profugiorum ab aerumna libri*, ed. Giovanni Ponte [Genoa: Tilgher, 1988], 17).

52. Bracciali Magnini (Cardini 2010, 981 n. 36) says Plato's erotic epigram can be found in Diogenes Laertius, *Lives of the Eminent Philosophers* 3.29: "Star-gazing Aster, would I were the skies, / To gaze upon thee with

a thousand eyes." Contarino (166 n. 31) also mentions a poem cited in Aulus Gellius, *Attic Nights* 19.11.2, and in Macrobius, *Saturnalia* 2.2.15, but this was a different poem, one about Agathon not Aster (*aster* in Greek means *stella* in Latin), and it was also cited by Diogenes Laertius, *Lives of the Eminent Philosophers* 3.23. The Stella poem was admired by humanists and quoted in Guarino's *Life of Plato* (1429).

53. Bracciali Magnini (Cardini 2010, 981 n. 37) points to Cicero's famous letter to Lucceius (*Letters to Friends* 5.12) as the allusion here.

54. Bracciali Magnini (981 n. 38) suggests Plutarch, *Life of Cato the Elder* 24 and 33, as the allusion's source, but the same episode is alluded to also in Plutarch, *Comparison between Aristides and Cato* 6.1–2.

55. M. Licinius Crassus was famously wealthy. For the story of the forged will, Contarino (166 n. 33) rightly points to Cicero, *On Duties* 3.18.73–75.

56. This appendix is found only in the authoritative Oxford manuscript (O), but Mariangela Regoliosi has shown that the note was probably written by Alberti himself: see Mariangela Regoliosi, "Un'orazione funebre umoristica: Il *Canis* dell'Alberti," in *Alberti Lvdens* 23.2 (2020): 161–69, at 161. The Latin text of the note was first printed in Cardini 2010, 589. On the Bodleian manuscript, see Elisabetta Arfanotti, "Scheda 15," in *Leon Battista Alberti. La biblioteca di un umanista*, 282–86.

57. Alberti was fond of this classical contrast between seeming and being: see note 28 to the translation of *On the Advantages*. This would also suggest that this appendix note is by Alberti himself.

MY LIFE

1. Bracciali Magnini (Cardini 2010, 999 n. 1) says Alberti's words about the attainments befitting a liberally educated person echo Cicero's words about the orator instructed in the liberal arts (*De oratore* 1.16.73). She also refers to *De oratore* 3.32.127 for the idea of the liberal arts, but another phrase from the same dialogue may have been in Alberti's mind when he claims that nobody should be considered an orator unless they are accomplished in all the arts worthy of a free person (2.17.72). It is also worth noting that in the concluding phrase in this first sentence, about

the leading young men, the word *primarius* is one of Alberti's favorite terms: it recurs later in the autobiography (section 5) and is used also in *On the Advantages* (4.39, 4.167), in *The Life of St. Potitus* (3), and in many other works: see McLaughlin, *Leon Battista Alberti*, 30–32. The emphasis on primacy and excellence is obviously connected with his constant aspiration to originality.

2. One model for this description of Alberti's mastery of all the arts was Livy's description (39.40) of Cato the Elder, especially the phrase about his versatile genius, which he could turn to any art: see the edition of Fubini and Menci Gallorini (cited in the Bibliography), 34. The all-rounder Cato appears regularly in Alberti's works as a positive model. This opening idea of Alberti being versatile in any art quickly passed into the reception of the humanist, since Lapo da Castiglionchio makes this very point when he describes Alberti in his *Dialogus de curiae commodis* (1438): see Albanese, "Leon Battista Alberti nella storiografia letteraria e artistica," 56.

3. The wording here suggests that the passage recalled by Alberti ("quod aiunt") is from another author, in this case Cicero, *On Old Age*. This was a text he knew well, as he had his own personal copy of the text — now in the Marciana, MS Lat. VI 205 (3086): see Francesca Mazzanti, "Scheda 61," in *Leon Battista Alberti. La biblioteca di un umanista*, 402–3. The Cicero passage states that after each stage of life a person tires of the enthusiasms of that previous stage, until, finally, when the old tire of their own enthusiasms, their satiety of life ushers in the time when the old person is ready for death (Cicero, *On Old Age* 20.76). The point of this intertextual allusion seems to be that even Alberti's brilliance as a youth has to be seen in the context of a life that will eventually reach old age. For this and other echoes of Cicero's work in *My Life*, see McLaughlin, "Alberti and Burckhardt," 161–62. There is a similar motif in a passage from one of the versions of Donatus' *Life of Virgil*, the so-called Donatus Auctus, which recounts some of the poet's famous *sententiae*, one of which concerned satiety: see *The Virgilian Tradition. The First Fifteen Hundred Years*, ed. Jan M. Ziolkowski and Michael C. J. Putnam (New Haven: Yale University Press, 2008), 352. Since other motifs from that biography are also present in Alberti's autobiography (the author's ill-health, his desire to burn

some of his works, his battles with envious critics, his witty replies), it is quite possible that Alberti had this passage in mind here as well.

4. The cathedral mentioned here, "our biggest church," refers to Florence's Cathedral, Santa Maria del Fiore, whose dome was constructed by Filippo Brunelleschi, to whom Alberti dedicated the vernacular version of his treatise on painting, *Della pittura* (1435–36).

5. In this long sequence about his physical accomplishments, Alberti may have been thinking of another passage from Cicero, *On Old Age* 16.58, where it is said that certain sports are appropriate to the young, not to the elderly, such as feats of arms, horse riding, the javelin, club and ball, swimming and running (five of the seven activities mentioned by Cicero feature in Alberti's description here).

6. His brother was Carlo Alberti, also born illegitimate, who was the dedicatee of *On the Advantages*. Alberti specifies that he played music for his own pleasure and not for public performances, which would have been considered ignoble: see James Hankins, "Humanism and Music in Italy," in *The Cambridge History of Fifteenth-Century Music*, ed. Anna Maria Busse-Berger and Jesse Rodin (Cambridge: Cambridge University Press, 2015), 231–62, esp. 234–36 and note 28.

7. Probably an allusion to the fact that after his father's death in 1421, Alberti's relations refused to pay him and his brother Carlo the money left them by their father, leading to the family quarrels that Battista often alluded to.

8. The first redaction of the *Philodoxeos*, written in 1424, circulated for ten years as though it had been written by a little-known ancient writer Lepidus (*lepidus* means charming, witty), but then in 1434 Alberti openly claimed authorship of the comedy and revised it for what became the second and definitive redaction of the play, which he then dedicated to Leonello d'Este in 1437. For the texts of the two redactions, see Leon Battista Alberti, *Philodoxeos Fabula*, ed. Lucia Cesarini Martinelli, *Rinascimento*, ser. 2, 17 (1977): 111–234.

9. This allusion to the memory of names and of things is reminiscent of the mention of both Lucullus and Hortensius as having great memories, the former for things, the latter for words, as found in Cicero, *Academica*

2.1.2; Alberti makes a similar distinction regarding his dog's memory: see note 32 to the translation of *My Dog*, where again Cicero's *Academica* is the source, and also McLaughlin, "Alberti's *Canis*," 64–65.

10. On this mathematical-scientific "turn" in Alberti, see Luca Boschetto, *Leon Battista Alberti e Firenze*, 72 n. 4; David Lines, "Leon Battista Alberti e lo studio di Bologna," *La vita e il mondo di Leon Battista Alberti. Atti dei Convegni internazionali VI Centenario della nascita di Leon Battista Alberti. Genova, 19–21 febbraio 2004* (Florence: Olschki, 2008), 2:377–95. As Lines points out (esp. p. 387), natural philosophy meant primarily the study of Aristotle's *Physica*, *De caelo*, and *De anima*. These texts would have been studied in the arts faculty rather than in the faculty of law, where he had previously been studying.

11. Loredana Chines in her edition of the *Life* (70 nn. 3–4) claims that *Ephebia* here refers to Alberti's *Amator*, a Latin work written in response to his brother Carlo Alberti's *Ephebia*, but the precise relationship between Carlo's *Ephebia* and Battista's *Amator* is still not clear (Cardini 2010, 119). Chines also suggests that *De religione* is in fact one of the early *Intercenales*, entitled *Religio*. The *Deifira* was a vernacular work on the evils caused by love.

12. *Vidua* was a novella-like story about a widow, written in Latin, and included in Book 11 of the *Intercenales*. *Defunctus* was one of the longest of the *Intercenales*, but was not assigned to any particular book.

13. On Alberti's method of composition, see Roberto Cardini, "Le *Intercenales* di Leon Battista Alberti. Preliminari all'edizione critica," *Moderni e Antichi* 1 (2003): 98–142; Id., "Un nuovo reperto albertiano," *Moderni e Antichi* 2–3 (2004–5): 81–100; Lucia Bertolini, "Come 'pubblicava' l'Alberti: ipotesi preliminari," in *Storia della lingua e filologia. Per Alfredo Stussi nel suo sessantacinquesimo compleanno*, ed. Michelangelo Zaccarello, Lorenzo Tomasin (Tavernuzze-Impruneta: SISMEL, 2004), 219–40. The motif of the author wanting to burn his books before they were published derives from the lives of Virgil written by Donatus and others.

14. Alberti was fond of the contrast found in classical moral witers between seeming and being: see the English translation of *On the Advantages*, note 28, and *My Dog*, note 35.

15. Chines notes (74–75 n. 9) that the autobiographical protagonist Philoponius, in two early *Intercenales*, *Erumna* and *Pupillus*, recalls similar abuses at the hands of his relatives.

16. Aside from the New Testament source (Christ's Sermon on the Mount in Matthew 5), a similar doctrine is taught in Plato's *Gorgias* and *Apology*, which Alberti could easily have known in Leonardo Bruni's translations.

17. For the significance of the list of different kinds of artisans mentioned here, see McLaughlin, *Leon Battista Alberti*, 8–10. On Burckhardt's distortion of this passage, see Id., "Alberti and Burckhardt," 151–53, and the Introduction to this volume. There is a similar passage in Book 3 of the *Momus*, where Socrates questions a cobbler about his art: see Leon Battista Alberti, *Momus*, ed. and trans. Virginia Brown and Sarah Knight, I Tatti Renaissance Library 8 (Cambridge, MA: Harvard University Press, 2003), 252–61; and, in fact, the motif of the artisans' unusual and recondite piece of knowledge occurs there verbatim (p. 259).

18. In his conversations with artisans and his pretense of ignorance, Alberti was clearly imitating Socrates: see McLaughlin, *Leon Battista Alberti*, 8–11, 60–61.

19. This phrase about never betraying secrets repeats almost verbatim the same idea in *My Dog* (51): see note 38 to the translation of *My Dog*.

20. Chines (80 n. 10) observes that Alberti's habit of dictating the first draft of his works accounts for the oral dimension of early drafts and the complex philology behind his texts: see the bibliography cited at note 13 above. *The Fly* was composed in just this way, according to its dedicatory letter to Cristoforo Landino.

21. Alberti lived in Venice between 1415 and 1418: since he was between only eleven and fourteen years of age at that time, in this passage he was presumably talking of another occasion when he was in Venice: see Stefano Borsi, *Leon Battista Alberti tra Venezia e Ferrara* (Melfi: Libria, 2011).

22. The vernacular version of *Della pittura* was completed in 1435–36 and dedicated to the architect Filippo Brunelleschi, in time for the opening of his Duomo in Florence, July 1436; the Latin version, *De pictura*, was completed later, probably 1439–41, and dedicated to Giovanfrancesco Gon-

zaga. For the dating of the two redactions, see Lucia Bertolini, "Nouvelles perspectives sur le *De pictura* et sa réception," in *Alberti: Humaniste, architecte*, ed. Françoise Choay and Michel Paoli (Paris: Ecole nationale supérieure des Beaux-Arts: Musée du Louvre, 2006), 33–45.

23. Presumably, a kind of camera obscura or diorama.

24. The Homeric epithet for Dawn was *erigeneia* (meaning "early born"): it appears already in the first line of Book 2 of Homer's *Odyssey*. It is still not certain how many Greek texts Alberti was able to read in the original: certainly some, but others he read in Latin translation or gained knowledge of them through some intermediate Latin source, as here: see Lucia Bertolini, *"Grecus sapor." Tramiti di presenze greche in Leon Battista Alberti* (Rome: Bulzoni, 1998), esp. 21–22.

25. Alberti regularly mentions what we would call his work ethic. The wording about never ceasing to meditate or comment on things seems to be a conflation of Cicero's praises of two orators in his *Brutus*, namely Caius Piso and Hortensius (78.272, 88.302). As has been said, this was one of Alberti's favorite Cicero texts: see Maria Luisa Tanganelli, "Scheda 62," in *Leon Battista Alberti. La biblioteca di un umanista*, 404–5; see also Martin McLaughlin, "Alberti e le opere retoriche di Cicerone," in *Leon Battista Alberti e la tradizione*, 180–210, esp. 184–85. Alberti also attributes a keen work ethic to the subjects of his two mock encomia, *My Dog* and *The Fly*: see McLaughlin, "Alberti's *Canis*"; and Id., "Alberti's *Musca*." On the whole subject of work in Alberti, see Claudia Bertazzo, "The Rhetoric of Work in Leon Battista Alberti's Writings," in *Rhetorics of Work*, ed Yannis Yannitsiotis et al. (Pisa: Pisa University Press, 2008), 161–85; Juliann Vitullo, "*Otium* and *Negotium* in Alberti's *I libri della famiglia*," *Annali d'Italianistica* 32 (2014): 73–89; Marianna Villa, "L'etica del lavoro nel Quattrocento letterario," ibid., 91–116.

26. As with his work ethic, Alberti often mentions his own sense of humor and even attributes humorous qualities to his pet dog and the fly in his mock encomia.

27. The inclusion of a collection of witty sayings was a feature of the ancient biographies by Greek writers such as Diogenes Laertius and Plutarch, whose works were being translated into Latin around this time.

The importance of Diogenes Laertius' work for Alberti's autobiography was first pointed out by Cecil Grayson, "Il prosatore latino e volgare," in *Convegno internazionale indetto nel V centenario di Leon Battista Alberti* (Roma-Mantova-Firenze, 25–29 aprile 1972) (Rome: Accademia Nazionale dei Lincei, 1974), 273–286, at 273 n. 2.

28. Alberti's strong misogynistic streak is in evidence here and in section 57, as well as in many other works.

29. The phrase in the Latin original—"rerum omnium suavissimum amari liberale tempus"—is ambiguous, and different editors have adopted different punctuation, syntactical solutions, and translations. In their edition Fubini and Menci Gallorini (p. 75) offered the following punctuation: "rerum omnium suavissimum: 'Amari liberale tempus.'" In their introduction they suggested that it means something antithetical, along the lines of "Time, which brings us and frees us from bitterness" (Fubini and Menci Gallorini, 45). They also note that Alberti's replies in this section 59 are modeled on the double set of replies in Plutarch, *The Dinner of the Seven Wise Men* 153A–D, and on some of the sayings attributed to Thales in Diogenes Laertius' *Life of Thales* 1.35–37. Grafton quotes these sources too, but his translation suggests a more pessimistic view of time, "Time which makes free with bitterness," though he is aware that elsewhere Alberti's views on time are more nuanced: Grafton, *Leon Battista Alberti*, 24. David Marsh's version is similarly pessimistic: "Time, that liberally dispenses bitterness" (Marsh, "The Self-expressed," 133). However, the fact remains that there are no other instances of "liberalis" with a genitive in Alberti's works. In addition, the use of the adjective "amarus" as a noun meaning "bitterness" is very rare. Cardini and Regoliosi's text punctuates the phrase as two questions, not one, "rerum omnium suavissimum? 'Amari.' liberale? 'tempus'" (Cardini 2010, 994), so Bracciali Magnini's Italian version in the same edition runs as "quale la più dolce? 'Essere amati'; quella copiosa? 'Il tempo'" (Cardini 2010, 1006). This seems the best solution, since Alberti had a neutral rather than totally pessimistic view of time—see the famous passage in the third book in Alberti, *I libri della famiglia*, ed. Romano, Tenenti, and Furlan, 207–8. Similarly, Watkins translates the phrase as two questions: "What sweetest, 'To be loved and appreciated.' What most freely given, 'Time'" (Wat-

kins, 13). It is typical of Alberti's technique of *variatio* that he does not reproduce Thales' answers verbatim or in the same order: where the Greek philosopher had said that the greatest thing was space, and the commonest was hope, Alberti says the greatest thing was hope; where Thales said the wisest thing was time, Alberti says time was the most copious thing; and where Thales said the sweetest thing was success, Alberti says the sweetest thing was to be loved. For his technique of varying and splicing his ancient sources, see note 12 to the translation of *My Dog*.

30. Referring to summary executions during political disturbances by defenestration or hanging from the windows of the public palace.

31. Nestor was the mythical aged king of Pylos who helped Telemachus in his search for his father, Ulysses. Alberti mentions him in his vernacular dialogue *Theogenius* as a paragon of the wisdom of old age: see Alberti, *Opere volgari*, ed. Grayson, 2:70, 102.

32. Fubini and Menci Gallorini read "forum putridum nodo non teneri" (p. 75), meaning something like "that a rotten gangway could not be held secure by a rope"; but Cardini reads "fenum putridum" (Cardini 2010, 995), and Bracciali Magnini translates "fieno marcio non si annoda" (Cardini 2010, 1006).

33. Chines (92 n. 25) explains that the "capri ficus" was a wild fig, a sterile fig, which was useful only for feeding goats, and refers to Pliny's discussion in *Natural History* 15.21.79–80.

34. Chines (92 n. 26) suggests that Alberti is referring to the bloody events of 1425 in Ferrara, when Parisina, the young wife of Niccolò III d'Este, was executed along with her lover, Ugo Aldobrandino, the older illegitimate brother of Leonello d'Este: Leonello would become one of Alberti's patrons. Bracciali Magnini (Cardini 2010, 1007 n. 12) argues that the reference to Niccolò III's reign as something in the remote past suggests that at least this part of *My Life* was composed after Niccolò's death in 1441.

35. Chines (92–93 n. 27) reminds us that Alberti, like many intellectuals of the time, believed in astrology, even writing out his own horoscope in his copy of Cicero's *De legibus*, another manuscript that survives from his

library: see Maria Luisa Tanganelli and Sara Donegà, "Scheda 60," in *Leon Battista Alberti. La biblioteca di un umanista*, 396–402 (with a reproduction of the horoscope at 397). See also Roberto Cardini, "Biografia, leggi e astrologia in un nuovo reperto albertiano," in *Leon Battista Alberti umanista e scrittore*, 1:21–90.

36. Paolo dal Pozzo Toscanelli (1397–1482) was a famous Florentine mathematician, cosmographer, and astronomer, a friend of Alberti who dedicated the first book of his Latin *Intercenales* to him. No trace of Alberti's letters to Toscanelli remains.

37. Grafton, *Leon Battista Alberti*, 23–24, notes that Alberti's claims to prophetic powers here could have been inspired once more by Diogenes Laertius, *Life of Thales* (1.26), which attributed similar capacities to the ancient philosopher.

38. A superhuman power of prediction was a standard element in saints' lives, and this tradition might also have influenced Alberti here: see Michel Paoli, "Autoportrait d'humaniste." And the detail of the ray in his chest echoes the same motif in the portrait of Potitus in *The Life of St. Potitus*, section 3.

39. On Alberti's use of pseudonyms, see Martin McLaughlin, "Da Lepidus a Leon Battista Alberti: metamorfosi onomastiche e anonimizzazioni nell'Italia del Quattrocento," in McLaughlin, *Leon Battista Alberti*, 19–37.

40. According to Bracciali Magnini (Cardini 2010, 1008 n. 15), the passage here about putting up with pain, cold, and heat reworks the descriptions of Sulla's and Catiline's tolerance of hardship in Sallust's and Cicero's works. Chines (95 n. 30) suggests another possible source for Alberti's tolerance of such things, in Livy's description (21.4) of Hannibal's tolerance of heat and cold, which is then followed by details of how he ate and drank moderately and was often found sleeping covered only by his military cloak. She refers also to Sallust's portrait of Catiline putting up with incredible levels of hunger, cold, and lack of sleep (Sallust, *The War with Catiline* 5.3).

41. On Alberti's tolerance of cold, Marsh, "The Self-expressed," suggests a possible source in Diogenes of Sinope's ability to withstand extremes of heat and cold in his famous barrel, as recounted by Diogenes Laertius,

Lives of the Eminent Philosophers 6.23. Perhaps even closer to Alberti's motif of riding bareheaded in the coldest of weather is Cicero, *On Old Age* 10.34, where Cato the Elder says that Massinissa at the age of ninety still rode on horseback and would not be induced by either rain or cold to cover his head.

42. This idea is articulated in a rather everyday context here (Alberti overcoming his dislike of garlic and honey), but it is decontextualized in Burckhardt's portrait of Alberti and associated instead with something more exalted, namely the passage about his prophetic powers. The concept of being able to achieve anything one wants becomes almost a slogan for the "universal man of the Renaissance": see McLaughlin, "Alberti and Burckhardt," 156–57; see also the Introduction to this volume. The same idea is mentioned in the second book of *De familia*: "People say that man can achieve what he wants. If you try, as I have said, with all your strength and skills, I have no doubt that in whatever field you operate, you will reach the first and highest level of perfection and renown" (Alberti, *I libri della famiglia*, ed. Romano, Tenenti, and Furlan, 169; my translation).

43. In this and in the following remark to himself in section 86, Alberti explicitly identifies himself as the subject of the autobiography, Leon Battista: see Luca Boschetto, "Tra biografia e autobiografia," 93–94.

44. It is possible that the praise of nature here derives from the praise of the sight of fields and trees in another favorite text of Alberti's, Cicero's *On Old Age* (16.57), especially as that passage precedes another important moment in the classical dialogue, the praise of Xenophon's *Oeconomicus*, which would be the model for the third book of *De familia* (*On Old Age* 17.59).

45. The original Latin sentence here uses the superlative *lepidissimo* (very charming, witty) of his dog, which hints at the fact that *My Dog* is also a self-portrait: *lepidus* is one of Alberti's favorite adjectives and has a special resonance in his works. As noted above, he attributed the first redaction of his comedy *Philodoxeos* to a fictitious ancient writer of comedies, Lepidus, and it is also the name of a character who is very like Alberti himself in a number of the *Intercenales*.

46. For this unusually open attitude to bad writers, see the Introduction and McLaughlin, "Alberti and Burckhardt," 153–54.

47. What is now called the photic sneeze reflex (i.e., feeling the need to sneeze when looking at the sun) was discussed already in antiquity, e.g., pseudo-Aristotle, *Problems* 33.4.

48. Chines notes (100 n. 33) that the night owl singing on the roof is a sign of ill omen in *Convelata*, one of the *Intercenales* (Cardini 2010, 435)

49. Lazy and sleepy men manifest a phlegmatic temperament, which according to Galenic theory was caused by an excess of the cold humor of phlegm.

50. Bracciali Magnini (Cardini 2010, 1010 n. 16) sees a parallel idea in Alberti's vernacular work *Villa*: "If it seems easy to you to request something, it will be even easier for me to deny you what you ask for" (Alberti, *Opere volgari*, ed. Grayson, 1:360).

51. Already in the middle ages, Bologna was known as "la dotta e la grassa" (the learned and fat): it was famous for its university and for its good food. Chines (102 n. 35) notes that Petrarch mentions these aspects of the city in *Seniles* 10.2. Like Petrarch before him, Alberti had studied canon and civil law in Bologna, probably from 1421 to 1428. He mentions the high costs of studying there in *On the Advantages*, section 4.19–25.

THE FLY

1. Cristoforo Landino (1424–98) was an admirer of Alberti. Around the time of Alberti's dedication of *The Fly* to him, he dedicated to Battista the first redaction of his Latin love lyrics, *Xandra* (ca. 1443–44). In his dedicatory poem he mentions a number of ludic works, including Catullus' poems on Lesbia's sparrow, Martial's learned epigrams (Landino calls him the Spanish dog), and Alberti's *The Fly* (vv. 32–34 of poem 1.13): see Cristoforo Landino, *Poems*, trans. Mary P. Chatfield, 26. Later in his *Prolusione petrarchesca* (1467), he praised Alberti for his contribution to the development of the vernacular, and in his *Proemio al commento dantesco* (1481), he singled out his literary variety, famously comparing him to a chameleon, since he takes on the very color of the thing he is talking

about: see Cristoforo Landino, *Scritti critici e teorici*, ed. Roberto Cardini (Rome: Bulzoni, 1974), 1:35–36, 120. Landino even portrayed Alberti as one of the principal speakers in his major Latin dialogue, *Disputationes Camaldulenses* (1473). On the question of the dating of *The Fly* and *Xandra*, see Alessandro Perosa, "Miscellanea umanistica," in *Annali della R. Scuola Normale Superiore di Pisa*, serie 2, 7 (1938): 73–80: Perosa argues (p. 76) that *The Fly* was composed before Alberti's departure from Florence on March 7, 1443. Grayson in his edition (*Opuscoli inediti*, 18–21) also puts the date as between late 1441 and March 1443.

2. For the Greek text and the English translation of Lucian's *Eulogy of the Fly (Encomium Muscae)*, see *Lucian*, with an English translation by A. M. Harmon, 8 vols. (Cambridge, MA: Harvard University Press, 1913), 1:81–95. Guarino da Verona (1374–1460) was in Constantinople between 1403 and 1408, when he first translated Lucian's eulogy into Latin, and he published the *Musce collaudatio vel explicatio* in 1440, when he dedicated it to Scipione Mainenti. He later sent a copy of his version to Alberti in 1441, and the latter immediately decided to compose, not a translation, but a Latin rewriting of the original. See *Das Lob der Fliege von Lukian bis L. B. Alberti*, ed. Billerbeck and Zubler (cited in the Bibliography), esp. 41–53 (introduction to Guarino's and Alberti's versions), 182–90 (for the Latin text of Guarino's translation), and 192–232 (for the Latin text of Alberti's *Musca*).

3. Marco Parenti was a friend of Alberti who often acted as his agent in his absences from Florence: see Luca Boschetto, *Leon Battista Alberti e Firenze, ad indicem*. His son Piero produced a vernacular version of Alberti's *Canis*: see Gabriella Albanese and Rossella Bessi, *All'origine della guerra dei cento anni. Una novella Latina di Bartolomeo Facio e il volgarizzamento di Poggio Bracciolini* (Rome: Edizioni di Storia e Letteratura, 2000), 301; and the posthumous article by Cecil Grayson, "Piero di Marco Parenti's *volgarizzamento* of Alberti's *Canis*," in *Alberti Lvdens* 22.2 (2019): 51–55.

4. The "famous philosopher" was probably Socrates: see Xenophon, *Memorabilia* 1.1.11, in Xenophon, *Memorabilia and Oeconomicus*, with an English translation by E. C. Marchant (Cambridge, MA: Harvard University Press, 1923), 9. This work was translated into Latin by Cardinal

Bessarion in 1442: see David Marsh, "Xenophon," in *Catalogus Translatio- num et Commentariorum: Medieval and Renaissance Latin Translations and Commentaries. Annotated Lists and Guides*, ed. Virginia Brown, Paul Oskar Kristeller, F. Edward Cranz (Washington, DC: The Catholic Univer- sity of America Press, 1992), 75–196, at 166. For the identification with Socrates, see Luca Boschetto, "Ricerche sul *Theogenius* e sul *Momus* di Leon Battista Alberti," *Rinascimento* ser. 2, 33 (1993): 3–52, at 33 n. 68. However, Maria Letizia Braccciali Magnini (Cardini 2010, 1025 n. 1) sug- gests it was Democritus, because of what is said in Cicero, *On Divination* 2.13.30, and certainly Democritus's phrase quoted by Cicero ("nobody looks at what lies at their feet but instead they scan the regions of the sky") seems to be echoed by Alberti here. Contarino in his edition of the text (Alberti, *Apologhi ed elogi*, 174 n. 3) notes a similar motif in the *Theo- genius*: "Other living creatures are content with what is appropriate to them; but only humans are always investigating new things and making themselves enemies to others" (*Opere volgari*, ed. Grayson, 2:92).

5. Presumably, he is thinking primarily of the first half of Book 4 of Vergil's *Georgics*.

6. Inachus' daughter was Io, famously metamorphosed into a cow after Jupiter had seduced her (Ovid, *Metamorphoses* 1.568–667); and according to Vergil, the polluted blood of a dead cow could give birth to bees (*Geor- gics* 4.285). The paradoxical idea that flies are descended from the mythi- cal centaurs is invented by Alberti. He backs up this claim with a fake reference to the "linen books," which supposedly contained the earliest annals of Rome: they are mentioned by Livy on several occasions (4.7, 4.13, 4.20, 4.23).

7. Bellona was the Roman goddess of war.

8. This whole anti-bee polemic is a jocular attack on Vergil and other ancient writers who praised bees for providing a model for human soci- ety: see Hartmut Wulfram, "Alberti's attack on Virgil in the *Musca*," in *Alberti Lvdens* 23.2 (2020): 171–90.

9. On the martial qualities of the Getae tribe, see Solinus, *Collection of Memorable Things* 15.3; another source might have been Ovid, *Letters from the Black Sea* 1.7.12. Alberti's sentence here begins "Getis quidem," but the

Oxford manuscript (O) has this variant: "Mavorti quidem genti, Getis, quod muscas imitari conata sit . . ." (That martial race, the Getae, is egregiously praised . . .). On this and other philological questions, see Donatella Coppini, "Leon Battista Alberti si corregge. Il caso della *Mosca Riccardiana*," in *Leon Battista Alberti. La biblioteca di un umanista*, 51–56.

10. Alberti probably read about leaders such as Agesilaus, Pyrrhus, and Fabius Maximus in Plutarch's *Lives*, which he could have read in the original Greek or more probably in the Latin translations of the *Lives* that were being carried out in the first half of the Quattrocento: see Pade, *The Reception of Plutarch's Lives*, cited above. Interestingly, Plutarch wrote the life of Pompey the Great as the Roman parallel to Agesilaus (mentioned here), and Alberti later in this text makes a reference to Pompey (see below, note 32).

11. According to the *Souda*, Timotheus' music made Alexander the Great leap from his seat and ride into battle. There are references to the power of his music on Alexander after capturing Persepolis. However, as Grayson first suggested in *Opuscoli inediti*, 49, note, Alberti was perhaps confusing Timotheus with the musician Antigenides, mentioned by Plutarch in his *The Fortune or Virtue of Alexander the Great* 335A: see Plutarch's *Moralia*, trans. Frank Cole Babbitt and others, 16 vols. (Cambridge, MA: Harvard University Press, 1927–2004), 4:431. Grayson and Contarino (178 n. 6) note that Alberti also mentions this legend in the *Profugiorum ab aerumna libri* (*Opere volgari*, ed. Grayson, 2:108). But Bracciali Magnini (Cardini 2010, 1027 n. 6) thinks Alberti was correct in saying it was Timotheus of Miletus who had this effect on Alexander (she mentions Dion of Prusa and Athenaeus as possible sources).

12. Grayson (*Opuscoli inediti*, 49, note) and Contarino (178 n. 7) suggest that Alberti's source here was Lucian, *De saltatione* (*The Dance*) 10, as does Mario Bonaria, "La *Musca* di L. B. Alberti: Osservazioni e traduzione," in *Miscellanea di studi albertiani* (Genoa: Tilgher, 1975), 47–69, at 57 n. 43: "[The Spartans] do everything with the aid of the Muses, to the extent of going into battle to the accompaniment of flute and rhythm and well-timed step in marching; indeed, the first signal for battle is given to the Spartans by the flute": see *Lucian*, trans. A. M. Harmon, 5:225.

13. The idea that the kite was effeminate comes from Isidore, *Etymologies* 12.7.58, according to Grayson (*Opuscoli inediti*, 50, note). Isidore says that its Latin name, *milvus*, derives from *mollis avis* (literally, "a soft bird"). For the legend about the Gauls' lack of bravery in meeting a second attack in battle, see Livy 10.28.4.

14. The notion that a fly can lay an elephant low comes from Lucian, *Encomium muscae* 6.

15. The idea of the vulture as a lucky bird might have come from Livy 1.7, which mentions the twelve vultures that appeared as Romulus was building the future city of Rome and which led to the murder of Remus. But Contarino (180 n. 10) argues that Alberti's wording shows that it is Plutarch's account (*Roman Questions* 93) that he has in mind, since it mentions, like Alberti, the fact that the vulture was believed to be the most righteous of all creatures, never harming nature: "it is the most harmless of birds to men, since it neither destroys any fruit or plant nor injures any domesticated animal" (Plutarch, *Moralia*, trans. F. C. Babbitt, 4:139–41). It is possible that Guarino's partial translation of the *Roman Questions* (1437–39) might have been Alberti's source: see Francesco Becchi, "Humanist Latin Translations of the *Moralia*," in *Brill's Companion to the Reception of Plutarch*, ed. Sophia Xenophontos and Katerina Oikonomopolou (Leiden: E. J. Brill, 2019), 458–78, at 461. Grayson (p. 50, note) quotes Pliny, *Natural History* 10.12.28, though there Pliny is talking about the kite.

16. The legend that certain gems fall from the night sky is found in Pliny, *Natural History* 37.56.151, 37.59.164, 37.65.176; it is also mentioned in Isidore, *Etymologies* 16.5, 16.17, 16.24. See Wulfram, "Alberti's Attack on Virgil in the *Musca*," 177 n. 2.

17. Grayson (*Opuscoli inediti*, 51, note) suggests as source for this Spartan custom Xenophon, *Constitution of the Lacedaemonians* 5, translated by Francesco Filelfo around 1430. Bonaria ("La *Musca*," 57 n. 46) points also to Herodotus, *History* 1.65; Plato, *Laws* 1.625C, 625I, 781A; Plutarch, *Life of Lycurgus* 12 and 26; Athenaeus, *Deipnosophistae* 4.16. Though of these authors we have evidence only for Alberti reading Herodotus in Greek in the 1440s (in the passage added to Book 1 of *De familia* about the hard-

ness of the Egyptians' skulls): see Lucia Bertolini, "Per la biblioteca greca dell'Alberti," in *Leon Battista Alberti. La biblioteca di un umanista*, 101–3, at 102.

18. Bonaria ("La *Musca*," 58 n. 47) quotes as his source Plutarch, *Life of Cato the Elder* 25.3, a passage alluded to in Alberti, *De familia*, Book 4: see Alberti, *I libri della famiglia*, ed. Romano, Tenenti, and Furlan, 421.

19. Lucian's account of the fly's mating habits had been fairly objective: "In mating, love, and marriage they are very free and easy. The male is not on and off again in a moment, like the cock; he covers the female a long time. She carries her spouse, and they take wing together, mating uninterruptedly in the air, as everyone knows" (Lucian, *The Fly*, in *Lucian*, trans. A. M. Harmon, 1:89). Alberti turns this description of mating into something much more heroic, seeing it as one fly nobly carrying another tired fly on top of it. Aeneas was famed for his *pietas*, but given the wording here, Alberti was referring precisely to the words in the first book of the *Aeneid* where "pius Aeneas" says he is carrying his Penates with him and that his fame is known beyond the skies (1.378–79). Aeneas carrying his father is also mentioned in Alberti's *Profugiorum* Book 2, where he goes on to quote in Latin *Aeneid* 2.726–29 (*Opere volgari*, ed. Grayson, 2:143).

20. An allusion to the "civil" wars of bees mentioned by Vergil at the beginning of the fourth book of the *Georgics* (4.67–87).

21. Grayson (*Opuscoli inediti*, 52, note) and Bonaria ("La *Musca*," 58 n. 50) rightly suggest Pliny, *Natural History* 8.43.104, as the source.

22. This recalls the passage in the *Theogenius* Book 2 that states that even a small insect such as a fly can prove fatal to men (*Opere volgari*, ed. Grayson, 2:90).

23. Lake Trasimene and Cannae were the scenes of two of the bloodiest battles between the Romans and Hannibal's Carthaginian army in the Second Punic War: Alberti would have known about these famous battles from many sources, but particularly Livy 22.4–7 (Trasimene) and 22.43–50 (Cannae).

24. Alberti's words explicitly state that this is a quotation from a poet: in fact, it is from Martial's poem about the slopes of Vesuvius after the eruption of 79 CE (*Epigrams* 4.44.7).

25. Julius Caesar himself in *The Gallic War* 4.15 boasts of having killed over 400 men, not over 400,000. Grayson says Solinus, *Collection of Memorable Things* 3, is Alberti's source here, but another Solinus passage (*Collection of Memorable Things* 1.106) mentions 1,192,000 men killed by Caesar. Contarino (182 n. 16) and Bracciali Magnini (Cardini 2010, 1029 n. 13) suggest that Alberti was referring to Augustus, whom he mentions in the *Theogenius* as having killed 90,102 men (*Opere volgari*, ed. Grayson, 2:94), a figure that curiously resembles the figure given by Solinus, at least in its digits.

26. Alberti's phrase "non invita, uti aiunt, Minerva" alludes to Horace's famous phrase "invita Minerva" (literally, "if Minerva is unwilling," i.e., if the poet lacks inspiration): see Horace, *Art of Poetry* 385.

27. For the source of this claim, Grayson (*Opuscoli inediti*, 54, note) points to Plutarch, *Against the Stoics on Common Conceptions* 1083D: see Plutarch, *Moralia*, trans. Harold Cherniss, 13.2:851–53. But Bonaria ("La Musca," 60 n. 55) quotes Valerius Maximus, who says that Strabo had such wonderful eyesight that from the port of Lilybaeum (in Sicily, not the Piraeus, as here) he could see the Carthaginian fleet emerging from its port (*Memorabilia* 1.8.ext.14). Pliny supplies more detail, saying Strabo could even tell the actual number of ships emerging from the harbor (*Natural History* 7.21.85). However, in a vernacular work, Alberti says that the source for this story is Varro (*Profugiorum*, Book 2, in *Opere volgari*, ed. Grayson, 2:145), and this detail allows us to say that Solinus was the source, since he mentions both Varro and Strabo (*Collection of Memorable Things* 1.99), as Ponte points out: see Leon Battista Alberti, *Profugiorum ab aerumna libri*, ed. Giovanni Ponte (Genoa: Tilgher, 1988), 59 n. 19. There seems to be an echo of this in his autobiography, when Alberti mentions that some Greek visitors were able to see in one of his "demonstrations" a fleet at sea, thanks to his observation room (*My Life* 38). Again, Alberti's fascination with the eye and sight is evident here.

28. In this and the other episodes mentioned in this paragraph, Alberti mockingly mentions trivial pieces of knowledge about classical mythology. The Circe episode is in Homer, *Odyssey* Books 10 and 12, but Alberti could have known about it from many other sources.

29. The legend of the hiding of Osiris' body in a chest and casting it into the Nile comes from Plutarch, *On Isis and Osiris* 13, 356C, 17, 357F; see Plutarch, *Moralia*, trans. F. C. Babbitt, 5:34–44. It was found by his wife Isis and their son Horus, but the fact that Osiris' body was ritually "discovered" every year by his devotees means that this piece of knowledge is also useless.

30. The legend about the blemishes on Helen of Troy's bottom is rather obscure, but Grayson (*Opuscoli inediti*, 54, note) pointed out that it was still being mentioned in Pierre Bayle's *Dictionnaire historique et critique*, 3rd ed. (Amsterdam: P. Brunel et al., 1730), 2:701–3.

31. These slightly obscene details about Ganymede and Andromache are made up by Alberti. Wulfram, "Alberti's Attack on Virgil in the *Musca*" (183 n. 42), notes that, with the exception of Isis and Osiris, all these characters are mentioned in the *Aeneid*, which is thus again implicitly being mocked.

32. According to Bonaria ("La *Musca*," 61 n. 58) and Bracciali Magnini (Cardini 2010, 1030 n. 16), the source for Pompey's reticence is Valerius Maximus, *Memorabilia* 3.3.2, which tells the story of how a certain Pompeius was prepared to place his finger in the fire rather than give information to the enemy king Gentius; but this episode took place in 169 BCE, so it could not have been Pompey the Great. It may be that Alberti mistook this Pompeius for the later more famous Pompey; alternatively, the source might have been *Memorabilia* 6.2.4, where Pompey the Great is praised for his impassive bearing when facing insults. For Alberti's knowledge of Valerius Maximus, see Ida Mastrorosa, "La tradizione memorialistico-antiquaria romana in Leon Battista Alberti: Valerio Massimo e Gellio," in *Leon Battista Alberti e la tradizione*, 383–405. Another possible source, Plutarch, says that nobody "remained more constant in his adversity" than Pompey: see Plutarch, *Life of Pompey*, 1.2, in *Plutarch's Lives*, vol. 5, *Agesilaus and Pompey; Pelopidas and Marcellus*, trans. Bernadotte Perrin (Cambridge, MA: Harvard University Press, 1917), 117. This is a possibility since it seems that Iacopo Angeli da Scarperia's Latin version of the life of Pompey was in circulation in the first decade of the Quattrocento: see Pade, *The Reception of Plutarch's "Lives" in Fifteenth-Century Italy*, 1:122–23. Not surprisingly, there are several examples of Al-

berti's own self-restraint in his autobiography. For others who refused to talk, Grayson (*Opuscoli inediti*, 54, note) points to the story of Mucius Scaevola in Valerius Maximus, *Memorabilia* 3.3.2, and he also cites Alberti's *Profugiorum*, which openly acknowledges Valerius as the source for Scaevola placing his hand in the fire and Pompey placing his finger in it rather than talking (*Profugiorum*, Book 1, in *Opere volgari*, ed. Grayson, 2:113).

33. The detail about Domitian capturing and killing flies with a sharp dagger comes from Suetonius' life of Domitian in *Lives of the Caesars* 3.1. Wulfram, "Alberti's Attack on Virgil in the *Musca*," 184–85, suggests that this episode too is an attack on the ideology of the *Aeneid*, since in the poem Aeneas was the mythical founder of the race of Roman emperors. A more recent source for Alberti might have been Pier Paolo Vergerio, *The Character and Studies Befitting a Free-Born Youth*, section 32: see *Humanist Educational Treatises*, ed. and trans. Craig W. Kallendorf, I Tatti Renaissance Library 5 (Cambridge, MA: Harvard University Press, 2002), 40.

34. According to Solinus, this was Socrates (*Collection of Memorable Things* 1.73). Grayson (*Opuscoli inediti*, 56, note) quotes *Profugiorum*, Book 1 (*Opere volgari*, ed. Grayson, 2:111–12), which mentions Socrates' ability to confront any misfortune with an unchanged face

35. Alberti makes a similar pun concerning music in *My Dog*: "canendi modos": see the English translation of *My Dog*, note 43.

36. The first six notes of the musical scale in Latin were based on the first syllables in the lines of a famous medieval hymn to St. John the Baptist by Paulus Diaconus (*Ut queant laxis resonare fibris, mira gestorum famuli tuorum, solve polluti labii reatum* . . .): ut, re, mi, fa, sol, la. Alberti inverts the order of the last two pairs of notes to produce: ut, re, sol, la, mi, fa.

37. Bracciali Magnini (Cardini 2010, 1032 n. 23) points out that the marsh of Maeotis is today the Sea of Azov, and was the legendary homeland of the Amazons.

38. The sources of the legend of Pythagoras sacrificing to the Muses after discovering his famous theorem are Diogenes Laertius, *Lives of the Eminent Philosophers* 8.12; Cicero, *On the Nature of the Gods* 3.36.88; and

Vitruvius, *De architectura* 9, proem 7. Bracciali Magnini (Cardini 2010, 1032 n. 24) says Alberti is here conflating the Cicero and Vitruvius sources and suggests that the final phrase about "that amazing geometric figure which allows us to measure height" (*geometrica illa altimetra*) refers to some device that could offer a practical application of Pythagoras' famous theorem. This in turn may be connected with Alberti's interest in calculating the height of towers in the opening pages of his *Ex ludis rerum mathematicarum* (ca. 1450).

39. In fact, as we shall see, Alberti goes on to be anything but succinct, as he adds many more erudite allusions in what follows.

40. On Plato's wanderings, the sources are Diogenes Laertius, *Life of Plato*, in his *Lives of the Eminent Philosophers* 3.6–7, 3.18; and pseudo-Plato, *Letter 7*. For other possible sources, see Alice Swift Riginos, *Platonica. The Anecdotes Concerning the Life and Writings of Plato* (Leiden: Brill, 1976), 61–85.

41. Diogenes Laertius says it was a bronze ball he held in his hand (*Life of Aristotle* in *Lives of the Eminent Philosophers* 5.16). Many such anecdotes about Aristotle are mentioned in Ingemar Düring, *Aristotle in the Ancient Biographical Tradition* (Göteborg: Elanders Boktryckeri Aktiebolag, 1957).

42. There is a similar idea in *Theogenius* (*Opere volgari*, ed. Grayson, 2:91), which mentions a senator who died from drinking milk with a hair in it, a philosopher who died eating a grape seed, and another famous Roman who died eating a cake.

43. Alberti will have known of Afranius' dictum from Aulus Gellius, *Attic Nights* 13.8.1. Afranius' emphasis on practice as well as on the memory of things will have appealed to Alberti. On Alberti's use of Gellius, see Ida Mastrorosa, "La tradizione memorialistico-antiquaria romana," in *Leon Battista Alberti e la tradizione*, 1:405–14.

44. Here, Alberti seems to have confused Pliny the Elder, who perished in the eruption of Vesuvius in 79 CE, with Empedocles, who jumped into Mount Etna some time in the fifth century BCE. This was probably a deliberate "mistake" since *The Fly* has a strong pro-Roman dimension, and in other works Alberti correctly quotes Empedocles' suicide: for instance, in the vernacular version of Walter Map's *Dissuasio Valerii* (*Opere*

volgari, ed. Grayson, 2:370). For other Roman examples in *The Fly*, see McLaughlin, "Alberti's *Musca*," 18–19, 24 n. 49.

45. Aristotle, *On the Generation of Living Things* 4.8.777A7–8.

46. Pliny, *Natural History* 14.7.58, quotes Alexander the Great's physician Androcydes saying to the king that when he was about to drink wine he should remember that wine was the blood of the earth.

47. There are many sources for this episode, but two seem to have verbal echoes: Cicero, *On Ends* 5.19.50; and Livy 25.31.9. Livy's greater visual emphasis on the "tumult" of the captured city seems to be echoed in Alberti's phrasing here. Other possible sources are Valerius Maximus, *Memorabilia* 8.7.ext.7; Plutarch, *Life of Marcellus* 19.4–6 = 308E–309A. Archimedes is one of Alberti's heroes, and the episode of his death is the final classical exemplum in Book 3 of *Profugiorum ab aerumna libri*, where the account is much more detailed (*Opere volgari*, ed. Grayson, 2:182–83).

48. Grayson (*Opuscoli inediti*, 60, note) points to Gellius, *Attic Nights* 2.18.6, as the source for the phrase.

49. Bracciali Magnini (Cardini 2010, 1034 n. 29) notes that Alberti differs from Lucian (*Encomium* 5), who had stressed the fly's capacity to escape the spider's trap.

50. The Sabines were an ancient warlike race in Italy, and in the early history of Rome, the Romans fought a fierce war against them, recounted in Livy 1.9–45. But it is possible that if we want to find a precise source for Alberti's allusion here, it might be Plutarch, *Life of Numa* 1.4, where we are told that the Sabines attributed their military valor to the fact that they were originally colonists from Sparta.

51. As Bracciali Magnini observes (Cardini 2010, 1034 n. 30), the allusion to the member of the Alani tribe who briefly captured the Armenian king Tiridates with a lasso comes from Josephus, *The Jewish War* 7.249–50 (= 7.7.4). See McLaughlin, "Alberti's *Musca*," 24 n. 50.

52. For Arion, Grayson (*Opuscoli inediti*, 61, note) quotes Aulus Gellius, *Attic Nights* 16.19, a chapter devoted to Arion's story.

53. Once more Alberti mentions the famous deeds and sayings of his subject, just as he had done for his dog (*My Dog* 62); he had also attrib-

uted famous deeds and sayings to his dog's ancestors (*My Dog* 10). See also the English translation of *My Dog*, note 9. He even provides two lists of his own sayings in *My Life* 41–76, 89–107. The wording suggests again that Alberti is ending his eulogy just as Diogenes Laertius often ended his life of a philosopher with a mention of his famous deeds and sayings.

54. Contarino (194 n. 31) states that "Caspiumque montem" here is not a scribal error for "Caspiumque mare," saying that there was a real "mons Caspius," a mountain range that separated Media from Armenia and was referred to by Pomponius Mela, Pliny, and Tacitus. Coppini's edition prefers the reading "Casiumque montem" (Cardini 2010, 1023): Casius was a sacred mountain in northwestern Syria, mentioned by Herodotus (*Histories* 2.6), Pomponius Mela (*Chorographia* 3.74), Lucan (*Bellum civile* 8.858, 10.434), and Pliny (*Natural History* 5.18.80, 12.55.124). Any of these could have been Alberti's source here. Perhaps the first mention in Pliny might have attracted his attention more than the others, since Pliny says that from that lofty mountain, at the last watch of the night, one can see both the night sky to the West and the dawn to the East (5.18.80).

Bibliography

ON THE ADVANTAGES AND DISADVANTAGES OF LITERATURE

EDITIONS

Leonis Baptistae Alberti Opera. Edited by Girolamo Massaini. Florence: Bartolomeo de' Libri, ca. 1499 = Universal Short Title Catalogue (USTC) 998089.

De commodis litterarum atque incommodis; Defunctus. Edited by Giovanni Farris. Milan: Marzorati, 1971. With an Italian translation.

De commodis litterarum atque incommodis. Edited by Laura Goggi Carotti. Florence: Leo S. Olschki, 1976.

De commodis litterarum atque incommodis. Edited by Mariangela Regoliosi. In *Leon Battista Alberti: Opere latine,* edited by Roberto Cardini, 19–50. Rome: Istituto Poligrafico e Zecca dello Stato, 2010. With an Italian translation.

De commodis litterarum atque incommodis. Edited by Mariangela Regoliosi. 2 vols. In the series *Edizione Nazionale delle Opere di Leon Battista Alberti.* III. *Trattatistica Morale I.* Florence: Edizioni Polistampa, 2021.

ENGLISH TRANSLATION

The Use and Abuse of Books. De Commodis Litterarum atque Incommodis. Translation and introduction by Renée Neu Watkins. Prospect Heights, IL: Waveland Press, 1999.

THE LIFE OF ST. POTITUS

EDITIONS

Opuscoli inediti di Leon Battista Alberti: "Musca"; "Vita S. Potiti." Edited by Cecil Grayson. Florence: Leo S. Olschki, 1954. Facsimile reprint with a preface by Cesare Vasoli. Pisa: Edizioni della Normale, 2005.

Vita S. Potiti. Edited by Elena Giannarelli. In *Opere latine,* ed. Cardini, 123–65. With an Italian translation.

MY DOG

EDITIONS

Grayson, Cecil . "Il *Canis* di Leon Battista Alberti." In *Miscellanea di studi in onore di Vittore Branca*, vol. 3: *Umanesimo e Rinascimento a Firenze e Venezia*, 193–204. Florence: Leo S. Olschki, 1983. Reprinted in Cecil Grayson, *Studi su Leon Battista Alberti*, edited by Paola Claut, 359–72. Florence: Olschki, 1998.

Alberti, Leon Battista. *Apologhi ed elogi*, 142–69. Edited by Rosario Contarino. Genoa: Costa & Nolan, 1984. With an Italian translation.

Canis. Edited by Mariangela Regoliosi. In *Opere latine*, ed. Cardini, 963–92. With an Italian translation and notes by Maria Letizia Bracciali Magnini.

MY LIFE

EDITIONS

Leonis Baptistae Alberti Commentarius de coniuratione Porcaria, cui praemittitur Vita eiusdem scriptoris. In *Rerum Italicarum scriptores*, edited by L. A. Muratori, vol. 25, coll. 293–304. Milan: Societas Palatina in Regia Curia, 1751.

Leonis Baptistae de Albertis Vita. In *Opere volgari di Leon Battista Alberti*, edited by Anicio Bonucci, 1:xc–cxvii. 4 vols. Florence: Tipografia Galileiana, 1843. With an Italian translation.

Anonymi Leonis Baptistae Alberti Vita. In *Philippi Villani Liber de civitatis Florentie famosis civibus*, edited by G. C. Galletti, 141–48. Florence: G. Mazzoni, 1847.

Fubini, Riccardo, and Anna Menci Gallorini. "L'autobiografia di Leon Battista Alberti: Studio e edizione." *Rinascimento* ser. 2, 12 (1972): 21–78.

Autobiografia. Edited by Roberto Cardini and Mariangela Regoliosi. In *Opere latine*, ed. Cardini, 987–1014. With an Italian translation.

Autobiografia e altre opere latine. Edited by Loredana Chines and Andrea Severi. Milan: Rizzoli, 2012. With an Italian translation.

ENGLISH TRANSLATION

Watkins, Renée Neu. "L. B. Alberti in the Mirror: An Interpretation of the *Vita* with a New Translation." *Italian Quarterly* 30 (1989): 5–30.

THE FLY

EDITIONS

Opuscoli inediti di Leon Battista Alberti: "Musca"; "Vita S. Potiti." Edited by Cecil Grayson. Florence: Leo S. Olschki, 1954. Facsimile reprint with a preface by Cesare Vasoli. Pisa: Edizioni della Normale, 2005.

Leon Battista Alberti: Apologhi ed elogi. Edited by Rosario Contarino, 172–94. Genoa: Costa & Nolan, 1984. With an Italian translation.

Billerbeck, Margarethe, and Christian Zubler. *Das Lob der Fliege von Lukian bis L. B. Alberti. Gattungsgeschichte, Texte, Übersetzungen und Kommentar.* Berne: Lang, 2000.

Alberti, Leon Battista. *Musca.* Edited by Donatella Coppini. In *Opere latine*, ed. Cardini, 1015–38. With an Italian translation and notes by Maria Letizia Bracciali Magnini.

SELECTED MODERN STUDIES

Alberti Lvdens: In memory of Cecil Grayson. Edited by Francesco Furlan, Martin McLaughlin, and Hartmut Wulfram. Published as special issues of *Albertiana*, 22.2 (2019) and 23.2 (2020).

Boschetto, Luca. *Leon Battista Alberti e Firenze. Biografia, storia, letteratura* (Florence: Leo S. Olschki, 2000).

———. "Tra biografia e autobiografia: Le prospettive e i problemi della ricerca intorno alla vita di L. B. Alberti." In *La vita e il mondo di Leon Battista Alberti. Atti dei convegni internazionali del Comitato nazionale VI centenario della nascita di Leon Battista Alberti: Genova, 19–21 febbraio 2004,* 1:85–116. 2 vols. Florence: Leo S. Olschki, 2008.

Bracciali Magnini, Maria Letizia. "L. B. Alberti, *Canis* 10–27. Fonti e problemi." In *Nel cantiere degli umanisti: Per Mariangela Regoliosi*, edited by Lucia Bertolini, Donatella Coppini, and Clementina Marsico, 2:777–826. 2 vols. Florence: Polistampa, 2014.

Cardini, Roberto. "Alberti o della nascita dell'umorismo moderno." *Schede umanistiche* 1 (1993): 31–85.

———. "Biografia, leggi e astrologia in un nuovo reperto albertiano." In *Leon Battista Alberti umanista e scrittore*, 21–190.

———. *Mosaici. Il Nemico dell'Alberti*. Rome: Bulzoni, 1990.

Enenkel, Karl A. E. "Der Ursprung des Renaissance-Übermenschen (*uomo universale*): die 'Autobiographie' des Leon Battista Alberti." In Enenkel, *Die Erfindung des Menschen: Die Autobiographik des frühneuzeitlichen Humanismus von Petrarca bis Lipsius*, 189–228. Berlin: De Gruyter, 2008.

Garin, Eugenio. "Studi su Leon Battista Alberti." In Garin, *Rinascite e rivoluzioni. Movimenti culturali dal XIV al XVIII secolo*, 133–95. Bari: Laterza, 1975.

Grafton, Anthony. *Leon Battista Alberti. Master Builder of the Italian Renaissance*. New York: Hill and Wang, 2000.

Grayson, Cecil. *Studi su Leon Battista Alberti*. Edited by Paola Claut. Florence: Leo S. Olschki, 1998.

Kircher, Timothy. *Living Well in Renaissance Italy: The Virtues of Humanism and the Irony of Leon Battista Alberti*. Tempe, AZ: Arizona Center for Medieval and Renaissance Studies, 2012.

Leon Battista Alberti e la tradizione. Per lo 'smontaggio' dei 'mosaici' albertiani. Atti del Convegno internazionale del Comitato Nazionale VI centenario della nascita di Leon Battista Alberti: Arezzo, 23–24–25 settembre 2004. Edited by Roberto Cardini and Mariangela Regoliosi. Florence: Polistampa, 2007.

Leon Battista Alberti: La biblioteca di un umanista. Exhibition catalogue, Biblioteca Medicea Laurenziana. Edited by Roberto Cardini and others. Florence: Mandragora, 2005.

Leon Battista Alberti: Opere volgari. Edited by Cecil Grayson. 3 vols. Bari: Laterza, 1960–73.

Leon Battista Alberti umanista e scrittore. Filologia, esegesi, tradizione. Atti del Convegno internazionale del Comitato Nazionale VI Centenario della nascita di Leon Battista Alberti: Arezzo, 24–26 giugno 2004. Edited by Roberto Cardini and Mariangela Regoliosi. 2 vols. Florence: Polistampa, 2007.

Marsh, David. *Lucian and the Latins. Humor and Humanism in the Early Renaissance*. Ann Arbor: The University of Michigan Press, 1998.

——. "The Self-expressed: Leon Battista Alberti's Autobiography." *Albertiana* 10 (2007): 125–40.

McLaughlin, Martin. "Alberti and Burckhardt: The Construction of a Myth." *Albertiana* 20.1 = n.s. 2 (2017): 145–63.

——. "Alberti's *Canis*: Structure and Sources in the Portrait of the Artist as a Renaissance Dog." *Albertiana* 14 (2011): 55–83.

——. "Alberti's *Musca*: Humour, Ethics and the Challenge to Classical Models." In *Authority, Innovation and Early Modern Epistemology: Essays in Honour of Hilary Gatti*, edited by Martin McLaughlin, Ingrid D. Rowland, and Elisabetta Tarantino, 8–24. Cambridge: Legenda, 2015.

——. "Humanist Translations and Re-writings: Lucian's *Encomium of the Fly* between Guarino and Alberti." In *Making and Rethinking the Renaissance: Between Greek and Latin in 15th–16th Century Europe*, edited by Giancarlo Abbamonte and Stephen Harrison, 95–108. Berlin: De Gruyter, 2019.

——. *Leon Battista Alberti: La vita, l'umanesimo, le opere letterarie*. Florence: Leo S. Olschki, 2016.

Paoli, Michel. "Autoportrait d'humaniste en athlète prodigieux: L'*Autobiographie* et la plaquette 'L. Bap.' de Leon Battista Alberti." *Letteratura & Arte* 1 (2003): 135–43.

Pearson, Caspar. *Leon Battista Alberti: The Chameleon's Eye*. London: Reaktion, 2022.

Regoliosi, Mariangela. "Gerarchie culturali e sociali nel *De commodis litterarum atque incommodis* di Leon Battista Alberti." In *Sapere e/è potere. Discipline, dispute e professioni nell'Università medievale e moderna. Il caso bolognese a confronto. Atti del Convegno Bologna 13–15 aprile 1989*, edited by Luisa Avellini, 1:151–70. 2 vols. Bologna: Istituto per la Storia di Bologna, 1990.

Robinson, Christopher. *Lucian and His Influence in Europe*. London: Duckworth, 1979.

Index

❦❧❦

337

Publication of this volume has been made possible by

The Myron and Sheila Gilmore Publication Fund at I Tatti

The Robert Lehman Endowment Fund

The Jean-François Malle Scholarly Programs and Publications Fund

The Andrew W. Mellon Scholarly Publications Fund

The Craig and Barbara Smyth Fund
for Scholarly Programs and Publications

The Lila Wallace–Reader's Digest Endowment Fund

The Malcolm Wiener Fund for Scholarly Programs and Publications